Europe in the International Economy
1500 to 2000

In memory of Sidney Pollard

Europe in the International Economy 1500 to 2000

Edited by

Derek H. Aldcroft

Research Professor in Economic History, Manchester Metropolitan University, UK

Anthony Sutcliffe

Special Professor, Department of History, University of Nottingham, UK

Edward Elgar
Cheltenham, UK • Northampton, MA, USA

Published by
Edward Elgar Publishing Limited
Glensanda House
Montpellier Parade
Cheltenham
Glos GL50 IUA
UK

Edward Elgar Publishing, Inc.
136 West Street
Suite 202
Northampton
Massachusetts 01060
USA

A catalogue record for this book
is available from the British Library

Library of Congress Cataloguing in Publication Data

Europe in the international economy 1500 to 2000 / edited by Derek H. Aldcroft,
    Anthony Sutcliffe.
       1. Europe—Economic conditions. 2. Europe—Foreign economic relations.
    I. Aldcroft, Derek Howard. II. Sutcliffe, Anthony, 1942–
    HC240.E8177 1999
    337.4—dc21   99–12897
                                                     CIP

ISBN 1 85898 670 2 (cased)
Printed and bound in Great Britain by MPG Books Ltd, Bodmin, Cornwall

Contents

Figures and tables

FIGURES

TABLES

vii

Contributors

Derek H. Aldcroft is Research Professor in Economic History at the Manchester Metropolitan University and Visiting Professor at Anglia Polytechnic University. Formerly Professor and Head of Department in the Universities of Sydney and Leicester, he has published widely in modern British and European economic history. His latest works include *Studies in the Interwar European Economy* (Ashgate, 1997), with Steven Morewood, *Economic Change in Eastern Europe since 1918* (Edward Elgar, 1995) and with Michael Oliver, *Exchange Rate Regimes in the Twentieth Century* (Edward Elgar, 1998).

James Foreman-Peck is Economic Adviser at HM Treasury. Formerly Fellow of St Antony's College, Oxford and Professor of Economic History at the University of Hull, his research interests have focused on industrial policy and history and on the international economy. His edited *European Industrial Policy: The Twentieth Century Experience* will be published by Oxford University Press in 1999.

Edwin Horlings is a postdoctoral researcher at the University of Amsterdam, specializing in quantitative macroeconomic history and in the relationship between economic growth and the quality of life. His main publications are: *The Economic Development of the Dutch Service Sector: Trade and Transport in a Pre-modern Economy* (1995); 'Private consumer expenditure in the Netherlands, 1800–1913', *Economic and Social History in the Netherlands*, 7, 1995, 8–40; and 'The Quality of Life in the Netherlands, 1800–1913: Experiments in Measurement and Aggregation', in J. Komlos and J. Baten (eds), *The Biological Standard of Living in Comparative Perspective*, 2 (Franz Steiner Verlag, 1998).

Steven Morewood is currently a Lecturer in International History at the University of Birmingham. He has taught widely at several universities including Warwick, Manchester and Leicester. He is the co-author of the widely acclaimed *Economic Change in Eastern Europe since 1918* (Elgar, 1995) and contributed the closing chapter to the third edition of Derek Aldcroft's *The European Economy 1914–1990* (Routledge, 1993). The twentieth century European economy, especially its post-1945 aspects, have figured prominently in his teaching. His research interests include the economic dimensions of Britain's relative economic decline *vis-à-vis* the world power role 1945–1970.

Sidney Pollard, who died suddenly as this book went to press, was one of the greatest economic historians of the post-war era. In more than thirty books and over one hundred articles he dealt with almost every aspect of the industrialization process and its effects, concentrating on Britain and, more recently, the continent of Europe. Educated at the London School of Economics, he moved to the University of Sheffield in 1950. Becoming Professor of Economic History there in 1963, he built up a strong Department of Economic History (later the Department of Economic and Social History). He became a frequent visitor to universities outside the UK and in 1980 he moved to a professorship at the University of Bielefeld. In retirement he returned to Sheffield where his prolific output continued until his death.

Anthony Sutcliffe is Special Professor in the Department of History, University of Nottingham. As editor of *Planning Perspectives*, his main interests lie in the history of urban and regional planning, but he has a broader commitment to international studies. Recent publications in the history of the cinema and the history of art reflect his enthusiasm for visual and experiential approaches to reality. His contribution to this volume was preceded by his *An Economic History of Western Europe since 1945* (Longman, 1996).

Jan Luiten van Zanden is Professor of Economic History at the University of Utrecht. Among his publications are *The Rise and Decline of Holland's Economy* (Manchester University Press, 1993), *The Transformation of European Agriculture in the 19th Century* (Free University Press, 1994), with Marjolein't Hart and Joost Jonker (eds), *A Financial History of the Netherlands* (Cambridge University Press, 1997), *The Economic History of the Netherlands 1914–1995* (Routledge, 1998) and with Lee Soltow *Income and Wealth Inequality in the Netherlands 16th–20th century* (Het Spinhuis, 1998).

Preface

The early versions of the chapters in this volume were presented and discussed at a meeting of the contributors held in Leicester in July 1998. We would like to thank the Economic History Society for a generous grant towards the cost of the conference.

We are also grateful to Dr Peter Musgrave of the University of Leicester who kindly allowed us to read the typescript of his new work on early modern Europe.

It is with deep regret that the editors learned of the death of one of the contributors, Sidney Pollard, shortly after he had completed the final draft of his chapter for this volume. It is fitting, therefore, that this volume be dedicated to the memory of Sidney Pollard, who over a long and productive career contributed so much to scholarship in economic and social history.

DHA/AS
January 1999

Introduction: Europe in the international economy 1500 to 2000

Over the last half millennium Europe has witnessed great changes in its political and economic history. But what stands out above all is Europe's striking rise in economic power from the sixteenth to the nineteenth century, to a position of world dominance through to 1914. followed by the undermining of its position after the First World War. Since the Second World War, western Europe has regrouped and recovered much of its former importance and now looks to be on the threshold of moving towards a new and unified configuration for the first time since the Roman Empire. Even eastern Europe, sadly retarded under Communist ideology and Soviet domination, eventually began to resume its place in the capitalist system of Europe in the 1990s.

Europe's unique rise in world terms took place in the context of its relatively small area; it is the second smallest of the world's continents as conventionally defined by geographers, occupying about 8 per cent of the earth's surface. As a large peninsula of the Eurasian land mass, Europe's area was less than a quarter of Asia's, and a third of Africa's. However, the European littoral enjoyed very good sea access and the small area of the European land mass meant that much of the interior had good links with the sea. A high rainfall and a temperate climate sustained a system of broad, deep rivers which iced over only in the very north of the continent. Most of Europe enjoyed fertile soil and adequate rainfall. Only two mountain ranges, the Alps and the Pyrenees, were serious obstacles to movement.

From the time of the Roman Empire, Europe began to generate a degree of standardization in institutions and mentalities, through the Roman Catholic Church and feudalism. Economic development, however, did not occur evenly throughout Europe. By the later Middle Ages, northern Italy was the leading economic region. From the seventeenth century, the most striking developments were to take place in the northwest, in northern France, the Low Countries and England. It was within this region that modern industrialization was launched in the later eighteenth century, to be followed by imperialism in the nineteenth century.

Explaining its rise to predominance is certainly one of the important themes in European history, but it is by no means the only one. Equally important and interesting is the uneven incidence of its development whereby so much took place in the north-west corner of the continent, along with its overseas appendages, while eastern and southern Europe eventually lagged far behind. Moreover, this success did not happen overnight: the industrial revolution certainly changed the scale and scope of the whole exercise but it could never have happened without a long period of slow progress towards that goal. Late developers have often discovered to their cost that modern economic growth and high income levels cannot be had for the asking. It takes time and preparation before they can be achieved – centuries, in fact, in the case of Europe.

The regional dimension takes on another form apart from the contrast between the west and the south and east. Was the nation state the arbiter of progress or should we take a pan-European approach, as Pollard (1973) has done where development is partly oblivious to national frontiers and spills over into regional development blocs?

Finally, what of failure? The twentieth century has been a very turbulent one which at one stage brought Europe to her knees, only to see her rise again, like a phoenix from the ashes, not to pole position as in the previous century, but certainly to being a key force in global economic and political affairs. More recently, this seems to have been given added emphasis through the evolving organizational structure towards a federated Europe. But is big so beautiful? Past experience suggests that large empires or dynasties crumble in time, because they become too cumbersome, overcentralized, bureaucratic and lacking in internal dynamism. Of course there are many differences between the European Union and the great dynasties of the past, and the United States has been the dominant exemplar since 1945, but in a modern guise the EU may have some of the characteristics of former structures which could render it ill-equipped to meet the challenges of more competitive systems.

•   •   •   •   •

The rise of the western world and the gradual extinction of the once glittering civilizations of the past have long fascinated historians. How was it that a large collection of small, feudal and often warring polities managed to consolidate and gain the upper hand, so that by the sixteenth century they were taking the lead in political and economic affairs? After all, in the early Middle Ages, when Europe was a mosaic of principalities, bishoprics, feudal lordships and city states with overlapping authority, 'nothing like a centralised state existed anywhere in Europe' (Tilly 1992,

39–40), and no one would have held out much hope for the future welfare of Europe, let alone foreseen an integrated continent.

We know of course that in western Europe at least the economic variables became distinctly more favourable as time went by: income levels, capital accumulation, trade volumes, productivity and human skills improved, albeit often slowly and erratically, so that the foundations of modern economic growth were being laid. But the obvious question is, why not elsewhere? Why was Europe, or to be more precise, north-west Europe, so unique in this respect?

The answer to this conundrum possibly lies partly in the differing political and institutional frameworks between east and west. The large empires and dynasties of the past, which had once shown so much promise, the Roman, Islamic, Chinese, Indian and Ottoman, eventually became too big and unwieldy, bureaucratic and militaristic, so that they stifled individual initiative and intellectual and political inquiry. 'Like parasites ... agrarian elites sapped their dominions in those areas where progressive economic behaviour was most likely, trade and capital accumulation' (Chirot, 1985, 183). Often they were little more than military despotisms bent on preserving or enhancing their power by exacting tribute from impoverished subjects who were left with little more than bare subsistence. The overhead costs of state to provide for the upkeep of large armies, administrative bureaucracies and parasitical elites were therefore heavy and tended to weaken the strength of the empires over time (Kahn, 1979, 30–31). Furthermore, they rarely managed to retain control over an entire cultural region for very long since the very forces which brought the dynasties together in the first place were also those which made for their disintegration.

Of course, Europe itself was not immune from the stultifying effects of overweening empires from time to time: the Carolingian Empire which expired in the ninth century was an early example; the rise to dominance of the Habsburg Empire was of comparable stature, though one should bear in mind that the Habsburgs repulsed the Ottoman threat to Europe. But while they, in combination with the Ottoman Empire, managed to crush scientific progress, nonconformist religious thought, intellectual inquiry and middle class values in much of southern and eastern Europe, they failed, as Chirot (1985, 183) notes, to gain control of the north-west sector of the continent: northern Germany, the northern Low Countries, France, Switzerland and England. Significantly, it was these areas which spawned the initiative and vitality for the rise of the western world.

It may therefore be a blessing in disguise that a unified European Empire failed to materialize to dominate the whole continent, otherwise its history could have been quite different, if the experience of other large dynasties is anything to judge by. Fortunately, when mediaeval Europe, or at least the west, emerged from the fragmented control of individual rulers, it did not fall into the hands of monolithic dynasties and so avoided some of the pernicious features of the great Empires of the east. Instead western Europe crystallized into a number of distinct states which replaced the multiplicity of political units of the late mediaeval period with more organized and homogeneous nation states with fairly clearly defined boundaries. In this respect the history of Europe is unique since, as Cobban (1969, 30) points out, at no time had such a considerable group of nation states survived in geographical proximity and close association over a period of many centuries. It is true that mobilization for war continued to be a dominant activity among the new European states, but this has been seen as a major factor explaining why 'states expanded, consolidated and created new forms of political organization' (Tilly, 1992, 70, 74; Kennedy 1988).

What is important to note is that this new political configuration in the west was both more competitive and more liberal than its counterparts elsewhere. In brief, it provided greater economic security and a corresponding increase in the rights to property (P. Anderson 1974, 420, 429; J.L. Anderson 1991, 61). In time it removed or modified some of the more inhibiting characteristics of feudal society which helped to reduce market transaction costs and strengthen the links between effort and reward.

The importance of institutional change to economic progress has long been recognized. Cunningham (1904, 152–69, 261–2), for example, touched upon many of the key issues which were later elaborated in more rigorous form by the work of North and Thomas (1970; 1973; North, 1981). For economic enterprise to thrive it is important that the institutional and legal framework protects individual property rights, reduces the costs of economic transactions and facilitates resource flows. In addition, it should protect the economic agent from undue exactions on the part of a repressive state. Only in north-west Europe can it be said that a framework conducive to economic progress was gradually established from the late mediaeval period. Wherever else one looks, be it mediaeval Europe, the eastern civilizations, eastern Europe in the nineteenth and early twentieth centuries, or the Third World today, this is not the case. Private property in mediaeval Europe was in constant danger of violation by plunder or expropriation on the part of both individuals and the polity; the same was true in nineteenth-century eastern Europe, where corrupt and despotic rulers matched those of many contemporary Third World countries today. The great dynasties of India, China and the Ottoman Empire were essentially feudal and regressive and provided little incentive for individual initiative and inquiry lest this undermined the basis of feudal power.

Perhaps the most striking manifestation of the disjuncture between east and west was in the way the legal framework changed in the latter in regard to market transactions and property rights. The rise of the nation state in the west was accompanied by the revival of Roman law, which is generally regarded by many observers as the most effective legal system for encouraging capitalist transactions. The main advantages of Roman law are that it allows the establishment of rights to property, provides a means of defining and enforcing contracts, and establishes a systematic and coherent framework for the purchase, sale, lease, hire, loan and transfer of goods and assets. The foundation of a firm legal basis for property rights and economic transactions, without which modern capitalism could not flourish, was first developed in western Europe (Tilly, 1992, 100). Elsewhere the legal basis was very poorly developed. Nineteenth-century eastern Europe lagged far behind, with many regions having progressed little from the pillage, plunder and corruption stage of earlier centuries. Likewise, the legal systems of the east, India, China and Japan, are not generally considered to be very favourable to economic enterprise and individual initiative (Caldwell, 1977, 54).

Such changes that did take place in western institutions and structures did not happen overnight. They evolved gradually and erratically over a long period of time to provide a framework that was conducive to economic transactions and entrepreneurial endeavour. Again one should stress that most of the advances were concentrated in the north-west corner of the Europe, the region that became the dominant core of the continent.

Yet how advanced was Europe by the eighteenth century? Views differ on this issue quite considerably. There are those writers who would argue that Europe did not have a clear lead until the early nineteenth century. Tilly (1992, 171) for example, doubts whether the European powers could claim to have led the world economically before the later eighteenth century. Ramirez-Faria (1991, 1) reckons that, up to the eighteenth century at least, Europe could not claim to have been more than *primus inter pares*, despite 'a towering but subjective sense of her own superiority.' Added weight to such views comes from Bairoch's quantitative studies of global income and levels of industrialization, which suggest that differences between countries and regions were quite small before the great upsurge in industrial development from the late eighteenth century onwards (Bairoch 1981; 1982; 1991). He claims that the gap between the richest and poorest country circa 1750 was probably in the range 1.0 to 1.6, and as low as 1.0 to 1.3 if broader regions such as western Europe and China are considered. In fact, the per capita income of China may have been marginally higher than that of the whole of Europe in 1750. Similarly, the data for levels of industrialization seem to confirm this picture.

It should be stressed that the figures for this period are highly conjectural, as Bairoch is the first to admit. Nevertheless, it does appear that the enormous gap between rich and poor nations with which we are familiar today did not exist in the eighteenth century. On the other hand, there is still reason to believe that western Europe had already stolen a march on the rest of the world. In fact Bairoch himself is prepared to concede that the richest parts of Europe (England, France and the Low Countries) had a 20 to 40 per cent income superiority over the average of that of the future Third World (Bairoch, 1991, 31). This would seem to have logic in the light of subsequent developments which are difficult to explain satisfactorily unless there had already been favourable movements in a whole range of economic variables, including capital accumulation, mercantile activities, technological changes, educational levels, urban development and, ultimately, the ability to surmount the dreaded Malthusian population barrier.

Indeed, many writers would argue that European advances can be located well before the eighteenth century and that there is little doubt that western Europe at least was well in the lead before the industrial revolution. Cipolla (1981, 300) for example, felt that global history after 1500 could not be properly understood without taking into account the impact of European culture, economy and technology. Landes (1969, 13–14) argued that western Europe was already comparatively rich before the industrial revolution by comparison with other regions of the world and it was this that made it ready for the breakthrough into modern economic growth. McNeill (1963, 653; 1979, 376) traced the roots of European dominance back to the sixteenth century and maintained that by 1700 the wealth and power at Europe's command clearly surpassed anything that other civilized communities of the earth could muster. Snooks (1996, 258) is even more emphatic: 'By 1500 Europe had equalled, if not exceeded, the technological achievement of any former or contemporary civilization.' Similarly, Jones (1981, 41, 183) argues that a decisive gap between Europe and Asia was emerging before modern industrialization. A wealth of detail on Europe's burgeoning industrial and technological capabilities from 1600 onwards is provided by Goodman and Honeyman (1988; see also Chirot, 1985, 192–3).

Such changes suggest that the springs of modern economic growth are to be located way back in time and quantitative estimates on incomes, however fragile, indicate that income growth was taking place, albeit slowly and erratically, for many centuries. This was certainly the case in England according to latest estimates (Persson, 1988; Snooks, 1990; 1996) and may also be true of other parts of western Europe (Landes, 1969, 14; Maddison, 1982, 6–7). The grim Malthusian picture painted by some continental historians may not be wholly consistent with what was actually happening in practice.

In fact, staving off the Malthusian demon may have been the crucial element in enabling Europe to make the transition to modernity. Though population grew very slowly in pre-industrial times in both Europe and the wider world (down to 1750, the world rate of change was 0.06 per cent a year, with little variation between continents), population pressures were experienced periodically by Europe and eastern civilizations (Livi-Bacci, 1992, 31–6). These were usually relieved by the famous Malthusian checks of war, pestilence, plague and famine, rather than by any permanent upward shift in the supply schedule to accommodate an enlarged population, hence the very slow growth in population over the long haul. Population changes could sometimes prove fatal to unyielding regimes, as Goldstone (1991, 476) explains: 'Population growth in the context of inflexible economic and social institutions is fully capable on its own of producing income polarization, élite conflict, and state breakdowns as the cases of Ming China and Ottoman Turkey demonstrate.'

In this respect it has been argued that western Europe was in a uniquely favourable position. It was never suffocated by the acute population pressures which afflict many Third World countries today or which faced some of the eastern civilizations in the past. Though pre-industrial Europe's population did sometimes outstrip the capacity to sustain it in the short term, the population problem never became so acute as to upset seriously the balance of the environment. And in the long term, western Europe was able to surmount the Malthusian trap.

This was accomplished in two ways. Western Europe was more successful in containing population pressure by virtue of its unique family life cycle pattern, whereby abstinence from marriage (high proportion of celibrates) and a late age of marriage for women combined to restrain fertility levels. This pattern seems to have prevailed in England, France, the Low Countries, Scandinavia, Germany and Switzerland, as also, significantly, in Japan. Thus western Europe was able to adjust its population more readily to the economic environment, whereas in most other parts of the world early marriage and high fertility rates had the reverse effect. Thus 'early modern Western Europe and Tokogawa Japan enjoyed certain advantages from the point of view of fomenting economic growth: a more favourable age structure; and less pronounced population instability' (McNeill, 1996, 25, 34; Laslett, 1988, 235–8).

On the other side of the equation, western Europe's supply capability improved steadily during the early modern period, to a point where it was possible to cope with population-driven expansion from the eighteenth century onwards (Komlos, 1989a, 247–8; 1989b, 204–5). There is evidence to suggest that in much of western Europe both the agrarian and non-agrarian sectors of the economy had been responding positively for some time, so that it became possible to support a growing population. By the eighteenth century, western Europe's agrarian system was capable of meeting additional population pressure when it came, not initially by raising overall living standards, but by preventing them from fading away as they had sometimes done in the past when confronted by somewhat less rigorous population changes (Bairoch, 1989; Mokyr, 1976, 23–4; Grigg, 1992, 2, 33).

Thus through a combination of restrained fertility and a long-run improvement in supply capability, western Europe was able to keep the Malthusian devil at bay. In other words, population never became a serious constraint to development as it has been elsewhere, especially in many Third World countries in the later twentieth century, with population growth rates at least twice those experienced by European societies at their peak in the nineteenth century. Early developers rarely had population growth rates much above 1 per cent a year, which seems to have been an upper threshold for successful modernization (Bairoch, 1975, 204).

A further indication of Europe's increasing pre-eminence is its role in trade. By the early nineteenth century, Europe was by far the dominant force in international trade, accounting for 69 per cent of world trade in 1720 and 77 per cent by 1800. The west European shares were 42 and 61 per cent, respectively, with Britain way out in the lead, followed by Germany, France and the Low Countries, in that order (Chisholm, 1982, 60). Although a significant proportion consisted of intra-European trade, it also reflected the active exploitation by European traders of the new opportunities for intercourse in both the Old and New Worlds from the sixteenth century onwards. The New World also had another role to play, that of providing Europe with an additional resource base and an outlet for surplus population. What Jones refers to as the 'ghost acreages' in the newly discovered lands served to improve man–land ratios and helped to stabilize population densities in the European core. By contrast, population densities in India, China and the Ottoman Empire, which were already high by European standards, tended to increase further between 1500 and 1800 (Jones, 1981, 83; Reynolds, 1985, 29).

Western Europe, along with its overseas appendages, was therefore in a much more favourable position than the rest of Europe or the eastern civilizations to accumulate a margin above subsistence through its strong mercantile connections, which also had an important social class dimension: they provided western Europe with a wealthy urban bourgeoisie which, according to Batou (1990, 464), was noticeably lacking in Asia, the Middle East and China, and for that matter in eastern Europe. The European instinct to accumulate capital over many centuries, in contrast to the more destructive properties of Eastern civilizations, is indicative of the long-run origins of the development process, which emphasize the continuity of that process rather than the concept of a dramatic structural break (Komlos, 1989a, 203–5).

Not all writers would agree with the emphasis frequently placed on the uniqueness of the European environment for modern economic growth. In fact some have taken grave exception to the Eurocentric approach to world development and to the very concept of the 'European miracle'. One of the fiercest critiques of the diffusion thesis has rejected outright the previous notions of the long-term superiority of Europe (Blaut, 1993, 206). Modern economic growth, Blaut argues, could have happened anywhere, at least before 1492, since Europeans were in no way more modern, more advanced, more rational or intellectually brighter than the inhabitants of other civilizations. Nor were they necessarily more culturally disposed to economic endeavour than their counterparts elsewhere (though see Landes, 1998, for a different view). What gave Europe the upper hand was her geographic proximity to America and the immense wealth obtained there by Europeans and later also in Asia and Africa. Capitalism became centred in Europe, it is argued, 'because colonialism gave Europeans the power both to develop their own society and to prevent development from occurring elsewhere' (Blaut, 1993, 152–3, 206). Marxist writers have also made some very large estimates of Europe's gains from the plundering of other continents (Caldwell, 1977, 55).

Blaut's thesis is both stimulating and provocative and certainly deserves attention. There is obviously some merit in re-examining the Eurocentric emphasis on modern development which has permeated the literature and the textbooks for so long. No one would probably now take exception, in the light of modern research, to the notion that eastern civilizations were more advanced than Europe in the Middle Ages (Abu-Lughod, 1989; Smith, 1991; Landes, 1994; Hodgson 1993), but there is a big question mark as to whether they were able to maintain their earlier progress, and Blaut probably underestimates the advances made in Europe by the sixteenth century. According to Abu-Lughod (1989, 361), the crucial fact is that the fall of the east preceded the rise of the west. The disintegration of what she calls the Afro-Eurasian system after circa 1350 was followed by the rise of a new, European, system in southern and western Europe in the sixteenth century, as Europe filled the power vacuum in the east, first through the Portuguese, then the Dutch and finally the British. More to the point, the idea that the rise of Europe's predominance was largely a product of geographic accident, namely Europe's convenient location to the Americas which allowed her to exploit the resources of the New World, and subsequently those of Asia and Africa, does somewhat strain the reader's credulity. The more so in that Blaut does not demonstrate in any great depth the interconnections between colonialism and development.

There is no doubt that colonial expansion and the accompanying mercantile activity contributed to western development, as we have already acknowledged, but there is a danger of overemphasizing its role, as O'Brien and Prados de la Escosura (1998, 38) have recently cautioned: 'arguments that reify the expansion of western Europe overseas into the engine of its economic success compared to other continents ... should be resisted and severely qualified'. Colonial trade and investment accounted only for a relatively small part of aggregate economic activity even for the Netherlands and England (Musgrave, 1999, ch. 7). The long-term benefits of colonial endeavour were decidedly mixed. The Iberian peninsula eventually gained very little from it, nor did the Dutch for that matter, and for most countries that subsequently led the way in modern economic growth it was of minor importance, often costing more than it was worth. The British, and to a lesser extent the French, were the major beneficiaries. But there is no conclusive evidence to support the extreme 'dependency theory' view that the emergence of global income inequality was largely the product of western exploitation, even though the influence of the great powers was not always beneficial to the periphery (Ramirez-Faria, 1991, 261; Valerio, 1992, 131). That apart, it would be legitimate to argue that colonial expansion was largely a European phenomenon simply because the Europeans were more advanced and enterprising than their Asian and African counterparts by the sixteenth century.

In his recent and often controversial study, Musgrave (1999, chs 5, 7) not only questions the primacy of Europe *vis-à-vis* Asia but also raises doubts about the conventional thinking regarding the leading position of north-west Europe. He argues that it was Europe, rather than Asia, that was underdeveloped in the early modern period, and that the Europeans came to Asia as marginal players and utilized the highly developed commercial structure already there. He also takes issue with the traditional notion that western Europe, or rather northern Europe in his north–south divide, was at the cutting edge of development, claiming that, until well into the eighteenth century, Europe's industrial heartland was still located in the south, which looked nearer to an industrial revolution than the more backward north. The problem with this interpretation is how to explain why the roles were suddenly reversed. Musgrave's answer is the series of heroic and risky gambles in technology which tipped the scales in the north's favour.

War is often seen as an important catalyst, but whether for good or evil is a matter for debate. We are still a long way from being able to draw up a final balance sheet of the costs and benefits of war (O'Brien, 1996). On a broad view it would appear that the best economic performance has occurred during periods when there has been an absence of major conflict and with a hegemonic core state dominating the system: for example, much of the nineteenth century after 1815, when Britain was the leading nation, and the period 1945–73, when the United States held sway. Most other periods experienced multi-centre competitive systems and were inherently unstable. Twentieth-century experience tells us that war can be totally destructive, leading to a serious loss of growth. Similarly, the 300 or more years down to the Congress of Vienna were rarely free of conflict, dynastic struggles, balance of power conflicts and commercial rivalries among the major European countries (Bergeson and Schoenberg 1980, 244–6). No doubt they produced a spur to military technology and arms production but, since the greater part of state budgets were gobbled up by war, resulting frequently in serious public finance problems, it is debatable whether any net benefit accrued. However, Tilly (1992, 70–74) argues that the major mobilizations for war were the means by which states expanded, consolidated and created new forms of political organization. Military rivalry therefore underlay both the creation and ultimate predominance of European national states which eventually became the prototype for the whole world.

Whatever the ultimate reasons for the rise of the west, the fact remains that Europe, along with its overseas appendages, was the driving force in economic development from the sixteenth century through to the First World War. But if Europe's rise to greatness took many centuries to reach full maturity, it was squandered very quickly in the first half of the twentieth century. Within little more than a generation, war and depression had brought Europe to its knees. Statesmen and policy makers must also shoulder some of the blame for the disintegration, since they failed to create a viable European structure after 1918. Perceptive observers at the time were all too aware of Europe's political and economic weaknesses, but statesmen and others in high office, imbued with the glories of the past, failed to recognize or chose to ignore them. As Thomson (1966, 601) noted, they 'failed to appreciate that modern war is a revolution, and that the economic world of 1913 had already passed into history as much as had the Habsburg and Romanoff Empires'. The League of Nations made a similar point in their study of inter-war commercial policy published in 1942 (League of Nations, 1942,154–5).

Though self-generated flaws contributed to Europe's collapse in the first half of the twentieth century, allowing the United States to become the world's dominant economic and political power, Europe was spared the ignominy of total eclipse. A new lease of life began soon after the Second World War, at least for western Europe. Partly through her own exertions and partly by dint of American military and economic involvement as a result of the Cold War, western Europe experienced a spectacular revival. Some world systems analysts would see this as a mere extension of the former modern Eurocentred world system, by which the United States enabled the old core 'to preserve by economic means the privileges it forfeited through decolonization' (Abu-Lughod, 1989, 370). One may question the veracity of the colonial disconnection, given that its beneficial aspects were fast disappearing anyway, but the revamped hegemony of the west was all too apparent. The question is how stable is this unicentred system; will the balance eventually swing back to the east, with the rise of Japan, East Asia and, latterly, China? Or will it become a bipolar system, as under the Roman and Han Empires? Alternatively, with the emerging new configuration in Europe and the continued resilience of the United States at a time when the economies of East Asia are becoming more unstable, the hegemony of the west may be preserved for some time to come. Much will no doubt depend upon the success or otherwise of the European integration process, and especially whether the poorer outlier territories of southern and eastern Europe can be accommodated into what has been for so long a rich western club.

BIBLIOGRAPHY

Abu-Lughod, J. (1989), *Before European Hegemony: The World System AD1250–1350*, New York: Oxford University Press.

Anderson, J.L. (1991), *Explaining Long-term Economic Change*, Basingstoke: Macmillan.

Anderson, P. (1974), *Lineages of the Absolutist State*, London: New Left Books.

Bairoch, P. (1975), *The Economic Development of the Third World since 1900*, London: Methuen.

Bairoch, P. (1981), 'The main trends in national income disparities since the industrial revolution', in P. Bairoch and M. Lévy-Leboyer (eds), *Disparities in Economic Development since the Industrial Revolution*, London: Macmillan.

Bairoch, P. (1982), 'International industrialization levels from 1750 to 1980', *Journal of European Economic History*, 11.

Bairoch, P. (1989), 'Les trois révolutions agricoles du monde développé: rendements et productivité de 1800 à 1985', *Annales*, 44.

Bairoch, P. (1991), 'How and not why: economic inequalities between 1800 and 1913: some background figures', in J. Batou (ed.), *Between Development and Underdevelopment: The Precocious Attempts at Industrialization of the Periphery, 1800–70*, Geneva: Droz.

Batou, J. (1990), *Cent ans de résistance au sous-développement: l'industrialisation de l'Amérique latine et du Moyen-orient au défi européen, 1700–1870*, Geneva: Droz.

Bergeson, A. and R. Schoenberg (1980), 'Long waves of colonial expansion and contraction, 1415–1969', in A. Bergesen (ed.), *Studies of the Modern World System*, New York: Academic Press.

Blaut, J.M. (1993), *The Colonizer's Model of the World: Geographical Diffusionism and Eurocentric History*, New York: The Guilford Press.

Caldwell, M. (1977), *The Wealth of Some Nations*, London: Zed Press.

Chirot, D. (1985), 'The rise of the west', *American Sociological Review*, 50.

Chisholm, M. (1982), *Modern World Development*, London: Hutchinson.

Cipolla, C. (1981), *Before the Industrial Revolution: European Society and Economy, 1000–1700*, London: Methuen.

Cobban, A. (1969), *The Nation State and National Self-determination*, London: Collins.

Cunningham, W. (1904), *An Essay on Western Civilisation in its Economic Aspects*, Cambridge: Cambridge University Press.

Frank, A.G. (1990), 'The thirteenth-century world system: a review essay', *Journal of World History*, 1.

Goldstone, J.A. (1991), *Revolution and Rebellion in the Early Modern World*, Berkeley, CA: University of California Press.

Goodman, J. and K. Honeyman (1988), *Gainful Pursuits: The Making of Industrial Europe*, London: Edward Arnold.

Grigg, D. (1992), *The Transformation of Agriculture in the West*, Oxford: Blackwell.

Hodgson, M.G.S. (1993), *Rethinking World History: Essays on Europe, Islam and World History*, Cambridge: Cambridge University Press.

Jones, E. (1981), *The European Miracle*, Cambridge: Cambridge University Press.

Kahn, H. (1979), *World Economic Development, 1979 and Beyond*, London: Croom Helm.

Kennedy, P. (1988), *The Rise and Fall of the Great Powers: Economic Change and Military Conflict from 1500 to 2000*, London: Unwin Hyman.

Komlos, J. (1989a), *Nutrition and Economic Development in the Eighteenth Century Habsburg Monarchy: An Anthropometric Study*, Princeton, NJ: Princeton University Press.

Komlos, J. (1989b), 'Thinking about the industrial revolution', *Journal of European Economic History*, 18.

Landes, D. (1998), *The Wealth and Poverty of Nations: Why Some Are So Rich and Some Are So Poor*, New York: Norton.

Landes, D.S. (1969), *The Unbound Prometheus: Technological Change and Industrial Development in Western Europe from 1750 to the Present*, Cambridge: Cambridge University Press.

Landes, D.S. (1994), 'What room for accident in history? Explaining big changes by small events', *Economic History Review*, 47.

Laslett, P. (1988), 'The European family and early industrialization', in J. Baechler, J.A. Hall and M. Mann (eds), *Europe and the Rise of Capitalism*, Oxford: Blackwell.

League of Nations (1942), *Commercial Policy in the Interwar Period*, Geneva: League of Nations.

Livi-Bacci, M. (1992), *A Concise History of World Population*, Oxford: Blackwell.

Maddison, A. (1982), *Phases of Capitalist Development*, Oxford: Oxford University Press.

McNeill, J.R. (1996), 'The reserve army of the unmarried in world economic history: flexible fertility regimes and the wealth of nations', in D.H. Aldcroft and R.E. Catterall (eds), *Rich Nations–Poor Nations: The Long-run Perspective*, Cheltenham, UK and Brookfield, US: Edward Elgar.

McNeill, W.H. (1963), *The Rise of the West*, Chicago: University of Chicago Press.

McNeill, W.H. (1979), *A World History*, Oxford: Oxford University Press.

Mokyr, J. (1976), *Industrialisation in the Low Countries, 1795–1850*, New Haven, CT: Yale University Press.

Musgrave, P. (1999), *The Economy of Europe in the Early Modern Period*, Basingstoke: Macmillan.

North, D.C. (1981), *Structure and Change in Economic History*, New York: Norton.

North, D.C. and R.P. Thomas (1970), 'An economic theory of the growth of the western world', *Economic History Review*, 23.

North, D.C. and Thomas, R.P. (1973), *The Rise of the Western World: A New Economic History*, Cambridge: Cambridge University Press.

O'Brien, P.K. (1996), 'Global warfare and long-term economic development, 1789–1939', *War in History*, 3.

O'Brien, P.K. and L. Prados de la Escosura (1998), 'The costs and benefits of European imperialism from the conquest of Ceuta, 1415, to the Treaty of Lusaka, 1974', in C.-E. Núñez, (ed.), *Debates and Controversies in Economic History: Proceedings of the Twelfth International Economic History Congress*, Madrid: Fundación Ramón Areces.

Persson, K.G. (1988), *Pre-industrial Economic Growth: Social Organization and Technological Progress in Europe*, Oxford: Blackwell.

Pollard, S. (1973), 'Industrialisation and the European economy', *Economic History Review*, 26.

Ramirez-Faria, C. (1991), *The Origins of Economic Inequality between Nations: A Critique of Western Theories on Development and Underdevelopment*, London: Unwin Hyman.

Reynolds, L.G. (1985), *Economic Growth in the Third World, 1850–1950*, New Haven, CT: Yale University Press.

Smith, A.K. (1991), *Creating a World Economy: Merchant Capital, Colonialism and World Trade, 1400–1825*, Boulder, CO: Westview Press.

Snooks G.D. (1990), 'Economic growth during the last millennium: a quantitative perspective for the British industrial revolution', paper presented to the Tenth International Economic History Congress, Leuven, Belgium.

Snooks, G.D. (1996), *The Dynamic Society: Exploring the Sources of Global Change*, London: Routledge.

Thomson, D. (1966), *Europe since Napoleon*, Harmondsworth: Penguin.

Tilly, C. (1992), *Coercion, Capital and European States, AD 990–1990*, Oxford: Blackwell.

Valerio, N. (1992) 'Some remarks about growth and stagnation in the Mediterranean world in the XIXth and XXth centuries', *Journal of European Economic History*, 21.

1. The rise of the European economy 1500–1800

J.L. van Zanden and E. Horlings

Since the days of Adam Smith (1776) economists and economic historians have asked the question how the rise to world pre-eminence of the European economy in the centuries before 1800 can be explained. How is it possible that, in an economy in which decisions over investment, consumption and production are spread over many millions of decision makers – individuals, households, governments, (family) firms – a systematic tendency came to operate which led to the long-term increase in productivity? Why was Europe able to produce almost continuous advances in technology and how did these new technologies spread over those many millions of productive units? Why did not population growth 'eat up' the gains that were made in the field of production? What role was played by the creation of a 'world economy': the expansion of European trade with and control over the Americas and parts of Asia and Africa? Or were the changes in the rural basis of society, the creation of a (rural) proletariat and the rise of commercialized agriculture more fundamental for the advance of the European economy?

Again, since the days of Adam Smith there has been (perhaps) agreement on one fundamental point: that it was the rise of the market economy that was the driving force behind many of these changes. The market created strong incentives to find new technologies and new patterns of specialization that were more efficient than the old ones; the market coordinated the economic decision making of these many millions of entrepreneurs in such a way that they were 'forced' to accept more productive solutions to old problems; those who did not lost their competitive edge and saw their incomes decline. The big question is, however, how to explain this 'rise of the market economy'. What were the conditions under which it could become the dominant mode of organization of the economy during the Middle Ages and the early modern period? And, related to this first question, is the problem of when it became dominant: during the 'crisis' of the seventeenth century, or during the 'crisis' of the late Middle Ages, or even before.

It is beyond the scope of this chapter to summarize the extensive debate on these issues,[1] but a number of different interpretations can be mentioned. In much of the literature the development of the market economy is seen as an autonomous process, which in itself was creating the conditions for its own long-term dynamics. The 'heroes' of this interpretation are the merchants who started trading on a small scale in the early Middle Ages, thereby profiting from the lack of regional economic integration which created large price differentials between different parts of Europe. They slowly expanded their networks, acquired political independence in cities, became involved in the financing of princes and states, gained influence over the state through representative bodies (the Cortes, the Parliament) as a result, continued to accumulate capital, penetrated manufacturing (through proto-industry, for example), engaged increasing numbers of wage workers, and so on. Finally, this process resulted in an integrated market economy which made possible high levels of specialization and productivity. The creation of a world economy in the sixteenth century gave an enormous boost to this process as it meant new opportunities for rapid growth of international trade and at the same time supplied the fuel for it: the gold and silver that Spain robbed from Latin America.

Two schools take issue with this gradualist (or Smithian) interpretation. The Marxists have argued, following Marx's famous Chapter 24 of the first volume of *Das Kapital*, that the 'primitive accumulation of capital' meant in the first place the separation of producers from the means of production. Because, according to Robert Brenner, for example, independent producers in agriculture – let us call them peasants – have no incentives to produce for the market, they will block the development of the market economy. Instead, a class of wage labourers has to be created (and its antipode, a class of commercial farmers) in order to create the preconditions for capital investments and productivity growth in the countryside. This could only be done through political force, through the dispossession of the peasantry with the help of the state. As a result, class conflict lay at the roots of the rise of market economy (see Brenner, 1985).

Another, increasingly influential, interpretation focuses on the institutions that enable the individual producer to produce for the market and lower the risks of market participation. Predator states, already present in the writings of Smith, may seriously harm progress in that direction because the profits of specialization to the producer will be directly skimmed off by them (Jones, 1988; North, 1990). Legal systems and informal rules may create the wrong incentives; markets may be ill-organized and taxes on market production so excessive that it does not pay for a peasant to step up his output. In the writings of Douglass North (1990) the relationship between the bourgeoisie and the state is considered fundamental; he has especially focused on the interaction between differential processes of state formation in England and Spain to show the implications of these processes for long-term economic development.

These fundamental issues will be discussed to some extent in the course of this chapter. Following North, we will begin with a short digression into the institutional framework that made the rise of Europe possible; in a few pages we try to summarize thoughts about the contributions of households, families and the state to this success story. Then we proceed with the fundamental problem of specialization in agriculture: when will peasants want to step up production for the market? After this brief discussion of the role of agriculture in economic development, we will move on to the two sectors that in a way functioned as engines of economic growth: manufacturing and international services. Finally, we will ask the question why growth was so slow in Europe during the early modern period, and why it accelerated after 1780 (in Britain) or 1820 (in the rest of western Europe).[2]

THE CHANGING ECONOMY OF THE HOUSEHOLD

In a classic paper Hajnal (1965) has formulated the proposition that, in the early modern period, Europe west of the line Leningrad–Trieste was characterized by a special 'European marriage pattern', of which the features were that men and women tended to marry at a very late age (on average after their 25th and 23rd birthday respectively) and that a relatively large proportion of them remained single. Research carried out since has shown how important this European marriage pattern was for demographic development; the age at first marriage has been identified as the single most important variable determining long-term population growth (Wrigley and Schofield, 1981). Moreover, this age at first marriage responded quite accurately to socioeconomic pressures; when real wages went down and it became more difficult to set up a household, people tended to postpone marriage, and population growth slowed down consequently. Conversely, economic expansion resulted in the growth of employment and higher wages, and led to an expansion of the labour supply in the long run. This 'homeostatic regime' created a certain balance between the forces of population growth and those of economic change; through these 'preventive checks' population growth in western Europe remained in step with the long-term increase in productive capacities (ibid.).

The timing of the emergence of this European marriage pattern is still rather unclear; Hajnal suggested that it came into existence in the fifteenth and sixteenth centuries. Research carried out since has confirmed this hypothesis for England and the Low Countries (Razi, 1993; Van Zanden, 1998b). However, this does not yet offer an explanation of its appearance. A number of issues seem to be at stake here. In the first place, the European marriage pattern, which was characterized by nuclear families, was radically different from the marriage patterns we find outside Europe, where the extended family dominated, in the sense that the (not so) youngsters themselves took the decision with whom and when they married. This was especially the case in the lower income classes, where the parents could not back up their authority with much private property and the transfer of it was not an important part of the marriage contract. The strong position of the adult children may to some extent be explained by the teachings of the Catholic Church, which preached the doctrine that marriage was in the end a contract between two persons before the eyes of God. The bottom line of this was that, as soon as man and wife had promised to marry, they were bound to their promises, which seriously limited parental control over these matters (Bange and Weiler, 1987).

But perhaps much more fundamental was the development of the labour market. In England and Holland in the fifteenth century, men and women could actually acquire an independent position as they had the option to gain an income from wage labour – either as a day labourer or as a maid or servant in another household. This influenced negotiations with their parents (who, of course, preferred to exercise parental authority over this decision) in a radical way. Many could and in fact did leave the household at an early age (that is, at an age when they were about to be married in other societies). Many left for the cities temporarily, to become migrant workers, or more permanently, to become, for example, apprentices or servants (Razi, 1993; Seccombe, 1992). Consequently, there was a close correlation between the rise of the labour market and the appearance of the European marriage pattern.

The European marriage pattern therefore meant that, in contrast to societies in which the marriage was the result of a decision of the patriarchal heads of two extended families who 'exchanged' a young woman or a young man for a certain amount of goods, a new household was set up by the couple themselves. This brought about a close link between *economic* decision making (can we afford to set up a new household?) and *demographic* decision making, as marriage implied having children. Setting up a new household was considered to be an investment decision: have we built up enough 'credit', are our employment prospects stable enough to take the big step? The fortuitous result of that connection was the 'homeostatic regime' that has been analysed so convincingly by

Wrigley and Schofield (1981). Moreover, it gave an enormous impetus to the development of the labour market; as real wages declined and it took more and more years to build up enough 'credit' to start a new household, young men and women, in the best years of their lives, were increasingly dependent on wage labour. The sharp decline in real wages we find all over Europe in the sixteenth century may perhaps be partly explained by this perverse reaction of labour supply (although after marriage certainly a large proportion of the men remained dependent on wage labour).

THE DIALECTICS BETWEEN STATE AND ECONOMY

There seems to be broad agreement between Marxists (Brenner), institutional economists (North) and 'Smithian' economic historians (Jones) that the state could pose a serious threat to economic development. Whenever producers were able to generate wealth, the state was tempted to pressure them into financing the public deficit, or to raise taxation on trade and market production, in short, to channel the proceeds of economic growth into its own coffers. In the short run such a policy meant that its power basis was strengthened, but in the long run it killed the goose that laid the golden eggs. On the other hand, merchants (and industrial entrepreneurs) needed the backing of a strong state; in the centuries before 1800 the differences between trade and war were often only marginal and all large merchant empires were built as much on military power as on economic superiority. Moreover, the state was needed for the creation of a stable institutional framework for national and international exchange. Therefore, since the birth of capitalism, the entrepreneur and the prince, on the one hand, needed each other badly, but on the other hand, were unable to live together peacefully as their interests, certainly in the short run, conflicted constantly. Successful economic development was only possible when a precarious balance between the state and the economy was maintained.

One of the reasons behind Europe's economic miracle was its feudal legacy. In the period between 800 and 1000, the political system of Europe disintegrated into many small entities, governed by feudal lords. An intensive competition between the many hundreds of kingdoms and lordships began, in which warfare and preparation for war played a crucial role (Tilly, 1990). The more a territorial unit was able to generate resources for this, the more it could consolidate and expand into a larger, more powerful unit. These resources had to be generated by the economy.

Feudal levies, derived from an unspecialized and relatively unproductive peasant population, were the initial means to generate this surplus. Increasingly, taxes from trade and industry and loans from wealthy citizens came to play a decisive role, however. This process of state formation created larger units for exchange, in which (to some extent) common rules were applied and communications between the various parts of the kingdom were enhanced; in other words, transaction costs were being reduced by the expansion and consolidation of states. Consequently, the expansion of trade could follow (and reinforce) this process of creating larger, more unified territorial units.

From an evolutionary perspective this process can be analysed as follows. The many hundreds of states of tenth-century Europe can be considered as a large number of experiments with different 'mutations' of the institutions which might, on the one hand, stimulate economic development and would, on the other hand, skim off part of its proceeds to the treasury. Those states that were most successful in finding efficient solutions to this institutional problem were likely to prosper, expand at the expense of others and in the end dominate the European state system. Moreover, states were able to learn from each other: they could copy, for example, successful mercantile policies, or learn from unsuccessful experiences (such as frequent devaluations to increase the income from minting).

A successful series of experiments was characterized by a political structure in which the bourgeoisie was itself in control of the state. This solved the problem of the tension between the prince and the entrepreneurial class. The mediaeval communes attempted as much as possible to gain independence from monarchs in order to be able to regulate the economic and political affairs of the cities themselves. The city states of Italy, the partly independent cities of Flanders (which constantly had to battle with their counts over independence), the near-independent cities of the Holy Roman Empire and, finally, the autonomous cities of the Netherlands that would later form the Dutch Republic, were throughout the Middle Ages and the early modern period focal points of economic development. But, as the case of the Italian city states shows perhaps most convincingly, they were by their nature unable to form strong, centralized states and were therefore bound to fall prey to the large territorial states that came into existence during the early modern period (Tilly, 1990). This inability was a factor behind the tragedy of Italy in the sixteenth and seventeenth centuries, of Flanders after 1580, of the German towns after 1618, and in a way also of the Netherlands after 1795; and the loss of independence invariably brought about the loss of economic dynamism. This class of experimental 'mutations' was in the long run unable to continue the competition with France and England.

Within these 'victorious' territorial states, the central issue was the balance of power between the prince and his (wealthy) citizen. How much say in political affairs was to be delegated to those who paid the taxes and funded his majesty's debts? And, perhaps even more importantly, how was this power to be delegated: through systems of patronage and clientism to a few wealthy magnates, or through formal rules and laws which would in principle apply to all? The most important constraint in the search process for efficient solutions was the position of the prince himself. Because his main motive was to increase his power base and income, it was unlikely that he would accept reforms which would seriously limit his influence. Hence, to summarize a very complex story in a few words, a number of revolutions were necessary to break his power. The Dutch Revolt (against the king of Spain) of the 1570s can be viewed as an early example of such a revolution. The classics here are, of course, the English Revolution of the 1640s leading up to the Glorious Revolution of 1688, and the French Revolution of 1789 (which in its revolutionary fervour and military aggression swept away many comparable pre-modern institutions in the neighbouring countries).

The result of these transformations was, at least in the more successful countries, an institutional framework in which secure property rights were established (North, 1990), in which an equilibrium between the state and the economy was maintained through many checks and balances. Many regions and countries did not (at first) profit from these experiments. Even Tuscany, for example, became a stagnant economy as a result of its exploitation by a small urban elite (Epstein, 1993); the Spanish case, documented by North and Thomas (1973), is an even more classic example of stagnation caused by a predator state (see also Thompson and Yun, 1994). The uneven process of economic development can therefore be partially explained by the different relationships between state and economy in Europe in the early modern period.

THE COMMERCIALIZATION OF AGRICULTURE

If we agree that the rise of the market economy was the most important process that propelled western Europe forward on its way to world hegemony in the nineteenth century, one of the most fundamental problems to solve is the rise of commercialized agriculture. Why did peasants in some parts of Europe begin to work for the market relatively early, whereas this process seems to have stagnated in large parts of Europe until well into the eighteenth and nineteenth centuries?

One way to approach this problem is by trying to find out which factors influence the decision-making process of rural households who can allocate resources between different activities: to produce for the market or to produce for home consumption. From an economic perspective, such a process can be analysed as being caused by changes in the 'relative profitability' of market production versus subsistence production, by the amount of goods (or of leisure) that can be gained by putting the resources of the household into one of the two alternatives. In this section the most important factors responsible for a change in this choice process are briefly analysed in order to explain why peasants commercialized in some periods and under some circumstances.

When a peasant is producing for a small local market – say for the local landlord and for a few craftsmen who consume agricultural products – he will be confronted by a sharply declining demand curve; in other words, the 'terms of trade' of market production will decline rapidly when output for the market is increased. Therefore, in such a situation, he may act rationally when he limits market output beyond a certain point. However, declining prices of agricultural products can in some instances be compensated for by the productivity growth that is made possible by specialization. In general one can argue that the productivity of subsistence production is bound to be relatively low. Specialization is by definition absent, economies of scale cannot be realized, learning effects are probably small and, given this state of affairs, there is not much scope for technological change. It is part of the basic teachings of economics since Adam Smith that market production does offer scope for specialization, economies of scale, learning effects and technological change; in other words, a shift towards increased production for the market will generally mean that the factors of production can be used much more intensively and productively than in subsistence production. As a result of these changes which accompany the process of commercialization, the relative 'profitability' of market versus subsistence goods will probably tend to increase when the benefits of specialization are being reaped; therefore, after a certain point, commercialization may become a self-reinforcing process.

The second factor which determines the change towards specialization, the terms of trade for agriculture, is also related to the extent of the market this sector is producing for, and its capacity to absorb surpluses. One of the driving forces behind the commercialization of agriculture was the growth of cities and of employment opportunities outside agriculture in general, which created markets for agricultural products (Wrigley, 1978; Grantham, 1989). Another was technological change in the non-agricultural sector, which drove down the prices of industrial products in the long run. Especially during the great upswings in the European economy – the sixteenth century, the eighteenth century and after – the relative prices of most industrial and colonial products did fall relative to the prices of foodstuffs, which meant that the incentives for peasants to produce for the market became stronger. In the regions where the progress of industry and international trade was concentrated – in Flanders, Holland and England successively – prices of manufactured commodities fell quite rapidly; the growth of international trade meant that also in the rest of Europe relative prices of industrial products tended to decline.[3] In this way, technological and organizational advances in the rest of the economy stimulated the commercialization of agriculture.

The final factor that is involved is related to the organization of the marketing system and to the institutional structure of the society at large. In a Pareto-optimal, neo-classical world, there are no costs involved in market transactions: every producer and consumer has perfect information about the state of the market and perfect foresight of the future development of the market. In practice, transactions are costly, because the buyer and the seller have to spend time and money going to the market place, they have to transport their commodities, pay tolls, excises and other charges, pay for brokers and merchants who bring parties together and so on. Other costs are involved in acquiring the necessary information about the state of the market, the current prices and in negotiating about the buying and selling prices. The fact that transaction costs exist, and that they are probably higher the less developed a market system is, means that it is rational for a peasant to eat the rye and the potatoes he has cultivated himself, and not to sell it to the market and buy it in return whenever he needs it for consumption. Large landowners, in a similar way, may prefer to provision their households from their own estates to save on transaction costs (Campbell, 1997).

To this concept of transaction costs must be added the costs that are associated with the risks and uncertainties of market production. The transformation from autarky to commercial farming evidently involves investments in seeds, implements, livestock and so on: in other words, transition costs. Moreover, a switchback into autarky will also be costly: it will mean that the farmer has to learn to make subsistence goods again, whereas the members of the household have become used to the superior quality of manufactured goods. These 'transition costs' become more important when participation in the market is considered to be a risky affair, because farmers cannot predict the future development of (relative) prices and of transaction costs. Moreover, production for the market may mean that new forms of dependence are created or old ones are revived; middlemen who supply capital, seed or other inputs to the farmer, in return for buying the new crops in advance, may turn into Shylocks; tax farmers and landlords may skim off the new wealth that is being created by the efforts of the peasant. Finally, the quality of the institutional framework, the legal protection of property rights, may determine whether it is worthwhile for a farmer to engage in increased market production.

Again a dynamic view of these costs is helpful. It is obvious that when agricultural surpluses increase it becomes profitable to invest in the improvement of marketing systems, for example in the establishment of many new, more decentralized markets, in the improvement of infrastructure to reduce transport costs, and so on. A larger turnover will probably increase competition between different (groups of) merchants, which will reduce trade margins and the power of the middlemen. In a completely competitive marketing system the middleman will be reduced to the role of servant of buyers and sellers. In the long run, therefore, increased market production will probably tend to lower transaction costs substantially. There are, however, important qualifications to this 'rule' (or better, hypothesis). Princes and cities might become dependent on taxes levied on trade, which was one of the 'easiest' sources of income of early modern states. The recurrent crises in state finances may induce states to increase taxation in such a way that transaction costs are increased substantially, which will in the long run tend to kill the goose that lays the golden eggs (see Epstein, 1993). The long-run dynamics of these transaction costs are therefore also dependent on the institutional framework in which the farmers operate.

The 'dynamics' of transaction costs, which probably will tend to decline when the volume of market production increases, means that the 'terms of trade' between agricultural market goods and manufactured goods are not a static phenomenon, but might become favourable for the peasants when the process of commercialization continues. This implies that the dynamic, long-run trade-off between subsistence production and market production may be much more favourable than the short-term terms of trade that peasants will perceive at a certain point in time. In other words, as a result of the dynamic advantages of specialization there exist multiple equilibria; at a certain point a peasant may be in complete equilibrium when he restricts market production to a trifle, but once exogenous forces – the growth of external demand from a big city – have pulled him out of this point, a dynamic process of commercialization may begin, resulting in the rapid growth of output and productivity.

PRODUCTIVITY GROWTH IN AGRICULTURE

The approach outlined in the previous section is able to explain the 'stylized facts' of European agricultural development much better than the 'classic' Malthusian/Ricardian interpretation, which focuses on the tensions between population growth and the supply of foodstuffs from agriculture. Slicher van Bath showed in 1963 that levels of *land productivity* (measured as yield ratios) in the countries bordering the North Sea rose significantly in the early modern period, whereas in other parts of Europe not much progress was made. An analysis of the pattern of crop yields at the beginning of the nineteenth century tends to confirm this picture (Table 1.1). The high level of productivity in the countries around the North Sea (including Ireland) is immediately apparent. In this region a crop yield of 20 hectolitres per hectare is quite normal (the cultivation of rye in the Netherlands is a notable exception). The yield ratio in this core region is about 10. Going south, production per hectare gradually

Table 1.1 Estimated crop yields and yield ratios for 12 countries in about 1800 (crop yields in hl per ha)

| | Crop yields | | | | Yield ratios | | | |
	Wheat	Rye	Barley	Oats	Wheat	Rye	Barley	Oats
England	20.3		29.3	32.5	11.3		12.7	9.0
Ireland	19.9		31.2	32.9				
Netherlands	18.9	15.4	27.7	28.8	11.2	7.5	14.2	11.1
Belgium	19.6	20.8	25.3	25.1	11.5	12.2	14.1	13.2
France								
north	14.4	12.1	14.0	15.4	6.6	5.5	6.9	8.5
south	10.1	9.7	12.3	14.5	6.2	5.5	6.6	7.1
total	12.2	10.8	13.5	15.2	6.4	5.5	6.8	8.2
Italy	6.9	7.6	10.1	9.9	4.1	4.4	5.0	5.2
Spain	7.0	4.0	9.0	9.5	4.5	2.5	7.0	
Germany								
4 dept.	13.7	13.2	20.4	25.8	7.1	7.1	6.7	8.0
total	13.7	12.5	13.5	17.0				
Austria	12.8	12.9	19.2	19.3	4.0	4.0	4.6	5.2
Sweden					6.0	5.9	5.9	5.0
Russia					3.0	3.1	3.1	3.6

Source: Van Zanden (1998a).

declines. In the Bassin de Paris, productivity is quite close to the level around the North Sea (for wheat, the most important grain, the yield was about 17 hl and the yield ratio almost 7). However, south of a line drawn between La Rochelle and Mulhouse, it begins to drop towards Mediterranean levels (Clout, 1980). Along this southern axis the yield ratio generally declines less than production per hectare because less and less seed was used per hectare. In the far south of Spain they sometimes used less than 1 hl of seed per hectare, compared to about 2 hl in the North Sea countries (Amalric, 1983, 29). This may also explain the relatively high yield ratios to be found in some parts of Southern Italy (Agro Romano, Sicily) (Aymard, 1973; Revel, 1982). Around the Mediterranean, production per hectare stood at 8 to 10 hl, with a few high points (Sicily); this level was approximately 50 per cent lower than in the Low Countries and England. Towards the east, yield ratios fell sharply to 3 hl in Russia, partly due to a slight increase in the amount of seed used.

The very high level of land productivity found in the region around the North Sea area is, according to Slicher van Bath (1963; 1967) and more recent research (Van Zanden, 1998a), the result of developments between 1500 and 1800. It is much more difficult to measure the level of *labour productivity*. Wrigley (1987) has developed a way of 'guesstimating' this important variable (or rather, to estimate the number of mouths fed by every one hundred people working on the land) which uses data on the urbanization ratio linked to estimates of the non-primary working population in the countryside. This method rests on the premise that long-term per capita consumption of agrarian products was stable between 1500 and 1800. A second premise is that only a very small proportion of agrarian production was traded internationally (see also Persson, 1988). The sole exception to this rule seems to have been the Netherlands, but we can include the Dutch in our calculations by estimating the percentage of grain imported for human consumption. Wrigley himself has only published estimates of 'labour productivity' in British and French agriculture. However, similar calculations have been made for a number of other countries using estimates of the urbanization ratio published by De Vries (1984) (see Table 1.2).

The following picture emerges from these data: in western Europe labour productivity generally increases (with the possible exception of Belgium between 1500 and 1700), while stagnation prevails in the rest of the continent. As early as 1500, labour productivity in the Low Countries is noticeably higher than elsewhere, but the upward movement is only sustained in the north; in Belgium a U-shaped development can be found. Labour productivity increases substantially in England, while growth is much more modest in France.

Table 1.2 Rough estimates of the number of mouths fed by 100 people working in agriculture 1500/20–1800

	1500/20	1600		1700	1800
England/Wales	132	143		182	248
Belgium	173	160		192	233
Netherlands	177		219[a]		277
France	138	145		158	170
Italy	133	143		122	129
Poland	100	101		101	105
Spain	114	130		122	129

Note: [a]1670.

Sources: England/Wales and France: Wrigley (1987,187); for other countries, see Van Zanden (1998a).

In contrast to these dynamics, Italy, Poland and Switzerland are distinguished by stability; only in Spain do we see any progress, first in the sixteenth century and again in the eighteenth century. It should be noted, however, that since these estimates are based exclusively on the urbanization ratio they take no account of the growth of non-agricultural employment in the countryside in southern and eastern Europe in the seventeenth and eighteenth centuries (for example, as a result of the emergence of proto-industry). It is therefore quite likely that they underestimate the increase in labour productivity.

This reservation does not, however, alter the main conclusion of this analysis, namely, that the long-term development of labour productivity and land productivity was analogous. In other words, there was no trade-off between the growth of land and labour productivity, as one would expect on the basis of the Ricardian approach. On the contrary, in the North Sea region (consisting of England, Belgium and the Netherlands and parts of northern France) there is a strong correlation between the growth of land and labour productivity: both grew strongly in periods of rising urbanization, and stagnated in years of declining demand for agricultural products. The Flemish case is very interesting, as it shows that a strong decline in demand for agricultural products – as a result of a series of urban crises, of which the occupation by the Spanish army after 1580 was only the final blow to the urban system – went together with an absolute decline in land and labour productivity. During the seventeenth and eighteenth centuries the urban system and the agricultural sector recovered again. This U-shaped development was also demonstrated in the work of Neveux (1980) and Morineau (1970) on agricultural productivity in the French–Belgian border region and has been confirmed by the research of Thoen and Vandenbroeke into grain yields per hectare in Flanders between c. 1450 and 1800. The development of agriculture in England and Holland is more straightforward; here we find an almost continuous growth of labour and land productivity, which seems to correlate closely to the long-term development of these two economies. On the other hand, in the rest of Europe, where the urban economy was much less dynamic between 1500 and 1800, the growth of agricultural productivity was rather slow or, in some cases, almost absent. The result of these diverging trends was that, at the beginning of the nineteenth century, a core region with high levels of productivity had come into existence: the North Sea area. The more one moved away from this core region, the lower the level of agricultural productivity was.

A final implication of the approach outlined here is that commercialization often had very different consequences for the different groups of peasants. Large and small farmers faced different relative costs of subsistence versus market goods. Because of the availability of much 'underemployed' labour, the small farm had a competitive advantage in subsistence production (with a low level of labour productivity), whereas it faced higher transaction costs (and probably higher risks) for its much smaller surplus of market goods. This may explain why peasants with smallholdings were in almost every part of Europe considered to be 'obstacles' to the modernization of agriculture (Hoffman, 1996, 14ff); they were, as a result of their specific combination of resources, placed at a disadvantageous position in comparison with the large farmers who could much more easily expand market production.

On the other hand, large farmers often were the pioneers of increased commercialization and were able to reap the dynamic profits of that process, in the form of increased returns to labour, land and capital, and declining transactions costs. Their superior access to land, capital and markets meant that they profited the most from the expansion of market opportunities. The competition in the market for land did the rest: because they were able to pay higher rents, they were able to accumulate more land at the expense of the peasants with smallholdings, which resulted in a dual structure of landownership, in which a small group of farmers owned or rented most of the land and the peasants became landless labourers.

The results of these differential incentives for commercialization were quite dramatic. In many regions of western Europe the commercialization went together with the growth of large farms and the proletarianization of the labour force. Developments in the English countryside are very well known in this respect; during the early modern period, and especially during the agricultural revolution of the eighteenth century, smallholdings almost disappeared from the countryside, and consolidated farms, on which wage labour was employed on a large scale, came to dominate the agricultural sector (Allan, 1992). On the continent, the polarization in the countryside was less radical, but here too one can witness comparable changes in the most commercialized regions. In the Sea Provinces of the Netherlands, large farms and wage labour also became the norm (Van Zanden, 1994, 164). In the most commercialized part of France, the Bassin de Paris (Jacquart, 1967), and in large parts of Belgium (but not in Flanders), the same process of polarization was taking place. It can therefore be suggested that commercialization went together with a strong increase in inequality in the countryside.

This interpretation implies that proletarianization of the peasantry and the rise of a class of large farmers were the consequences, not the causes, of the commercialization process. We propose that the hypothesis of Brenner, that the creation of a class of rural labourers preceded the commercialization of agriculture, should be turned on its head.

TECHNOLOGICAL AND ORGANIZATIONAL CHANGE IN INDUSTRY

Industry was, already in the centuries before the industrial revolution, a relatively dynamic part of the economy. A very rough impression of these dynamics can be derived from various estimates of the long-term development of the European iron industry (Table 1.3). Although these estimates are not completely consistent, they suggest that, on balance, production per head probably trebled during the early modern period. The growth in iron production was concentrated in a few specific regions. In England, there was a rapid expansion of the industry in the sixteenth century, followed by a period of more gradual growth. In Sweden, the expansion took place in the seventeenth century, under the influence of Dutch merchants who effected a major modernization of the Swedish iron industry using technical expertise developed in Liège (Nijman, 1991, 231). The tempo of growth increased throughout Europe in the eighteenth century; probably only Spain experienced a fall in iron production during this period (Pounds and Parker, 1957, 24). Important innovations in the British iron industry, where coal was introduced as the main source of fuel, were responsible for an enormous growth in iron production in that country. But in France too, and to a lesser extent in Germany where these innovations were barely applied, production increased very rapidly. In the eighteenth century France was actually the largest iron producer in western Europe, although production per head remained below that of England and Sweden.

Table 1.3 Estimates of the development of production in the iron industry
of western Europe 1500–1790 (in 1000 tonnes)

	Total G&H	Total Sprangel	Total kg/capita	Great Britain	Sweden	France	Germany
1500		40	0.65	1	5	12	5
1600	125		1.6	17	7[a]		
1700	165		2.0	24	28[a]	25	30
1740/50		145–80	1.5–1.9	27	40[a]		
1790	335		2.2	80	50	140	50

Note: [a]based on data of exports of iron.

Sources: Total: Goodman and Honeyman (1988, 172); corrected to exclude the Russian Empire with Pounds and Parker, (1957, 27); total: Sprangel (1969, 305-21); Great Britain: Riden (1977, 442-59); Sweden: Nijman (1991, 231); France and Germany, 1500: Mulhall (1898); 1700 and 1790: Pounds and Parker (1957, 27); De Vries (1984, 36).

It is extremely uncertain whether the growth of the iron industry is typical of European industry as a whole. Unfortunately, it is impossible to single out other branches of industry where production must have risen even more sharply. These would largely have been relatively new industries, such as printing, paper making, sugar refining, the tobacco industry, the silk industry, the cotton industry, diamond cutting and the distilling of gin. The supply of industrial products at the end of the eighteenth century was infinitely richer than at the beginning of the sixteenth century, owing to the rise of all sorts of new industries which swelled the market with new products, from coffee, tobacco and sugar to carriages, musical instruments and wigs. Dramatic growth was also visible in the mining of coal, driven by the increasing scarcity of wood (as a fuel) and by the growing demand for energy. Estimates of the output of British mines reveal a spectacular rise, from 210 000 tons in 1551/60, to almost 3 million tons in 1681/90, to more than 10 million tons in 1781/90 – an increase by a factor of 49 in 230 years (Wilson, 1977, 124). Similarly, in the mining region of Liège total output increased from about 25 000 tons in 1510 to more than 500 000 tons in 1812 (Unger, 1984, 237). However, in most cases coal replaced a declining supply of wood, which makes it difficult to interpret this as a clear sign of economic growth (Wilkinson, 1973).

In contrast to the growth sectors – the new industries, those linked to the commercial sector and those linked to the industrial revolution (coal and iron) – there were of course the more 'traditional' sectors, which experienced a much less rapid expansion. In the seventeenth and eighteenth centuries beer brewing was declining almost everywhere in western Europe, thanks to the rise of alternative drinks such as coffee, tea and gin. In Belgium, estimated annual beer consumption per capita declined from 156 litres in 1610/15 to 108 litres in 1760/65 (Blomme *et al.*, 1994, 20). According to Richard Yntema, the fall was even more dramatic in Holland: from 301 litres per capita in 1622 to 38 litres in 1795 (Yntema, 1992, 128)! The meat industry must also have lost much of its significance, owing to the fall in the consumption of meat. It seems, however, that the list of industries which declined is much shorter than the list of expanding sectors. Perhaps the iron industry, with more than a doubling of production per head between 1500 and 1750, is roughly typical of industry as a whole during this period, but this cannot be more than a guess.

Behind this relatively strong growth of the output of manufacturing (and of international services) were complex interactions between supply and demand factors. Technological change was obviously very important; although many great inventions had already been made during the Middle Ages (for example, printing, gunpowder and many applications of wind and water power), it was the early modern economy which was able to reap the gains from them in full. Learning effects, economies of scale and the gradual spread of minor adaptations of existing techniques made possible an almost continuous growth of productivity in industry and shipping. The long-run supply curve of new industries such as printing, sugar refining, distilling and diamond cutting, and perhaps also of many of the long established industries, such as shipbuilding or metal working, obviously had a downward slope: production costs tended to decline with the scale of production. Specialization processes, of which Smith's pin factory is the classic example, also contributed significantly to these productivity increases; the urban centres of the textile industry saw a continuing increase in the number of specialisms involved in the production process. The rise of proto-industry (putting-out) is another example of important organizational changes which made possible large reductions in production costs.

In view of this shape of the long-term supply curve, the expansion of demand for these products was also of fundamental importance; only a growing demand for non-agricultural products and services made it possible to realize the full potential of the early modern technology. This meant that, to begin with, the growth of population (density) and the rise of cities stimulated the development of industry and trade; moreover, the increase in productivity that resulted from this interplay of a rising demand and falling production costs also induced peasants (who saw their terms of trade improve) to increase market production, which would in its turn again stimulate the growth of output of industry and services. Therefore, in periods of rising population numbers and growing urbanization – in the sixteenth and the eighteenth centuries – the relative prices of industrial products (and of imported colonial products) declined, that is, relative to the prices of agricultural products. The sixteenth century price revolution, triggered by the import of American silver and gold, acted in a similar way. European expansion into the Americas and the creation of a 'world economy' in the same period boosted shipping and trade, and created new markets for the industrial products of Europe.

In view of this state of affairs, it becomes clear why many states thought that capturing a larger share of the European pie of international services and (export) industry would have important effects on the national economy. Structural transformation (the growth of cities and of employment outside agriculture in general) was the key to productivity growth in the agricultural sector; the growth of industry and trade would be to some extent self-reinforcing: it lowered production costs and consequently increased international competitiveness. Acquiring a larger share in international trade could therefore have large multiplier effects on 'the wealth of nations'. This helps to explain the mercantilist policies that were devised by the territorial states to increase their share in international business.

INTERNATIONAL TRADE

World trade provided opportunities beyond the limits of domestic markets and agricultural productivity. Potential demand and supply far exceeded that of regional and national economies: international trade involved large numbers of producers and consumers and was characterized by low transaction costs because of its large volume and easy communications. A large and accessible world market made possible a scale of production and degree of specialization that could not be achieved on the basis of home demand. In general, export production was subject to less regulation and more competition, which encouraged technological and organizational innovations. Consequently, the expansion of international trade after the Middle Ages was one of the most dynamic elements of the early modern European economy.

Grain illustrates the way in which international trade could affect regional economies. In the late Middle Ages, rising water levels forced the farmers of Holland (the western part of the Netherlands) to abandon grain production. Many shifted to livestock and dairy production, took up non-agricultural professions (such as fishing) or moved to the cities (Van Zanden, 1991). The supply of basic necessities instead shifted towards producers in other parts of the Netherlands and, above all, in eastern Europe. This was the beginning of the large-scale Baltic trade that became the foundation of the Amsterdam staple market in the next centuries. Polish and German grain producers responded to the increased demand from western

Europe by expanding their operations, albeit by intensifying feudal methods of exploitation. Thus the international grain trade encouraged urban expansion, agricultural specialization and productivity growth in Holland.

International trade within Europe was largely an equal exchange of goods based on comparative advantages. Trade went along with the rise of an intricate system of international payments, specialized shipping, banking, insurance and large-scale export and processing industries. However, the market was not altogether free. Competition was tempered by mercantilist (protectionist) policies and trade monopolies. Governments tried their best to force competing nations out of markets by political and sometimes military means.

Yet the greatest addition to world markets had little to do with free markets or unbridled competition. Instead it was based on conquest. There already existed commercial relations with other continents, such as the overland trade with the Far East. In the fifteenth century Europe – Spain and Portugal in particular – began to expand its economic interests into Asia, Africa and America. Mercantilist theory argued that a nation's wealth could only grow by achieving a favourable balance of trade. Since the world was still comparatively 'small', it seemed more appropriate to exclude foreign competitors than to try and gain in competitive strength. Under the circumstances, colonial expansion was the logical solution. European dominance in world trade can to some extent be considered a function of its economic development. Capitalist mentality and the forces of the market economy provided the drive for expansion. The native populations of the New World (North and South America, Australia) were no match for European military technology and the ecological consequences of the invasion (Crosby, 1986). In other parts of the world superior technology and economic organization gave the Dutch, British, French, Portuguese and other Europeans a dominant position in trade (Wallerstein, 1980). The very nature of its economic development, centred around the growth of a capitalist market economy, explains the success of the colonial expansion and world trade hegemony of western Europe.

The primary economic aim of merchants and conquerors was to create a protected niche in the world market without competition from other European nations. Intercontinental expeditions were concerned mainly with trade. It was very attractive to secure a monopoly in the trade in such goods as pepper, cloves or coffee. Exotic products yielded tremendous profits on the markets of Europe. America was the notable exception. Discovered by accident and mistaken for India, its economic properties (astonishing wealth) were considered given, so that the Spaniards and Portuguese opted to annex the continent rather than to negotiate with local leaders. In addition, they attached greater value to gold and silver than to trade.

In Asia, the European invasion began with the control of individual seaports. In the early sixteenth century, Portugal literally conquered the Indian Ocean with the explicit intention of monopolizing the trade in spices. Dutch and British merchants took over in the seventeenth century. They had greater military strength and a more efficient commercial organization based on public limited companies (the East India Companies). However, with a few notable exceptions, it was not until the nineteenth century that the colonial powers shifted their attention from trade to government and began to incorporate their 'possessions' into their respective empires.

Sheer profit motivated governments and merchant associations to turn to outright exploitation. Native agriculture was obliged to produce valuable export crops, usually by threat of force, at low wages or prices, and even at the expense of subsistence production. Indonesia provides two telling examples. The Dutch East India Company (*Verenigde Oostindische Compagnie*) wanted to monopolize the trade in cloves. To that end they first restricted production to part of the Moluccas, a group of islands in the eastern part of the archipelago. Feudal structures were used to organize the production and collection of cloves. Inter-island trade was strictly controlled to prevent smuggling, even though this raised the price of rice and textiles. At the same time, the purchase price of cloves was deliberately held low to boost profits. The result was a highly profitable monopoly at the expense of those who actually produced the cloves (Van Zanden, 1991, 79–84). In the nineteenth century the same method of exploitation was used on a much larger scale. Under the so-called 'cultivation system' (*Cultuurstelsel*) of 1832, Javanese peasants were forced to set aside a substantial part of their land for the production of export crops, sugar and coffee in particular. In return, they received a very low price, so that the proceeds went almost entirely to the Dutch.

Where indigenous labour was scarce, slaves were used to produce the desired commodities, especially in the Americas. The Spaniards used Indian slaves to extract gold and silver. The islands and coastal regions of the Caribbean sprouted numerous plantation economies, based entirely on (African) slave labour and with few ties, if any, to the region itself. Their sole purpose was to produce such desirable commodities as sugar, tobacco and coffee for the European market. Harsh labour conditions generally resulted in high mortality among slaves. Hence European demand for tropical arables stimulated the slave trade, which brought into being the famous commercial triangle between Europe, Africa and the Americas. The plantation economies were little more than production facilities run by merchants from the motherland. The more populous and advanced colonies in time became markets for European manufactures, textiles in particular. Access to many colonies was granted only to national merchants. Only Britain was able to capture its colonial markets by competitive strength.

Colonial expansion resulted in an enormous inflow of goods and bullion, which had a substantial economic impact. Massive imports of gold and silver from South America may have brought about the price revolution of the sixteenth century. Spices, coffee, sugar, tobacco and other tropical commodities – including the potato – permanently changed European consumer preferences. Intercontinental trade, the richest of trades considering the large share of high-grade products, had significant forward and backward linkages to shipbuilding, textile manufacturing, processing industries, financial and professional services, and to armament production.

Intra-European trade gave a similar impetus to the rest of the economy. The links between world trade and home production were nonetheless relatively weak. On a macroeconomic scale, exports rarely accounted for more than 5 per cent of gross agricultural and industrial output. International trade therefore only had direct economic significance for specific regions and sectors. These regions were by no means constant. There was a sequence of market leaders, from Venice in the late Middle Ages, Spain and Portugal in the sixteenth century, the Dutch Republic in the seventeenth century and Britain thereafter. Estimates of the size and distribution of the European merchant fleet help identify the regional shifts in trade (see Table 1.4). Around 1500, the south of Europe reigned supreme. A century later the 'golden age' gave the Dutch a dominant position in world trade. And between 1670 and 1780, the centre of trade shifted from the Dutch Republic to Great Britain and, to a lesser degree, France.

Table 1.4 Estimates of the size and regional distribution of the European merchant fleet 1500–1780

	Total fleet size (000 tons)	Capacity per 1000 inhabitants (tons)	Regional shares in European fleet capacity				
			Southern Europe	Netherlands	Great Britain	France	Hansa
1500	200–250	3.2–4.0	40	16	10–12	?	20
1600	600–700	7.7–9.0	25	33	10	12	15
1670	1000–1100	12.8–14.1	20	40	12	8–14	10
1780	3372	30.7	15	12	26	22	4

Sources: Romano (1962), Vogel (1915), Lane (1966, 5–20) Van Zanden (1987, 587), Wilson (1977, 129).

THE ORIGINS AND SPEED OF ECONOMIC GROWTH

The early modern economy has often been described as a Malthusian zero-growth environment that ended when the industrial revolution took off. Industrialization marked the beginning of an era of rapid economic growth and structural change, yet it is theoretically impossible for an economy to remain completely stagnant. Its functioning depends on the decisions and preferences of a multitude of individuals whose behaviour would have to be absolutely consistent and complementary for there to be a 'stationary state'. Even if, for some reason, a situation of perfect order were achieved, the economy would still be subject to exogenous shocks. Change was consequently inevitable. In the long run, the direction of change was probably biased upwards. Once it has been acquired, knowledge (for example, of new techniques, methods of production or forms of organization) is rarely lost. Economic experience is preserved and enhanced by on-the-job training and learning-by-doing, while the general body of knowledge is protected through the institutionalization of scientific research and technological experience in universities, guilds and other organizations, as well as in writings.

There is plenty of evidence that early modern Europe experienced growth. A simple though crude measure of long-term improvement is the rate of urbanization. De Vries's estimates reveal a continuous process of urban growth in early modern Europe. On average, the share of the total population living in cities rose from 5.6 per cent in 1500 to 10 per cent in 1800 (De Vries, 1984, 39, 45). Even though the percentages and gains were modest and regional differences were considerable, there were two notable exceptions, namely the Mediterranean in the seventeenth century and the Low Countries in the eighteenth century.

A more revealing indication is provided by research into patterns of economic growth. Recent research into the long-term development of output and income in a number of European countries before 1800 has resulted in very rough estimates, which are presented in Table 1.5 (they are made comparable by setting the UK level of 1820 at 100) (for full details, see the discussion in Van Zanden, 1997). The results of this comparison can be briefly summarized. Long-term stagnation is revealed on the periphery: Italy, Spain and Poland. Between 1500 and 1750, GDP per capita in these countries first fell, then rose, after which a certain recovery set in (at least in Spain and Poland). Only in Spain, however, was GDP per capita possibly somewhat higher in 1820 than in 1570.

Compared with the stagnation of southern and eastern Europe, the countries bordering the North Sea show relatively gradual (Belgium) or rapid (England) growth in the early modern period. These estimates show a rough doubling of GDP per capita in England between 1520 and 1820; the Van Zanden estimates for Holland imply a much more modest rise of only about 50 per cent for the same period, and the extent of the increase in Belgium was probably even smaller.

Table 1.5 Estimates of the development of GDP per capita at constant prices in six European countries 1500–1820 (UK 1820 = 100)

	1500	1570	1650	1700	1750	1820
UK	45–49[a]	45[a]	54[a]	68	81	100
Netherlands	60	60	98	97	95	89
Belgium	55	65	63	66	72	74
Italy	75–76[a]	62–66	71	71	62–66	62
Spain	0	55–61	49–62	50–56[a]	51–53	61
Poland	51–60	48–56	48–55	40–46	34–37	46
Unweighted average	57–60	55–58	63–67	65–67	66–67	72
Coefficient of variation	0.17[b]	0.14	0.25	0.25	0.29	0.26

Notes:
[a] Intrapolated.
[b] Excluding Spain.
Italy – first estimates date from 1380 and 1450.

Source: Van Zanden (1997).

Consequently, economic disparities within Europe tended to increase in the long run. These were rather small during the sixteenth century. The gap between the richest regions (Flanders and northern Italy) and the poorest (England or Poland) in about 1570 was at most 30 per cent (of the level of the richest) and probably even smaller. Differences increased sharply during the seventeenth century as a result of the rise of Holland and the decline of Poland and Spain, but this was compensated partially by the rise of England and the decline of northern Italy and Flanders relative to the 'European average'. In the second half of the eighteenth century, international disparities seemed to reduce slightly, owing to the increase in GDP in Poland and Spain (and to the stagnation in Holland). In 1820, the spread around the mean was even smaller than in 1700 or 1750, although at that time England was certainly running increasingly ahead of the continental countries.

The growth record that emerges from these data can be looked at in two ways. It is clear that, over the long term, population growth was more than compensated by the increase in production whereby in 'Europe' – the average of these six countries – production per capita between c.1500 and c.1820 increased by an average of some 25 per cent (of which almost 10 per cent occurs after 1750). In total, the population in these six countries increased by 91 per cent between 1500 and 1800. The Malthusian pessimists, who saw a growing tension arising between population and resources, were therefore not right, if we go by these data: the growth of population was clearly matched by a somewhat larger increase in output. But likewise the hopes of the optimists are only met in patches; economic growth, in the sense of growth in per capita production, was not normal in western Europe, but rather an exception to the rule – certainly before 1700. In Holland, there occurred only one 'growth spurt' in a period of 300 years, and this was probably also the case in Belgium; moreover, growth in Holland was partly achieved at the expense of Flanders/ Brabant, whose economy declined at the same time. On balance, growth was very modest indeed in these six countries, taken as a whole; on average, GDP per capita increased by only 25 per cent in a period of 300 years, and this growth was mainly due to the inclusion of the most dynamic parts of Europe (England and Holland) in our sample.

The estimates presented here also give food for thought on the exceptional development of the British economy between 1500 and 1800 (see Table 1.6). Much of the older literature, which focused on the 'miracle' of the British industrial revolution, has stressed the dynamic development of the British economy between c. 1760 and c. 1850. According to the esti-

Table 1.6 Estimated growth of GDP per capita at constant prices 1570–1913 (compound average annual growth rates %)

	1570–1750	1750–1820	1820–1870	1870–1913
UK	0.3	0.3	1.3	1.0
Netherlands	0.3	–0.1	1.1	0.9
Belgium	0.1	0.0	1.4	1.1
Italy	0.0	–0.1/0.0	0.6	1.3
Spain	–0.0/–0.1	0.5	0.5	1.2
Czechoslovakia/ Poland[a]	–0.2	0.3/0.4	0.6	1.4
Six countries	0.1	0.1	1.0	1.2
Western Europe[b]	–	–	1.0	1.3

Notes:
[a] 1570–1820, Poland; 1820–1913, Czechoslovakia.
[b] Twelve countries.

Sources: Table 1.5, Maddison (1995).

mates presented here, what is much more surprising is the consistent growth of GDP during the preceding period. Demographic studies confirm this interpretation: England was the only region in Europe with a virtually continuous increase in population and in the urbanization ratio between 1500 and 1800. The data on the development of the shipping fleet, iron production and coal output suggest a similar story. The English share showed almost continuous advance; progress in the other countries was often short-lived and tended to peter out after a number of generations. These findings are of special importance to the debate on the question, 'why was England first?' (Crafts, 1977; Landes, 1998). Seen in the very long perspective of the three centuries before 1800, the fact that the crucial acceleration of economic (industrial) development took place in England does not seem to be mere coincidence, but the almost 'natural' continuation of its strong performance since (at least) 1500. Yet even in Britain growth was much slower before 1820 than thereafter. Therefore the question should be raised why European growth was so slow and uneven.

The nation state is commonly regarded as the standard unit of measurement for macroeconomic historians. However, what if the analysis were to focus on a single dynamic region, such as Holland, the south-east of England, the city states of northern Italy or the Paris Basin? The province of Holland has been described as the first 'modern' economy, with advanced institutions, a skilled workforce, high urbanization rates and agricultural productivity, and close ties to the world market (De Vries and Van der Woude, 1995; De Vries, 1973). Its per capita income was higher than anywhere else and would not be surpassed until the early nineteenth century. Other regions of the Netherlands benefited from the dynamic development of Holland, but they could not copy its success. In England progress had a wider foundation. Gradual improvements in institutions and technology (for example, early political centralization and the enclosure movement) made for a sustained rise in per capita income, whereas in Holland growth ended after 1670. Yet even the economic achievements of England were made in a few select regions. Thus a regional focus can reveal success stories that are obscured by nationwide growth rates. On the scale of national states, advances were more modest and obstacles to productivity growth more pronounced.

Regional fragmentation seems to have been one of the defining features of the early modern economy. Infrastructural inadequacies created physical barriers between regional commodity markets and, to a lesser extent, factor markets (Pounds, 1985, 427). The bulk of trade consisted of low-value, high-volume products, agricultural commodities, building materials and fuel, that had high transport costs relative to their value. Moreover, in order to cope with the difficulties of transport and communication, interregional trade relations were maintained by an intricate network of middlemen, thus adding to the costs of distribution. The result was a situation of high transaction costs, slow communications and low volumes of interregional trade (cf. Braudel, 1982). There was no 'national' market, although there will always have been a degree of trade, capital flows and migration between regions. Instead, large parts of the pre-modern economy were characterized by large economic variations between small and relatively autonomous regional markets whose coexistence and interaction may be seen as one of the principal features of the pre-modern economy. International (long-distance) trade was an exception, characterized as it was by low transaction costs and highly integrated markets for labour, capital and goods.

Fragmented markets made for a high degree of economic uncertainty and risk. Institutions emerged as a rational solution, providing a measure of stability in a highly volatile economy (Boserup, 1970, 81–6; Olson, 1982, 2–16; Persson, 1988, 35–41). Yet, in the course of time, as markets expanded and opportunities arose for the use of new techniques and organizations, institutions could become obstacles in the way of change. O'Brien provides a telling example in his article on path dependency. In the Middle Ages the peasants of France had obtained a strong hold on their land, whereas the property rights of British peasants were not nearly as secure. As a result, the enclosures that transformed and improved English agriculture could not be achieved in France. This slowed down the release of labour from agriculture, which helps explain why England industrialized first (O'Brien, 1996). Institutional rigidity could severely hamper the growth of productivity, since every economic improvement required additional effort to break down the barriers to change and, hence, raised the costs of (or lowered the returns to) innovation (Ames and Rosenberg, 1963; De Vries, 1981, 216–18).

In short, inadequate transport technology and infrastructure created an environment of small and ill-integrated markets at highly varying levels of development. The limited extent of the market inhibited the introduction of innovations and increases in scale, while it encouraged the emergence or strengthening of institutions and regulations aimed at controlling (or subduing) competition and reducing overall economic risk. The inability of most regions to achieve a sustained increase in productivity imposed a demand constraint on the economy, while the dangers of economic life reinforced the non-economic constraints to change. Large regional differences in development, the limited growth potential of individual markets (especially the least accessible ones) and the low yield and uncertain prospects of infrastructural investments discouraged entrepreneurs and capital owners from trying to remove market imperfections (for example, by constructing new roads and canals), especially when more profitable alternatives were available. The absence of sustained productivity growth was therefore to some extent inherent to the pre-modern economy.

The pre-industrial economy did change and the evidence suggests mild progress in the long run. Cities were hot spots of growth in the pre-industrial world. Rural industries did generate significant innovations – for example in mining, paper-making and textile production – but cities had a comparative advantage. The economies of scale inherent in the high density of population gave rise to an advanced division of labour and specialized production as well as a low level of transaction costs. Government, administrative services, financial and specialized distributive services, medical services and other types of highly skilled labour were predominantly found in the cities. The relative success of the urban economy was essentially based on the extent of its market. Urban density made for low transport costs and a high level of aggregate demand; cities were generally centres of interregional and international trade, and the majority of people relied on wage labour for their survival and were thus compelled to purchase rather than produce the foodstuffs and industrial goods they consumed. Yet cities could not exist or grow on their own account. The relative size of the non-agrarian population depended largely on the productivity of regional agriculture as well as on the possibility of interregional and international trade. The urban monopoly on long-distance trade provided opportunities for economies of scale and specialization beyond the limits imposed by the size of the city or the productivity of local agriculture. The best recipe for growth was to gain control of a share in world trade by exploiting and enhancing the city's comparative advantages. The drawback of economic expansion based on international trade was that it made urban development highly dependent on the city's ability to maintain a competitive edge over other port cities. The long-term economic strength of a city was ultimately determined by the extent to which the urban economy was interwoven with the domestic or regional economy. On the other hand, the beneficial effects of urban density diminished with rising distance. Their scope was limited further by the market imperfections and institutional obstacles of the pre-industrial economy. In addition, given the prominent role of urban agglomerations and the short range of density effects, urban growth will have widened the gap between 'modern' and 'traditional' regions.

From the end of the eighteenth century growth began to accelerate as the economies of Europe, led by Britain, entered the age of industrialization. Notwithstanding considerable international differences in the speed and timing of economic growth, the nineteenth-century development of

Europe was generally characterized by sustained productivity gains, rapid population growth, urbanization and a structural shift from agriculture to industry and services. Where did the transition come from? The remarkable thing is that the European (national) industrial revolutions, in some form or another, all occurred roughly between 1780 and 1913. Given that there were considerable international differences in resource endowments and population density, the transition cannot be explained on the level of individual economies. In all likelihood the diffusion of technological, organizational and institutional knowledge was a necessary part of the process.

The most radical kind of change was the introduction of strategic inventions with far-reaching effects on productivity growth, such as Newcomen's atmospheric steam engine in coal mining and the many applications of steam power such as railway transport and steamships. (Landes, 1969; Szostak, 1991, 289–302; Price, 1975). Such macro innovations reduced the amount of inputs per unit of output, they substituted an abundant resource (such as coal) for a scarce one (such as wood), and they often had inherent economies of scale (such as new transport technologies). The industrial revolution as a 'wave of gadgets' is still an attractive idea.

However, technology was not the only source of radical change. A factor specific to the nineteenth century was the impact of the Napoleonic wars on the political and institutional landscape of Europe. Napoleon's drive for domination wiped out feudal structures in large parts of Europe and changed the course of state formation (for example, in Belgium, Germany, Italy and the Netherlands). In some areas, most notably Belgium, the continental blockade fostered the growth of industries that would otherwise have been unable to withstand English competition. In general, the nineteenth century witnessed the redefinition of the economic role of government, which involved increasing intervention, such as public participation in railroad investments. Political centralization and active intervention were ultimately instrumental in the removal of market imperfections and institutional obstacles. These radical changes were common to every industrializing nation in Europe, albeit to varying degrees. One reason for the international similarity was the crucial importance of the diffusion of innovations. Britain could act as the proving ground of new production methods by virtue of its good infrastructure, stable and centralized government, sound economic institutions and vast colonial empire. Once improved and, above all, proven, new techniques and forms of organization spread to other countries on the European continent. More important than mere diffusion was the fact that, rather than providing a single economy with a comparative advantage, the innovations of the late eighteenth and early nineteenth centuries eventually opened up the world market and, hence, provided all countries with new opportunities to innovate and expand production.

NOTES

1. See, for example, Wallerstein (1974), North and Thomas (1973) and the contributions to Aston and Philpin (1985).
2. The debate about when and why Europe overtook China as the most dynamic and prosperous economy is beyond the scope of this chapter; for two 'extreme' interpretations, see Landes (1998) and Frank (1998). We suggest that the two elements of the institutional framework discussed briefly – the competitive state system and the European marriage pattern – may have been of fundamental importance in this process.
3. This statement is based on as yet unpublished research, based on evidence from Poland (Kula, 1976, 116–7), Holland (calculated from Posthumus, 1943–64), England (Nef, 1937; Phelps Brown and Hopkins, 1981, 44–57), Austria (calculated from Pribram, 1938) and Tuscany (Malanima, 1994).

BIBLIOGRAPHY

Allan, R.C. (1992), *Enclosure and the Yeoman*, Oxford: Clarendon Press.

Amalric, J. (1983), 'Dans les Espagnes du XVIIIe siècle: une agriculture bloquée?', *Aux origines du retard économique de l'Espagne XVIe – XIXe siècles*, Paris: Editions du CNRS.

Ames, E. and N. Rosenberg (1963), 'Changing technological leadership and industrial growth', *Economic Journal*, 73, 13–31.

Aston, T.H. and C.H.E. Philpin (eds) (1985), *The Brenner Debate*, Cambridge: Cambridge University Press.

Aymard, M. (1973), 'Rendements et productivité agricole dans l'Italie moderne', *Annales E.S.C.*, 28, 475–98.

Bange, P. and A.G. Weiler (1987), 'De problematiek van het clandestiene huwelijk in het Middeleeuwse bisdom Utrecht', in D.E.H. de Boer and J.W. Marsilje (eds), *De Nederlanden in de late Middeleeuwen*, Utrecht: Het Spectrum, pp. 393–409.

Blomme, J., E. Buyst and H. van der Wee (1994), 'The Belgian economy in a long-term perspective', paper session 'Economic Growth and Structural Change', Milan.

Boserup, E. (1970), *The Conditions of Agricultural Growth: The Economics of Agrarian Change under Population Pressure*, London: Allen & Unwin.

Boserup, E. (1981), *Population and Technology Change*, Oxford: Blackwell.

Braudel, F. (1982), *Civilization and Capitalism*, vol. 2: *The Wheels of Commerce*, London: Weidenfeld and Nicolson.

Brenner, R. (1985), 'Agrarian class structure and economic development in pre-industrial Europe', in T.H. Aston and C.H.E. Philpin (eds), *The Brenner Debate*, Cambridge: Cambridge University Press.

Cameron, R. (1985), 'A new view of European industrialization', *Economic History Review*, 38, 1–23.

Campbell, B.M.S. (1997), 'Matching supply to demand: crop production and disposal by English demesnes in the century of the Black Death', *Journal of Economic History*, 57, 827–58.

Canny, N. (ed.) (1994), *Europeans on the Move: Studies on European Migration 1500–1800*, Oxford: Oxford University Press.

Clark, G. (1987), 'Productivity growth without technical change in European agriculture before 1850', *Journal of Economic History*, 47, 419–32.

Clarkson, L.A. (1972), *The Pre-industrial Economy in England 1500–1750*, New York: Schocken Books.

Clout, H. (1980), *Agriculture in France on the Eve of the Railway Age*, London: Croom Helm.

Crafts, N.F.R. (1977), 'Industrial revolution in Britain and France: some thoughts on the question "Why was England first?"', *Economic History Review*, 30, 429–41.

Crafts, N.F.R. (1985), *British Economic Growth during the Industrial Revolution*, Oxford: Clarendon Press.

Crosby, A.W. (1986), *Ecological Imperialism: The Biological Expansion of Europe 900–1900*, Cambridge: Cambridge University Press.

Davids, K. (1992), 'Technological change and the economic expansion of the Dutch Republic, 1580–1680', *Economic and Social History in the Netherlands*, 4, 79–104.

Deane, P. (1969), *The First Industrial Revolution*, Cambridge: Cambridge University Press.

Deane, P. and W.A. Cole (1964), *British Economic Growth 1688–1959: Trends and Structure*, Cambridge: Cambridge University Press.

Epstein, S.R. (1993), 'Town and country: economy and institutions in late medieval Italy', *Economic History Review*, 46, 453–77.

Frank, A.G. (1998), *ReORIENT: Global Economy in the Asian Age*, Berkeley: University of California Press.

Goodman, J. and K. Honeyman (1988), *Gainful Pursuits: The Making of Industrial Europe 1600–1914*, London: Arnold.

Grantham, G.W. (1989), 'Agricultural supply during the Industrial Revolution: French evidence and European implications', *Journal of Economic History*, 49, 43–72.

Griffiths, R.T. (1982), 'The creation of a national Dutch economy: 1795–1909', *Tijdschrift voor geschiedenis*, 95, 513–37.

Hajnal, J. (1965), 'European marriage patterns in perspective', in D.V. Glass and D.E.C. Eversley (eds), *Population in History*, London: Arnold, pp. 101–43.

Hoffman, P.T. (1996), *Growth in a Traditional Society: The French Countryside 1450–1815*, Princeton: Princeton University Press.

Hymer, S. and S. Resnick (1969) 'A model of an agrarian economy with non-agricultural activities', *American Economic Review*, 59, 493–506.

Jacquart, J. (1967), *La crise rurale en Ile-de-France, 1550–1670*, Paris: Presses Universitaires de France.

Jones, E.L. (1988), *Growth Recurring: Economic Change in World History*, Oxford: Clarendon Press.

Kula, W. (1976), *An Economic Theory of the Feudal System: Towards a Model of the Polish Economy*, London: NLB.

Landes, D. (1969), *The Unbound Prometheus*, Cambridge: Cambridge University Press.

Landes, D. (1998), *The Wealth and Poverty of Nations*, New York: W.W. Norton.

Lane, F.C. (1966), *Venice and History*, Baltimore: Johns Hopkins University Press.

Maddison, A. (1995), *Monitoring the World Economy, 1820–1992*, Paris: OECD.

Malanima, P. (1994), 'Changing patterns in rural living conditions: Tuscany in the eighteenth century', in A.J. Schuurman and L.S. Walsh (eds), *Material Culture: Consumption, Lifestyle, Standard of Living, 1500–1900*, Milan: Electa pp. 115–24.

Mokyr, J. (1985), 'The Industrial Revolution and the new economic history', in J. Mokyr (ed.), *The Economics of the Industrial Revolution*, London: Allen & Unwin, pp. 1–52.

Morineau, M. (1970), *Les faux-semblants d'un démarrage économique: agriculture et démographie en France au XVIIIe siècle*, Paris: Colin.

Mulhall, M.G. (1898), *A Dictionary of Statistics*, London.

Nef, J.U. (1937), 'Prices and industrial capitalism in France and England', *Economic History Review*, 7, 155–85.

Neveux, H. (1980), *Les grains de Cambrésis (fin du XIVe – début du XVIIe siècles)*, Paris: Presses Universitaires de France.

Nijman, D.G. (1991), 'Louis de Geer (1587–1652), vader van de Zweedse industrie?', *Tijdschrift voor geschiedenis*, 104, 213–32.

North, D.C. (1990), *Institutions, Institutional Change and Economic Performance*, Cambridge: Cambridge University Press.

North, D.C. and R.P. Thomas (1973), *The Rise of the Western World: A New Economic History*, Cambridge: Cambridge University Press.

O'Brien, P.K. (1996), 'Path dependency, or why Britain became an industrialized and urbanized economy long before France', *Economic History Review*, 49. 213–49

Olson, M. (1982), *The Logic of Collective Action: Public Goods and the Theory of Groups*, Cambridge, MA: Harvard University Press.

Persson, K.G. (1988), *Pre-industrial Economic Growth: Social Organization and Technological Progress in Europe*, Oxford: Oxford University Press.

Phelps Brown, H. and S.V. Hopkins (1981), *A Perspective of Wages and Prices*, London: Methuen.

Posthumus, N.W. (1943–64), *Nederlandsche prijsgeschiedenis*, Leiden: E.J Brill.

Pounds, N.J.G. (1985), *An Historical Geography of Europe 1800-1914*, Cambridge: Cambridge University Press.

Pounds, N.J.G. and W.N. Parker (1957), *Coal and Steel in Western Europe*, London: Faber and Faber.

Pribram, A.F. (1938), *Materialien zur Geschichte der Preise und Löhne in Österreich*, Vienna: Ueberreuter.

Price, R. (1975), *The Economic Modernisation of France*, London: Croom Helm.

Razi, Z. (1993), 'The myth of the immutable English family', *Past and Present*, 140, 1–44.

Revel, J. (1982), 'Rendements, production et productivité agricole: les grands domaines de la Campagne romaine, XVIIe–XVIIIe siècles', in J. Goy and E. Le Roy Ladurie (eds), *Prestations paysannes, dîmes, rente foncière et mouvement de la production agricole à l'époque préindustrielle*, I, Paris: Editions de L'E.H.E.S.S., pp. 227–36.

Riden, P. (1977), 'The output of the British iron industry before 1870', *Economic History Review*, 30, 442–59.

Romano, R. (1962), 'Per una valutazione della flotta mercantile europea alla fine del secolo XVIII, *Studi in Onore di Amintore Fanfani*, V, Milan: Giuffre.

Seccombe, W. (1992), *A Millennium of Family Change: Feudalism to Capitalism in Western Europe*, London: Verso.

Slicher van Bath, B.H. (1963), 'Yield ratios, 810–1820', *AAG Bijdragen*, 10.

Slicher van Bath, B.H. (1967), 'The yields of different crops, mainly cereals, in relation to the seed c.810–1820', *Acta Historiae Neerlandica*, 11, 78–97.

Smith, A. (1776), *An Inquiry into the Nature and Causes of the Wealth of Nations*, London.

Sprangel, R. (1969), 'La production du fer au Moyen Age', *Annales E.S.C.*, 24, 305–21.

Szostak, R. (1991), 'Institutional inheritance and early American industrialization', in J. Mokyr (ed.), *The Vital One: Essays in Honor of Jonathan R. T. Hughes* (Research in economic history, Supplement 6), Greenwich/London: J.A.I. Press, pp. 287–308.

Thompson, I.A.A. and B. Yun Casalilla (eds) (1994), *The Castilian Crisis of the Seventeenth Century*, Cambridge: Cambridge University Press.

Tilly, C. (1990), *Coercion, Capital, and European States, AD 990-1990*, Cambridge: Basil Blackwell.

Unger, R.W. (1984), 'Energy sources for the Dutch Golden Age: peat, wind, and coal', *Research in Economic History*, 9, 221–53.

Ville, S.P. (1990), *Transport and the Development of the European Economy, 1750–1918*, Basingstoke: Macmillan.

Vogel, W. (1915), 'Zur Grosse der europäischen Handelsflotten im 15., 16. und 17. Jahrhundert', *Festschrift Dietrich Schäfer*, Jena.

Vries, J. de (1973), 'On the modernity of the Dutch Republic', *Journal of Economic History*, 33, 191–202.

Vries, J. de (1976a), *The Dutch Rural Economy in the Golden Age, 1500-1700*, New Haven/London: Yale University Press.

Vries, J. de (1976b), *The Economy of Europe in an Age of Crisis, 1600–1750*, Cambridge: Cambridge University Press.

Vries, J. de (1981), *Barges and Capitalism: Passenger Transportation in the Dutch Economy, 1632–1839*, Utrecht: HES Publishers.

Vries, J. de (1984), *European Urbanization 1500–1800*, London: Methuen.

Vries, J. de (1994), 'The industrial revolution and the industrious revolution', *Journal of Economic History*, 54, 249–70.

Vries, J. de and A.M. van der Woude (1995), *Nederland 1500–1815. De eerste ronde van moderne economische groei*, Amsterdam: Balans.

Wallerstein, E. (1974), *The Modern World-System I*, New York: Academic Press.

Wallerstein, E. (1980), *The Modern World-System II*, New York: Academic Press.

Wilkinson, R.G. (1973), *Poverty and Progress*, London: Methuen.

Williamson, J.G. (1984), 'Why was British economic growth so slow during the industrial revolution?', *Journal of Economic History*, 44, 689–712.

Wilson, C. (1977), 'The British Isles', in C. Wilson and G. Parker, *An Introduction to the Sources of European Economic History 1500–1800*, New York: Cornell University Press, pp. 115–54.

Wrigley, E.A. (1978), 'A simple model of London's importance in changing English society and economy 1650–1750', in P. Abrams and E.A. Wrigley (eds), *Towns in Societies: Essays in Economic History and Historical Sociology*, Cambridge: Cambridge University Press, pp. 215–43.

Wrigley, E.A. (1987), 'Urban growth and agricultural change: England and the Continent in the early modern period', in E.A. Wrigley (ed.), *People, Cities and Wealth*, Oxford: Blackwell, pp. 157–93.

Wrigley, E.A. and R.S. Schofield (1981), *The Population History of England 1541–1871: A Reconstruction*, Cambridge: Cambridge University Press.

Yntema, R.J. (1992), 'The brewing industry in Holland, 1300–1800: a study in industrial development', dissertation, University of Chicago.

Zanden, J.L. van (1987), 'De economie van Holland in de periode 1650-1805: groei of achteruitgang?', *Bijdragen en mededelingen betreffende de geschiedenis der Nederlanden*, 102, 562–609.

Zanden, J.L. van (1991), *Arbeid tijdens het handelskapitalisme. Opkomst en neergang van de Hollandse economie 1350–1850*, Bergen: Octavo.

Zanden, J.L. van (1994), *The Transformation of European Agriculture: The Case of the Netherlands*, Amsterdam: Free University Press.

Zanden, J.L. van (1997), 'Pre-modern economic growth: the European economy 1500–1800', Paper for the 4ème Journées Braudéliennes, NIAS.

Zanden, J.L. van (1998a), 'The development of agricultural productivity in Europe 1500–1800', *Neha-jaarboek*, 61.

Zanden, J.L. van (1998b), 'An economic interpretation of the European marriage pattern', paper, CORN workshop on the Rise of the European Marriage Pattern, Cambridge.

2. The Europeanization of the international economy 1800–1870

Sidney Pollard

The world economy in this period stood under the sign of the industrial revolution, a development which by 1800 was gaining strength in Britain, where it had had its origins, and by 1870 had affected much of western Europe and the United States. But while the bundle of changes referred to as the 'industrial revolution' is usually thought of as occurring in the western economies only, in fact, it also altered and very much enlarged the role of Europeans in the world economy. It propelled European actions onto a world stage, so that the rest of the world was forced to adjust to European rhythms. In an astonishing burst of dynamism, ancient empires were conquered, or at least forced to admit European traders and entrepreneurs on privileged terms, while 'empty' territories, thinly populated by societies inferior to Europeans in technology, were occupied, adding altogether an area 10 times the land surface of western, central and northern Europe for settlement and development (Youngson, 1966, 139). No wonder people came to speak of the 'European century' (Bairoch, 1976a, 19).

Perhaps the clearest developments were those affecting world trade. This now turned into an exchange of primary products from overseas countries for manufactures from Europe. Moreover, while earlier it was mostly luxury goods, marginal to economic life, which were traded, now increasingly it was bulk commodities, some of which had a key role in their economies, such as raw cotton, wool or coal, which entered international trade. This occurred not least because of the technical improvements in the means of transport, which themselves were one aspect of the industrial revolution. It also signalled the emergence of industrial out of the previous commercial form of capitalism.

International trade increased at an accelerating pace. The average annual percentage rates of increase have been calculated as follows:

1785–1830: 1.37
1820–1840: 2.81
1840–1860: 4.84
1860–1870: 5.53

World trade multiplied sevenfold in those decades; by 1870, Europe and North America accounted for 80 per cent of it (Rostow, 1978, 49, 70–71, 74). Some of the causes of this development are treated in the rest of this chapter, which is structured as follows. The first section traces the developments in Europe. The second section deals with the period in three chronological divisions, 1800–1815, 1815–1847/50 and 1847/50–1870. The third section discusses the impact on the non-European world. There is a brief conclusion.

THE INDUSTRIALIZATION OF EUROPE

Great Britain was the country of the classical industrial revolution – the first one to which the term was applied by contemporaries. Among the most obvious aspects of the process were the technological inventions and innovations: spinning machines, including jennies, frames and mules spreading from cotton to woollens, worsteds and flax, followed by power-loom weaving, coke-based iron making on a very much larger scale than hitherto, mining engineering, steam engine making and machine tools: these are among the most commonly quoted and enumerated. Later in the nineteenth century were added the railway (1825–30), the hot blast in iron making (1828), Bessemer steel (1856) and the Siemens open-hearth method of steel making (1860s). Besides these, which were very much in the public eye, mechanical and chemical ingenuity was applied successfully to a host of other industries and processes, including crucible steel, silver plating and electroplating, textile bleaching and dyeing, non-ferrous metallurgy, the production of gas, the making of pottery, glass, paper, tinplate, steel pens and other metalware, lace, brewing and printing . . . the list is endless. There were similar striking innovations in transport and in industrial organization. In each of these, beside the obvious 'macro-inventions' there were numerous and often unsung 'micro-improvements' (Mokyr, 1994, 15). Productivity per man in agriculture rose in parallel. All of these necessarily required enormous changes in organization, in finance, in employment conditions, living and working conditions, in social structures and industrial relations. Urbanization and the increase of traffic seemed inevitable concomitants.

Recently, some doubt has been cast on the concept of an industrial revolution itself (for a recent review, see Mokyr, 1993, 1). One apparent justification for this view is the slow overall growth of the economy, as calculated in modern terms. What does 'slow' mean in this context? Certainly, the growth rate of the British economy between, say, 1780 and 1850 or 1870, was lower than those of Europe and the Far East in the recent post-war 'golden age'; at the same time, it was much faster than anything that had been seen before. Statistical accuracy is difficult to secure over any length of time when the composition of national income changed fundamentally, and it is not surprising, therefore, that there have been some divergences in recent estimates. According to Crafts and Harley, income rose by 1.0 per cent a year in 1760–1801 and by 1.9 per cent in 1801–31, while total factor productivity (TFP), the increase in income or output not due to increased inputs, rose by only 0.1 per cent and 0.35 per cent a year, respectively. Feinstein's older estimate was markedly higher, at 1.1 per cent and 2.7 per cent for income and 0.2 per cent and 1.3 per cent TFP, respectively (Crafts and Harley, 1992, 718). Over long periods, even such apparently low rates of growth are not negligible. National income *per head* rose as shown in Table 2.1.

Table 2.1 National income per head, Great Britain, at constant (US$ of 1970) prices

Year	Crafts (1985)	Deane and Cole (1967)
1760	400	250
1800	430	300
1830	500	500
1870	900	900

Source: Harley (1993, 194).

Growth accelerated in the middle of the nineteenth century, as improved technology covered increasing shares of the total economy. Thus one of the best known inventions of the later eighteenth century, Watt's steam engine, generated 35 000 HP in 1800; by 1870, that had grown sixty-fold to 2 million HP. Industrial production showed a healthy rise (see Table 2.2).

Growth rates were even higher, indeed quite spectacular, in some of the leading industries, which thereby enlarged their shares in the total. Thus, according to Harley, the cotton industry showed a *productivity* increase between 1780 and 1860 of 1.9 per cent a year, worsteds 1.3 per cent, woollens 0.6 per cent, iron 0.9 per cent and canals and railways 1.3 per cent. Together with shipping, all the 'modernized' sectors averaged 1.2 per cent a year, with agriculture at 0.7 per cent and the rest nowhere. McCloskey's estimates are considerably higher than this. What this means in terms of output is that cotton *production*, for example, rose from an index of 0.8 in 1770 to 100 in 1841, or some 120-fold, metal in the same period rising 14-

Table 2.2 Industrial production, Great Britain (index 1913 = 100)

1800	5.07
1830	11.5
1850	21.2
1870	38.4

Source: Crafts and Harley (1992, 726–7).

fold and mining more than 6-fold (Harley, 1993, 181, 200). Numerous improvements and a changing variety and quality of products could also be found in the neglected remainder of industries, though possibly of a different order of magnitude (Berg and Hudson, 1992; Landes, 1993).

It is perhaps puzzling that, while these striking changes were put through in Britain, nothing comparable took place on the continent for the space of up to half a century, though in many respects several countries and regions there appeared to have enjoyed rather similar economic, social and legal preconditions to industrialization. It was only after the Napoleonic wars that successful efforts were made to catch up with Britain. By then, however, Britain had a long lead and was still racing ahead, the gap probably being at its widest around the 1860s. Of many key 'modern' products, Britain produced more than the rest of Europe put together. The proportions of some products of the European totals accounted for by Britain are shown in Table 2.3.

Table 2.3 British share of some European products (per cent)

	1800	1830	1870
Pig iron production	29	45	58
Raw cotton consumption	65	66	57
Coal production	85	78	63
Railway mileage open	—	90	24

Source: Bairoch (1976a, 129).

The total *per capita* level of industrialization in 1860 stood at an index of 64 for Britain, compared with 28 for Belgium and 26 for Switzerland, the next highest; in a comparison of *absolute* manufacturing output, however (on an index of UK in 1900 = 100), Britain was then at 45, Belgium at 3 and Switzerland at 2 (Bairoch, 1968, 1102–7; 1976a, 138; 1976b, 281,284). On the basis of 2 per cent of the world's population, Britain's share of *world* manufacturing output in 1870 has been estimated at 32 per cent (North, 1961, v). In the light of these data, it seems curious that there should be some who would deny the significance of the British industrial revolution.

The British economy was not only more developed than any on the continent, it was also differently structured. This arose in part out of Britain's dominant commercial position even in the eighteenth century, before the onset of industrialization, and was boosted by her successful blockade of Europe in the French wars which, incidentally, deprived her enemies of most of their colonies. Building on that commercial dominance, in addition to her early industrialization, Britain came to occupy a unique specialized place in the international division of labour, importing not merely raw materials, but also basic foodstuffs, in return for manufactured exports, earlier, and to a greater extent, than others. She was thus in a position to let her agriculture – itself far more productive per man and per acre than the continental – occupy a declining share while enlarging the mining and manufacturing part of the economy. Thus, on the basis of her national income level of 1840, Britain had 47.3 per cent of her male labour force in industry, compared with 25.3 per cent in the rest of Europe when it reached the same level of income, and for 1870 the figures were still wide apart at 49.2 per cent and 36.5 per cent, respectively. Additionally, Britain's financial sector was more developed at any given point of time (Crafts, 1985, 62–3).

Britain became a major channel of trade between overseas territories and the continent. A significant part of Britain's trade consisted of the re-export of overseas produce. Britain also supplied much of the capital, short-term and long-term, which flowed outward from Europe, and encouraged and fostered the development of supplies from overseas. Her specialization thus had more than a national ambit; the country performed significant tasks for the whole of Europe. In fact, much of the economic impact which Europe had on the rest of the world in those decades was simply the result of British action; by looking at Britain's overseas economic relations, we are encompassing the major part of Europe's role in the world economy. We appear almost to be entitled to speak of a British, rather than a European century. By the end of the nineteenth century, people were to speak of the *Pax Britannica*, though that had a distinctly political ring.

It is not clear why so much of continental Europe (there were some exceptions) played a lesser role. Europe had not lacked energy or initiative in other ages: why in this age did so many of the merchants and sea captains, explorers and conquerors, as well as inventors and entrepreneurs, come from the United Kingdom, and relatively so few from elsewhere (and why were so many of the latter found among the Americans)? Was there some special spring released by industrialization and the complex changes with which it was necessarily accompanied, which drove society forward and would, in due course, supply the energies of the rest of Europe also, when it reached a comparable economic stage?

Britain's special role was, perhaps, nowhere more evident than in the area of overseas trade. The volume of her foreign trade was growing a good deal faster than industrial production. Total trade (imports and exports combined) rose from about 24 per cent of national income at the beginning of the century to an average of 79 per cent in the 1860s; in volume it increased tenfold between the beginning of the century and 1870. The trade of other countries was growing rapidly also, and in the case of some smaller countries it even formed a higher proportion of their national product. As far as can be ascertained, Britain conducted about one third of the world's trade in 1800, a share which fell to one quarter by 1870 (Rostow, 1978, 70–1; Mulhall 1892, 128–9).

British trade was made distinctive by its slant towards regions outside Europe (see Table 2.4). Thus the major part of European trade with what is nowadays called the Third World and particularly with Asia, was conducted by Britain. In the course of the century, the *share* of British trade to Asia, mostly to India, grew, largely at the expense of North American trade, which was itself still expanding in absolute terms. In the 1860s, the largest trading partners outside Europe were the United States with £593 million (12.2 per cent of the total), India, just below that at £542 million (11.2 per cent) and, a long way behind them, Australia (£231 million or 4.8 per cent) (Mulhall, 1892, 133). The American trade was somewhat down in the 1860s because of the Civil War.

Table 2.4 Regional percentages of total trade 1830–60

	Europe	North America	South America	Asia	Africa	Oceania
			Exports to			
1830						
from UK	46.7	25.5	11.5	12.8	2.5	1.0
from continent	82.0	6.6	6.3	3.8	1.3	—
1860						
from UK	34.3	16.6	12.0	25.7	3.2	8.2
from continent	82.0	5.8	5.8	3.1	3.2	0.1

Source: Bairoch (1976a, 88).

The largest single item in British trade in this period was cotton. Being the first material the manufacture of which was mechanized, it was the first to lead foreign trade onto a higher stage. At times, in the late 1790s and early 1800s, some three-quarters of the *increase* in British exports were due to cotton, and even in the period 1814/16 to 1844/6 nearly half the growth of exports was accounted for by it (Crouzet, 1985, 228). In absolute terms, yarn exports rose almost 40-fold between 1800 and 1860, and the exports of piece goods more than 40-fold, from £12 million to £507 million in those years. In terms of value, cotton goods exports increased a hundredfold between 1784/6 and 1872/4.

As was to be expected, exports went mostly to Europe in the early years of the century, most overseas territories still lacking the means to buy them, or still shutting themselves off from imports; moreover, the existing means of transport might have been unable to cope with the quantities that were carried later. As the century wore on, European countries, which had imported British yarn to supply their handloom weavers, began to introduce modern mills themselves, and cotton goods exports increasingly went farther overseas, India, the Levant and Latin America becoming the leading customers. Other leading export commodities were woollen and worsted goods and iron and iron products, particularly rails and railway equipment from the 1840s onward. Generally, over four-fifths of the rising spate of British exports consisted of products of the 'modern sector' industries, created or transformed in the industrial revolution.

Britain was also much the most important market for the exports of overseas countries. She took 42 per cent of the exports of the whole of the rest of the world in 1800, and still took 26 per cent in 1873. Of the American raw cotton exports she received 85 per cent, and she took half the exports of Asia, Africa and South America combined (Imlah, 1958, 167; Hanson, 1980, 55). There were broadly two types of imported commodities: foodstuffs together with tobacco, increasing because of the growing population and its rising prosperity, and raw materials for manufacturing and construction (see Table 2.5).

The two halves of the table cannot be linked together because of the very different basis of calculation, but each half by itself shows strong growth. The consumption of tea, with sugar, was spreading among the working classes, helped by the gradual abolition of the sugar duties from 1846 onwards, the year when the Corn Laws also were abolished. Consumption *per head* of tea and sugar rose nearly fourfold in this period, and of tobacco it doubled. The imports of wheat began to rise sharply at the end of our period. Coffee is the odd man out; it is assumed that the Beer Act of 1830, which cheapened the price of beer, held back

Table 2.5. Major imports into Britain 1800–1870 (£ million)

	Average of years	Coffee	Sugar	Tea	Timber	Raw cotton	Raw wool
Official values							
GB	1800/2	3.9	5.2	2.4	0.6	1.9	0.4
UK	1854/6	3.9	12.1	8.5	1.7	30.1	2.8
Current values							
UK	1854/6	1.6	10.7	5.3	10.2	22.5	7.2
UK	1868/70	4.9	15.7	10.9	12.5	55.2	15.6

Source: Mitchell (1962, 289, 291, 299).

the spread of coffee as a popular drink. The increases in the textile raw materials speak for themselves.

Britain was also the largest exporter of capital by far into overseas territories, including the United States; she stood out starkly in this respect among European countries (Crafts, 1984, 451). She was also much the most important source of emigrants until well past the middle of the century. Capital exports and migration are treated further below.

At the end of the French wars, Britain found herself in possession of the largest overseas empire. There has been much controversy over whether the empire constituted a benefit or a loss, both to the home country and to the colonies, and to what extent Britain pursued an active imperialist policy. With these controversies we are not concerned, except to note that while Britain repeatedly rejected demands to incorporate regions in Africa and South America into the empire, there were also examples of active expansion, into New Zealand and British Columbia, and in the occupation of naval and trading stations in the Cape Colony, Aden, Singapore and Hong Kong among others, while the East India Company, which administered the Indian sub-continent until 1858, added large territories to its possessions.

In practice, over 20 per cent of Britain's trade was with Empire countries, and the share of manufacturing exports going to imperial possessions rose to 35 per cent in 1860 and 41 per cent in 1870 (Cain and Hopkins, 1993, 167). Yet the other great colonial powers, such as Portugal and the Netherlands, were not among the early industrializers, while Belgium and Switzerland, which were among the pioneers, did not possess any colonies (Mokyr, 1993, 75). It seems that it was economic strength, not colonial possession, which was the basis of Britain's industrial and commercial dominance.

On the European continent it was France which constituted much the strongest economic power over most of our period. The relative positions of some continental countries are presented in Table 2.6. The table, though complex at first sight, will repay closer study, but note that columns A and B should not be compared directly with each other, as they are based on different prices. C and D, on the other hand, do show the actual progress.

Table 2.6 European countries, income and industry

| | GDP per head 1830* 1870 (in US$ (in US$ of 1960) of 1990) | | Per capita industrialization (index UK 1913 = 100) 1800 1860 | | Total manufacturing capacity, 1860 (index UK 1900 = 100) |
	A	B	C	D	E
UK	346	3263	16	64	45
France	264	1858	9	20	18
Germany	245	1913	8	15	11
Italy	265	1467	8	10	6
Belgium	295	2640	10	28	3
Switzerland	276	2172	10	26	2
Netherlands	347	2640	—	—	1
Spain	263	1376	7	11	4
Sweden	194	1664	8	15	1
Austria–Hungary	250	1875**	7	11	10
Russia	170	—	6	8	16

Notes: *These are rough estimates. **Austria only.
Sources: Column A: Bairoch (1976b, 286), Column B: Crafts (1997, 306), Columns C and D: Bairoch (1982, 281), Column E: Bairoch (1982, 284).

In per capita terms, France's domestic product is seen to have been well below Britain's and to have declined further in relation to the British in this period. Bearing this in mind, together with the technological backwardness of some French industries precisely in the sectors which had taken the lead in British industrialization, it used to be the rule to describe the period of industrialization for France in the nineteenth century in terms of retardation and disappointment. Explanations were not lacking. France, it was said, had lost some of her most valuable sugar colonies in the Revolution and the wars, and her former strength in colonial trade, together with the prosperity of her rich Atlantic ports, had been undermined. The markets for cheap machine-produced goods had come to be dominated by Britain, while handicraft manufacture was handicapped by high relative French wages compared with countries further east. The Revolutionary settlement had created a large peasant class, rooted to its land and unwilling to move into the industrial towns. For the new industries, France lacked coal, in quantity, quality and ease of location. Inland distances were great and the transport network underdeveloped. Government was expensive, interfering and frequently misguided; the high tariffs in the early decades of the century removed the spur of British competition, while the *Banque de France* used its powers to inhibit the rise of local and regional banks. Finally, the attitude of the French entrepreneur, seeking security and clinging to tradition rather than embracing competition and change, came in for criticism (for example, Trebilcock, 1981, ch. 3; also Caron, 1979, 36ff). Her share of the world's industrial production slipped from 20 per cent in 1820 to 16 per cent in 1860; in 1870, on a different basis, it had dropped to 10 per cent, lying for the first time well below Germany's (Rostow, 1978, 52).

In recent years a reaction has set in. France, it has been argued, did not fail or falter on the path to modernity; she just chose a different route from Britain, with which she is unfairly compared. Being a much larger country, she had a broader agricultural sector, which made it less necessary to sell goods abroad in order to feed her population. Since Britain had pre-empted the overseas markets for cheap mass production, she did well to concentrate on quality goods, where her skills, her taste and designs gave her the edge, and she was able to dominate the European markets in fashion goods. Her industrialization proceeded 'upstream', from finished articles to semi-manufactures, rather than the other way round, which had been the British way. Above all, French population growth was much slower than that of Britain, and statistics in terms of growth per head were thus more favourable to France than absolute data, and at times even showed her doing better than the United Kingdom (Crouzet, 1985, 348). It might be argued, indeed, that all the efforts of British technical ingenuity and the exploitation of British industrial labour merely served to provide for Britain's rising population what France could do for her relatively stagnating one more smoothly and at lower social costs. By one set of calculations, French industrial labour was actually more productive than the British, partly because it was engaged in high-quality production, creating higher values, and it was merely the low productivity of French agriculture which kept down the country's comparative overall figures (O'Brien and Keyder 1978, 51,91; Cameron and Freedeman, 1983).

The truth, as so often, lies somewhere in the middle (see Table 2.7). It cannot be denied that France was slow to adopt the new cost-reducing

Table 2.7 French production (index 1885–90 = 100)

	Consumption goods	Investment goods
1810	17.92	18.93
1830	26.32	26.11
1850	44.14	37.88
1870	72.15	70.02

Source: Lévy-Leboyer (1968, 800).

technology, or to expand into promising new product markets. Apart from some isolated cases, neither machine spinning nor coke iron smelting and puddling made much headway before 1815, and even afterwards they trailed far behind Britain and used out-of-date British technology. Pig iron production, for example, was 1 187 000 tons in 1870, less than a fifth of Britain's 6 059 000 tons. Steel production in 1871 amounted to 80 000 tons, against 334 000 tons; cotton spindles, 6.8 million in 1867, against 34.2 million (Mitchell, 1993).

Yet, at the same time, France never lost contact with the best technology of the day. Her chemists, mathematicians, artillery and naval designers led the world. No other country could match the theoretical grounding joined to practical experience of the *Corps des Mines* or the Bridges and Roads Department inherited from the eighteenth century. If French ironmasters were slow to adopt coke smelting, that was not wholly unreasonable in view of the cheap wood supply as compared with the expensive coal to be brought in from a distance. From the mid-1820s, France pioneered the design of water wheels and turbines, making use of the country's cheap water power, and there were innumerable innovations in the French textile trade, including the Jacquard loom and the Heilmann wool combing machine. From the 1840s onwards, French engineers began to move abroad as they were sought after to build Europe's railways, just as the British had been in the 1830s. The Napoleonic *École des Arts et Métiers* (1803) and the *École Centrale des Arts et Manufactures* (1828) were widely envied abroad. As befits an advanced industrial country, French exports consisted overwhelmingly (80 per cent in 1830, 70 per cent in 1860) of manufactures, led by silk, cotton and woollen fabrics. Imports consisted mostly of industrial raw materials, including silk, cotton, wool and skins and hides, together with sugar. In this respect, as in the level of industrial output per head, France was still far ahead of most of the rest (Crafts, 1984, 54).

According to the latest statistics, national income in real terms grew in this period at around 1.5 per cent a year, and industrial output grew at just under 3 per cent. Among the 'industrial revolution' industries, in which France was said to have lagged, annual growth rates (per cent) were as follows:

	1820–50	1851–73
Coal	4.9	6.1
Pig iron	1.7	5.2
Cotton goods	3.7*	0.08
*1831–50 (Fohlen, 1970, 224)		

These were respectable rates, comparing well with those of the rest of the continent. They look better still in per capita terms in view of the slow growth of population.

France had much the best road system in Europe and in the first half of the nineteenth century had greatly extended her canal network. Railway building began on a large scale in the 1840s. By 1850, about 2500 km were open to traffic, and by 1870 the figure was 17 500 km (Caron 1983, 32). Railway construction helped to develop the French iron and engineering industries as well as the country's investment banking skills, and played a large part in overcoming the disadvantages of distance of many of the industrial regions. At the same time, it is clear that no other nation (apart from Britain) could have assembled the resources to build the Suez Canal, opened in 1869.

Outside Europe, however, the role of France was very minor compared to that of the United Kingdom. Imports increased about nine-fold between 1800 and 1870 and exports some 11-fold; as a proportion of GNP, trade rose from 13 per cent in 1830 to 41 per cent in 1870, but it would be difficult to see trade as an engine of growth, or to credit France with contributing greatly to world development outside Europe. Most of French trade was within Europe, as was also indeed her rising foreign investment. In 1860, 75 per cent of her exports went to Europe and North America; in 1880 this had risen to 81 per cent (Caron, 1979, 109). French exports to Algeria, occupied and increasingly penetrated from 1830 onward, fluctuated around 4–7 per cent of the total. There were also commercial treaties with Tunis in 1830 and with Morocco in 1856. By 1860, there were some 200 000 French immigrants in Algeria; emigration out of France was otherwise extremely limited. With the loss of Saint Domingue in 1791, France lost her most prolific source of sugar, but significant supplies were developed from some of her remaining islands, including Martinique, Guadeloupe and Réunion. Trade with Latin America had a downward tendency, and trade with Asia did not rise beyond a fluctuating 1–4 per cent of French commerce.

The links between most of the remaining European countries and overseas territories were even more tenuous than those of France. Germany, soon to grow into the leading industrial power on the continent, consisted until 1870 of a collection of independent states, of which a growing number were associated within a Customs Union (*Zollverein*) but, apart from that, treated trade between each other as foreign trade, while confusing the statistics by conducting a good deal of their overseas trade through the Netherlands. In terms of the 'modern' industrial sector, the territories that were to become Germany, which started from a much lower level, were catching up with and overtaking France in 1850–70; by 1870, coal output was 26 million tons, against the French 13 million tons, pig iron 1.261 million tons, against 1.187 million tons, and steel, in 1871, 143 000 tons against 80 000 tons. It was particularly in railway building, often considered the 'leading sector' in the German industrial revolution, that Germany had outperformed her western neighbour; over the key years 1851–69, the railways absorbed between 10 and 20 per cent of total investment, and the equivalent of around one-third of the home iron production, while creating an engineering industry out of practically nothing (Fremdling, 1983, 124, 127).

Despite a rapidly expanding mercantile fleet, which grew from 291 000 register tons in 1816 to just over a million register tons in 1870 (Hoffmann, 1963, 104), foreign trade played a lesser part in Germany than in most other countries in their industrializing phase, running at a constant share of 10 per cent of world trade in our period (Bairoch, 1976a, 77). Of German exports, 92 per cent went to European countries and another 2 per cent to North America, while 4 per cent went to South America. There was some flourishing trade with Brazil after its independence; four ships from Brazil, for example, landed in Hamburg in 1815, the number increasing to a peak of 137 vessels in 1824, to decline thereafter (Zorn, 1976, 391). There were commercial treaties with the United States, with Brazil in 1827, and with other Latin American states in the 1830s and 1840s, but little came of them. Germany was, however, a major source of overseas emigration from the 1840s onwards.

The remaining two early industrializing countries in Europe were Belgium and Switzerland. The Belgian economy resembled the British most closely; with a long tradition in metallurgy and textile production, the country also had plenty of coal and iron resources, easy internal transport facilities (improved by an early railway network), the British example across the water and good access to neighbouring France and

Germany, as well as a government more inclined to favour business than much of the rest of Europe, where the landed elites were still in power. Belgium was the first country on the continent to install coke smelting of iron and the Cort system of puddling and rolling. Precocious spinning machines were installed in 1798 (wool) and 1801 (cotton). Other modern industries benefiting from the cheap coal supplies were paper and glass. Table 2.6 shows Belgium's high standing on the continent in terms of income and industrialization; in per capita terms, her output of coal, iron and machinery, and her railway network were closest to the British, and her exports per head even higher.

The United States were the main overseas trading partner, but Belgium also had some trading relations with Latin America. In the years when she was joined to the Netherlands, it was Belgian calicoes which were sent to the East Indian colonies of Java and Madura by the Dutch semi-official monopoly Trading Company (NHM), in return for tropical products, though this overseas market was lost after Belgian independence in 1830 (Mokyr, 1976, 32–3; Bairoch, 1976a, 270–5).

The Swiss experience was in many ways in complete contrast to this. Without coal, iron ore or access to the sea, and surrounded by large protectionist countries with which the cantons could not even negotiate as a single state before the middle of the century, Switzerland seemed ill-equipped for early industrialization. Her assets included a skilled, well-educated labour force, some capital accumulations, plenty of water power and a trading tradition made necessary by the fact that the country could not feed itself in grain. The first mechanized cotton mill which started up in 1801 in St Gall did not remain an isolated enterprise but was followed rapidly by others. By 1814, there were 152 000 cotton spindles; by 1870, there were 1.8 million. Machine building and engineering developed next, and the Swiss conquered their foreign markets with high-quality products, in cottons, in embroidered goods, in silk and, not least, in the making of watches, though that remained on a putting-out basis, with a high degree of division of labour rather than a factory industry (Bergier, 1983, 203–25).

Unique to Switzerland was the concentration on overseas markets, necessary in part because neighbours were both politically unstable and protectionist. About 1845, no less than 64 per cent of exports went overseas, with the United States as the main market, and only 36 per cent to Europe. By 1862, these proportions were reversed following the free-trade drive in Europe started by the Anglo-French commercial treaty of 1860. Even then, of total exports of Fr. 418.7 million, there went to the United States Fr. 75 million (18 percent), to Latin America Fr. 12–13 million (3 per cent), to the East Indies Fr. 17 million (4 per cent) and to the

Levant Fr. 48–52 million (11–12 per cent), or altogether 36–37 per cent of total exports. Per head, Swiss exports greatly exceeded those of Britain and even of Belgium, being (in current US dollars) 18 in 1840, as against 10 for Britain and 7 for Belgium, and in 1880, 50, against 30 and 43 (Veyrassat, 1990; Bairoch, 1990, 106; 1976a, 276–7).

Italy and the Habsburg monarchy started on their drive to industrialization somewhat later, as is evident from Table 2.6, but both had advanced regions – Bohemia and the Vienna basin in Austria–Hungary, and the northern triangle in Italy – which were not far behind the pioneers. The overseas trade and shipping connections of both were mainly to the Levant, in addition to trade with the United States. Scandinavia started out later still, though it developed very rapidly after 1870. Sweden and Denmark had some minute colonial possessions, but the main impact of Sweden and Norway on overseas territories was their heavy emigration after 1850, particularly to the United States.

Russia was the last of the European powers to industrialize, but because of her size she carried much weight, as is evident from Table 2.6, though her delayed development caused her share of world trade to fall from 9 per cent in 1800 to 5 per cent in 1870 (Rostow, 1978, 70–1). The country was *par excellence* an exporter of food and raw materials. Russia's drive into Central Asia, therefore, could not have been fuelled by industrialization at home; it was, in fact, mainly politically induced or the result of buccaneering activity in frontier regions, and possibly also linked to her population increase. In 1826, Russia took two provinces from Persia, the island of Sakhalin was occupied in 1855, Bukhara was incorporated into the Tsar's realm in 1868 and Khiva in 1873. Trade with the latter two regions was put at £5 million a year by Mulhall (1892, 366), rather more than other estimates. Russian traders also encouraged the growing of cotton in northern Persia (Issawi, 1971).

There remain the colonial powers, the Netherlands, Spain and Portugal. As a consequence of the earlier Dutch 'golden age', the Netherlands' income per head was still among the highest in Europe, despite the delayed industrialization, and there were large foreign investments, mostly in Europe. The Dutch colonies were by far the richest of any continental country's. Java, briefly occupied by the British in the French wars, was restored in 1816, and the penetration of Sumatra, Borneo and other East Indian islands followed. Protective measures were introduced to prevent British trading dominance. The Dutch Trading Company (NHM) was set up in 1824, largely financed and its interest guaranteed by the king, and given some monopolistic powers. It became integrated with the so-called *Cultuurstelsel* (cultivation system) developed from 1830, under which native farmers were to set aside a proportion of their land for certain export produce, to be delivered to the NHM at low prices, the benefits to go to the state as a form of taxation and to the company. Later in the century private traders took over much of the system. The main products sent to the Netherlands were coffee, sugar and tobacco, in return for which Dutch cotton products were sent out. Trade with the East Indian possessions formed a large element in Dutch foreign commerce. By the end of our period, the net gain to the home country was calculated at £3 million a year (Mokyr, 1976, 104; Mulhall, 1892, 332).

As a result of the Napoleonic invasion of the Iberian peninsula in 1807–8, both Spain and Portugal lost the bulk of the vast empires they had inherited from their days of glory. Even before that, however, the industrial weakness of the home economy had prevented their full use as markets for manufactures, despite the prohibition of colonial manufacturing as late as 1785 in Brazil and 1800 and 1801 in Spanish America. By then, Britain had muscled in, both as trader and as supplier of manufactures, and Spain's share of world trade had fallen from 10 per cent in 1780 to 3 per cent in 1800 and 2 per cent in 1870, while the value of Portuguese exports to her colonies fell from 10 million cruzeiros in 1800–1801 to 2.5 million in 1820 (Rostow, 1978, 70–71; Boxer, 1969, 385; Halperin Pereira, 1986, 287–90). By 1860, Spain's modern industry was rated at a mere 3–5 on an index of the UK = 100, and Portugal's at 0.5–1 (Bairoch, 1976a, 172).

After the loss of her South American mainland colonies, Spain was left with Cuba, Puerto Rico and the Philippines, beside the Canaries. Cuba developed into a major supplier of sugar as well as tobacco, and in the period 1815–80, as much as one-quarter of Spanish exports went there (Prados, 1987, 135). Portugal was left with long stretches of African coast, as well as some islands off Africa and small settlements in the Indies and China. Though prevented by Britain from engaging in the slave trade north of the equator, the main export of Portuguese Angola in our period consisted of slaves to Brazil.

Thus there were great variations in Europe. Taking it as a whole, however, it was Europe which provided the dynamic, the entrepreneurship and some of the key resources to fuel the unprecedented economic growth of the age on a world scale. Among 'modern' products, European production of pig iron increased 16-fold between 1800 and 1870, coal output 14-fold, raw cotton consumption 21-fold and railway mileage between 1840 and 1870 some 36-fold. European exports in constant prices rose 12-fold in 1800–1870. With only just over 20 per cent of the world's population, the share of Europe in world trade, and the share of intra-European trade fluctuated around 70–80 per cent, leaving only 20–30 per cent for the rest of the world. At the same time, virtually all of the overseas trade and the necessary investments overseas were financed by credits from Europe (Bairoch, 1976a, 61, 81, 129; 1974, 13; Mulhall, 1892, 128–9; Woodruff, 1966, 313).

Europe and North America were so dominant that some attempts to register data for world trade or production, such as Mulhall's, saw nothing wrong in simply ignoring all other regions of the globe, or entering notional figures for them. According to one calculation, while exports per head in 1860 amounted to $20.70 in current dollars in Britain, to $7.30 a head in the rest of western Europe, to $8.85 in North America and to $5.60 even in South America, the figure was a mere $0.35 in Asia and $0.45 in Africa (Bairoch, 1974, 566, 579; Hanson, 1980, 21). Trade thus played in Europe a quite different part from that in the overseas territories, and this has to be borne in mind when considering the impact of Europe on the rest of the world.

THE EUROPEAN IMPACT ON THE REST OF THE WORLD

The years 1800–1815 were dominated by warfare in Europe. Blockade and counter-blockade, Berlin and Milan decrees and the Orders in Council were the background to naval actions in which Britain succeeded in cutting the European countries off from their colonial territories and from most other supplies. She became almost the sole re-exporter of colonial goods to the continent (Crouzet, 1985, 277ff, 301; Drescher, 1977, 148–9). It was from this period onwards that British concepts of the law of the sea began to be increasingly accepted worldwide. The notion that the enormous costs of the finance of war, including subsidies to the allies, 'crowded' out industrial investment in Britain and slowed down industrialization has not found universal acceptance (Hueckel, 1973, 373; Harley, 1993, 216–23; Ward, 1994, 58–9; Mokyr, 1987, 294ff).

As always, the neutrals tended to gain most. Protected by the war from direct British competition, the American cotton industry enjoyed a big spurt. Though it was hit badly by British imports when peace returned, the foundations of the industry which had been laid then held firm (M. B. Hammond, 1966, 258; Rostow, 1978, 120; Jeremy, 1981, 258). North American shipping also did well, temporarily becoming a major carrier across the Atlantic. How far the rest of the economy benefited from the prosperity engendered in the coastal towns is subject to some dispute (North, 1961, 47, 231; Adams, 1980; Goldin and Lewis, 1980; Lipsey, 1994, 3, 54–6; Kutz, 1986, 208–12).

There were two other major effects of the European war on overseas territories. One was the prohibition of the slave trade enacted by Britain in 1807, followed by Sweden in 1813 and the Netherlands as well as some South American states in 1814; Denmark had led the field in 1803. Though it took around half a century to be fully effective, a start had been made towards the abolition of slavery altogether (Eltis, 1987; Green, 1976; Drescher, 1977). The other was the achievement of independence by Latin American countries from Spain and Portugal respectively, noted above. Britain took on the role of supplier of manufactures, credit and shipping services, creating a kind of informal colonial relationship with the whole of Latin America (Lynch, 1985, 46; Platt, 1972, 24–33; Winn, 1976, 100–102; Cain and Hopkins, 1993, 279–80).

It was in the period 1815–50 that a new type of trade emerged, on a larger scale and with greater effect on the trading partners than anything that had gone before. Among the commodities which now became significant, raw cotton was symbolic: it was the single most important export item of the United States, and import item into Britain. The rise of the United States as leading supplier was astonishing. Output rose from an average of 60 million lb a year in 1802–4 to 2241 million lb in 1860; from supplying 9 per cent of the world's exports in 1801, the figure rose to three-quarters by 1860. From 1815 until the late 1830s at least, raw cotton was a key factor, and has even been described as the 'major expansionary force', the 'pivot', on which American growth hinged. Among the reasons for its success was the enterprise of the population of the southern states, the use of slaves, capital from Britain and, later, from the northern states, and free land available ever farther west, as eastern lands became progressively exhausted. The United States was also the only major supplier who succeeded in building up a large cotton textile industry in its own territory (Fogel and Engerman, 1971, 312; Bruchey, 1967, 82ff; R.J. Hammond, 1966, 43–4, 67, 83; North, 1961, 67).

During the Civil War, US exports slumped drastically, but the 'cotton famine' of the early 1860s was a misnomer. At first, large stocks helped out; later, by 1864–5, supplies from elsewhere had fully taken up the slack. Taking the Third World as a whole, cotton exports tripled in value between 1840 and 1860, then tripled again in the period to 1880, though much of this was due to the rise in prices (Hanson, 1980, 34–6; Bairoch and Etemad, 1985, 30; Farnie, 1979, 261). The largest contribution came from India, where raw cotton exports increased 20-fold between 1820 and 1870, to dominate the British market during the cotton famine; quality, however, remained low, despite the efforts of government and of the (Lancashire) 'Cotton Supply Association', established in 1857, to improve it. Egypt, where a French expert made the first experiments with planting cotton in 1819, did much better in terms of quality, and her exports went up sixfold between the 1830s and the 1860s. In neither of these was it necessary to employ slaves, nor was it in Brazil, the other expanding source, where cotton was produced by small farmers. In the West Indies and elsewhere, exports tended to decline (Bruchey, 1967, 7; Harnetty, 1972, 44, 86; Ellison, 1965, 98; Issawi, 1966, 389, 416; Graham, 1972, 75; Dutt, 1902, 272; Platt, 1972, 257).

While the rise in the European imports of raw cotton symbolized the expansion of the new industrialism, sugar, the next weightiest traded commodity, increased with rising incomes. World sugar output doubled between 1840 and 1870; in Britain, the price fall associated with the reduction in foreign sugar duties in 1846 led to a doubling of consumption within 10 years. The output of the British West Indies stagnated, though there was a shift towards Barbados, Trinidad and Guiana. Elsewhere the big increases in exports occurred in Cuba, which rose to produce a quarter of the world's sugar, using the most advanced equipment, Brazil, Mauritius, Réunion and, towards the end of the period, Java. Sugar was widely associated with slavery; when slavery was abolished, contract labour tended to replace it at once (Engerman, 1983, 640; Deerr, 1949–50, 198ff, 490; Mintz, 1985, 73; Curtin, 1965, 443; Hanson, 1980, 34–6; Green, 1976, 229).

One other industrial raw material traded overseas may be looked at in some detail: wool. This, too, was produced even outside Europe on the initiative and under the control of Europeans, and with credit supplied by Europeans. In Australia, it was British emigrants who got together the first flocks, initially by the import of Saxon merinos. By culling and selective breeding they produced high-grade wool much in demand in Britain. As it could take up to two years between shearing and the arrival of payment, merchant or bank credit, furnished first from London and later from local houses, was a necessity. By 1870, Australia produced 10 per cent of the world's output, and half the British consumption came from imports (McMichael, 1984, 101–2; Butlin, 1994, 187–8; Rostow, 1978, 459). Argentine flocks grew at a similar pace, but it was only in the 1880s that the quality of their wool became fully acceptable (Platt, 1972, 258).

Trade in some other products grew at a similar pace. Guano from Peru reached a peak of 302 000 tons in its export to Britain in 1858. Cocoa consumption in Britain went up from 440 000 lb in 1831 to 7.2 million lb in 1871. West African palm oil exports to Britain increased from 1000 tons in 1810 to 10 000 tons in 1830 and about 50 000 tons in the 1860s (Mathew, 1970, 113; Mulhall, 1892; Hopkins, 1973, 128). Table 2.8 lists other exports of all 'Third World' (less developed) countries of which details exist.

In Britain, to name one receiving country, imports of metals, in millions of pounds at constant prices, went up from 0.1 in 1820 to 6.0 in

Table 2.8 Exports of the less developed countries 1840–80 ($ million)

	1840	1860	1880
Coffee	32.2	53.7	114.5
Copper	5.0	16.1	12.7
Hides and skins	1.0	7.9	25.3
Jute		1.5	22.0
Opium	6.1	47.7	79.3
Rice	2.0	20.1	55.3
Silk	9.9	39.8	34.2
Tea	25.7	26.4	65.2
Tin	1.1	4.3	10.8
Tobacco leaf	1.5	7.6	10.3
All LDC exports	238.0	543.2	1107.0

Source: Hanson (1980, 36).

1870, of timber in the same years from 2.0 to 12.5 and of skins and hides from 0.4 to 4.9 (Schlote, 1976, 139ff). Among other products entering overseas trade were indigo, alpaca, rubber, rape seed, gum, peanuts, timber, teak and cinchona and, at the end of the period, wheat. Some of these products, like Indian raw cotton, had a long tradition, their export being boosted by European demand; the production of others, like Peruvian guano or Assam tea, was started *ab ovo* on European initiative.

Many of the tropical products supplied to Europe were grown by slaves. Slavery was one of the most drastic and catastrophic ways in which Europe affected the lives of overseas people. The actual enslavement was carried through by Africans on Africans, but the Europeans entered at the stage of transshipment and, later, employment. The nineteenth century did not invent slavery – it abolished it, against the opposition not merely of the plantation owners in the Americas, but of many leading Africans, who were inclined to stress the benefits to their economies derived from the export of slaves (Evans and Richardson, 1995, 674–5; Hopkins, 1973, 119).

The drive to eliminate, first the slave trade, and later slavery itself, came almost singlehandedly from the leading industrial nation, Great Britain. Using her navy to intercept the slave ships, and her diplomatic power to persuade other nations to support her drive, she gradually reduced the trading, beginning with her own prohibition in 1807, first north of the equator, and finally across the whole Atlantic by around 1860. To the 1830s, the decline in the shipping of slaves to the United States and the

British Caribbean was compensated by a vast increase in trade to Brazil and Cuba, so that annual figures remained between 50 000 and 60 000 until around 1840. They fell to 43 000 a year in the 1840s, to 14 000 in the 1850s, when Brazil ceased trading, and to a mere 4000 in the 1860s. Including the pre-prohibition years, the total for 1801–70 came to 2.9 million slaves sent to the Americas (Eltis, 1987, 249; Curtin, 1969, who has much lower figures in his Table 67; Leveen, 1975). Actual slave holding was abolished in the British West Indies in 1834–8, in Ceylon in 1837, British India in 1843, the French territories in 1848, the Netherlands East Indies in 1860, the United States in 1865, in Spanish America at various dates between 1846 and 1885, and in Brazil over the period 1871–88. After slave imports had ended in the Americas, East Africa continued for a time to supply slaves to the Arabian peninsula and to Persia.

Yet the need for labour on the plantations remained, and powerful interests were involved to see that it was met. The immediate answer was to bring in contract labour from poor or overpopulated countries. The West Indies began recruiting in numbers in India in 1844, the first arrivals reaching the Caribbean in 1845. By 1865, over 96 000 Indians had come, in addition to some 14 000 Chinese (Green, 1976, 276ff; Watts, 1990, 474; Tinker, 1974). Cuba recruited possibly as many as 150 000 from China in 1847–75, Mauritius received 116 000 from India over the period 1839–49, and other receiving areas included Peru, Malaya and Sumatra, the latter accepting labourers both from China and from Java. In practice, five-year contracts became common to work off the cost of transport and provide for the labourers' keep and a small cash payment, and up to 10 years to earn the return journey. In spite of 21 emigration Acts passed by India between 1837 and 1864, conditions were harsh and many died on the long journey; immigration into British Guiana was halted in 1848–51 for that reason. The workers had virtually no civil rights and were little distinguished from slaves. Nevertheless, many opted to stay in the West Indies at the end of their indenture (Knight, 1970, 116–9; Engerman, 1983; Curtin, 1990, 176; Adamson, 1975; Shirras, 1931, 596).

There was some involuntary migration also of Europeans in the form of British convicts to Australia during 1788–1853 (and in 1867 to Western Australia). However, it was the voluntary emigration of Europeans overseas which numerically put the enforced migration of coloured people wholly in the shade. That stream of migrants created possibly the single most important impact of Europe on the rest of the world. Large though it seems in the decades to 1870, it was to be greatly exceeded in the decades thereafter.

Data, as in all these cases, are doubtful and authorities differ. This is partly due to problems of definition, such as how to define 'temporary' migrants or returnees, and partly to the inadequate collection of data by the authorities in the first place. In the early years of the century, emigration from Europe was a mere trickle, comparable to that of the eighteenth century, but it began to increase in the 1830s. For one authoritative estimate, see Table 2.9.

Table 2.9 European emigration, by decades 1820–70 (thousands)

Decade	Gross emigration	Net emigration	Implied ratio (%)
1820–30	152	152	100
1831–40	599	529	95
1841–50	1713	1539	90
1851–60	2589	2201	85
1861–70	2315	1856	80

Source: Willcox (1931, 89)

In total this may have been four times as large as the migration of slaves. Up to the 1840s, most of these came from the United Kingdom; from the 1840s onward, when the potato blight struck and the continent suffered the crisis of 1847 and the revolutions of 1848, Germany became a second major source. By the 1860s, when the total had risen to 281 000 a year, Scandinavia became important, at 24 000 emigrants annually (Bairoch, 1976a, 113).

Motives for the movement were mixed. Some sailed in the optimistic hope of betterment, perhaps in the hope of acquiring cheap land or, in the 1850s, to join the gold rush in California or Australia. But the first mass exodus, in 1847–54, when over 2 million sailed for America alone, showed that it could also be poverty and hunger which drove them out. In time, information on the overseas areas improved, the reception at the other end was better organized, and the journey became less hazardous and cheaper. The cost of crossing the Atlantic from Britain, for example, fell from £12–20 at the beginning of our period, for a journey lasting at least 40 days, to as little as £2.17s.6d (£2.88) by sail and £4.15s.0d (£4.75) by steam, when it took but 14 days (Thomas, 1973, 95–6). The British government encouraged emigration, particularly to the Antipodes, in part to secure the colonies and in part to get rid of an assumed 'surplus' population. Thus the Colonial Land and Emigration Commission helped some 39 000 to migrate to Australia by 1869, at a cost of £4.8 million (Erickson, 1976, 122). The largest numbers, however, went to the United States, which received some two-thirds of the European emigrants in 1821–80.

The effect of immigration on 'new' or 'empty' territories was decisive. Without it, there would have been no Australia, New Zealand or much of Canada as they came to develop. But even to territories with an existing population, such as the United States or the River Plate, nineteenth-century immigration added not merely numbers, but desperately needed skills and practices. For the United States, skilled British workers can be shown to have helped the cotton and woollen industry and carpet weaving from the 1820s, hosiery, coal mining and iron puddling in the 1830s and 1840s, cutlery, pottery in the 1840s . . . the list is almost endless. It has been calculated that the value added by the immigrants in the 1840s was equivalent to the total home investment of the United States. Similarly, in Latin America, European merchants and craftsmen were commonly the necessary leaven to get the mass going (Uselding, 1971; Berthoff, 1953; Erickson, 1957; Platt, 1972, 39–40).

With the migrants, Europe sent capital. The export of capital, like emigration, started from small beginnings in the early century and, like the stream of migrants in the first half of the century, it originated mostly from the United Kingdom. Much of the world's overseas trading was financed by short-term credit also from Britain. France contributed the bulk of the remainder. The favourite method was using bills, handled by brokers and ultimately held by bankers, though by the mid-century specialist discount houses, using their own funds, had emerged in London. In the United States some lenders were repaid in part in shares or bonds of the enterprises they helped with credit. In the less sophisticated parts of the world, unused to paper money, the rising prices of the precious metals pointed to a shortage of them. This was resolved with the striking gold finds in California and Australia. World output of gold, fluctuating around half a million ounces in 1801–40, rose to almost 2 million ounces in 1840 with the increase in Russian production, and to over 6 million in the next two decades (Vilar, 1976, 331).

As far as long-term investment is concerned, there is some evidence that, to the end of the eighteenth century, Britain may have been a net international borrower; the transformation into a net lender occurred some time before 1815 (Brezis, 1995). Traditionally, in Europe, foreign loans were taken up by governments, not private agencies, and this practice continued as lending overseas began, since distance precluded close observance or control by the lenders over private borrowers. Investment occurred in big waves or 'manias', fuelled by a form of mass psychosis. The first of these manias ran up to a peak in 1825, and was centred on lending to South American governments and mining companies. The latter hoped to restart the gold and silver mining interrupted by revolution and war; the former appeared commercially sound as well as attractive to liberal sentiments. There were, however, no productive assets created, and of the £20 millions invested, all but those lent to Brazil were in default by 1827. It took some 30 years to achieve returns (Platt, 1972, 36–7). There was some investment also in Canada and Australia.

A second wave, reaching its peak in 1836, went mainly to the United States. In the northern states, canals and other means of transport were the main targets, prompted by the success of British canals and of the Erie canal. In the southern states, British investors were happy to support the extension of cotton growing, mainly by providing capital for local banks; by 1838, 88 per cent of the investments in American banks were made in the south, the proportions being exactly reversed for means of transport (Williamson, 1964, 103). Much of this lending was done indirectly by taking up state bonds, the states then making the actual investment. When they defaulted, as they soon did, the creditors had no redress. Total American borrowings abroad are estimated at $78 million in 1800 and $87 million in 1820, rising to a peak of $297 million in 1839, to decline thereafter before rising once more to $379 million in 1860. Altogether, 14 per cent of American assets were owned abroad in 1800 and 7 per cent still in 1850. That capital inflow was of great significance up to 1830; after that, though it increased in bulk, it played a declining part in the American economy (Lipsey, 1994, 12, 14; North, 1960, 578–81; 1961, 219–20; Imlah, 1958, 137). In Australia British governmental investments topped £300 000 a year from 1817, and from 1830 substantial private funds were added (Butlin, 1994, 63, 183).

In total, £39 million had been invested by British capitalists by 1854 in Latin America and £65 million in the United States, plus £13 million elsewhere. The bulk of the £260 million British foreign investment outstanding at the time was, however, still concentrated in Europe (Kenwood and Lougheed, 1971, 43; Jenks, 1963, 63).

India formed the great exception to all this; whatever British capital was invested there was swamped by the movement in the opposite direction. This arose from the fact that the East India Company, starting as a tax-raising as well as a trading concern, also became in effect the government until 1858. Its primary object was to maximize profits for the shareholders and perks for the officials, and these were derived both from the surplus arising from taxing the Indian population and from trading, until 1813 as a monopoly, with continuing monopoly rights in the trade to China until 1833. In that time, the company required an annual surplus to be sent to Britain, not merely to run its affairs and pay its dividends in London, but also to pay the pensions of retired officers as well as servicing an increasing state debt. It was done by ensuring that India achieved a large export surplus, directly in the trade with the

United Kingdom and indirectly by a surplus with China, which had a positive balance with Britain in turn. The trading surplus averaged £4 million a year in the 1830s (exports £11 million against imports £6.9 million), rising to £5 million from the 1840s, except for the mutiny year and the years which followed (Chaudhuri, 1966, 345, 355–8; Dutt, 1902, 11, 159, 343; Rostow, 1978,515; Desai, 1969, 256). Savings and capital thus went out of India, not into it. Something of a similar nature, on a much smaller scale, took place in the Netherlands East Indies.

Much of the competitive advantage and success registered by Europeans overseas they owed to their superior technology. Together with their commercial energy, which may be considered to have been a product of Europe's unique history, it allowed them to unlock the economic treasures of overseas territories in a manner not available to the native populations (Headrick, 1981, 4–9). There was, however, one field where technological progress benefited all simultaneously: improvements in ocean shipping. There were two major aspects to this: steam replacing sail, and iron and steel replacing timber, while world tonnage itself was growing fast.

Exact data for the earlier period are, as ever, hard to come by. British registered tonnage, listed at 1 292 000 tons in 1792, had doubled to about 2.5 million tons by the end of the Napoleonic war. It then grew slowly, reaching 2.8 million tons by 1840, but thereafter more than doubled to 5.7 million tons by 1870. World tonnage was estimated at 9 million tons in 1850 increasing to 16.8 million tons in 1870, but that included some 2.7 million tons on American lakes and rivers, while probably excluding some shipping in overseas countries (Davies, 1985, 46; Fayle, 1933; Mitchell, 1962, 221).

The first regular steamboats were launched in the United States in 1807 and in Scotland in 1812. By the 1820s, they plied across the English and Irish channels and on American inland waterways, and by the 1830s they had begun to be used for trade to the Mediterranean. Something like a breakthrough occurred around 1840, as engines were improved and paddle wheels were replaced by screws in due course. The company that was to become the P&O undertook regular sailings to Gibraltar in 1837 and to Alexandria in 1840; from 1842, a continuation was established from Suez to India, later to the Far East. Meanwhile Cunard introduced a regular service to Canada in 1840, using four steamers, and a service to the Pacific coast of South America began in 1838. In 1850, 1800 vessels called at Alexandria, 2600 in 1862, and a total of 32 000, of 12.5 million tons, between 1863 and 1871(Issawi, 1966, 413–15). By then steamers were plying on many rivers, even in India and Africa.

Steamships paid off where speed and reliability were paramount concerns – usually subsidized also by mail contracts. From the early passenger services they gradually spread also to cargo vessels, to make trade respond more flexibly to demand, aided by a telegraph cable from Europe to America in 1866, and from Britain to India in 1870. On long journeys where speed was less essential, however, sailing vessels which had no fuel costs and wasted no space on coal were still much cheaper, even after the opening of the Suez Canal in 1869, while their design improved under competition. The tea 'clippers', bringing tea from China to London in the 1850s, represented a high point in the art of shipbuilding. Even in Britain, sail tonnage still outnumbered steam by 4:1 in 1870; for the world as a whole, the ratio was 5.3:1.

Larger ships were more economical, and iron (and later steel) permitted ship sizes to increase vastly beyond the capability of timber. There were problems, however, such as the fouling of the hulls in tropical waters, which was prevented for timber ships by copper sheathing. From the late 1860s onwards, iron shipbuilding began to overtake timber construction. Taking all these changes together, the increasing efficiency of shipping was reflected in falling ocean freight rates: American export freight rates, for example, declined from an index of 238 in 1816 to 100 in 1830 and a low of 42 in 1858–60, to rise again to 81 in 1869–71 (North, 1958, 549; 1971, 173).

Growth and modernization, it will be seen, accelerated from the mid-century; the period 1850–70 thus forms, in some way, a transition to the very much faster integration of the world economy with Europe that was to occur in the decades after 1870. One innovation which symbolizes that integration better than most was the construction of railways in all parts of the globe. In Europe, they had spread outwards from the north west to all regions, to a total track length of well over 60 000 miles by 1870. Overseas, they were constructed both for existing traffic in populated areas and for opening out empty lands for development. They represented a massive investment effort, together with huge demands for iron, for engineering equipment and for skilled management and labour. Most of these came from Europe.

The exception to this, as to so much else, was to be found in the United States. There the first pioneer lines were built in the early 1830s, at the same time as in Britain, and despite the much smaller population, the length of track roughly kept pace with Europe until 1860, by which time around 32 000 miles had been built in both. Between 1849 and 1860, construction in the United States proceeded at an average of more than 2000 miles a year. Up to 1840, New England and the south shared in much of the construction; subsequently, most of the mileage was built in the mid-Atlantic and mid-western states (Williamson, 1964, 115–8; Wicker, 1960, 506). In the years of the Civil War, in the 1860s, construction fell behind the European rate, but still continued at an average of 2000 miles a year. It was then that the astonishing rail connection to the Pacific coast, by the Central Pacific and Union Pacific railways, was made, between 1862 and 1869. Built across thousands of miles of empty, and in part very difficult, terrain, it showed that slow progress in other continents was not so much due to physical difficulties, as to economic and industrial backwardness and the lack of enterprise and foresight of the kind possessed by the Americans.

The American railway system was built up by private companies, though with some state help, including land grants. In the early years, much iron and equipment was imported from Britain; later on native production caught up with demand. There was also much European capital invested in American railways; one estimate puts it at one quarter. Conversely, 60 per cent of British investment in the United States was in railway shares and bonds (Jeremy and Stapleton, 1991, 40–3; Woodruff, 1966, 119–125). Canada's early railways also used much foreign, British and American capital. Given the large distances and the small population, there had to be a government guarantee of interest to attract the investor (Jenks, 1963, 198–200; Baskerville, 1981, 314, 324).

Outside North America, railway building was still in its infancy in 1850–70, with one exception: India. Here the earlier flow of capital was reversed, and British capital flooded into India for investment in railways. The reason for this was a guarantee of interest by the Indian government, mostly at the rate of 5 per cent. Considered a gilt-edged investment at a time when British consols yielded very much less, there was no shortage of money from Britain. All told, some £95 million was spent in this way between 1845 and 1875, total British investment in India being around £160 million. Since shareholders would receive their interest payments whatever the losses, construction was wasteful, badly managed and corrupt. Costs per mile were £17–18 000 instead of the planned £8000. As a result, the government decided to take over building itself in 1869. The railways, as built, made large losses up to the end of the century and beyond, which were met by the Indian government. The whole thus represented a vast annual transfer of funds from the Indian taxpayer to the British investor, some 40 per cent of the costs having actually been spent in Britain in the first place. For the cost of 890 million rupees, an annual sum of 44 million rupees had thus to be transferred (Rothermund, 1988, 32–3; Headrick, 1981, 185–8; Charlesworth, 1982, 44).

By 1870, some 5000 miles had been constructed, following in outline the plan proposed by the Marquis of Dalhousie, Governor General in 1848–56. In the long term, the railways proved useful for India's development, but at the time they ran well ahead of needs and placed a heavy burden on the country's budget. It has been argued, with much justification, that a system of canals and irrigation channels would have done far more good at the time.

Egypt was another area in which some early railway building took place. A line from Alexandria to Cairo was started in 1853 and completed in 1856, followed by a railway from Cairo to Suez in 1857. These, the first railways in Africa, turned out to be profitable. In Latin America, government interest guarantees were an early requirement, and much of the initiative and the capital came from Britain. With some building starting in the 1850s, by 1870 there were some 500 miles open in Brazil and Argentina, 450 miles in Chile, mostly around the capital cities, 250 miles in Peru and 215 miles in Mexico. Comparatively speaking, however, railway building outside Europe and North America was lagging badly. By 1850, the mileage constructed there was still negligible. By 1860, it had risen to 1685 miles and in 1870 to 9035 miles (more than half of which were in India). This represented no more than 7 per cent of the world total (Léon, 1978, 578; Mulhall, 1892, 495; 1971, 72).

There was European overseas investment also in other infrastructure projects, such as roads and canals in India from the late 1830s, roads in Egypt and in parts of Latin America, docks and harbours, as well as banks in Latin America, the Ottoman Empire and India, and tea and other plantations in India. Above all, there was the Suez Canal, constructed in 1862–9, representing an investment of some £16–18 million. Productive enterprises of this kind usually could service their foreign capital themselves, or had government interest guarantees. It was often quite different in the case of loans to governments, the other major investment target of foreign capital. British colonial governments and American federal, state and municipal loans were reasonably safe. According to one estimate, foreign holdings of American railway shares and debentures rose from $52 million in 1853 to $243 million in 1870, while holdings of public authority obligations had risen from $159 million to $1107 million in the same years (Williamson, 1964, 259). Much of this was British, but German, Dutch and other European capital was also involved. As for Australia, foreign capital, which in the 1860s represented 5.2 per cent of national income, also considered it safe. It was in Turkey and Latin America that loans to governments, subscribed with apparent abandon by European financiers on the advice of supposedly knowledgeable merchant banks, soon ran into defaults and endless series of recycling and new loans to service the old ones.

Britain was much the largest foreign lender at the time, her approximately £260 million outstanding in 1855 and £770 million in 1870 representing two-fifths of the world total, as well as the bulk of the sums lent outside Europe. France, the next largest lender, at about £200 million and £500 million outstanding at those dates, invested three-quarters of it in Europe, and virtually all the remainder in the Mediterranean region

(Bairoch, 1976a, 10 1; Trebilcock, 1981, 176–9; Woodruff, 1966, 150; Cain and Hopkins, 1993, 173; Kenwood and Lougheed, 1971, 43–5).

The acceleration of the flow of overseas migration in those years has been noted above. Two-thirds of British migrants between 1843 and 1870 left for the United States, and another 30 per cent for imperial territories (Thomas, 1973, 57). Germans and Scandinavians also made mainly for the United States, while the increasing numbers migrating to Argentina and Brazil were made up mostly of Spaniards, Portuguese and Italians, with a sizeable German minority moving to Brazil. The largest losses by emigration in 1850–70, as a share of the home population, were recorded by Ireland, Norway, Scotland and England (Baines, 1991, 10).

One other impact of Europe on overseas territories deserves mention: the introduction of the practices of European medicine. Although, like so much else, becoming fully effective only after 1870, the foundations were laid before then. At the beginning of the century European medical practice, with its bleeding, purging, the application of mercury and the like had hardly been superior to the mixture of superstition and practical common sense found elsewhere. It scored thereafter by the growing pursuit of systematic observation and research, which it began to apply also to the colonies.

Progress was made mainly in four geographical regions. In the West Indies, a number of Scots doctors had begun by the late eighteenth century to treat tetanus and lockjaw, as well as undertake smallpox inoculation among the slave population. On the West African coast, the original interest was in the high mortality of Europeans. Systematic enquiries into yellow fever were made in 1849–52, and the benefits of the practice of boiling the drinking water, of avoiding swamps and seeking the high ground were also noted as protection against dysentery and malaria, among others. Against malaria or 'fever', the cinchona bark had been known to be effective in South America; now quinine could be isolated and commercially produced and it was used widely, almost routinely, by the 1840s (Curtin, 1965, 344–54; Headrick, 1981, 62–7).

In India, cholera was a main scourge, wreaking havoc among the troops; as late as the 1860s, units would lose half their men within eight years of arrival as a result of that and other diseases. Quartering them in married homes rather than in crowded barracks helped somewhat, but other obvious remedies for the general population, such as prohibiting the mass pilgrimages in which the illness was particularly liable to spread, could not be applied for political reasons. Since India was thought to be the source of world cholera epidemics, the international conference held in Constantinople in 1866 paid particular attention to that country. As part of concerted action to deal with disease, Provincial Sanitary

Commissions were established in 1864 and spread to most provinces in 1866–7 (Arnold, 1986; Ramasubban, 1988).

Algeria, where many Europeans had settled since the French colonization in 1830, received much attention from French medicine. Reports from 1851 onwards traced malaria, smallpox, cholera, typhus, syphilis and discussed remedies. In 1835, a service of French itinerant doctors was created and regular services were planned in the 1840s. Local traditions and Muslim religious practices made it difficult to deal with sources of disease of long standing, such as garbage heaps, cesspools and polluted water supply, and the population distrusted European doctors in general; but in 1863, the principle of vaccination was accepted, and the first Arab doctors began to apply it (Marcovich, 1988). As a result of all this work, the death rates of Europeans and of slaves were brought down, but it is not known how far the native populations benefited.

Taking the period 1800 to 1870 as a whole, the extra-European territories had greatly strengthened their linkage to the advanced countries of Europe and North America. Growing at over 3 per cent per annum, the exports of Spanish America, the British colonies and India, taken together, increased from £37 million in 1800 to £348 million in 1870, their share of world trade actually going up from 12 per cent to 16 per cent and perhaps to as much as 18 per cent (Bairoch and Etemad, 1985, 19, 52; Bairoch, 1976a, 86; Mulhall, 1892, 128).

Yet in their general development they had fallen badly behind. This was not merely so in the high-tech industries, where the Third World, with 71 per cent of the world's population, had only 7 per cent of the total steam horse-power, and still less, a mere 3 per cent of the fixed horse-power excluding locomotives and steamships, it produced only 0.4 per cent of the output of pig iron, and it possessed only 0.03 per cent of cotton spindles in 1870 (Mulhall, 1892, 545; Bairoch, 1976a, 176; 1982, 288). Even in the more traditional crafts they had declined from a position around 1800 when countries like India, China or the Ottoman Empire were at an economic level not too dissimilar from western Europe, to 1870 when that near-parity had become completely out of reach. Even their absolute level of industrialization had declined, by one calculation from an index of 99 in 1800 (UK 1900 = 100) to 67 in 1880; as a proportion of world manufacturing production, the Third World's percentage had fallen more dramatically from 68 in 1800 to 37 in 1860 and a mere 21 in 1880 (Bairoch and Lévy-Leboyer, 1981; Bairoch, 1980, 34; 1982, 275, 291–2). With the loss of economic power had come the loss of political power, as many of these overseas countries had to submit to freer trade, open ports, control over their finances and legal privileges for foreigners. Most of them were also hopelessly in debt to the west.

Their relatively high share of world trade they owed to their export of primary products, some countries becoming wholly and dangerously dependent on one or two products only (see Table 2.8). It is worth noting that, apart from the trade figures, little statistical information on Third World countries appeared to be available in the west; either their data were ignored, or a nominal small figure was inserted (Mulhall, 1892, 129,132; 1971, 37,42). Not merely economic policy, but also statistical interest was Eurocentred.

The reasons for this dropping behind are many and varied. It cannot have been lack of natural resources, for many of these overseas territories are richly endowed. It cannot have been their concentration on primary production, as is often alleged, for that did not hold back the United States or the colonies of white settlement. The origins must lie in the social and historical sphere, in the restrictions imposed by the colonial powers, in the lack of preparation, the lack, as Sir Arthur Lewis put it, of an 'investment climate' (Lewis, 1978, 10). Whatever the cause, it was not surprising that many in those countries thought that contact with the west had been detrimental to them, or even that they became poor *because* the others had become rich.

THE OVERSEAS WORLD

We may now turn to a brief review of some of these overseas countries. Among them, the development of the United States was unique, for, starting as a 'colonial' type of economy and in fact expanding primary exports at a fast rate, by 1870 the country had become a major industrial power, about to become the leading industrial economy in the world. The occupation of the vast areas of land west of the Appalachians was one of the major events in American as well as in world economic history in this period. As late as 1870, the United States was still essentially an agrarian state, but agriculture formed a shrinking proportion of employment and output. It was manufacturing which showed the most astonishing growth.

Leading in the first decades of the century was the cotton textile industry, in which value added rose from $16 000 in 1805 and $930 000 in 1820 to $48.4 million in 1860. Using British technology at first, it added its own innovations before long, such as an improved throstle, the cap and ring spindle and a different form of factory organization (Zevin, 1971, 123; Jeremy, 1981, 213; North, 1961, 172–5). Other leading industries were coal mining and iron mining and smelting (mostly still with charcoal), but in fact much of the growth was in traditional craft-based industries: while total factor productivity in cotton, with 1820 = 100, rose to 261 in 1860, it increased to a respectable 206 even in boots and shoes. American technology was by then leading Britain in wood-working machinery, in high-pressure steam engines, in ring spindles and in what has become known as the 'American system of manufacture', the mass production of composite articles using interchangeable parts (Sokoloff, 1986, 696–7; Hounshell, 1984; Rosenberg, 1972, 87ff). By 1870, the United States was producing 23 per cent of world industrial output. Manufactured products were beginning to compete in world markets and by the 1860s, the share of final manufactures in American exports had reached 15.7 per cent (Gallman, 1960, 43; Bairoch, 1982, 292; North, 1961, v; Davis *et al.* 1972, 568). All this was achieved in spite of the massive destruction wrought by the Civil War of 1860–65 and the loss of productivity in the south following the freeing of the slaves in 1865.

The United States was rich in land and other natural resources as well as in capital, but short of labour, and one would therefore have expected different priorities and technologies from those of the United Kingdom. The Americans did indeed tend to go for innovations that were labour saving even at the expense of using resources lavishly, yet the two economies moved closely in step. There even seemed to be a common rhythm, slow growth in Britain being associated with exports of capital and capital goods to the United States and a high rate of investment there, and vice versa (Williamson, 1964; 1995; Rostow, 1978, 159; Thomas, 1973).

Some of the linkages between American economic growth and the influence of Europe, and especially of the United Kingdom, have been discussed above. They include capital investment, immigration, technology and, not least, the inheritance of a social and legal system favouring enterprise. Europe also furnished the main market for American primary product exports, creating an export-led growth in a critical period: 'The major market for goods in the first part of the nineteenth century lay outside America . . . As far as the westward movement was concerned, it was primarily the demand for cotton and then wheat (and flour) that was critical' (North, 1956, 496; see also Lipsey, 1994, 59).

Canadian economic developments showed many similarities, though with a time lag. Population being thinner on the ground meant that greater government support was needed in the building of the early canals and railways. The main export products were timber, which had its chance after the Continental Blockade cut off the traditional supply from the Baltic, and wheat and its products, which overtook timber in the second half of the century. The opening up of the country after 1800 was performed by British immigrants and capital, mainly for British markets, though after 1850 the American market became increasingly important (Marr and Paterson, 1980, 72ff).

The economies of Australia and New Zealand were the creation of the nineteenth century by European, mostly British, immigrants, the native Maori population of New Zealand managing to keep a better hold on their land than the Australian aborigines. Australian population growth was slow at first, consisting mainly of convicts and their guards and, as late as 1850, the total had reached only 334 000. In 1851 came the gold discoveries, and no fewer than 59 000 people landed in Melbourne in 1852 alone. By 1870, the total had risen to close on 2 million. New Zealand's gold was discovered 10 years later, and its population grew to 177 000 in 1867 (Shann, 1948, 173; Butlin, 1994, 28, 38; Cruickshank, 1931, 180).

Before that, however, the Australian economy had been put on a more solid footing by the discovery that sheep would flourish in some of the inland territories, and by the skill of the breeders in producing wool of the highest quality. Wool exports, at 41 million lb in 1850, covered one-quarter of the total British consumption, rising to one-half by 1870. Total Australian commerce had grown from £3 million in 1840 to £57 million in 1870, of which Britain took 60 per cent of exports and 75 per cent of imports. By then, the country's income per head was the highest in the world, well above that of the United Kingdom and the United States, the next highest (Butlin, 1962, 10; 1994, 189; Mulhall, 1892, 124; McMichael, 1984, 101–3; Maddison, 1991, 6–7).

The West Indies were among the overseas territories which changed least in this period. Having been developed by Europeans from the seventeenth century onwards, they continued in the nineteenth to be 'the place where England finds it convenient to carry on the production of sugar, coffee and a few other tropical commodities . . . the trade with the West Indies is hardly to be considered an external trade, but more resembles the traffic between town and country' (John Stuart Mill, 1848; cited in Mintz, 1985, 42).

As the production of cotton shifted to mainland America, sugar became, if anything, even more critical to the West Indian economy in the nineteenth century; in 1860, it accounted for 60 per cent of their exports, against 6 per cent for the next biggest item, coffee (Hanson, 1980, 149). The critical change was the abolition of slavery, with the consequent temporary loss of production in the British colonies in 1834–8 and in the French in 1848; this gave Cuba and Puerto Rico their chance. However, Barbados, British Guiana and Trinidad also raised their output, as did Martinique and Guadeloupe; only Jamaica, among the larger islands, declined badly, making up the loss in part with coffee (Watts, 1990, 234, 321).

The former Spanish colonies on the American mainland formed a somewhat heterogeneous group. At one extreme were the small Central

American republics, poverty-stricken and backward, whose total exports between them came to a mere $6 million in 1860, compared with $20 million for the British West Indies, $23 million for Cuba and $5.5 million for Costa Rica (Hanson, 1980, 139). At the other extreme were the more advanced countries at the southern tip of the continent, Chile, Argentina and possibly Uruguay.

Chile was the most industrialized and most Europeanized of the republics, distinguished also for generally paying its debts in time after resuming repayment in 1842. Copper and the nitrate of soda were leading among her exports, and these increased fivefold between 1844 and 1873. Argentina, with her wide, open grasslands and her temperate climate was potentially the most prosperous country in the region, the one most likely to develop like Australia or New Zealand. However, the country suffered from monetary confusion and, for long periods, political anarchy. From the 1860s, the country took to sheep farming and wool exports, which by 1880 formed nearly half the total. General economic development came late, but then it was remarkably fast, including the building of the railways in the 1860s, which attracted both capital and immigrants from abroad to begin to fill up the vast inland spaces (Hanson, 1980, 146; Ferns, 1960, 320f).

Uruguay was also well placed for cattle raising, but politically a buffer state, which actually tried repeatedly in 1839–48 to get Britain to take it over as a protectorate. Peru was the other main exporter in the region, on the basis of the guano trade from 1841 onwards. Though the trade was in the hands of British firms, it yielded most of the country's tax revenue, at least until the 1870s. There was also sugar, produced in part by Chinese coolie labour. Bolivia became a main exporter of tin, while Mexico restarted some silver mining after gaining independence. Most of the capital and the economic initiative came from Europe, but in general it either extended itself only to enclave sectors to service the export industries or channelled the proceeds abroad, or both. What was missing, by comparison with the English-speaking colonies similarly endowed by nature, was a go-ahead middling class of farmers, craftsmen, traders and professionals.

Brazil entered upon treaties with Britain and other countries in 1810, which in effect allowed the much better equipped United Kingdom to replace Portugal as the main supplier of manufactured goods and trading services to the Latin American country, reinforcing her privileged position with the treaty of 1827 (Marques, 1972, I, 456). Britain continued to be the leading foreign lender and investor; she supplied much of the infrastructure for the coffee-growing region, though the product was sent mainly to the United States and the continent of Europe (Cain and Hopkins, 1993, 298; Peláez 1976, 279).

At the beginning of the century, sugar was the main export product, with cotton and coffee not far behind. From the 1830s, coffee took off: it formed 41 per cent of exports by value in the 1840s and 68 per cent in the 1860s, Brazil becoming the world's major supplier (Graham, 1985, 749). The shift from sugar to coffee also involved a geographical shift, from the north-east, the Bahia and Pernambuco region, to the 'South Central Region', mainly the Paraiba valley, helping to build up the populations of São Paolo, Rio de Janeiro and Minas Gerais, including, incidentally, a considerable German minority (Naylor, 1931, 160f; Mulhall, 1971, 474; Mauro, 1986, 349). Sugar and coffee were worked by slaves, and Brazil became the major slave-importing country in our period. Britain forced it to renounce the slave trade in 1850, and abolish slavery itself between 1871 and 1888, the last American country to do so.

India was by far the most important trading partner with Europe after America; British India was also much the most populous part of the British Empire. Its area under British governance was repeatedly enlarged even at the height of *laissez-faire* policies in the mid-nineteenth century, when the Punjab, Berar and Nagpur, Sind and Oudh, beside Burma, Assam, and other territories were annexed. The East India Company lost its trading monopoly to Britain in 1813, its monopoly of the China trade in 1833 and finally handed over all political power to the British government in 1858. Its primary objective had always been to make money for its shareholders, not to govern a colony, and it managed to use both its taxing powers and its trading to fulfil its primary task as well as allowing its chief servants to become extremely wealthy.

In Bengal and adjacent territories the tax collection power was transferred to local landowners, or Zemindars. The actual sums were fixed by the 'permanent settlement' of 1793, which in many areas placed an enormous burden on the peasants. Elsewhere, the peasants were taxed individually, being granted title to their land. The land tax generally provided half the total revenue and fluctuated around 6–8 per cent of gross national produce and 15–50 per cent of the peasant's net income (Léon, 1978, III, 236; IV, 560–63; Stokes, 1973, 144, 149; Dutt, 1902, I, 371).

As noted above, the 'drain' of the large annual sums sent to Britain by the East India Company impoverished the country, reduced its savings and investment potential and, at the same time, inasmuch as the government was required to borrow to meet its obligations, enlarged the nominal debt of the government of India. The Indian taxpayer had to meet the cost of the British army there and of its various wars. On the positive side, Britain was said to have brought internal peace instead of chaos, to have unified the country administratively, to have established the rule of law and to have established appointments to the civil service by examinations, creating a college for it (Haileybury, 1906) long before similar practices were introduced into Britain (Panikkar, 1960, 1963; Morris, 1963; Knowles, 1928, 304–6).

Against all this, the chief indictment of the British administration of the Indian sub-continent was the destruction of its ancient handicrafts, particularly the production of cotton textiles, by the import of British machine-made goods. There can be no doubt of the change wrought on Indian foreign trade in this regard. While the large exports of cotton fabrics not only to Europe but also to southern Asia, the Middle East, Africa and even America at the beginning of the century collapsed in the 1820s, the yardage of English cotton cloth sold to India rose from 800 000 in 1814 to 51 million yards in 1830 and around 1000 million yards by 1870, making India much the largest foreign market for Lancashire (Bairoch, 1980, 34; Parthasarathi, 1998, 85). A large literature exists to deplore this development as part of a general attack on nineteenth century 'capitalism' and 'imperialism'.

It might well be argued that hand spinners and handloom weavers would have lost out against the machine no matter who governed the country, but there is no doubt that the British government, which maintained a prohibitive tax against Indian imports into Britain while forcing virtual free trade on India, with a minimal tariff on imports, greatly speeded the process. Typically, in 1862, the pressure by Lancashire cotton industrialists led to a reduction in import duties from 10 per cent to 5 per cent, despite the desperately needed revenue in India (Harnetty, 1965; Dutt, 1902, I, 205, 261).

Yet, in a controversy which clearly has political undertones, it has also been asserted that the harmful effects of the manufactured imports have been greatly exaggerated. For one thing, weavers were able to survive for a long time by using cheap British yarn, by producing intricate patterns for the luxury trade, and by turning to silk goods, the exports of which were increasing. Other crafts might even benefit from growing markets and by building and repairing equipment (Twomey, 1983, 50; Ghosal, 1964, 131; Farnie, 1979, 103–4). Besides, measured against the vast size of India, the effects of imports could easily be exaggerated; as late as 1837, cotton imports were estimated to amount to no more than 6 per cent of Indian consumption, and 10 per cent in 1850. Transport away from the coast was still primitive, village craftsmen still kept their local customers, and a dual economy persisted for a long time (Marshall, 1990, 112–13; Thorner, 1950, 7; Robb, 1992, 102; Charlesworth, 1982, 32–3; Hanson, 1980, 27).

India's exports consisted overwhelmingly of primary commodities. In the 1820s and 1830s, indigo and opium occupied the top two places. As indigo declined after 1830, opium became, and remained, the leading item (China being the main importer), representing 33 per cent of exports by value in 1860, with cotton a temporary second. Other important items were rice, sugar, seeds, tea from Assam and, towards the end of the period, jute, of which India had a world monopoly (Hanson, 1980, 148; Mulhall, 1971, 225). By that time the first modern plants in mining and manufacturing began to appear, mainly on European initiative, including a cotton mill in Bombay in 1856 (founded by a Parsi) and a jute mill in Calcutta in 1855 (Rothermund, 1988, 51,56; Rostow, 1978, 515).

There were some similarities in the history of the Dutch East Indies, particularly as regards the official policy of making the transfer of large funds to the home country a main aim of policy. The export surplus over the whole period 1833–70 amounted to fl.800 million, running towards the end at an annual £3 million (Léon, 1978, 537; Mulhall 1971, 332). There is some controversy regarding the effects on the native population of the 'cultivation system' noted above, imposed in 1830 and wound down in 1870, though most judgments tend to be negative. There is no doubt, however, that it led to a substantial increase in the exports of key commodities, exceeding even the targets planned by van den Bosch (Baasch, 1927, 575; Deerr, 1949–50, 224; Furnival, 1944, 127, 167–89; Allen and Donnithorne, 1957, 168). Yet production for export used only a small share of the total cultivated area of the islands, taken together; the contractors were foreigners, in the majority Chinese, and where the 'system' prevailed, labour though technically free was tied to the soil. In sum, next to nothing was done to help the development of the native population.

China, though it was never turned into a colony, was nevertheless not immune from feeling some effects of the industrial revolution in Europe. Advanced for the time, and of vast size in relation to the rest of the world, China has been estimated to have possessed one-third of the world's total industrial capacity in 1800, and still 19.7 per cent in 1860 (Bairoch, 1982, 282, 292, 296). Though the government was traditionally hostile to foreign imports, Chinese customers were increasingly willing to buy European and American manufactures from the late eighteenth century onwards, to which were added raw cotton and opium from India in the nineteenth century. As a result of these imports, the traditional flow of silver into China to pay for the tea, the porcelain and silks widely demanded in Europe turned into a reverse flow of specie out of China from the 1820s at the latest. Opium was smuggled in, outside the control of the officially appointed Co-hong merchants in Canton, and when the opium imports became a flood in the 1830s, and China attempted to block the trade in 1839, the war of 1839–42 ensued, at the end of which Britain enforced the opening of other ports, some extraterritorial rights for her merchants and the cession of Hongkong. France and the United States soon obtained similar privileges, and these were much extended after the second opium war by the treaty of Tientsin in 1860 (Ward, 1994, 55–8; Greenberg, 1951, 112; Léon, 1978, 534).

Tea, the increasingly dominant Chinese export, was produced by hill farmers on a family basis, so that the opportunities for technical improvements, or rising productivity, were limited. By contrast, Lancashire cottons, with their sharply reduced prices, could capture ever larger markets; by 1868, China had become their second most important export market after India (Elvin, 1973, 282; Farnie, 1979, 120). Important though these trades were for the other countries, they hardly affected the large bulk of inland China, difficult of access except along rivers and canals, and resistant to change. Japan, which had shut itself off from the outside world for centuries, was forced to open its territories in the 1850s, and by the treaty of 1866 undertook not to raise tariffs above 5 per cent, while giving foreigners extraterritorial rights. The immediate effect was to damage some traditional manufactures with western imports, but the economy was transformed with remarkable speed from the 1870s onward.

In the Mediterranean region, the country which made the most determined and extensive effort to become part of the European drive to industrialization was Egypt. Its governor, Mohammed Ali, who took command in 1805 and left office in 1848, set out to turn it into a modern economy. An agricultural reform was accompanied by extensive irrigation and canal works, built by tens of thousands of peasants under a *corvée* type of forced labour. A wide range of industrial plants was set up with European experts and equipment from the advanced states of western Europe, including textile mills, glass works, sugar mills, paper works, leather working, sulphuric acid production, and a foundry and shipyard. School and colleges were founded, and students were sent to study in Europe. Mohammed Ali forced the peasants to sell their crops to him at a fixed low price, and the profits made by reselling them at higher prices helped to finance his industrial ventures. The work was continued by his successors, who built roads and encouraged railways and steam shipping. By 1872, there were 53 steamers plying the Nile, together with 9563 sailing boats. Meanwhile, Egypt had contributed some £8–11.5 million to the building of the Suez Canal, though the Khedive's holdings only amounted to £4 million, which had to be sold in 1875 (Issawi, 1966; Herschlag, 1964, 128).

Perhaps most impressive was the encouragement of the growing of long-stapled cotton. Crops were increased from 14 million lb per annum in the 1820s to 127 million lb in the 1860s. Total exports, which included wheat, sugar and other primary commodities, went up from just over

£E2 million a year in 1848–52 to £E13 million in 1863–72 (Mulhall, 1892; Issawi, 1966, 373; Richards, 1987, 215). Yet, despite these successes, Egypt failed to break through into modernity. Incomes remained low, and the modern sectors remained unviable enclaves; Mohammed Ali had merely succeeded in turning a subsistence economy into an export economy (Issawi, 1966, 361). Among the causes were lack of skill and ability among managers and workers alike, unwilling coerced labour, corruption, costly imported machinery and delayed spare parts, and lack of coal. Yet Egypt's soil was fertile, the climate was favourable, and other countries similarly endowed had succeeded in entering a continuous growth phase. By the end of the period the government had got into serious debt, aggravated by taking up foreign loans at usurious rates, the total reaching £35 million in 1873. It was forced to accept increasing fiscal control by foreign banking interests (Jenks, 1963, 314).

The Ottoman Empire was a classic example of an economy which, starting out from a level comparable with that of Europe in 1800, not only failed to keep up but actually experienced decline and deindustrialization. Some traditional craft industries survived, such as the production of silk robes, mother-of-pearl goods, damascene arms and morocco leather, but others, in particular cotton textiles, were destroyed by western manufactures. Political and economic weaknesses combined to oblige the Porte to conclude the commercial treaty of 1838 with Britain, which opened the country to foreign imports, limited import duties and privileged foreign merchants. Unlike local producers, these were exempt from the obnoxious provincial tariffs, and in 1856 the monopoly of coastal traffic was granted to foreigners. Contact with Europe encouraged the production of primary goods, such as raw cotton and tobacco, for export.

A major weakness was the incompetent and corrupt administration. From 1854, the government was forced to take up foreign loans, and in 1860 it privileged the foreign-run Ottoman Bank. Within very few years it became enmeshed in growing foreign indebtedness: by 1869, the empire owed £76 million abroad, of which it had received only about a half, and very little of which had gone into productive enterprises. The consequence was growing foreign control over Turkish administration in order to safeguard the interests of foreign investors (Issawi, 1966, 49,54; Herschlag, 1964, 48,62; Kasaba, 1988, 47; Inalcik, 1987, 383). A similar story could be told of Persia, forced open by treaty with Britain in 1841 (Issawi, 1971; Cain and Hopkins, 1993, 412). Persia's exports stagnated between 1830 and 1860 at $7 million per annum, while those of Algeria, Tunis and Morocco combined were $3.4 million and $12.6 million respectively, the growth being accounted for by French Algeria (Bairoch and Etemad, 1985, 92, 114).

The only other major European settlement in Africa was at its southern tip. The Dutch and, from 1806, the British picked the Cape for its strategic significance, but otherwise it held little attraction for settlers, with its harsh territory inland and no minerals, until the discoveries of diamonds at Kimberley in 1866 and of gold soon after. The European population increased from 27 000 in 1806 to some 175 000 in 1854, rising to over 400 000 in 1861 and to 1.5 million by 1877. At each stage blacks were in a majority, and by 1865 there were some 6500 Indians in Natal. About 90 per cent of the population was engaged in agriculture. An adaptation of native sheep did particularly well. From 1 million sheep in 1806, numbers rose to 8 million in 1865, and wool exports, rising from £30 000 per annum in 1840, reached their peak in 1872 at £3 million. The first railway was constructed in 1859, the harbour was deepened in 1860, and banking and shipping appeared, but real development had to wait for the last quarter of the century (Cain and Hopkins, 1993, 370; Beinart, 1998; Jaarsveld, 1975, 73, 156–7).

East African exports consisted mostly of slaves, with some gold traded northward. West Africa, on the other hand, developed closer relations with Europe as the slave trade gave way to the 'legitimate' trade in commodities. Exports consisted mainly of palm oil, groundnuts and timber, together with gum from Senegambia and wax, dyewoods and gold. Most of these lent themselves to production by peasant families rather than large plantations. The region imported textiles – some produced in India – tobacco, beads and firearms (Curtin, 1975, 327; 1990, 186; Davies, 1985, 67; Eltis, 1991, 111; 1987, 229). Commodity trade grew more than 20-fold between the 1780s and the 1860s as the slave trade shrank. Yet, as commerce reached £3.5 million a year, that still only represented £0.2 per head, compared with, say, £1.7 a head for Brazil at the time (Hopkins, 1973, 125; Eltis, 1991, 101). The region was still among the poorest and most backward in the world.

CONCLUSION

In the years 1800–1870, the interrelations between Europe and the rest of the world developed in a manner that was in many respects entirely novel. One obvious aspect of this was the amount of trade in commodities which multiplied many times over, tending towards a pattern in which Europe supplied manufactured goods, in return for primary products, food and raw materials from the rest of the world. Many European manufactures were new products which could not be produced at all overseas; others were more traditional, but could now be produced more cheaply by new methods in Europe. Of the inward traffic to Europe, also, some commodities were traditional, but faced increased demand because of rising populations or exhaustion of supplies in parts of Britain and continental Europe – timber and wheat were examples – while others were tropical products for which European conditions were unsuitable or which were found, or found in abundance, only in certain parts of the world. Some of these, in turn, had to be developed on European initiative.

Possibly of greater import was the movement of people. This was of many kinds. There were traders, adventurers and explorers, opening up closed markets and linking them with the rest of the world in traffic of all kinds. Far more numerous were settlers, driven by despair at home or hope overseas, who came to stay. Others went abroad temporarily, intending to make their fortune by privileges granted to Europeans or by skills acquired in Europe. Millions of people elsewhere were sold into slavery, or became near-slaves in a system of indenture.

In this manner, a single world was being created as never before, and few regions remained unaffected by those movements. The initiative came from Europe, some drive from North America being added in the later decades. It was the Europeans who peopled the territories that had been empty, or nearly so, before, and forced closed societies to open a window to the outside world.

What provided the drive for this worldwide initiative? How did it come about that this enormous energy was found essentially in parts of Europe only, and just at that time? Though there was a long run-up to it over previous centuries, there can be no doubt that the power was ultimately derived from the industrial revolution, which was transforming, first the British Isles, then Western Europe and which ultimately was to envelop the whole continent. Because of the early transformation of the British economy, and the British dominance in the world's commerce, shipping and naval power after 1815, it was the United Kingdom which supplied the larger part of the capital, the manpower, the manufactures and the initiative that radiated outward from Europe. Other leading countries were France and the countries with significant colonial possessions, the Netherlands, Spain and Portugal, but every European country played some part in the process. We are here essentially concerned with economic affairs, but have to note that impulses also came from the political and military initiatives of European states, while the state system, with the qualities it developed, was itself not unconnected with the continuing process of industrialization.

Broadly, the Europeans founded four types of overseas territories. First were the territories cleared and settled by people of European stock, which included North America and the 'white' British colonies. Here the settlers found congenial conditions in terms of climate, soil and accessibility.

Compared with the Europe they had left, land was plentiful and cheap and sometimes free altogether, though it might have to be cleared with an expenditure of effort, there was no traditional class of landlords to push down status or exploit the tillers of the soil economically, and government pressed lightly in terms of taxes or military service. Land being cheap and easily available, wages tended to be high, and mobility unhindered.

Though these territories all began as suppliers of primary products in return for European manufactures, as did the other overseas lands, they were distinguished by maintaining a high rate of economic growth and rising incomes and prosperity together with some signs of incipient industrialization. The United States had, in fact, become a major industrial power by 1870.

The second type comprised those territories colonized earlier from Europe, dominated by Europeans but containing large native or black populations. The Europeans had come to trade, or to exploit mines or plantations, but proved unable to raise incomes or modernize these countries in the same way as the first group. Cities with some trappings of European standards did come into existence, as well as estates or plantations in which the coloured population was subjected to old or new forms of exploitation. This period saw a huge increase in the output of primary products for the European markets, aided by improved means of transport across the seas. Latin America and the West Indies were the chief regions in this category, which thus ranged from the tropics to the temperate zone.

Countries with established governments and, usually, ancient civilizations before the arrival of the Europeans formed the third category. Some, including British India and the Dutch East Indies, were conquered outright. Others, including China, Japan, much of the rest of southern Asia, and the Middle East, were forced by war, by financial pressure or other means to admit Europeans as traders or in other capacities. Most of these countries had long traditions of craftsmanship, including much of a high artistic standard, of trade, of literacy and a settled political culture. Before industrialization, Europe had little to teach them in these regards, though the Europeans who arrived there might possess superior weaponry or military organization, together with the skill to use regional wars and civil wars to insinuate themselves into positions of influence and even of power. It was industrialization, directly and indirectly, which enabled them to force their goods, some of which came from other overseas territories, on these countries. Typically, there was some deindustrialization as a consequence of the competition of European manufactures, while modern industries developed only slowly.

Finally, there were regions with no highly structured native governments and limited European penetration, as in much of the African continent.

The dominance which Europe came to exert in this phase was based in the last resort on economic, mainly industrial, superiority and its derivatives, such as superior naval power or the existence of a class of self-confident entrepreneurs willing and able to override traditional obstacles. Yet the assumption guiding the Europeans (sometimes accepted even by the others) was that they were superior in other respects as well, including their social structure, their ethics and their religion, their political practices and even their racial characteristics. They thought of themselves as destined to rule the 'lesser breeds' of different colour. As yet, their strength was sufficient only to impose their trading conditions on the fringes of other civilizations, not to conquer more than a fraction of the non-European world or to penetrate their economies in depth. That was to follow in the next phase, as new technologies were to multiply further their power for good and evil.

BIBLIOGRAPHY

Adams, D.R. (1980), 'American neutrality and prosperity, 1793–1808: a reconsideration', *Journal of Economic History*, 40, 4.

Adamson, A.H. (1975), 'The reconstruction of plantation labour after emancipation: the case of British Guiana', in S.L. Engerman and E.D. Genovese (eds), *Race and Slavery in the Western Hemisphere*, Princeton: Princeton University Press.

Allen, G.C. and A.G. Donnithorne, (1957), *Western Enterprise in Indonesia and Malaya*, London: Allen & Unwin.

Arnold, D. (1986), 'Cholera and colonialism in British India', *Past & Present*, 113.

Baasch, E. (1927), *Holländische Wirtschaftsgeschichte*, Jena: Fischer.

Baines, D. (1991), *Emigration from Europe 1815–1930*, London: Macmillan.

Bairoch, P. (1968), 'Niveaux de développement économique au XIXe siècle', *Annales E.S.C.*, 20,6.

Bairoch, P. (1974), 'Geographical structure and trade balance of European foreign trade from 1800 to 1970', *Journal of European Economic History*, 3, 3.

Bairoch, P. (1976a), *Commerce extérieur et développement économique de l'Europe au XIXe siècle*, Paris/Hague: Mouton.

Bairoch, P. (1976b), 'Europe's gross National Product: 1800–1975', *Journal of European Economic History*, 5, 2.

Bairoch, P. (1980), 'Le bilan économique du colonialisme: mythes et réalités', *Itinerario*, 1.

Bairoch, P. (1982), 'International industrialization levels from 1750 to 1980', *Journal of European Economic History*, 11, 2.

Bairoch, P. (1990), 'La Suisse dans le contexte international aux XIXe et XXe siècles', in P. Bairoch and Martin Körner (eds), *La Suisse dans l'économie mondiale*, Geneva: Droz.

Bairoch, P. and B. Etemad (1985), *Structure par produits des exportations du Tiers-Monde 1830–1937*, Geneva: Droz.

Bairoch, P. and M. Lévy-Leboyer, (1981), *Disparities in Economic Development since the Industrial Revolution*, London: Macmillan.

Baskerville, P. (1981), 'Americans in Britain's backyard: the railway era in Upper Canada, 1850–1880', *Business History Review*, 55.

Beinart, W. (1998), 'The night of the jackal: sheep, pastures and predators in the Cape', *Past & Present*, 158.

Berg, M. and P. Hudson (1992), 'Rehabilitating the industrial revolution', *Economic History Review*, 45, 1.

Bergier, J.-F. (1983), *Die Wirtschaftsgeschichte der Schweiz*, Zurich: Benziger.

Berthoff, R.T. (1953), *British Immigrants in Industrial America 1790–1950*, Cambridge: Harvard University Press.

Boxer, C.R. (1969), *The Portuguese Seaborne Empire 1415–1825*, London: Hutchinson.

Brezis, E. S. (1995), 'Foreign capital flows in the century of Britain's Industrial Revolution: new estimates, controlled conjectures', *Economic History Review*, 48, 1.

Bruchey, S. (1967), *Cotton and the Growth of the American Economy 1790–1860*, New York: Harcourt Brace.

Bruchey, S. (1975), *Growth of the Modern American Economy*, New York: Dodd Mead.

Butlin, N.G. (1962), *Australian Domestic Product, Investment and Foreign Borrowing, 1861–1938/9*, Cambridge: Cambridge University Press.

Butlin, N.G. (1994), *Forming a Colonial Economy: Australia 1810–1850*, Cambridge: Cambridge University Press.

Cain, P.J. and A.G. Hopkins (1993), *British Imperialism: Innovation and Expansion*, London: Longman.

Cambridge History of the British Empire, II: The Growth of the New Empire 1783–1870 (1940), Cambridge: Cambridge University Press.

Cambridge History of Latin America, III: From Independence to c. 1870 (1985), Cambridge: Cambridge University Press.

Cameron, R. and C.E. Freedeman (1983), 'French economic growth: a radical revision', *Social Science History*, 7, 1.

Caron, F. (1979), *An Economic History of Modern France*, London: Methuen.

Caron, F. (1983), 'France', in P. O'Brien (ed.), *Railways and the Economic Development of Western Europe 1830–1914*, London: Methuen.

Charlesworth, N. (1982), *British Rule and the Indian Economy 1800–1914*, London: Macmillan.

Chaudhuri, K.N. (1966), 'India's foreign trade and the cessation of the East India Company's trading activities, 1828–1840', *Economic History Review*, 19, 2.

Crafts, N.F.R. (1984), 'Patterns of development in nineteenth century Europe', *Oxford Economic Papers*, 36.

Crafts, N.F.R. (1985), *British Economic Growth During the Industrial Revolution*, Oxford: Clarendon.

Crafts, N.F.R. (1997), 'The human development index and changes in standards of living: some historical comparisons', *European Review of Economic History*, 1, 3.

Crafts, N.F.R. and C.K. Harley (1992), 'Output growth and the British Industrial Revolution: a restatement of the Crafts–Harley view', *Economic History Review*, 45, 4.

Crouzet, F. (1985), *Britain Ascendant: Comparative Studies in Franco-British Economic History*, Cambridge: Cambridge University Press.

Cruickshank, D.J. (1931), 'New Zealand – external migration', in W.F. Willcox (ed.), *International Migrations*, New York: National Bureau of Economic Research.

Curtin, P.D. (1965), *The Image of Africa: British Ideas and Actions, 1780–1850*, London: Macmillan.

Curtin, P.D. (1969), *The Atlantic Slave Trade: A Census*, Madison: University of Wisconsin Press.

Curtin, P.D. (1975), *Economic Change in Precolonial Africa: Senegambia in the Era of the Slave Trade*, Madison: University of Wisconsin Press.

Curtin, P.D. (1990), *The Rise and Fall of the Plantation Complex*, Cambridge; Cambridge University Press.

Davies, P.N. (1985), 'British shipping and world trade: rise and decline 1820–1939', in T. Yui and K. Nakagawa (eds), *Business History of Shipping*, Tokyo: Tokyo University Press.

Davis, L.E. *et al.* (1972), *American Economic Growth*, New York: Harper & Row.

Davis, P. (1996), 'Nineteenth-century ocean transport', in P. Mathias and J.A. Davis (eds), *International Trade and British Economic Growth*, Oxford: Blackwell.

Deane, P. and W. Cole (1967), *British Economic Growth 1688–1959*, second edition, Cambridge: Cambridge University Press.

Deerr, N. (1949–50), *The History of Sugar*, 2 vols, London: Chapman & Hall.

Desai, T.B. (1969), *Economic History of India under the British 1757–1947*, Bombay: Vora.

Drescher, S. (1977), *Econocide: British Slavery in the Era of Abolition*, Pittsburgh: Pittsburgh University Press.

Dutt, R. (1902), *The Economic History of India*, London: Kegan Paul.

Ellison, T. (1965), *The Cotton Trade of Great Britain*, London: Cass.

Eltis, D. (1987), *Economic Growth and the Ending of the Slave Trade*, Oxford: Oxford University Press.

Eltis, D. (1991), 'Precolonial Western Africa and the Atlantic economy', in B. Solow (ed.), *Slavery and the Rise of the Atlantic System*, Cambridge: Cambridge University Press.

Elvin, M. (1973), *The Pattern of the Chinese Past*, London: Eyre Methuen.

Engerman, S. (1983), 'Contract labour, sugar and technology in the nineteenth century', *Journal of Economic History*, 43, 3.

Erickson, C. (1957), *American Industry and the European Immigrant 1860–1885*, Cambridge: Harvard University Press.

Erickson, C. (ed.) (1976), *Emigration from Europe 1815–1914*, London: Black.

Evans, E.W. and D. Richardson, (1995), 'Hunting for rents: the economics of slaving in pre-colonial Africa', *Economic History Review*, 48,4.

Farnie, D.A. (1979), *The English Cotton Industry and the World Market 1815–1896*, Oxford: Clarendon.

Fayle, C.E. (1933), *A Short History of the World's Shipping Industry*, London: Allen & Unwin.

Ferns, H.S. (1960), *Britain and Argentina: The Nineteenth Century*, Oxford: Clarendon.

Firestone, O.J. (1960), 'Canada's external trade and net foreign balance 1861–1900', in Conference on Research in Income and Wealth, *Trends in the American Economy in the Nineteenth Century*, Princeton: Princeton University Press.

Fogel, R.W. and S.L. Engerman, (eds) (1971), *The Reinterpretation of American Economic History*, New York: Harper & Row.

Fohlen, C. (1970), 'The Industrial Revolution in France', in R. Cameron (ed.), *Essays in French Economic History*, Homewood: Irwin.

Fremdling, R. (1983), 'Germany', in P. O'Brien (ed.), *Railways and the Economic Development of Western Europe 1830–1914*, London: Methuen.

Furnival, J.S. (1944), *Netherlands India: A Study in Plural Economy*, Cambridge: Cambridge University Press.

Gallman, R.E. (1960), 'Commodity output 1839–1899', in Conference on Research in Income and Wealth, *Trends in the American Economy in the Nineteenth Century*, Princeton: Princeton University Press.

Ghosal, R.H. (1964), 'Changes in the organisation of industrial production in the Bengal presidency in the early nineteenth century', in B.N. Ganguli (ed.) *Readings in Indian Economic History*, Bombay: Asia Publishing House.

Goldin, C.D. and F.D. Lewis, (1980), 'The role of exports in American economic growth during the Napoleonic Wars 1793–1807', *Explorations in Economic History*, 17, 1.

Graham, R. (1972), *Britain and the Onset of Modernization in Brazil, 1850–1914*, Cambridge: Cambridge University Press.

Graham, R. (1985), 'Brazil from the middle of the nineteenth century to the Paraguaian war', in L. Bethell (ed.), *Cambridge History of Latin America*, Vol. 3, Cambridge: Cambridge University Press.

Green, W.A. (1976), *British Slave Emancipation: The Sugar Colonies and the Great Experiment 1830–1865*, Oxford: Clarendon.

Greenberg, M. (1951), *British Trade and the Opening of China 1800–1842*, Cambridge: Cambridge University Press.

Halperin Pereira, M. (1986), 'Portugal and the structure of the world market in the XVIIIth and XIXth centuries', in W. Fischer *et al.* (eds), *The Emergence of a World Economy 1500–1914, vol. I, 1500–1850*, Wiesbaden: Steiner.

Hammond, M.B. (1966), *The Cotton Industry: An Essay in American Economic History*, New York: Johnson.

Hammond, R.J. (1966), *Portugal and Africa 1815–1910: A Study in Uneconomic Imperialism*, Stanford: Stanford University Press.

Hanson J.R. (1980), *Trade in Transition: Exports from the Third World 1840–1900*, New York: Academic Press.

Harley, C.K. (1993), 'Reassessing the Industrial Revolution: a macro view', in J. Mokyr (ed.), *The British Industrial Revolution: An Economic Perspective*, Boulder: Westview.

Harnetty, P. (1965), 'The imperialism of free trade: Lancashire and the Indian cotton duties, 1959–62', *Economic History Review*, 18, 2.

Harnetty, P. (1972), *Imperialism and Free Trade: Lancashire and India in the Mid-Nineteenth Century*, Manchester: Manchester University Press.

Headrick, D.R. (1981), *Tools of Empire: Technology and European Imperialism in the Nineteenth Century*, New York: Oxford University Press.

Herschlag, Z.Y. (1964), *Introduction to the Modern Economic History of the Middle East*, Leiden: E.J. Brill.

Hoffmann, W.G. (1963), 'The take-off in Germany', in W.W. Rostow (ed.), *The Economics of Take-Off into Sustained Growth*, London: Macmillan.

Hopkins, A. G. (1973), *An Economic History of West Africa*, London: Longman.

Hounshell, D.A. (1984), *The American System of Mass Production 1800–1932*, Baltimore: Johns Hopkins University Press.

Hueckel, G. (1973), 'War and the British economy, 1793–1815: a general equilibrium analysis', *Explorations in Economic History*, 10, 4.

Imlah, A.H. (1958), *Economic Elements in the Pax Britannica*, Cambridge: Harvard University Press.

Inalcik, H. (1987), 'When and how British cotton goods invaded the Levant market', in H. Islamoglu-Anan (ed.), *The Ottoman Empire and the World Economy*, Cambridge: Cambridge University Press.

Issawi, C. (1966), *The Economic History of the Middle East 1800–1914*, Chicago: University of Chicago Press.

Issawi, C. (ed.) (1971), *The Economic History of Iran 1800–1914*, Chicago: University of Chicago Press.

Jaarsveld, F.A.v. (1975), *From van Riebeeck to Vorster 1652–1974*, Johannesburg: Perskor.

Jenks, L.H. (1963), *The Migration of British Capital to 1875*, London: Nelson.

Jeremy, D. (1981), *Transatlantic Industrial Revolution: The Diffusion of Textile Technologies Between Britain and America, 1790s–1830s*, Oxford: Blackwell.

Jeremy, D. and D.H. Stapleton, (1991), 'Transfers between culturally-related nations: the movement of textile and railway technologies between Britain and the United States, 1780–1840', in D. Jeremy (ed.), *Industrial Technology Transfer: Europe, Japan and the USA, 1700–1914*, Aldershot: Edward Elgar.

Kasaba, R. (1988), *The Ottoman Empire and the World Economy: The Nineteenth Century*, New York: State University.

Kenwood, A.G. and A.L. Lougheed, (1971), *The Growth of the International Economy 1820–1960*, London: Allen & Unwin.

Knight, F.W. (1970), *Slave Society in Cuba during the Nineteenth Century*, Madison: University of Wisconsin Press.

Knowles, L.C.A. (1928), *The Economic Development of the British Overseas Empire*, Vol. I, London: Routledge.

Kutz, M. (1986), 'Aussenhandel und Krieg 1789–1817', in W. Fischer *et al.* (eds), *The Emergence of a World Economy 1500–1914*, Part I, 1500–1850, Wiesbaden: Steiner.

Landes, D. S. (1993), 'The fable of the dead horse: or, the Industrial Revolution revisited', in J. Mokyr (ed.), *The British Industrial Revolution: an Economic Perspective*, Boulder: Westview.

Léon, P. (ed.) (1978), *Histoire économique et sociale du monde*, vols 3 and 4, Paris: Colin.

Leveen, A.P. (1975), 'A quantitative assessment of the impact of British suppression policies on the volume of the nineteenth-century slave trade', in S. Engerman and E.D. Genovese (eds), *Race and Slavery in the Western Hemisphere: Quantitative Studies*, Princeton: Princeton University Press.

Lévy-Leboyer, M. (1968), 'La croissance économique en France au XIXe siècle', *Annales E.S.C.*, 23, 4.

Lewis, W.A. (1978), *The Evolution of the International Economic Order*, Princeton: Princeton University Press.

Lipsey, Robert E. (1994), *US Foreign Trade and the Balance of Payments, 1800–1913*, Cambridge, MA: NBER.

Lynch, J. (1985), 'The origins of Spanish American independence', in L. Bethell (ed.), *Cambridge History of Latin America*, vol. 3, Cambridge: Cambridge University Press.

McMichael, P. (1984), *Settlers and the Agrarian Question: Capitalism in Colonial Australia*, Cambridge: Cambridge University Press.

Maddison, A. (1991), *Dynamic Forces in Capitalist Development*, Oxford: Oxford University Press.

Marcovich, A. (1988), 'French colonial medicine and colonial rule: Algeria and Indochina', in R.M. Macleod and M. Lewis (eds), *Disease, Medicine and Empire*, London: Routledge.

Marques, A.H. de O. (1972), *History of Portugal, Vol. I: From Lusitania to Empire*, New York: Columbia University Press.

Marr, W.L. and D.G. Paterson (1980), *Canada: An Economic History*, Toronto: Gage.

Marshall, P. G. (1990), *Bengal: The British Bridgehead in Eastern India 1740–1828*, Cambridge: Cambridge University Press.

Mathew, W.M. (1970), 'Peru and the British guano market, 1840–1870', *Economic History Review*, 2nd series, 3, 1.

Mauro, F. (1986), 'Structure de l'économic interne et marché international dans une époque de transition: le cas de Brésil, 1750–1850', in W. Fischer *et al.* (eds), *The Emergence of a World Economy 1500–1914: Part I, 1500–1850*, Wiesbaden: Steiner.

Mintz, S.W. (1985), *Sweetness and Power: The Place of Sugar in Modern History*, New York: Viking-Penguin.

Mitchell, B.R. (1962), *Abstract of British Historical Statistics*, Cambridge: Cambridge University Press.

Mitchell, B.R. (1993), *International Historical Statistics: Europe 1750–1988*, London: Macmillan.

Mokyr, J. (1976), *Industrialization in the Low Countries 1795–1850*, New Haven: Yale University Press.

Mokyr, J. (1987), 'Has the Industrial Revolution been crowded out? Some reflections on Crafts and Williamson', *Explorations in Economic History*, 24.

Mokyr, J. (1993), 'The new economic history and the Industrial Revolution', in J. Mokyr (ed.), *The British Industrial Revolution: An Economic Perspective*, Boulder: Westview.

Mokyr, J. (1994), 'Technological change 1700–1830', in R. Floud and D. McCloskey (eds), *The Economic History of Britain since 1700, I, 1700–1860*, Cambridge: Cambridge University Press.

Morris, M.D. (1963), 'Towards a reinterpretation of nineteenth-century Indian economic history', *Journal of Economic History*, 23.

Mulhall, M.G. (1892), *The Dictionary of Statistics*, London: Routledge.

Mulhall, M.G. (1971), *The Progress of the World*, Shannon: Irish University Press.

Naylor, D.O. (1931), 'Brazil', in W. F. Willcox (ed.), *International Migrations*, New York: National Bureau of Economic Research.

North, D.C. (1956), 'Iterative capital flows and the development of the American West', *Journal of Economic History*, 16, 4.

North, D.C. (1958), 'Ocean freight rates and economic development 1750–1913', *Journal of Economic History*, 18.

North, D.C. (1960), 'The United States balance of payments 1790–1860', in Conference on Research in Income and Wealth, *Trends in the American Economy in the Nineteenth Century*, Princeton: Princeton University Press.

North, D.C. (1961), *The Economic Growth of the United States 1790–1860*, Englewood Cliffs: Prentice-Hall.

North, D.C. (1971), 'Sources of productivity change in ocean shipping 1600–1850', in R.F. Fogel and S.L. Engerman (eds), *The Reinterpretation of American Economic History*, New York: Harper Row.

O'Brien, P. and C. Keyder (1978), *Economic Growth in Britain and France 1780–1914: Two Paths to the Twentieth Century*, London: Allen & Unwin.

Panikkar, K.M. (1960), *A Survey of Indian History*, Bombay: Asia Publishing House.

Panikkar, K.M. (1963), *Studies in Indian History*, Bombay: Asia Publishing House.

Parker W.M. and F. Whartenby (1960), 'The growth of output before 1840', in Conference on Research in Income and Wealth, *Trends in the American Economy in the Nineteenth Century*, Princeton: Princeton University Press.

Parthasarathi, P. (1998), 'Rethinking wages and competitiveness in the eighteenth century: Britain and South India', *Past & Present*, 158.

Peláez, C.M. (1976), 'The theory and reality of imperialism in the coffee economy of nineteenth-century Brazil', *Economic History Review*, 29, 2.

Platt, D.C.M. (1972), *Latin America and British Trade 1806–1914*, London: Black.

Prados, L.d.l.E. (1987), 'Foreign trade and the Spanish economy during the nineteenth century', in N. Sanchez-Albornoz (ed.), *The Economic Modernization of Spain 1830–1930*, New York: New York University Press.

Ramasubban, R. (1988), 'Imperial health in British India, 1857–1900', in R.M. McLeod and M. Lewis (eds), *Disease, Medicine and Empire*, London: Routledge.

Richards, A.R. (1987), 'Primitive accumulation in Egypt, 1798–1882', in H. Islamoglu-Inan (ed.), *The Ottoman Empire and the World Economy*, Cambridge: Cambridge University Press.

Robb, P. (1992), 'Peasants' choices? Indian agriculture and the limits of commercialization in nineteenth-century Bihar', *Economic History Review*, 45, 1.

Rosenberg, N. (1972), *Technology and American Economic Growth*, New York: Harper & Row.

Rostow, W.W. (1978), *The World Economy: History and Prospect*, Austin: Texas University Press.

Rothermund, D. (1988), *An Economic History of India*, London: Croom Helm.

Schlote, W. (1976), *British Overseas Trade from 1700 to the 1930s*, Westport: Greenwood.

Shann, E. (1948), *An Economic History of Australia*, Cambridge: Cambridge University Press.

Shirras, F. (1931), 'Indian migration', in W.F. Willcox (ed.), *International Migrations*, New York: National Bureau of Economic Research.

Silver, A.W. (1966), *Manchester Men and Indian Cotton 1847–1872*, Manchester: Manchester University Press.

Sokoloff, K.L. (1986), 'Productivity growth in manufacturing during early industrialization: evidence from the American north-east, 1820–1860', in S.L. Engerman and R.E. Gallman (eds), *Long-Term Trends in American Economic Growth*, Chicago: University of Chicago Press.

Stokes, E. (1973), 'The first century of British colonial rule in India: social revolution or social stagnation?', *Past & Present*, 58.

Thomas, B. (1973), *Migration and Economic Growth*, Cambridge: Cambridge University Press.

Thorner, D. (1950), *Investment in Empire: British Railway and Steam Shipping Enterprise in India, 1825–1849*, Philadelphia: University of Pennsylvania Press.

Tinker, H. (1974), *A New System of Slavery: The Export of Indian Labourers Overseas 1830–1920*, Oxford: Oxford University Press.

Trebilcock, C. (1981), *The Industrialization of the Continental Powers 1780–1914*, London: Longman.

Twomey, M.J. (1983), 'Employment in nineteenth-century Indian textiles', *Explorations in Economic History*, 20.

Uselding, P. (1971), 'Conjectural estimate of gross human capital inflows to the American economy: 1790–1860', *Explorations in Economic History*, 9, 1.

Veyrassat, B. (1990), 'La Suisse sur les marchés du monde', in P. Bairoch and M. Körner (eds.), *La Suisse dans l'économie mondiale*, Geneva: Droz.

Vilar, P. (1976), *A History of Gold and Money 1450–1920*, London: NLB.

Ward, J.R. (1994), 'The Industrial Revolution and British imperialism, 1750–1850', *Economic History Review*, 48, 1.

Watts, D. (1990), *The West Indies: Patterns of Development, Culture and Environmental Change since 1492*, Cambridge: Cambridge University Press.

Wicker, E.R. (1960), 'Railway investment before the Civil War', in Conference on Research in Income and Wealth, *Trends in the American Economy in the Nineteenth Century*, Princeton: Princeton University Press.

Willcox, W.F. (ed.) (1931), *International Migrations, II, Interpretations*, New York: NBER.

Williamson, J.G. (1964), *American Growth and the Balance of Payments 1820–1913*, Chapel Hill: University of North Carolina Press.

Williamson, J.G. (1995), 'The evolution of global labour markets since 1830: background evidence and hypotheses', *Explorations in Economic History*, 32, 2.

Winn, P. (1976), 'British informal empire in Uruguay in the nineteenth century', *Past & Present*, 73.

Woodruff, W. (1966), *Impact of Western Man: A Study of Europe's Role in the World Economy 1750–1960*, London: Methuen.

Youngson, A.J. (1966), 'The opening up of new territories', in *Cambridge Economic History of Europe, vol. VI, part I*, Cambridge: Cambridge University Press.

Zevin, R.B. (1971), 'The growth of cotton textile production after 1815', in R.W. Fogel and S.L. Engerman (eds), *The Reinterpretation of American Economic History*, New York: Harper & Row.

Zorn, W. (ed.) (1976), *Handbuch der deutschen Wirtschafts- und Sozialgeschichte, Band II. Das 19. und 20. Jahrhundert*, Stuttgart: Klett.

3. The zenith of European power 1870–1918

James Foreman-Peck

The years after 1870 saw the spontaneous emergence of a world economy, based primarily upon market exchange. Of course international economic relations around the world had been established for centuries, but technical and institutional changes greatly increased their intensity, interweaving the destinies of almost every part of the globe. As the principal industrial centre, western Europe – together with the north-eastern United States – drove the world economy by supplying technology, institutions, labour, capital and demand. 'Neo-Europe' reconstructed in other temperate zones of the world the civilizations, and even the place names, of the old world. The populous and ancient civilizations of Asia were also integrated into the burgeoning international markets for goods and factors of production. At the same time, European empires were extended (as well as those of Japan, the United States and, arguably, Ethiopia). The Titans of the mid-twentieth century, Russia and the United States, were primarily concerned with expansion across their adjacent land masses: Siberia for Russia and the western plains for the United States. Western Europe was thus left more or less a free hand in world politics.

Industrialization and urbanization in the west European 'core' were well established by 1870. The focus of this chapter therefore is how they spilled over into the wider world. Just as national economies did, international economic relations needed an institutional and organizational framework in which to operate. Understanding the operation of the European world economic order requires, first, a comprehension and assessment of these underpinning institutions. The second step is to consider the consequences of the organizations in integrating markets. The third is to examine core–periphery relations (or, for the geographically relaxed, relations between 'north' and 'south'), considering why some regions remained poor and the contribution of the European world order. The cataclysmic end of the order, with the First World War and the new relations established by the Versailles Treaty, goes some way to demonstrating the conditions underlying Europe's position in the world economy towards the end of the 'long nineteenth century'.

NINETEENTH-CENTURY INTERNATIONAL INSTITUTIONS

Underlying market economies, whether local, national or international are systems of law and enforcement. With sufficiently arbitrary and predatory rulers, or frequent wars and invasions, economic activity cannot flourish. Security is paramount. In settling the new worlds and subduing the old, western European military technology and organization went hand in hand. But for ordinary people in western Europe and in the overseas off-shoots, far more important than the weaponry were the living standards and life expectations that the related technology permitted. These were greater than ever before, despite expanding populations. Fundamentally, they depended on organizations and institutions that supported conventions and law, nationally and internationally; on rules that facilitated cooperation. The gold standard, diplomatic protocol, and common weights and measures were 'international public goods' that facilitated international exchange, or reduced international conflict, and so raised well-being (Eggertsson, 1991). The 'consumption' of these 'goods' by one nation did not reduce the 'consumption' by another, and the costs of their supply were negligible.

International Political Institutions

How did (European) sovereign states cooperate in maintaining an environment suitable for the growth of the international economy? Questions of national security were much less easy than commercial matters to delegate to international institutions. Nonetheless, attempts were made and international politics did become more cooperative during the nineteenth century.

The nineteenth-century 'Concert of Europe' arrangement, consisting of assemblies of accredited representatives of states to agree future policy, was revived at the end of the Crimean war in 1856. The 'Concert' accepted a protocol on the protection of neutral trade in time of war. A joint appointment of a director-general of the Danube River Commission was also agreed. Eight years later, the Concert at Geneva decided that, to ameliorate the suffering of war, military hospitals in the field should be neutralized. Unable to prevent the outbreak of a Russo-Turkish war in 1877, the Concert did restrict the spread of fighting. The 1878 Congress at Berlin, where Serbia was required to permit religious liberty, showed that multilateral diplomacy was ceasing to be a novelty. The Concert was based on supplying an international public good, the limitation of the spread, and regulation of the conduct, of war, if hostilities themselves could not be prevented.

Moving on to a higher level of diplomacy, the Hague Conferences are generally reckoned less successful. Initiated by a proposal to prevent war and the burden of arms races by disarmament, there was no international supervisory organization and no enforcement. More important, no nation wished to tie its hands, nor did most of them want to make that admission (for example, Albrecht-Carrie, 1958, 238, 254–5). As many as 26 nations signed the 1899 Convention of the Hague Conferences on laws and customs of war on land and a total of 44 nations were signatories to that of 1907. Later experience showed that the convention was more honoured in the breach than in the observance (Lyons, 1963, 305–6). Specific prohibitions of dumdum bullets, air raids, gas shells and submarines were all precluded in 1899 by the technologically most advanced powers.

Arbitration fared better, with the establishment of a court which began business in 1902, dealing with major incidents between Russia and Britain in 1905 and between France and Germany in 1909 (Lyons, 1963, 338–61). These were exceptions, though, nations generally preferring to deal with each other directly. Political cooperation through international organizations to limit international violence as a way of settling disputes had a long way to go. The large industrial states, not yet traumatized by world wars that revealed their national security shortcomings, still preferred traditional approaches. They had yet to see the full havoc that industrial technology and total war could wreak.

International Trade and Communications Regulation

Technological progress and booming trade more strongly raised the demand for and the supply of formal international economic cooperative institutions. The most obvious gains were in communications. Network industries, including the telegraph, the post and railways, classically require cooperation and are suitable for 'single issue' regulation and organization. National network owners, at least of similar sizes, have both an incentive to interconnect with other nations, to extend their service, and something to offer in exchange to other operators. Hence they are likely to reach agreement on the terms of interconnection.

In 1849 came the first telegraph treaties, pressed by the need for uniform standards. The Paris telegraphy conference of 1865 laid the groundwork for the International Office of Telegraphy at Berne, the forerunner of the International Telecommunications Union (ITU), to facilitate international through-traffic and agree charges. Since virtually all land telegraphy was state-operated by this date, negotiations took place, in effect, between government departments. Codding (1952) maintains that the ITU's success may be traced to its work being carried out almost exclusively by telecommunications experts. State agencies he regards as helpful for the implementation of agreed rules, unlike private companies such as John Pender's Atlantic Telegraph Company, whose high charges aroused even the private enterprise, free trade journal, *The Economist*, to favour telegraph nationalization.

The Universal Postal Union was a similar institution to the ITU, established in 1874. Railways too formed international organizations. Initiated by Prussia in 1846 with German railway cooperation, by 1914, 92 European railway systems had joined the original grouping (Lyons, 1963, 48, 51). By 1871 there was a European timetable, a development that originated with periodic meetings sponsored by Bavaria from 1860.

International trade was a much broader field with which nineteenth-century governments were concerned, for foreign trade was a source of revenue less likely than others to provoke adverse domestic reactions. The Cobden–Chevalier treaty of 1860 introduced the 'most favoured nation' clause into trade barrier negotiations. This principle might have been expected to spread free trade, but by the end of the nineteenth century trade negotiations had found ways around it. Extremely detailed specification of products, so that goods of interest to protectionist governments could be heavily taxed, despite international agreements, was one ploy. Maximum and minimum tariffs, and 'conditional most favoured nation' clauses allowed much more scope for bilateral bargaining. In the extreme, bilateral bargaining could trigger tariff wars, such as those between Russia and Germany and between Italy and France in the closing decades of the century. However, in a period of falling transport costs, Paul Bairoch (1989) concluded on balance that tariff barriers merely replaced previous natural barriers to trade. Quotas, which are far more destructive of trade in growing economies, were rarely employed, and thus there was less need for a world trade organization than in the period after 1945.

Europe felt the impact of development in the wider world when cheap foreign food grains entered on a large scale after 1870. Bairoch (1989) contends that they were the basic cause of the agricultural crisis that triggered a European return to protectionism, led by Germany in 1879. From 1892, another wave of increased protectionism broke on the continent. Germany's bilateral treaties reduced some of the impact and Italy remained rather liberal, whereas France raised tariffs, as did Russia and Spain.

The sugar trade was a particular focus of European government intervention, once it was discovered how to make sugar from beet. International policy illustrates how nineteenth-century empires internalized some of the 'spill-over' costs of agricultural subsidies, and 'linkage' reduced the stability of 'single issue' organizations. With large agricultural populations still, continental European states often subsidized beet sugar to reduce imports of cane sugar and then began to export. Free trade Britain acquired a sweet tooth at the expense of continental tax payers. On the other hand, the sugar-exporting British West Indies were impoverished by this unfair competition, and continental consumers frequently paid high sugar prices, thanks to cartelization.

Conventions in 1864 and in 1888 proved ineffective for getting rid of subsidies. Not until 1902, when the 'Sugar Union' emerged, was a workable cooperative solution found (Lyons, 1963, 103–10). European subsidies to beet sugar exporters and tariffs on imported sugar were ended at the 1902 Brussels convention agreed by Britain, Germany, Austria–Hungary, Italy, the Netherlands and Sweden. British legislation was passed in 1903 for a period of five years. Sugar prices duly rose in Britain. Russia remained outside the convention and therefore Russian sugar imports to the UK were taxed. The Russians retaliated with duties on Indian tea. This rather nullified one of the attractions of the legislation for the British government, which was the gains to the West Indies, the only colony which was not self-financing. The British confectionery industry was no more enthusiastic than the Russians. Together with the free trade doctrine of the Liberal government that had defeated a protectionist Conservative Party in the 1906 election, this industry hostility conspired to take Britain out of the Union in 1913. Without German opposition, the other Union members would have made sufficient concessions to keep Britain in, and save the Union. But once international politics became linked to a dispute within a single-issue international organization, the incentives to collaborate were severely weakened.

By the end of the century, unlike the situation in the 1860s, the British were less addicted to opium and derivatives than to sugar, partly because of a revision of medical opinion. Opium exports from India provided a major source of tax revenue for the Indian government but had gained notoriety in relations with China. Joshua Rowntree's *The Imperial Drug Trade* described the progress towards the elimination of the Indian export trade to China, despite the loss of Indian government revenue that suppression implied.

Although the international literature has focused on the rise of opium consumption in China during the nineteenth century, the United States was the world's largest market for non-medical morphine and cocaine in the early twentieth century. Throughout the nineteenth century, Britain herself imported opium mainly from Turkey and consumed large quantities: between 1840 and 1860, some 2–3 lb per 1000 population, or 127 therapeutic doses per annum per head of population (Berridge and Edwards, 1987). In 1885, 15.5 per cent of all prescriptions dispensed in Islington, London, contained opium. Medical practice towards the end of the nineteenth century was abandoning the drug, and also increasingly condemned recreational use of cocaine and morphine, a tendency which can be traced in Conan Doyle's 'Sherlock Holmes' stories.

The attempt to stamp out the international trade in 'noxious drugs' before the First World War illustrates the 'free rider' problem as a barrier to international cooperation, and the greater effectiveness of bilateral agreements. But international policies also hint that progress was being made by moral suasion and negotiation, only to be nullified by the outbreak of hostilities (Lyons, 1963, 371–9). First at the 1909 International Conference on Opium at Shanghai, then at the 1911 and 1912 conferences at the Hague, attempts were made to agree an international convention. Although 12 powers were represented, not one wanted to commit itself unless non-participating countries did so also.

A bilateral agreement between the British and Chinese governments in 1911 was more effective. Opium exports from British India were to be reduced at the same pace as opium poppy cultivation in China. By 1913, both Indian exports and Chinese production had almost ceased. But India was still in a weak position when wanting to block German exports of cocaine, which were creating an addiction problem in Rangoon (Foreman-Peck, 1997). Securing German cooperation in the suppression of the trade proved difficult – Germany was the major supplier of synthetic drugs and the India Office was unable to persuade the Foreign Office to press the matter 'until it put its own house in order'. Trade regulation of 'noxious drugs' by international negotiations was hardly draconian, but the first tentative steps were being taken.

International Property Rights in New Technology

In contrast to controlling the drugs trade, protection of international property rights was self-enforcing for large industrial nations; for them the incentives were to cooperate. Inventors were less than enthusiastic about displaying their ingenuity at the international exhibitions of the nineteenth century when foreigners could copy them without charge. Matters came to a head at the 1873 Vienna Exposition when foreign exhibitors hung back until a special protective law was passed (Lyons, 1963, 127). Thereafter the 1878 Paris Exposition gave the final impetus for an international agreement. The International Conventions for the Protection of Industrial Property of 1883 and 1900 recognized the gains from encouraging research and invention with a prospective pay-off from the entire world rather than from a single national market. Large industrial economies wanted protection for their own inventors, but small and less developed economies at first tried to 'free ride': using the rest of the world's inventions for free. By the beginning of the twentieth century signatories included the United States and most of Europe, Japan and Mexico, but not Spain and Russia.

Nineteenth-century Netherlands and Switzerland were among the states which took a free ride on the innovative efforts of those in larger countries, to the advantage of some of their manufacturers. Switzerland lacked any patent law until 1887, when legislation still left all processes unprotected, covering only inventions that could be represented by a model. The Swiss chemical industry was therefore able to concentrate successfully on the production of speciality dyes because German firms were unable to patent their own processes in Switzerland.

The Netherlands did not give patent protection until even later, in 1910. This helped the Jurgens brothers develop a French process for the manufacture of margarine after 1870. It was also very useful for Gerard Philips, who established an incandescent lamp factory at Eindhoven in 1891, making essentially Edison's carbon filament lamp with only minor modifications. By 1913, he was one of the largest manufacturers in Europe. A contributory factor to his success was that, in the early years, he was the only maker in western Europe not paying royalties to Swan/Edison. However, Dutch overseas patenting increased after the Netherlands signed the international patent convention, suggesting the policy had not been entirely beneficial, even to the Netherlands (Schiff, 1971).

Since Britain was a signatory of international patent agreements from the first, British experience was very different. British dyestuffs lobbyists worried about German blocking patents before the First World War. But Germany also had its problems. Aluminium manufacture in Germany made little progress before 1914 because of difficulties in upholding the patents for the Herault process. So the AEG group, which owned the Herault patents, established their plant at the Rhine Falls in Switzerland, where *all* process patents for aluminium were ineffective (Saul, 1978).

The principle of reciprocity ensured that patent recognition was self-enforcing. A participating country allowing patent violation could usually be brought to heel by the threat not to enforce that country's patents. But a state could always decide that the benefits from exploiting foreign inventions without payment were greater than receiving royalties from its own national inventions abroad.

Managing Default on Sovereign Debt

Hegemony was more apparent in the management of sovereign debt default towards the end of the nineteenth century, thanks to political linkages. But earlier a form of self-enforcement seems to have operated quite efficiently. Debtors had an interest in honouring agreements so long as they wished to have access to foreign borrowing in the future. For lenders, the (private, London-based) Corporation of Foreign Bondholders was the self-enforcing component of foreign lending, formalizing what operated informally before 1876. They aimed to prevent a state that had defaulted on bond servicing from raising another loan in the City unless it included a settlement for the cheated bondholders. By and large, the system worked, except when genuinely revolutionary governments took over and isolated themselves from world capital markets, as did Mexico and Russia after their revolutions respectively of 1910 and 1917. That London was the largest and most unrestricted international capital market increased the power of the Corporation.

Some evidence from the middle two quarters of the century consistent with private enforcement of payment being moderately effective in reducing the chances of default is presented in Figure 3.1 (calculated from Corporation of Foreign Bondholders, 1878). One half of those countries that defaulted in the first period made full repayment in the second, while only 27 per cent of those that paid fully in the first period defaulted in the second. Those that did not default in the first period were less likely than earlier defaulters to fail in the second. Payment performance improved; the incentives not to renege on agreements were apparently maintained by private enforcement, the market assessment of country risk improved and the size of the shocks in the two periods was different.

Lindert and Morton's study (1987, Table V) allows us to compare a period before the Corporation of Foreign Bondholders were active,

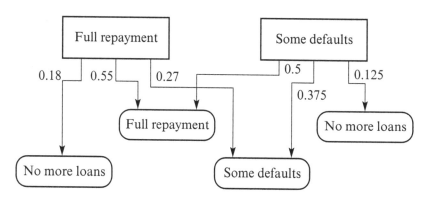

Figure 3.1 Historical transition probabilities of sovereign debt repayment and default 1822–76

1822–76, with years when they were supporting lenders' interests, 1880–1929. Among earlier full repayers in the early period, only 10.5 per cent became problem debtors in the later period: an even better result than in the third quarter of the century. Of those that were problems in the early period, 69.6 per cent were also defaulters in the later. Given that there were 19 in the first group and 23 in the second, the number and proportion of problem cases fell respectively between the two periods from 23 to 18 and from 55 per cent to 43 per cent: a small improvement. However, by the later period there were cases in which state international organizations supervised defaulted state finances, so that deterrent effects on default may not be solely attributable to the private international organization.

Lender government intervention between 1870 and 1914 with borrower governments, such as the 1902 blockade of Venezuela by German, Italian and British warships, was the exception rather than the rule. But in the last quarter of the nineteenth century it became apparent that the financial predicament of European governments could not be separated from politics. The same powers that comprised the 'Concert of Europe', regulated the affairs of defaulting nations, at least nominally. Turkish, Egyptian and Greek defaults on servicing foreign borrowings began the emergence of international financial bodies in the last quarter of the nineteenth century. Each was established to deal with a particular problem. Moreover, they were not truly international arrangements, being managed only, or mainly, by representatives of the lending states, or major powers with interests in the region. Specific taxes of all three states were hypothecated for debt service and were subject to supervision by an International Commission. As to their effectiveness, unilateral action seems to have had the greatest impact on the debtor economy. But it is extremely unlikely that the regime imposed on Egypt would have been acceptable in Greece or Turkey, either to the other 'Concert' powers or to the debtor states, and their financial predicaments were less acute anyway.

The International Gold Standard

National prices and interest rates tended to move more closely together; 'nominal convergence' was a characteristic of later nineteenth-century European and neo-European economies. This was achieved by national currency links with precious metals. The certainty of such financial stability undoubtedly facilitated trade, investment and migration.

Under the gold standard, as under any pegged exchange rate regime, domestic or foreign shocks to demand or supply could lead to balance of payments surpluses or deficits. These might be financed by gold outflows or inflows, although this practice was not typical in Europe. Financial assets were easier means of settlement. The first response was generally a change in interest rates. A lending economy such as Britain or France would staunch an outflow by a higher interest rate reducing lending. A borrowing country such as Canada or Argentina might face greater difficulties (Ford, 1989); a higher interest rate was much less likely to bring an increase in foreign investment. The burdens of adjustment were unequally distributed. But Britain, the biggest lender, or the Bank of England, was not entirely in control of world monetary affairs, the conductor of the international orchestra. The extraordinary pace of growth and size of the US economy by the beginning of the twentieth century meant that Britain was forced to adjust to US crises (Tullio and Wolters, 1999).

If an economy was tied to a gold standard, its government was obliged to exercise budgetary discipline. But whether the gold standard imposed a financial constraint on a government that was not already committed to small and balanced budgets must be doubted. As we show below, the Kingdom of Italy did not follow the precepts of liberal finance, even on the gold and silver standard, for the first 30 years.

The gold and silver standards were 'spontaneous' institutions but monetary unions were organizations created by governments for political ends. Monetary unions were like 'clubs' of adjacent states, one of which was always pre-eminent, or a prelude or concomitant of political union. In nineteenth-century western Europe they gave expression to national unification movements for Germany and Italy. On one interpretation, unions also offered a facade of economic cooperation behind which imperial struggles for European domination between France, Prussia and Austria–Hungary could be concealed. In no case was a central bank empowered to be a central banker for other sovereign states, although the Bank of France felt obliged to support Italian deficit financing.

Membership of the French-dominated Latin Monetary Union (LMU) certainly did not discipline Italian fiscal and monetary policies. Italy had formally adopted the French bimetallic standard in 1862, but continued to run a massive budget deficit until 1866. In that year the currency was declared inconvertible because of the pressures of another war with Austria–Hungary and the acquisition of Venetia. Italian notes depreciated by 20 per cent between 1866 and 1882 and bond prices fell by as much as 30 per cent.

Once the world price of silver in terms of gold began declining as it did from 1873, any (then bimetallic) Latin Union member state could gain a financial advantage by issuing silver coins. The silver coins were then exported to neighbour member states whose central banks were obliged to exchange the depreciated coins for gold at the agreed rate. Whereas France in 1874 agreed to limit her issue of silver coins that circulated with a higher face value than the metallic content warranted,

Italy could not be persuaded to cease minting them. As late as the 1878 International Monetary Conference, when the LMU moved to gold, Italy was still announcing her intention to continue coining silver.

France wanted the LMU to survive and so was willing to absorb Belgian and Italian silver and subsidiary coin at par. The Latin Union therefore paid for the 'monetization' of the Italian budget deficit. Even when Italian political friction with France over Tunis in the late 1870s sparked economic warfare in the 1880s, after Italy joined the Triple Alliance with Austria and Germany, free circulation of coins between the countries continued.

Why did France and Italy persist with the Union? Were there *mutual* benefits? Was the LMU a trade cost-minimizing organization for France and her trading partners? Belgium, Italy and Switzerland were always among the top six European trading partners of the French economy between 1850 and 1880. However, the United Kingdom was invariably the most important partner and Germany, always in the top six, surprisingly extended its role after the Franco-Prussian war by 1880. Intraregional LMU trade was around 30 per cent of total LMU trade in 1860 and 1870, falling to 26 per cent in 1880 (Flandreau, 1995). On the other hand, intra-European trade as a proportion of Europe's total trade was much greater, at almost two-thirds. The Latin Union was certainly not more integrated than Europe as a whole, yet that is what would be anticipated if the Union was driven by minimization of trading costs.

If the 1865 LMU Treaty reflected a spontaneous economic regrouping, institutionalizing an integration that had initially taken place without any government intervention, we might expect an Anglo-French monetary union as well. Of course the British had other fish to fry. Their trade and investment were far less Eurocentric than France's. And France was unlikely to accept Britain as a senior partner. Germany, to a lesser extent, was in the same position. Being smaller and weaker than France therefore was a requirement for LMU membership. This was mirrored in financial flows.

Another monetary union, lasting until the First World War, began when the Scandinavians formed their own bloc in 1873 and 1875, rather than enter the larger Latin Union. The Pan-Scandinavian movement of the 1840s and 1850s proved less successful than those pressing for Italian or German unification; it attracted mainly students and the middle classes, whereas the mass of the populations were demanding greater national independence (Derry, 1979, 238, 254). Indeed, Norway joined the Scandinavian Monetary Union later than Denmark and Sweden because of anti-Scandinavian sentiment. Norway was in many respects politically united with Sweden when monetary union began and proceeded to loosen political bonds while the union was in existence.

Outside monetary unions, central bank cooperation was rare. In principle, such cooperation can enhance the efficiency of monetary policy and therefore may have been able to reduce the severity of financial crises. Because each economy's policy spilled over to its trading partner, cooperation that took into account those repercussions could allow the attainment of collective policy objectives at lower cost. But nineteenth-century central bank cooperation was scarce (Flandreau, 1997). That they rarely supplied cooperative policies underlines the value of the gold standard as a device for reducing the demand for cooperative policies. The gold standard shrank the area in which agreement was necessary. It was an institutional device for achieving a form of cooperative equilibrium by reducing the demand for cooperation and the centrepiece of a liberal international economic order without leadership or hegemony.

MARKET INTEGRATION

In this international economic order, western Europe's offshoots, especially the United States, were most tightly integrated. They also expanded populations and incomes per head more rapidly than any other region. By comparison with Asia or Europe, these areas were sparsely inhabited in 1870. Europeans flocked to them in rising numbers throughout the nineteenth century, and their natural increase was extremely high as well. North America and Australia adopted British constitutions and economic practices. Latin America, which inherited the institutions of Spain and Portugal, and with much larger indigenous populations, experienced almost the same rate of population increase, though immigration played a smaller role.

Southern and eastern Europe remained poor, while Britain, the Low Countries, Germany and perhaps Scandinavia increased their economic lead over most other countries outside 'neo-Europe'. One of the characteristics that may have allowed western Europe to pull ahead of the rest of the world, even by 1820, was a greater openness to trade. According to Maddison (1995) exports were 1 per cent of world output in 1820, but for the United Kingdom the figure was over 3 per cent and for the United States, 2 per cent. People are more likely to trade with those closer to them, other things being equal. Table 3.1 points out that 68 per cent of European foreign commerce in 1860 and in 1910 was with other European states. So the larger the region or country, the less the external trade in relation to Gross Domestic Product (GDP), for given levels of economic activity. Yet what was distinctive about western Europe was the volume of intercontinental trade. And it was Britain that was unusual in specializing in this type of commerce; Table 3.1 shows that, in 1860, only 34 per cent of British exports were destined for Europe, whereas the average for continental Europe was 82 per cent. The European cotton textile industry, entirely dependent on raw materials only available in other continents, is perhaps the most spectacular example of the power of long- distance trade.

Table 3.1 The European focus of European exports 1830–1910: percentage of European exports destined for Europe

Area of origin	1830	1860	1910
Europe	72	68	68
Britain	47	34	35
Continent	82	82	78

Source: Bairoch (1974).

The new technologies of telegraphy and railways drove market integration on land masses, and at sea steam increasingly displaced sail. The Suez Canal gave steamships a major advantage on the Indian routes and contributed to the decline in freight rates. Even if towed through the canal, sailing ships could rarely sail all the way through the Red Sea. The impact of improvements in steamships on the routes left for sailing ships has been demonstrated statistically (Harley, 1971). Later, nineteenth-century sailing ships were forced to make greater voyages, such as between Europe and Japan. The China tea run in the 1860s was dominated by 'clippers' which later were transferred to the long-distance Australian wool trade.

Lower freight costs boosted flows of goods across national frontiers and caused convergence of prices. Wheat prices were almost equalized on both sides of the Atlantic Ocean by the outbreak of the First World War, but beef prices maintained a substantial differential, thanks to health regulations and transport difficulties (Harley, 1992). When Japan embarked upon a systematic westernization of many Japanese institutions and technologies, her exports and imports increased enormously. Japanese prices converged on those of the rest of the world as the country opened up to foreign trade. Average exportables prices rose at least three and a half times relative to the prices of importable products. Japanese gains from this liberalization were perhaps 65 per cent of 1858 real income by the 1870s (Huber, 1971). Changes in product prices alter rewards of the factors that make these goods.

Market integration also altered the relative prices of skilled and unskilled labour services, according to Adrian Wood (1994). Many commentators have noted that countries most successful at 'catching up' in skills, France, Germany and the United States in the nineteenth century, did not practise free trade. Temporary protection and judicious selection of infant industries at first sight appear to have made a major contribution. Learning by doing, perhaps encouraged by protection, may be essential for skills acquisition, and trade brings knowledge. Wood's view of the nineteenth century is that in the north the real wage of unskilled labour, unlike skilled labour, rose very slowly. The reason was an expanding supply due to population growth combined with migration, and slow growth of demand, since industrial development was initially skill-intensive.

Cheaper transport meant more land could be drawn into the world economy. Regions with abundant land but few people – like Australia – could specialize in supplying land-intensive commodities such as wool or wheat. In exchange, labour-abundant regions, such as England or the Low Countries, could offer labour-intensive products, such as textiles. In effect, trade made land less scarce in England and more scarce in Australia. Conversely, labour became relatively more scarce in England, and wages were higher relative to land rents than in the absence of trade. This is the thrust of the Heckscher–Ohlin trade theory.

Not only were products traded but factors of production moved internationally as well in the nineteenth century. Europeans migrated to other temperate zones and achieved high agricultural productivity because of land abundance and the application and modification of European techniques. Infrastructure investment (railways and ports in particular) financed by Europeans, largely the British, made their wheat, leather, wool and beef saleable in European markets. High productivity meant high earnings. But migration drove down these rewards towards the point where differences between the receiving and sending economies were sufficient to compensate for their relative advantages. The remaining earnings gap needed only to cover the costs of transport and the wages forgone while travelling, as well as the personal costs of leaving home. Migration helped convergence between the old and new worlds (Taylor and Williamson, 1997).

Late nineteenth-century intercontinental migrations were responses to shocks under fixed exchange rates, when domestic European growth was relatively sluggish relative to population growth. France, with a virtually stagnant population by 1870, was an exception. Most probably, the wide distribution of landed property and the Code Napoléon which required partible inheritance, reduced birth rates and thus the pressure to emigrate felt elsewhere in Europe.

Convergence of national aggregate incomes per head (roughly, or wages) does not imply convergence of regional output. Migration can radically reduce the population (and therefore the GDP) of a region, as in Ireland.

Convergence by depopulation stretches the meaning of the term, but it is certainly a possibility of open economy forces. Suppose transport developments lower grain prices, so that a gold-standard, primarily agricultural, area of small owner-occupier farmers can no longer compete. The implicit rent of land falls, farmers sell up and emigrate. Eventually, if there is an equilibrium, diminishing returns should ensure that, when sufficiently few people are left, those who remain will be as rich as any in the world. But the process may take many generations – if it works like that at all.

People were not usually forced to migrate, and they did not leave Spain in any great numbers. They could take other jobs, importing cheap grains and producing other goods or services, supposing that they could find any that allowed them to support a tolerable living standard. Exchange rate flexibility may accelerate the adjustment process (Sanchez Alonso, 1999). Cheaper grain imports might depreciate the exchange rate, raising import prices and reducing the prices of export products. Both price changes partly insulate the domestic grain-producing sector, encouraging the switching of resources into new export-oriented sectors. To the extent that fewer jobs are lost in the import-competing sector and more jobs created more quickly in export industries, external emigration is thus less necessary. Convergence of real wages would be reduced in the short term, though. By contrast, if labour was perfectly mobile internationally, the price of labour (allowing for non-pecuniary advantages and disadvantages) would be equalized. Exchange rate flexibility reduces external labour mobility but, in the case considered above, depreciation lowers real wages of those in work. The longer-term effects turn on the magnitude and the productivity of the switch into export industries. Thus the explanation for so little Spanish intercontinental migration in the generation before the First World War, in contrast to the rest of southern Europe, might be sought in the exchange rate regime. For many other European countries, however, factor price equalization under fixed exchange rates seems to fit the facts. Jeffrey Williamson (1996) finds real wage convergence from the 1840s much stronger than GNP, suggesting Heckscher–Ohlin is a tolerably satisfactory model for the north.

Business organization also responded to the globalization of the world economy. At the mid-century there was a cosmopolitan business class, with personal and financial connections in a number of countries (Jones, 1987). The Rothschild family and the Siemens brothers are two obvious examples. When nationalist pressures became stronger from the 1880s, cosmopolitanism was less popular, as markets became more integrated and jobs were threatened by foreign competition.

The new wave of business was the high-technology American manufacturing company, setting up subsidiaries abroad so as to reap the full advantages of their technical and managerial expertise. It was no accident that telecommunications was the most multinational of American enterprises. In this industry national determination to keep hold of the communications system clashed with the superiority of US technology. US subsidiaries in each country were the compromise.

An alternative to the large company with sophisticated management systems, much favoured in Europe, was cartels. By sharing markets and agreeing price, the pressures of competition could be avoided. By the outbreak of the First World War, there were 114 international cartels known to the public. However, most of them lacked substantial or sustained monopoly power, as McCloskey (1973) showed for the rails cartel.

CORE–PERIPHERY RELATIONS

Rising west European prosperity boosted the demand for products that could not be produced in Europe: the so-called 'colonial' goods, sugar from the West Indies, West African cocoa, tea from China, Brazilian coffee, American and Indian cotton as well as Chilean nitrate, gutta percha from Malaysia, Peruvian guano, African palm oil, Brazilian rubber, and indigo and opium from India. But these could also leave an exporting economy vulnerable to the fluctuating fortunes of a single crop. An extreme case was Brazilian coffee, accounting for 60 per cent of foreign exchange earnings and 50 per cent of world coffee exports between 1870 and 1890. It was no accident that the first commodity control scheme, to stabilize and buoy up export earnings, was introduced in São Paolo in 1906. However, single product export dependence was not invariably the rule. Brazil's neighbour, Argentina, had successfully diversified by 1913. Argentina earned 30 per cent of Latin American export revenues but accounted for only 9 per cent of the population (Bulmer-Thomas, 1994, 74).

Despite general export growth, the most ambitious collection of world national income statistics, by Angus Maddison (1995), controverts any general pattern of convergence since 1820 or even between 1870 and 1914. The arithmetic average of southern and eastern European countries' GDP per head rose by half between 1870 and 1914, whereas in western Europe the increase was 75 per cent. Incomes in the west were more than double those in the east by the outbreak of the First World War; the gap had widened since 1870.What was true of eastern Europe applied to Africa and most of Asia as well. Factor price equalization and convergence of incomes per head took place for a core of countries, but not for the periphery. This apparent lack of development, even when trade was growing, might be explained by Arthur Lewis's (1978) extension of his model of economic development with unlimited supplies of labour (Lewis, 1954) to the liberal international economy of the late nineteenth century.

There are two major components in a closed economy of the Lewis type: a modern, dynamic industrial sector, governed by market relations, and a traditional rural sector, where rewards of labour are unrelated to marginal productivity but determined by family and kinship. Labour is underemployed in the traditional sector, so that industrial/urban growth can siphon off 'surplus labour' from traditional agriculture without any reduction of output. GDP growth therefore increases as the share of the industrial/urban sector in total activity rises. When that sector's share is small, GDP growth is low.

When the dynamic sector is primary exports, export share in GDP grows with expansion of the sector. The effect on GDP depends on whether there is vacant land or whether land is diverted from food crops to exports. In the latter case there are gains from international specialization but GDP growth will be less than when more inputs are being utilized. Indeed, the expansion of the export sector and the export/GDP ratio are likely to be constrained by the availability of land, unless there is technical progress.

In his international model, Lewis focused on the segmentation of migration patterns between the tropics (the periphery or 'south') and the temperate zones (the core or 'north'). Mobility between regions was small but between sectors it was high. The north made and exported manufactures and the south produced and exported primary commodities. Both regions produced food (wheat, rice) which was also traded and therefore its price must have been the same across regions (ignoring tariffs and transport costs). (Coal rather uncomfortably straddles these distinctions.)

Productivity growth in export-oriented commodities was 'too fast' in one sense if it lowered the commodity terms of trade between southern exports and northern manufactures (Spraos, 1983, 40). But the main problem in Lewis's view was that productivity in the southern food sector was not high enough. Lewis (1978) concluded that Indians in the 1970s were poorer than US residents because US farmers were 11 times as productive as Indian farmers. The commodity terms of trade were merely a symptom.

Suppose each economy was 'small'. Then, although the above is true for north and south as a group, for each country, relative and absolute prices are fixed by world conditions. Changes in sectoral productivity then affect the size of their sectors. An increase in the productivity of primary exports raises the export/GDP ratio, GDP increases and resources flow into the export sector. If there was no immigration, GDP per head would rise by more. In Lewis's scheme, since there was southern surplus labour, it does not matter whether there was surplus labour or not within one southern economy, as long as free labour movement was allowed within the south.

Asian migration to nineteenth-century neo-Europe was prevented (Lewis, 1978, 192). Without this historical fact, falling transport costs would have driven productivity and living standards in the north down towards southern levels. Downward convergence of real wages might not occur (or at least, northern wages might not fall) if southern labour in unlimited supply was not a perfect substitute for northern labour. For example, if northern labour was skilled, and southern labour unskilled, they could be complements. Was Lewis right about the potential and actual impact of Chinese and Indian migration in the south? Not according to Table 3.2 below. Some southern economies grew quite markedly, while Indian and Chinese immigration was irrelevant to Brazil, Mexico and Japan.

Why were the two regions of the nineteenth-century world economy separately so open to labour movement, unlike the late twentieth century? One answer (Foreman-Peck, 1992) is that national governments in the north have become more pro-labour, or democratic, and less pro-land or pro-capital. Hence they are less willing than in the nineteenth century to enfranchise immigrants. The United States' political system was influenced by immigrants in the later nineteenth century – that is why it remained open – and the British Empire was committed to free internal movement of labour. In the south, land dominated governments and empires offer a sufficient explanation for the years before 1945. Immigration raises land values.

For Lewis, the core north determined the periphery south growth rate of 1870–1914 and the industrial urban sector determined the growth of the economy as a whole. If this dual economy operated at the world, as well as the national, level, we should not expect any convergence in the south towards the north until the surplus labour was exhausted. Indeed Lewis's views about the north are not consistent with convergence, through either Heckscher–Ohlin processes or technological diffusion.

The following south estimates show a rather mixed picture; the lowest initial income economies do not show the fastest growth. Only Brazil and Japan grew faster than the United Kingdom in this sample for 1870–1913 and therefore showed a tendency to converge (Table 3.2). The United States grew at twice the rate of the United Kingdom, which not even Japan matched. For the 1900–1929 sample, UK growth was very slow, at 0.5 per cent, so catching up was a less daunting target: Indonesia, the Philippines, Taiwan and Mexico joined Brazil and Japan in converging on the United Kingdom (Table 3.3). All the fastest growing economies by 1929 had high exports per head, consistent with high productivity growth in the primary export industries spilling over to other sectors, in contrast to the Lewis model. Slow-growth Thailand emerges as the oddity, since it did have surplus land on which rice exports were grown.

Table 3.2 Initial incomes and growth rates, selected countries 1870–1913 ($1980 prices)

	GDP per head 1870	Growth of GDP per head 1870–1913
Indonesia	413†	0.9/0.8
Japan	425	1.6
Thailand	506	0.4
Brazil	283	1.2
China	331	0.5
Ghana	292	0.9
India	345	0.6
Mexico	309*	0.8**
US	1591	2.0
UK	1875	1.0

Notes: * = 1877/8; ** = 1877/8–1910; † = 1880.
Source: Indonesia, Japan, Thailand: van der Eng (1992); others: Maddison (1983).

Table 3.3 Initial incomes, growth rates and exports per head, selected countries 1900–1929

	$1980 prices		$ current prices	
	GDP per head 1900	Growth of GDP per head 1900–1929	Exports per head 1900	Growth of exports per head 1900–1929
China	401	0.3	0.33	1.36
India	378	0.2	1.25	3.39
Indonesia	499	1.0	2.59	9.73
Philippines	718	1.4	3.14	12.70
Taiwan	434	1.3	2.32	27.82
Thailand	626	0	2.05	7.80
Brazil	436	1.4	10.12	14.05
Mexico	649	0.9	5.51	16.89
Japan	677	1.9	2.31	15.32
US	2911	1.8	18.63	42.35
UK	2798	0.5	34.41	77.73

Source: Derived from Maddison (1989).

Empire

An alternative explanation to surplus labour for the persistent poverty of the periphery is colonialism. Empire was the usual nineteenth-century conduit between, on the one hand, Europe and neo-Europe, and, on the other, the rest of the world. For the British and the Dutch governments, the principal interest was trade. European empires sometimes widened the sphere over which goods could move freely, though in other instances they may have been irrelevant or harmful to economic liberalism. Reversing causation, trade could precipitate the extension of European empire. However, European power politics (together with European technological advantages) gave a stronger impetus to imperialism. India became the jewel in the nineteenth-century crown of the British Empire, partly through conflict with the French. Africa was brought under European rule, as a sideshow to German politics between 1884 and 1900. Alternatively, it was not Bismarck who triggered the scramble for Africa but King Leopold of Belgium, whose 'crusade' for a 'private' colony in central Africa began in 1876. Ending the slave trade in central Africa and a mixture of 'commerce, Christianity and civilization' were the underlying conditions in either case (Pakenham, 1992, 286). The decaying Chinese Empire was divided into spheres of influence among the European powers and the United States, to prevent any one state gaining undue commercial advantage.

Whether for the colonized people the British Empire generated a net economic gain or loss depends on both valuations and on the character of the international economy that is assumed for purposes of calculation. The conclusion may well vary from territory to territory; the inhabitants of Yorubaland in West Africa might reasonably have regarded colonization as a rescue from endemic fighting, whereas many other Nigerian groups, such as the Fulani and the Benin empires, were capable of maintaining internal order and resisted European conquest. Broadly, the imperialists contended they were bringing civilization and religion, and those colonized by military force did not concede the point. Evidence from a later period suggests that colonies were more open to international trade than comparable independent states. Since there are mutual gains from trade, greater openness probably enhanced colonial material well-being (although more trade is not invariably preferable to less trade). Foreign investment is also likely to have been higher in the colonies than in an independent world.

The colonial regime shaped Indian economic development but the pattern was little different from those of Indonesia and China – the one colonized by the Dutch, the other nominally independent (Tomlinson, 1993, 92). Financial links between nineteenth-century Britain and her

Indian empire have always been particularly contentious. Indian national-
ists blame the 'drain' of remittances to Britain (for civil servants' pensions
and interest on loans to build Indian railways) for many of the Indian
economy's ills. On the other hand, India gained access to increasingly
cheap capital from the connection with Britain over the nineteenth century, even when the 'interest' on capital is interpreted broadly to include
the 'drain' money. India's financial problem at the end of the century was
that links with Britain were not close enough. The fall of the rupee
against the pound, which cost India a significant sum, stemmed from the
membership of the silver standard while Britain was on gold.

Generally, imperial powers inhibited or reversed the creation of a new
indigenous colonial administrative and military elite through indirect
rule, reinforcing traditional authority structures or employing European
administrators. Such policies should not necessarily have retarded economic development – indeed, quite the opposite if the Quakers, the Jews
and the Old Believers in Europe and Russia are pertinent examples. In
these cases exclusion from traditional, state-dominated, modes of
advancement diverted energies into business, arguably to the greater benefit of the economy and society in the long run.

What is a plausible alternative world that can provide a standard of
comparison for the colonial regimes? One imperfect standard is behaviour under subsequent independence but the difficulty of applying it
arises from the different intellectual and economic environment that
changed the behaviour of the former imperial powers as well. Another
approach is to examine those non-European powers that were not colonized. In Africa, Ethiopia and Liberia did not obviously perform better
that the colonised regions, and the Thai economy did not clearly expand
more rapidly than that of India.

Corresponding to gains or losses by colonial peoples are entries in the
imperialists' balance sheets. When the imperialists' benefit was the colony's
cost, then there was exploitation, but one party's gain was not necessarily the
other's loss. Although, for most of the imperial powers, colonies became a
considerable financial drain, the administration of the British Empire was a
model of economy. Great Britain, unlike most other powers, required its
dependencies to be self-supporting. Loans were expected to be repaid eventually. Even Britain, though, could not invariably enforce financial
self-sufficiency. In the 1890s, the British West Indies were one of the few
exceptions because the economy was so depressed, thanks to European sugar
subsidies, discussed above. Investment in empire was usually on commercial
terms and paid on average not particularly exciting returns. When the costs
of imperial defence are added in, the net benefits to Britain may well have
been negative, or very small, according to Davis and Huttenback (1986).

Michael Edelstein (1994) experiments with a number of alternative, non-empire worlds against which to measure costs and benefits to Britain. His distinctive innovation is to treat empire as a customs union and calculate the loss from exclusion if the colonies and the Indian Empire raised tariffs against Britain. India was important for British trade, and Algeria and Tunis for France. The Dutch colonial trade, stemming in part from government-owned coffee plantations, was principally based in what is now Indonesia. Spain traded intensely with the remnant of her Latin American empire, Cuba. But late-nineteenth-century formal and informal empires did not always exclude traders of other countries. With fairly strong assumptions, Edelstein can obtain gains from British Empire trade as high as 6.5 per cent in 1913. An alternative world he does not explore is one in which Britain exploited her monopsony power, and imposed optimum tariffs on formerly Empire imports. To the extent that Britain could shift the terms of trade against the colonial importers and in her favour, she could actually have been better off outside the Empire 'customs union'. For Avner Offer (1993) tariffs were not really the point; the benefits of empire were truly felt during the First World War, not only with colonial manpower but with colonial war materials and other resources.

THE END OF EUROPEAN SUPREMACY

Though it cemented some imperial links, the outbreak of war in 1914 ruptured the world economy, and it did so more severely as the war became more intense with the total blockades of belligerents. For non-belligerent countries such as those in Latin America, there were strong demands for strategic raw materials – Mexican oil, Peruvian copper, Bolivian tin and Chilean nitrates (Bulmer Thomas, 1994, 155–61). But by 1917, German U-boats were sinking half a million tons of Allied shipping each month.

Western Europe never recovered its late-nineteenth-century confidence after the pointless slaughter of Verdun and the Somme. The system of alliances that allowed virtually defeated nations to keep fighting, and the military technology of barbed wire, machine guns and artillery, killed perhaps 8 million (mainly) young men and permanently disabled another 7 million, to little obvious ultimate purpose (Kennedy, 1989, 328–54). 'The most enduring legacy of the war was social and political instability' (Feinstein *et al.*, 1997, 20). National boundaries in Europe multiplied, with the formation of roughly ethnic successor states to the Russian, Austro-Hungarian and German empires, and so too did national economic policies. Even Britain made the first dents in the policy of free trade with tariffs in 1915, supposedly to conserve shipping space.

Elsewhere protectionism became even more popular. The Ottoman Empire was fragmented mainly into 'mandated' territories, administered by Britain or France. Greece overplayed her hand by driving towards Ankara, triggering a Turkish nationalist response that forced a million refugees from Asia Minor into Greece.

With the peace, economic ostracism of Germany and the attempt to cripple her economy with heavy reparations continued severely to harm Europe as a whole and the rest of the world. The United States moved in to fill many gaps, especially investment in Latin America, but that did not avoid losses of world well-being from these misconceived non-cooperative policies. Of course, the damage from breaking existing relations is greater than the costs of not establishing those relations in the first place. So the war and the new order of the 1920s can, in one sense, only be taken as an upper-bound measure of the counterfactual of a world without the globalization of the years 1870–1914. A case in point is the expansion and then contraction of war-related industries – especially munitions, steel and shipbuilding – that created overcapacity and unemployment. Of particular concern to the world economy in the 1920s was the wartime resource shift into agriculture in neo-Europe to supply old Europe. Primary commodity prices were to be exceptionally weak in the 1920s. Farmers were likely to default on their debts and bring down those who had lent to them as well. These were the seeds of future crises.

The instability of the inter-war world economy contrasts with that of the generation before 1914. The earlier order evolved gradually, by trial and error, without any great plan or leader, whereas the radical social and economic transformations over the war period and the Versailles Treaty required a leap in the dark. Europe's loss of confidence as a result of the war was disguised by revolution in Russia and isolationism in the United States. Political and economic power is a relative concept. Only in 1941–2 did the speed with which the British, Dutch and French empires in the Far East collapsed under Japanese attacks reveal clearly how the world balance had been altered. European supremacy had been 'the Emperor's new clothes' for at least two decades.

CONCLUSION

Europe-originating international organizations and institutions in the nineteenth century gradually created the framework for the expanding world economy after 1870. Their success was due in part to their international acceptance, without coercion or hegemony, largely by spontaneous agreement. This achievement has been underestimated because the period ended in the senseless tragedy of the First World War. A buoyant world economy needed peace. Undoubtedly, the big failure ultimately was in international security arrangements.

Managing defaults on sovereign debt was perhaps the most political of economic activities, because of the implications for the delicate web of alliances and enmities in nineteenth-century Europe. Hypothecation of taxes for debt service was a more extreme treatment than would be expected from, say, the IMF or the World Bank in the late twentieth century. But these organizations often require policies such as the British applied to Egypt. The private organization, the Corporation of Foreign Bondholders, was quite effective in defaults where creditor country governments did not wish to be involved. That was easier because of the position of London in the nineteenth-century world capital market, but there was a similar organization in the United States, assuming prominence when London's pre-eminence was eroded. Their interests were similar; one would be unlikely to adopt policies that were not cooperative with the other.

Single issue economic institutions were largely self-enforcing, being based on the reciprocity principle, and so did not require enforcement and monitoring organizations. Although, for example, Spain chose to remain outside the international patent agreement, and businesses based in Spain were therefore able to exploit inventions made in other countries without paying charges, the Spanish market was small, and the revenue lost to world inventors was unlikely to have been significant. On the other hand, small open and more advanced countries might gain from 'free-riding' and establish an export trade generating a good deal of revenue, some of which should have accrued to the inventor if incentives were to be ideal. Trade regulation was similarly rather ambiguous, though the sugar agreement of 1902 was clearly a success.

The international economy was divided between a European and a non-European world (where the term 'European' includes 'neo-Europe'). The first group constituted a rich 'core' (excluding southern and eastern Europe for some purposes). The second was a poor 'periphery'. Together with the international organizations and institutions described, transport and communications improvements integrated markets and drove together product and factor prices between some regions and countries – the core. Others, the periphery, remained largely isolated from these processes. Migration was far more effective than trade in equalizing factor prices in different countries of the core. Hence separation of migration flows, the exclusion of Asian migrants from neo-Europe, ensured a divided world economy. Wages were not equalized between the two 'worlds'; indeed, they were not even equalized within the non-European world, despite migration.

Why did not European economic expansion pull up living standards in the non-European periphery? Surplus labour is not a satisfactory general explanation because the evidence of non-European economic performance is so mixed: some export-oriented economies supplying Europe – Japan, Brazil and perhaps Ghana (the Gold Coast) and Indonesia (the Dutch East Indies) – grew tolerably, while others did not. European colonialism does not seem any more empirically satisfactory a general explanation than surplus labour. Otherwise, Thailand and Ethiopia should have been star performers. Rigorous explanations must most likely be sought in the distinctive institutions of each economy.

BIBLIOGRAPHY

Albrecht-Carrie, R. (1958), *A Diplomatic History of Europe since the Congress of Vienna*, London: Methuen.

Bairoch, P. (1974), 'Geographical structure and trade balance of European foreign trade 1800–1970', *Journal of European Economic History*, 3.

Bairoch, P. (1989), 'European trade policy 1815–1914', in P. Mathias and S. Pollard (eds), *Cambridge Economic History of Europe*, vol. *VIII*, Cambridge: Cambridge University Press.

Berridge, V. and G. Edwards (1987), *Opium and the People: Opiate Use in Nineteenth Century England*, New Haven: Yale University Press.

Bulmer-Thomas, V. (1994), *The Economic History of Latin America since Independence*, Cambridge: Cambridge University Press.

Codding, G.A. (1952), *The International Telecommunication Union: An Experiment in International Cooperation*, Leyden: E.J. Brill.

Corporation of Foreign Bondholders (1878), *Fifth Annual Report of the Council*, London.

Corporation of Foreign Bondholders (1928), *Fifty Fourth Annual Report of the Council*, London.

Davis L. and R. Huttenback (1986), *Mammon and the Pursuit of Empire : The Political Economy of British Imperialism 1860–1912*, Cambridge: Cambridge University Press.

Derry, T.K. (1979), *A History of Scandanavia: Norway, Sweden, Denmark, Finland and Iceland*, London: George Allen & Unwin.

Edelstein, M. (1994), 'Imperialism: costs and benefits', in R. Floud and D. McCloskey (eds), *The Economic History of Britain since 1700, vol. 2 1860–1939*, Cambridge: Cambridge University Press.

Eggertsson, T. (1991), *Economic Behaviour and Institutions*, Cambridge: Cambridge University Press.

Feinstein, C.H., P. Temin and G. Toniolo (1997), *The European Economy between the Wars*, Oxford: Oxford University Press.

Flandreau, M. (1995), 'Was the latin monetary union a franc zone?', in J Reis (ed.), *International Monetary Systems in Historical Perspective*, London: Macmillan.

Flandreau, M. (1997), 'Central bank cooperation in historical perspective: a sceptical view', *Economic History Review*, 50.

Ford, A.G. (1989) 'International financial policy and the gold standard 1870–1914', in P. Mathias and S. Pollard (eds), *Cambridge Economic History of Europe, vol. VIII*, Cambridge: Cambridge University Press.

Foreman-Peck, J. (1992) 'A political economy of international migration 1815–1914', *The Manchester School*, 60.

Foreman-Peck, J. (1997), 'The long-run competitiveness of the British pharmaceutical industry', unpublished.

Harley, C. Knick (1971) 'The shift from sailing ships to steamships 1850–90', in D.N. McCloskey (ed.) *Essays on A Mature Economy: Britain after 1840*, London: Methuen.

Harley, C. Knick (1992), 'The world food economy and pre-World War I Argentina', in S.N. Broadberry and N.F.R. Crafts (eds), *Britain in the International Economy 1870–1939*, Cambridge : Cambridge University Press.

Holbraad, C. (1970), *The Concert of Europe:A Study in German and British International Theory 1815-1914*, London: Longman.

Huber, J. Richard (1971), 'Effect on prices of Japan's entry into world commerce after 1858', *Journal of Political Economy*, 79(3), May–June, 614–28.

Jones, C. (1987), *International Business in the Nineteenth Century: The Rise and Fall of a Cosmopolitan Bourgeoisie*, Brighton: Wheatsheaf.

Kennedy, P. (1989), *The Rise and Fall of Great Powers: Economic Change and Military Conflict from 1500 to 2000*, London: Fontana.

Lewis, W.A. (1954), 'Economic development with unlimited supplies of labour', *The Manchester School*, 22.

Lewis, W.A. (1978), *Growth and Fluctuations 1870–1914*, London: Allen & Unwin.

Lindert, P.H. and P.J. Morton (1987), 'How sovereign debt has worked', University of California Davis, Institute of Governmental Affairs, working paper n. 45.

Lyons, F.S.L. (1963), *Internationalism in Europe 1815–1914*, Leiden: A.W. Sythoff.

Maddison, A. (1983), 'A comparison of levels of GDP per capita in developed and developing countries, 1700–1980', *Journal of Economic History*, 43.

Maddison, A. (1989), *The World Economy in the Twentieth Century*, Paris: OECD.

Maddison, A. (1995), *Monitoring the World Economy 1820–1995*, Paris: OECD.

McCloskey, D.N. (1973), *Economic Maturity and Entrepreneurial Decline: British Iron and Steel 1870–1913*, Cambridge, MA: Harvard University Press.

Offer, A. (1993), 'The British Empire, 1870–1914: a waste of money?', *Economic History Review*, 46.

O'Rourke, K. and J.G. Williamson (1997), 'Around the European periphery, 1870–1913: globalization, schooling and growth', *European Review of Economic History*, 1.

Pakenham, T. (1992), *The Scramble for Africa 1876–1912*, London: Abacus (Little Brown).

Sanchez Alonso, B. (1999), 'What slowed down the mass migration from Spain in the late 19th century?', in J. Williamson and S. Pamuk (eds), *Long-run Economic Change in the Mediterranean Basin* (forthcoming).

Saul, S.B. (1978), 'The nature and diffusion of technology', in A.J. Youngson, (ed.), *Economic Development in the Long Run*, London: Allen & Unwin.

Schiff, E. (1971), *Industrialization without National Patents: The Netherlands 1869–1912; Switzerland, 1850–1907*, Princeton: Princeton University Press.

Spraos, J. (1983), *Inequalising Trade*, Oxford: Oxford University Press.

Taylor, A. and J.G. Williamson (1997), 'Convergence in the age of mass migration' *European Review of Economic History*, 1.

Tomlinson, B.R. (1993), *The Economy of Modern India 1860–1970*, Cambridge: Cambridge University Press.

Tullio, G. and G. Wolters (1999), 'A note on interest rate linkage between the US and the UK during the gold standard', *Scottish Journal of Political Economy*, 46.

Van der Eng, P. (1992), 'The real domestic product of Indonesia, 1880–1989', *Explorations in Economic History*, 29.

Williamson, J.G. (1996) , 'Globalization, convergence and history', *Journal of Economic History*, 56.

Wood, A. (1994), *North–South Trade, Employment and Inequality: Changing Fortunes in a Skill-Driven World*, Oxford: Clarendon Press.

4. The disintegration of Europe 1918–1945

Derek H. Aldcroft

In little more than a generation, Europe threw away a legacy that had taken centuries to accumulate. Norman Davies refers to the three decades between 1914 and 1945 as the period of Europe's eclipse, 'when Europe took leave of her senses'. In 1914, Europe still led the field in many things and European power and prestige were virtually unrivalled (Davies, 1997, 897, 899). By 1945, nearly all had been squandered or greatly diminished – her economic, political, military, colonial and cultural powers were but shadows of their former selves. The period of two world wars and a great depression left Europe in ruins, faced by the might of two extra-European nations, the United States and the USSR. Their dominance was predicted by Seeley as long ago as 1883 (Seeley, 1883, 87–8, 181, 334, 349–50). Though his prediction came home to roost, it was at a cost he certainly never contemplated.

EUROPE'S POSITION IN THE INTERNATIONAL ECONOMY

Though the neutral countries derived some benefit from the First World War, much of Europe suffered a serious setback to economic activity as a result of the losses, destruction and devastation caused by the conflict. Output and export levels were well down on those of 1913, even by 1920, while financial and transport systems were badly disrupted, inflationary pressures were severe and social and political forces highly unstable. Europe's trading contacts were also severely disrupted and many markets were lost for ever as former customers turned to alternative suppliers. The United States was undoubtedly the major beneficiary of Europe's indisposition, but the dislocation of war also fostered development in both industry and agriculture in many areas outside Europe, including the British Dominions, Latin America and Asia. While some of this could be regarded as hot-house development in response to Europe's diminished supply capability, it did mean that both import substitution and, subsequently, export competition would increase rather than diminish in the future to the detriment of European industry and agriculture. The extent of the shift in the balance of economic forces can be seen from the change in the regional distribution of world trade, with the Americas and Asia gaining world trade shares between 1913 and 1920 (from 22.4 to 32.1 per cent and 12.1 and 13.4 per cent, respectively), whereas Europe incurred a loss of more than 10 percentage points (Woytinsky and Woytinsky, 1955, 45).

The First World War certainly marked an important turning point in Europe's position in the international economy. Far more so than the Second World War, it produced a violent break in the continuity of development and the structures built up during the 'long nineteenth century', which presaged increasing dependence on the United States (Briggs, 1968, 48). Before the First World War, Europe, along with the United States, had dominated the international economy, generating some three-quarters of world income (Zimmerman, 1962, 54–5). A handful of countries (the United States, United Kingdom, France, Germany, Russia, Italy and Belgium) produced four-fifths of the world's industrial products, accounted for some two-thirds of world trade and owned two-thirds or more of the world's merchant shipping and liquid gold reserves. This high concentration of global income and wealth changed little in the aggregate during the inter-war period, but there were significant shifts in the distribution among the main countries. The wartime losses seriously damaged Europe's relative importance in trade, production and international investment. Even by the later 1920s, when there had been some recovery, most European countries had a lower share in world manufacturing production than in 1913, while Europe's overall trade share declined from 59 per cent to 48 per cent over the same period (Yates, 1959, 32–3, 48–50).

The United States, on the other hand, emerged as the richest and most powerful nation, replacing Germany as a leading creditor nation, and accounting for a greater share of world manufacturing production than the combined total of the major European producers (Table 4.1). During the following decade, when world trade stagnated, Europe's relative position tended to stabilize somewhat, largely owing to the relative setback of the American economy and the increasing importance of the totalitarian powers, especially the USSR and Germany. Thus the US, UK and French share in world manufacturing production declined from 59 per cent in 1929 to 42 per cent in 1938, whereas that of the USSR, Germany, Italy and Japan increased from 22 per cent to 38 per cent (Table 4.1).

As far as the free world democracies are concerned, the role of the United States is often seen as pivotal in the transwar period, though not

Table 4.1　Relative manufacturing shares (world output=100)

	USA	USSR	Germany	UK	France	Italy	Belgium	Japan	Total 8 powers
1913	35.8	5.5	15.7	14.0	6.4	2.7	2.1	1.2	83.4
1929	43.3	5.0	11.1	9.4	6.6	3.3	1.9	2.5	83.1
1938	28.7	17.6	13.2	9.2	4.5	2.9	1.3	3.8	81.2

Sources: Hillman (1952, 439), League of Nations (1945, 13).

always to good effect: first, in its dominating role after the First World War, when it failed to assert its leadership; then in leading the world into depression and subsequently failing to lead it out; and, finally, its contribution to the Second World War effort and reconstruction from 1941 onwards. But despite its powerful position, the United States was reluctant to assume a leadership role. Once the peacemaking exercise was completed, it made a strategic withdrawal from European affairs as isolationism took hold in the country, though for a time maintaining an arm's-length economic interest. A much weakened Europe became heavily dependent on the United States, even though the latter proved an unpredictable backer. She did little to provide leadership in world affairs, refusing to ratify the Versailles Treaty or join the League of Nations, while American economic policies often threatened Europe's stability in the 1920s: for example, the hasty withdrawal of reconstruction aid, restrictive import and immigration policies, gold sterilization measures, and rising interest rates and cutbacks in foreign lending in the late 1920s. For a time, at least from the mid-1920s onwards, when economic and political conditions became more stable, there seemed to be sufficient resilience to withstand temporary setbacks, provided the American economy remained healthy and it continued to pour dollars into Europe and the rest of the world. But once these supports were removed, there was nothing left to prop up the system. As the United Nations (1949, 66–77) commented in one of its early reports: 'The stage was thus set for the disturbances which culminated in the international financial crisis of 1931 and the subsequent disintegration of the international economy.'

During the 1930s, America was too absorbed with its own domestic affairs to give much attention to the European situation. The challenge was taken up by the main totalitarian powers who capitalized on the disarray caused by depression in the democratic camp. It was then but a short journey to Europe's nemesis. As Kennedy (1988, 291) remarks: 'In a remarkably short space of time, the clouds of war returned. The system was under threat, in a fundamental way, just at a moment when the democracies were least prepared, psychologically and militarily, to meet it; and just as they were less coordinated than at any time since the 1919 settlement.'

But why did Europe fail to regain its equipoise in the first decade after the war and become an integral part of the international economy? After all, experience since 1945 suggests that reconstruction and sustained recovery after a major war are not impossible. That they were never properly achieved after the First World War can be attributed, not simply to the severity of hostilities, but to the inept way in which post-war problems were handled. Three issues are especially relevant in this context: (1) the politics of the peace settlement; (2) the arrangements for the relief and reconstruction of Europe; and (3) the restoration of the international monetary system. In each case, the legacy of problems arising from defective policies served to weaken the European political and economic system, leaving it vulnerable to the shock of the the great depression. The repercussions of the latter further weakened Europe and finally, with Hitler's assistance, the disintegration of Europe was completed.

THE POLITICS OF PEACE

The post-war peace settlement effectively torpedoed any prospects of lasting peace and stability in Europe. It is true that over four and a half years of hostilities had seriously weakened Europe and that the balance of economic power, if not the political, had swung decisively westwards. But had the statesmen of the time been able to lay solid and sustainable foundations for Europe's peace and prosperity, this might not have mattered too much.

The first disaster was in the new geographical configuration of Europe. British statesmen, and no doubt the French too, had the quaint notion that, if the map of Europe was drawn along nationality lines, this would help to ring-fence Germany and weaken her power in east/central Europe (Jordan, 1943, 220). More idealistically, the Americans, taking their cue from President Wilson, pledged their support for national self-determination and democratic rights for the oppressed minorities of Europe. Thus, in contrast to the outcome, following the Congress of Vienna (1815), when the great powers gave little cognizance to the claims of smaller states, the peacemakers of 1919 adopted a far more generous attitude. The result was the 'Balkanization' of Europe as new and reconstituted states were granted full recognition.

In all fairness, it should be pointed out that the hands of the Allies were partly tied by the march of events. The collapse of old empires –

especially that of the Austro-Hungarian which they had not willingly envisaged until it actually happened, since it was still seen as a useful bulwark against Germany – left the way open for aspiring nationalities to lay claim to their cherished bits of territory. So the Paris Peace Conference was not in any real sense the arbiter of the new states since these had already emerged out of the disorder following the defeat of the enemy powers. 'All that the Conference could do was to register accomplished facts and delimit the frontiers of the new states, and even in this task its hands were far from free' (Cobban, 1944, 15). But in doing so they created a series of non-viable states which unleashed a 'whirlpool of national rivalries' (Perman, 1962, 4, 6; Macartney, 1939, 15–17; Schlesinger, 1945, 420, 435; Kiraly *et al.*, 1982, 35–6, 39–40, 493). Though space forbids full treatment here, it can be argued that the post-war territorial division of Europe exacerbated the national question and ethnic conflict. Some one-third of the inhabitants of the east European successor states were left stateless in the sense that they constituted national minorities. Thus the fact that nations were defined largely in ethnic terms served to heighten national perceptions of ethnic perfection, giving rise to demands for ridding nations of these 'alien' elements, who had once lived and worked fairly peacefully together, and fostering claims for the reconciliation of expatriates. 'Ethnic nationalism was to become an important force in fascist movements in these countries (Bideleux and Jeffries, 1998, 491).

Thus, unlike the economic sphere, there was no return to normality in international politics, to the nineteenth-century Congress system in which, according to Mowat (1923, 80–87), the sense of a community of responsibility among the great powers had been instrumental in averting at least seven great European wars before 1914. In other words, the war destroyed the traditional European balance of power for good, partly because of transformation within the great power structure itself, including challenges from two extra-European powers (the United States and Japan), and partly because the new states system was no longer amenable to pressures, as had been the case in the nineteenth century (Barraclough, 1964, 112–14). Unlike the former system, in which the bartering of peoples and provinces at the behest of the great powers was a practical reality, the post-war set-up never presented this option. However impractical the new territorial arrangements were from either a political or an economic point of view, the creation of sovereign states virtually precluded a subsequent review of the new configuration of Europe, since under the articles of the League of Nations the new states were endowed with an inalienable right to their new territories (Gathorne-Hardy, 1950, 25–6). That said, few countries, especially in central/east Europe, regarded the peace settlement as final, for the simple reason that they felt they had been robbed of lands and peoples that were rightfully theirs (Palmer, 1970, 180).

That the post-war peace settlement satisfied few, if any, of the European states is a well-known fact. Few treaty settlements can boast such a dubious honour (Hobsbawm, 1994, 31). However, from the point of view of the future political integrity of Europe, what mattered most was the situation at the centre, the security issue and the reaction of Germany to the peace terms, all three of which were closely interrelated.

Whether the peacemakers really believed they could provide long-term peace and stability in Europe through the creation of new states out of old empires is a moot point. Be that as it may, the fact is that almost from their inception the stage was set for later conflict – and not simply conflict through rivalry and tension between the smaller states themselves, though these were bad enough when territories and displaced populations were in dispute (Sharp, 1991, 195). But more important, from the long-term point of view in relation to Europe as a whole, was the inevitable power vacuum created through their very existence. The new and reconstituted states of east/central Europe were weak in every sense of the term, politically, economically and militarily. They also suffered from acute political and social tensions, partly due to their linguistic and ethnic diversity, while rivalry among them was fostered by territorial and nationality issues, fanned in turn by a growing sense of national identity (Kofman, 1997).

Thus, far from providing a bulwark against the incursion of a more powerful neighbour, they were 'destined to become the prey of any power which seized control of Central Europe, and no one was better fitted for that role than Germany' (Northedge and Grieve, 1971, 103). The vacuum left in east/central Europe by the disintegration of the Austro-Hungarian Empire therefore set the stage for later conflict. Newman (1968, 27, 58, 105–6, 201) repeatedly stresses the crucial role of this region in determining the subsequent distribution of power within Europe, and ultimately the continent as a whole. On the assumption that power vacuums do not remain open for long, since a predator nation will inevitably step in, this region provides a classic example since, as Newman says, the states in question were 'extremely weak reeds to place in the path of Germany, and they possessed few features that could lead to any hope of their being anything but satellites ... of Germany, Hitler or no Hitler' (Newman, 1968, 27). Whether they could have survived had there been greater mutual cooperation in the region is a very debatable point, but in isolation there was little hope once European security disintegrated in the 1930s (see Butler, 1941, 162).

Clearly, this interpretation of events obviates the need to evoke a *deus ex machina* in the guise of Adolf Hitler to explain the eventual political disintegration of Europe, since the seeds of destruction were already sown before his emergence on the scene. As Overy (1995, 289) has recently put it: 'Hitler played a part already written for him.' There were good reasons why Germany should be the one to play out this role, which Lenin had envisaged (Flood, 1989, 259). For one thing, there was no other obvious claimant for the throne; for one reason or another, the other possible candidates – Britain, France, Italy and Russia – were not in the running. Secondly, Germany emerged from the war as the strongest potential power on the continent, despite the losses and exactions imposed by the Treaty of Versailles (Weinberg, 1969). Thirdly, she had always coveted designs on the east – witness the wartime plan to colonize the region by setting up a chain of puppet monarchies in the conquered states from the Baltic to the Black Sea (Summers and Mangold, 1987, 274–5, 397). Such objectives were not obliterated by defeat in war. Indeed, the peace settlement gave Germany even greater cause for resentment and revenge. Whatever the rights and wrongs of the situation as polemicized by Keynes (1920) and Mantoux (1946), the fact is that Germany regarded the peace terms as harsh and iniquitous. They included loss of territory, assets and population in Europe and overseas, heavy financial reparations, restraints on rearmament and the occupation of key frontier zones, all of which it was hoped would contain German ambitions in the future. The crowning insult was the war guilt clause – the infamous Article 231 of the Treaty of Versailles. Finally, Germany was excluded at the outset from the League of Nations, which fostered the belief that it was a victors' club intent on imposing the terms of the peace settlement.

These impositions or penalties, and especially the war guilt clause and the heavy financial indemnities, caused burning resentment in Germany and provided her with strong motives to try and whittle away the onerous obligations and expand the empire eastwards. Moreover, in the final analysis, the prestige of the weak Weimar governments depended on success or failure in foreign policy above all else (Carr, 1947, 138–9). It is not without significance, therefore, that in the much trumpeted Locarno Treaty of 1925 Germany refused to guarantee her eastern borders, the pledges being confined to her western frontiers. This was no accidental oversight. Revisionism was the priority in foreign policy and containment in the east would have thwarted Germany's longer-term ambitions. These were evident under Stresemann's foreign policy in the 1920s, which sought to restore Germany as the greatest power in Europe (Orde, 1978, 209–10). What Hitler contributed to the cause was a fanatical racist doctrine rather than a totally new departure.

Locarno was in fact a charade in more senses than one. As Carr (1947, 97) first pointed out, it undermined the long-term sanctity of the Versailles Treaty and the League Covenants since it encouraged the notion that the Treaty provisions had in some way to be confirmed by subsequent arrangements to have binding force. Secondly, it gave Germany virtually a free hand in the east. It was an astute move originally conceived by Germany and supported by the Allies, especially the British, who were by then the losing interest in upholding the post-war settlement (Klein-Ahlbrandt, 1995), to pacify the French over the issue of security in Europe. The mutual security pact guaranteed the existing borders between France and Germany, including the demilitarized Rhineland, but the major flaw was that it failed to secure Germany's eastern frontiers (Young, 1997, 93–4). While it was hailed at the time as an important breakthrough in international diplomacy, following the tensions surrounding the Franco-Belgian occupation of the Ruhr, more sober reflection revealed its shortcomings. 'The era of Locarno suffused the international scene with an unreal glow which hid the fatal lesions in the European body politic' (Birdsall, 1941, 302).

From this time can be detected the beginnings of Germany's reintegration into Europe, which strengthened her position as far as revision of the terms of the peace settlement was concerned (Bretton, 1953; Henig, 1995, 44; Lentin, 1991, 27). Her hand was further strengthened in the latter regard by the fact that there was only limited resistance to her revisionist policies. The two obvious countries to uphold security and contain Germany were Britain and France, but for much of the time they were at loggerheads over Germany and other issues. As Young (1997, 77) notes, 'many Britons saw France as a trouble-making, militarist state, aiming at hegemony in Europe, while the French saw the British as unreliable, obsessed with profits and unwilling to enforce Versailles on the Germans, who were thereby encouraged to ignore its terms'. The two countries drifted in opposite directions in their attitude to Germany in particular and Europe in general. France was first and foremost concerned about security in Europe, which meant quelling Germany and sticking rigidly to the Versailles settlement. Britain, on the other hand, took a more relaxed stance, favouring gradual revision and the reintegration of Germany into the European political and economic system. Britain adopted an arm's-length approach to the affairs of Europe and the independence of new states was welcomed so long as it did not involve her active intervention, a fact which became only too apparent in the Austrian crisis of the early 1930s (Carsten, 1986, 215). This was especially the case in eastern Europe, whose fate was regarded with almost benign indifference until it was too late (Goldstein, 1997, 173–6). This attitude was perhaps understandable given Britain's extensive interests without Europe, but it did not help to restore the balance of power in which Britain above all had placed so much faith in the previous century and which had contributed much to its success (Carr 1942, 190–91; Newman, 1968, 202).

The French, to give them their due, adopted a much more positive approach, eventually concluding a series of mutual security treaties in eastern Europe, in the mistaken belief that these would help to avert any future German aggression. Unfortunately, France received only weak and intermittent support from her former wartime allies, especially in matters of security and containment. The fact was that the climate of opinion outside France was moving against her, in favour of German appeasement, while France herself was not strong enough to take matters into her own hands, even with the support of her little entente allies. And in fact, when she had done just that, as in the case of the Ruhr invasion at the start of 1923, things ended in disaster and redounded unfavourably on the French themselves.

Arguably, the League of Nations, the supranational body set up after the war, should have been the arbiter of dissension in Europe. Unfortunately, its effective role was weakened by Russian exclusion and American withdrawal, which meant that it came to be dominated by Britain and France, whose mutual distrust and rivalry rendered it largely impotent in matters of importance. The absence of American backing has been seen as the main reason for the League's limited influence in the affairs of Europe, especially with regard to security and disarmament (Henig, 1973, 175). As Birdsall (1941, 297) argued, the American withdrawal effectively sealed the fate of Europe:

> The defection of the United States destroyed the Anglo-American preponderance which alone could have stabilised Europe. It impoverished the authority and prestige of the League at its birth and it precipitated an Anglo-French duel which reduced Europe to the chaos from which Hitler emerged to produce a new chaos which he ... christened the 'New Europe'.

While the League made some important contributions in the economic field, especially in connection with the financial reconstruction of smaller countries, and resolved several border disputes, it had not the power or authority to ensure international peace when faced with the march of major aggressors – in turn Japan, Italy, Germany and Russia (Hayes, 1960, 128). As Davies (1997, 950) remarks, 'it played a major role in the management of minor issues and a negligible role in the management of major ones'.

What Europe needed most at this time was good Europeans to restore stability, but there were few of them to be found (Ross, 1983, 53). The trust and collaboration among the great powers, which had ensured that no one hegemon rose to dominate the continent in the previous century, were no longer there (Parker, 1969, 32). The powers themselves had either departed from the scene or were out of action for one reason or another. For most countries, great and small alike, questions of national sovereignty took first priority; the primacy of Europe came a poor second (Jacobson, 1983, 630, 644; Bridge and Bullen, 1980, 7).

RELIEF AND RECONSTRUCTION OF EUROPE

The peace settlement was also notable for what it did not do, and that is failing to make adequate provision for the economic reconstruction of Europe. Keynes lamented this fact in his vitriolic denunciation of the peace terms:

> The Treaty includes no provisions for the economic rehabilitation of Europe, – nothing to make the defeated Central Empires into good neighbours, nothing to stabilise the new States of Europe, nothing to reclaim Russia; nor does it promote in any way a compact of economic solidarity amongst the Allies themselves; no arrangement was reached at Paris for restoring the disordered finances of France and Italy, or to adjust the systems of the Old World and the New.
>
> The Council of Four paid no attention to these issues .... It is an extraordinary fact that the fundamental economic problem of a Europe starving and disintegrating before their eyes, was the one question in which it was impossible to arouse the interest of the Four. (Keynes, 1920, 211)

By the end of hostilities, much of continental Europe was destitute. There was a severe shortage of food, raw materials and equipment and a lack of hard currency earnings, especially dollars, to purchase supplies from abroad. Economic activity and trade had sunk to very low levels; in 1919, industrial production on average was about half the pre-war level and agricultural output was down by about a third (League of Nations, 1943b, 46). Many parts of Europe, especially in central and eastern Europe, were in desperate need of external assistance, not only to deal with the immediate needs of their starving populations, but also for the purposes of facilitating the rehabilitation of the devastated areas. There was, too, the task of consolidating new territories and populations and establishing new political and administrative systems at a time when famine and social disorder were rife and when border conflicts over disputed lands and populations continued apace.

Initially, it was recognized that large-scale relief would be required throughout Europe and that cooperation among the Allies, and especially the United States, from which most of the supplies would have to come,

was essential to effect it. For a time, that is during the Armistice period
from November 1918 to June 1919, things looked quite promising as relief
efforts were coordinated under the Supreme Economic Council. But the
experiment proved short-lived. The Americans were reluctant to get
embroiled in the affairs of Europe for any length of time, while inter-allied
cooperation rapidly disintegrated, partly because of Anglo-American
rivalry (Artaud, 1973, 17). Soon after the signing of the Versailles Treaty
with Germany (28 June 1919) inter-allied cooperation was terminated and
by the end of August official relief programmes had more or less been
wound up (League of Nations, 1943c, 12).

Most of the relief disbursed during the Armistice period consisted of
food supplies, together with small amounts of clothing; the bulk of these
supplies was provided under the auspices of the American Relief
Administration which had been established early in 1919, as the executive
agency of the Supreme Council with overall responsibility for European
relief. Under these arrangements some $1250 million of foodstuffs were
delivered to 20 European countries, mostly on credit terms or paid for in
cash (ex-enemy countries), with only about 20 per cent of relief deliveries
being in the form of outright gifts. When the official programme came to
an end in the summer of 1919 relief activities were largely confined to private and semi-official bodies which subsequently distributed a further
$500 million of supplies (largely foodstuffs) over a period of two to three
years, mainly in the form of gifts (League of Nations, 1943b. 34).

Given the scale of Europe's requirements, the Allied relief programme
was a mere drop in the ocean. It barely scratched the surface of the
immediate relief problem, and it did nothing to address the issue of
reconstruction. Hunger and poverty, especially among children, remained
acute. On average every child in central and eastern Europe was fed for
one month only by the American relief organization which distributed
the bulk of the official supplies. There was virtually no provision for raw
materials and equipment which Europe desperately needed to restore its
productive capacity. In fact, international action to promote the longer-
term reconstruction of Europe was conspicuous by its absence, despite
official recognition on the part of the United States that something
should be done to encourage the revival of Europe (see Costigliola, 1976;
Hogan, 1975; Leffler, 1979).

Failing adequate international action, most countries had to struggle
as best they could to obtain imports by using their limited currency
reserves or arranging private credits, though after 1920 the major source
of credit, the United States, dried up (League of Nations, 1943d, 68).
Their position was exacerbated by the post-war boom in commodity
prices caused by the worldwide scramble for raw materials, which left

much of continental Europe 'starved of primary products' (League of Nations, 1946a, 71). Data on post-war import volumes indicate that Germany and eastern Europe fared very badly in this period; total imports in 1919 and 1920 were only about one-third the pre-war levels, with negligible imports of raw materials, whereas the neutral countries fell short by only about 20 per cent and the western Allies exceeded their peacetime imports (League of Nations, 1943b. 19; Orde, 1990, 111).

The longer-term consequences of the failure to organize an adequate programme of reconstruction are especially relevant in this context. The inability to secure sufficient supplies, especially of raw materials and equipment, was an important factor accounting for the slow and erratic recovery in many European countries. It is true that some improvement was recorded over the very low levels of activity obtaining at the end of hostilities, but in 1920 industrial production was well below pre-war levels in many areas of Europe, up to 50 per cent in some parts of eastern Europe, and there was still a serious deficiency in agriculture. Even by 1925, economic activity in eastern Europe was still not fully back to normal (League of Nations, 1943a, 12; 1943b, 7–10).

Faced by insurmountable problems, including in some cases severe political and social disorders, governments were forced into extreme measures, including trade control, budgetary deficits, currency depreciation and inflation, to ease the situation. While these tended to impart a temporary boost to activity and employment, and probably staved off social unrest, the final consequences were often disastrous. In the extreme cases of Germany, Austria, Poland and Hungary, currencies collapsed under hyperinflation, real incomes of the bulk of the population declined, unemployment rose, savings were eroded and a complete loss of confidence led to capital flight. Thus the process of reconstruction had virtually to start all over again. As the League of Nations observed in one of its later publications, the whole economic and social organization of many countries was allowed to rot away and, 'when it was finally faced, it had ceased to be a general problem of transition and reconstruction and had become a problem of cutting the gangrene out of the most affected areas one by one' (League of Nations, 1943d, 70). It is rather ironic that the League itself had to step in, though not until the damage had been done, with financial rescue packages for several countries, notably Austria and Hungary in 1922 and 1924 respectively. Similarly a revised reparations programme for Germany was arranged in 1924 after the country had demonstrated, rather spectacularly, that it could not or would not meet the conditions of the original one.

The financial breakdown of several European countries in the early 1920s can be largely attributed to the failure to organize an effective programme of relief and reconstruction for the stricken areas. There was nothing to compare with the scale of operations mounted after the Second World War under the United Nations Relief and Rehabilitation Administration (UNRRA) and later via Marshall aid (see Killick, 1997). As a consequence, many countries were left in a parlous state, recovery was retarded and, when conditions did become more stable, several countries were forced to rely on private capital imports which later proved a source of strain (see below). Moreover, the difficult economic conditions of the early 1920s did little to further the cause of parliamentary democracy; if anything they alienated many citizens, especially those who had lost their savings in the turmoil of inflation. As Denise Artaud (1973, 16) points out, financial reconstruction was at the root of the problem and delay in bridging what was essentially a dollar gap in the transitional period proved fatal. Henig (1995, 39–40) goes further, believing that the failure of US governments to assist the regeneration of Europe through liberal credit facilities was an important factor in the failure to establish a lasting peace in Europe.

GOING BACK TO GOLD

If politics attempted to erect a new structural dimension for Europe, the reverse was true in the field of economics. Most contemporaries regarded the pre-war liberal economic system as something worth recapturing. The restoration of the former system – synonymous with free trade, free factor mobility, minimal state control and, above all, fixed exchange rates under a gold-based monetary system – was regarded by businessmen and politicians alike as a basic priority of policy (Arndt, 1944, 223). Indeed, throughout the 1920s, 'Ministers, officials, economists and businessmen alike continued to think about the broad issues of commercial policy in the light of the economic and political conditions obtaining in the prewar era and desired the readoption of long-run policies appropriate to these conditions' (League of Nations, 1942a, 154–5). Curiously, they failed to realize that the pre-war system was less robust than often imagined, as Keynes had pointed out on the opening page of his *Economic Consequences of the Peace* (1920, 1); that 'the economic world of 1913 had already passed into history as much as had the Habsburg and Romanoff Empires' (Thomson, 1966, 601). Financial leaders in particular were steeped in the economics of the past and most of them 'still inhabited a prewar dream world regulated by the gold standard' (Silverman, 1982, 298). They did not realize that what had been shattered by war could not easily be resurrected in its previous form; institutions and policies needed to be adapted to a different world and this should have been apparent from the very fact that some countries were already repositioning their commercial policies in the early post-war years.

What held uppermost in the minds of contemporaries was the currency question: specifically, restoring the pre-war international monetary system based on gold. The virtues of the gold standard were rarely questioned, and its resurrection was seen as the key to the return of world prosperity and economic stability. Both the Brussels and Genoa International Financial Conferences of 1920 and 1922 had stressed the urgency of returning to fixed gold parities (Orde, 1990, 229; Fink, 1984, 235; Kemmerer, 1944, 109–10). The same message had been transmitted loud and clear by the British Cunliffe Committee in 1918.

Whether the stabilizing properties of the gold standard were as important as many believed at the time is a moot point, but irrespective of any reservations on this score, there were sound practical reasons why statesmen should be anxious to restore the former international monetary system. Apart from the obvious reasons of prestige and national honour, of special relevance to certain countries such as France and Italy, the fact was that European currencies and international finance were in a state of chaos for several years after 1918. The floating exchange rate system which followed the general abandonment of gold during the war, or shortly thereafter, gave rise to large and erratic swings in currency values. Such violent movements, with the general trend downwards against the dollar, were associated with inflation and lax macroeconomic policies, all of which were seen as major impediments to European reconstruction and recovery. Pigou, in his memorandum to the Brussels Conference of 1920, had warned that wide fluctuations in exchange rates were a great hindrance to trade and credit transactions (Pigou, 1920, 12). Keynes was also well aware of the dangers to the revival of trade and investment after the war arising from extreme price and exchange instability, and in his memorandum on the exchanges of 1922 he advocated that the main European currencies should be stabilized as soon as possible, with other countries following subsequently (Moggridge, 1992, 377–8, 382–3). A similar view was expressed a few years later by the Head of the League of Nations Intelligence Service when he argued that exchange rate volatility had hindered European trade recovery (Loveday, 1931, 31). There was also a strong belief, though one perhaps exaggerated at the time, that floating exchange rates encouraged speculative activity which exacerbated fluctuations in rates and led to overtracking from true equilibrium values, a view which until recently became more or less the conventional wisdom as a result of Nurkse's work for the League of Nations (League of Nations, 1944). Thus monetary stabilization was seen as a solution to these undesirable tendencies and it would at the same time encourage governments to return to the good housekeeping practices in monetary and fiscal policies that had prevailed before 1914 (Bordo and Rockoff, 1996).

However, what eventually emerged fell short of the ideal of the former golden era. In contrast to the negotiated settlement on exchange rates after the Second World War, the process of currency stabilization in the 1920s was little short of a shambles. Despite resolutions passed by the Brussels and Genoa Conferences calling for a degree of coordination, at least among central banks, there was no systematic plan to stabilize currencies or groups of currencies simultaneously. This meant insufficient attention was paid to the vast changes which had taken place in world finance and economic conditions since 1914, and especially the changes in cost and price relationships of one country relative to another (Fink, 1984, 235; League of Nations, 1946b, 91).

In practice, currency stabilization proved a long-drawn-out process, which was still going on when the gold standard was near the point of collapse. Most countries acted independently of one another by stabilizing their currencies at different times as and when it best suited their needs, which often meant when they had managed to get their domestic financial systems under control. In this regard, delays were often encountered because of friction as to which groups in society should bear the cost of stabilization. This could lead to a war of attrition between the different socioeconomic groups until the more conservative elements managed to gain the upper hand and impose the costs on the weaker members of the community. France provides a classic example in this context (see Alesina and Drazen, 1991, 1173–4). In the convoluted process of securing political consolidation, little room was left for a rational consideration of the relative shift in costs and prices that had taken place since 1914 when choosing new exchange rates. The chief objective seems to have been to select a rate that was deemed to be defensible, although even this maxim was disregarded when matters of prestige and honour intervened, as in the case of Mussolini's defence of the lira, or when it was thought that a competitive edge could be gained by undervaluation, as in the cases of France and Belgium. The timing and process of stabilization were also influenced by the machinations of Montagu Norman and Benjamin Strong, who were keen to ensure that European countries did not select exchange rates that were too competitive (de Cecco, 1995, 122–4). Britain was also anxious to maintain her former role as a leading financial centre, which was one reason why Norman sought to induce countries to adopt the gold exchange standard.

As a consequence of the piecemeal and haphazard approach to currency stabilization, the revived system started out in a state of disequilibrium. Few countries had the correct rates and some of the major currencies were seriously out of line. The French and Belgian, and possibly the German, currencies were undervalued, while the reverse was true of the British, Scandinavian, Italian and Japanese currencies. This inevitably made it more difficult for countries to secure lasting balance of payments equilibrium. Fixed exchange rate systems in general are only as good as the sum of their individual components, and when these are out of kilter one with another the possibility of the system as a whole disintegrating are thereby enhanced. The League of Nations (1944, 114) summed up the situation as follows: 'The piecemeal and haphazard manner of international monetary reconstruction sowed the seeds of subsequent disintegration. It was partly because of the lack of proper co-ordination during the stabilization period of the 'twenties that the system broke down in the 'thirties.'

Misaligned exchange rates were far from being the only source of weakness of the restored standard, however. The format of the new standard differed appreciably from that before the war. Gold coins were generally withdrawn from internal circulation and the majority of countries adopted a modified form, the gold exchange standard, whereby a country's currency was linked to gold indirectly by holding reserves mainly in the form of foreign exchange (usually sterling or dollars) of countries with fully convertible currencies. The Bank of England, under Norman's direction, was largely responsible for promoting the adoption of the gold exchange standard, especially in those countries in which the Bank carried out stabilization plans (Kooker, 1976, 86–7). Of the 50 or so nations that were on some form of gold standard during part of the inter-war period, 32 adopted the gold exchange standard. While the exchange standard had the advantage of economizing on the use of gold, which at the time was thought to be in short supply, it also had the disadvantage that it pyramided potential gold claims on key currency centres which could prove fatal in times of crisis, especially for weak centres such as Britain, as became all too apparent in the financial crisis of the summer of 1931. A further source of danger came from those countries which aspired to move to a full gold standard at some future date, since this meant the ever-present threat of exchange conversion into gold for that purpose (Mouré, 1992, 264). The French, for example, never saw the exchange standard as more than a temporary expedient on the road to the full standard. Their attitude in this regard was reinforced by the fact that they were profoundly suspicious, perhaps with some justification, that the gold exchange standard was a ruse designed to consolidate Anglo-American hegemony in international finance (Silverman, 1982, 58). Their strong external position following *de facto* stabilization of the franc in 1926 enabled them to accumulate gold to the embarrassment of the British, as confidence in the franc encouraged the repatriation of errant funds.

Whatever the structural defects of the system, it should be stressed that it had to operate in a far less congenial climate than had obtained before 1914. Condliffe (1941, 102–3) reckoned that the restoration of the gold standard was a futile exercise, since the conditions for its successful operation were no longer present. The new standard was precarious from the start, he argued, because of increasing impediments to international trade, migration and capital movements, the growing inflexibility of price systems and the emergence of national monetary policies designed to deal more with domestic economic pressures. He might also have added the complications caused by the tangled network of war debts and reparations. On this interpretation, the failure of the system could scarcely be attributed to the mechanism itself, since no system could be expected to work satisfactorily under unsuitable conditions. As Ellsworth (1964, 396–402) noted, the balance of economic forces of the post-war world were responsible for undermining the international monetary system.

The fact that few countries were prepared to sacrifice, to the extent that had been the case before 1914, the stability of their domestic economies for the sake of external equilibrium, is scarcely surprising. Cyclical and structural problems loomed large in the post-war world and political pressures, due partly to the growth of mass electorates and other forces of social democracy, behoved governments to do something about them. Even Norman, the archetypal monetarist, was not oblivious to domestic considerations even when the Bank was 'under the harrow' in defending the overvalued pound sterling (Sayers, 1976, I, 225–34, 334; Dam, 1982, 58). This dichotomy of objectives partly explains why the 'rules of the game' of international monetary policy, however much they may have been observed in the breach before 1914, were less likely to be followed after the war as domestic priorities took increasing precedence (see McKinnon, 1996). In turn, it also explains the increasing concentration of gold in a small number of countries, especially the United States and France, as surplus countries failed to take appropriate action to counteract gold inflows, thereby exacerbating the position of deficit countries. The emergence of rival financial centres (New York and Paris especially) also challenged London's former predominance in international monetary relations. The system was therefore bereft of a hegemonic leader, which some see, though there has been much recent debate on this issue, as being crucial to the success of the gold standard before 1914 (Llewellyn and Presley, 1995; Aldcroft and Oliver, 1998, ch. 2). If international monetary stability required more than hegemonic dominance in the form of international cooperation, this too was not sufficiently robust (Eichengreen, 1989).

Thus, at a time when the system required greater management and international collaboration, it was found wanting. When the chips were down there was no one country prepared to defend and/or capable of defending the system, while sustained international cooperation among central bankers to manage the system eventually fell foul of political rivalries, the increasing emphasis on national policies, conceptual differences on monetary practice and limited support for the gold exchange standard. 'The gold exchange standard', writes Mouré (1992, 278) did not command sufficient support to attract the continuous co-operation advocated by the Genoa resolutions.'

Thus, given the manner in which it was restored and the way it was operated, the gold standard was a potentially destabilizing force in the 1920s. It was probably only a matter of time before it disintegrated since, once subject to undue pressures, countries were not prepared to sacrifice their domestic economies on the altar of the exchanges. For, when depression struck with force in the early 1930s, the gold standard, through the links forged by fixed exchange rates, became an independent source of contraction. Whether economic stabilization could have been achieved without jettisoning the gold standard, had the major countries adopted more appropriate measures to counteract the depression, is an interesting debating point which has been raised recently by several writers (Foreman-Peck *et al.*, 1996).

THE FRAGILE EQUILIBRIUM

Compared with the first half of the decade, the later 1920s appeared to hold out greater promise. Certainly, by then political and economic conditions were more stable than they had been for some years. The Locarno Treaty of 1925, the improved prospects for disarmament, the revised reparations deal (the Dawes Plan) with Germany in the previous year, along with the negotiated agreements on allied war debts, followed in August 1928 by the Kellogg–Briand peace accord denouncing war as a means of settling international disputes, all helped to ease international tension and reduce the danger of war. On the economic front there was also improvement. The great inflations had run their course, national finances were in better shape and currency stabilization had made good progress, while primary commodity prices had recovered from their post-war slump.

This more benign scenario was reflected in economic performance. The trade and output of European countries recorded more sustained advances than in the early 1920s, and eastern Europe tended to recoup some of the relative loss suffered earlier *vis-à-vis* western Europe. The strong domestic boom in America helped to stabilize the world economy and provided a source of capital for the impoverished nations of Europe.

Contemporaries were.generally optimistic about the future – the Americans especially, who, deluded by the roaring twenties, felt that an era of perpetual prosperity was at hand. With the benefit of hindsight, later writers have taken a more jaundiced view of the period. None of the descriptions is complimentary and all denote unstable equilibrium: a period of 'false stability' (Ross, 1983, 54), 'an era of illusions' (McDougall, 1979, 4), 'surface harmony and apparent economic prosperity' (Marks, 1976, 108). Friedman (1974, 107) described Europe as a mosaic 'ripe for collapse', while Condliffe (1941, 48) felt that the basic instability of the European economic system was concealed by the liberal credit flow from America. It was not a time of natural harmony in international economic relations, more 'a kind of armed truce' in which the participants were ready to take offensive action at the first sign of difficulty (Boyce, 1989, 66, 88).

These views have much to commend them. While the boom of the later 1920s may, to contemporaries, have seemed to augur well for the future, underneath the surface there were serious weaknesses which rendered the European economies vulnerable to shocks. These cascaded at the end of the decade to undermine the system.

According to Friedman (1974, 107), the British financial crisis of 1931 was the proximate cause of the disintegration of the European trading system. In his view, any shock would have served to initiate 'the contracting retaliatory process'. More important than the unique cause is the nature of the underlying structure and how it came to be in a position 'ripe for collapse'. This can be explained, he says, by 'The inherent debt structure after the war, hyperinflated currencies, the political and economic implications of Versailles, the legacy of wartime restrictions, and other conditions [which] all combined with the high degree of economic interdependence via trade to create a domino structure.'

While not denying that Europe was highly vulnerable to shocks from whatever source, issue can be taken with the sharp distinction which Friedman draws between the ultimate shock and the underlying structural weaknesses. In any case, it can be argued that there was more than one exogenous shock as far as Europe was concerned, and that initiating forces and structural factors were partly interrelated. Furthermore, some of the structural tensions identified have more relevance to the first half of the 1920s, while others of more fundamental significance for the later period are not mentioned. If for the moment we isolate the American downturn in the summer of 1929 and the restrictive import policy the following year (Smoot–Hawley Tariff) which can be seen as exogenous shocks, we are still left with three fundamental constraints which threatened the stability of

Europe: (1) price trends in an agrarian setting; (2) rising indebtedness; and (3) external imbalances and the role of the gold standard.

The first two constraints are especially relevant to the primary producing countries of Europe, though not exclusively, since foreign debt was an important element in the German context. Most of the countries of the region relied on world markets for the sale of their primary products, and they were also heavily dependent on imported capital for development purposes. In the later 1920s, western markets were becoming less open and, even more important, the terms of trade were turning against primary producers. Between the last quarter of 1925 and the third quarter of 1929, prices for agricultural products were 30 per cent lower than the average for 1923–5, while stockpiles rose by some 75 per cent (Ranki, 1983, 51–2). The overall terms of trade deterioration was somewhat less, though in the case of Turkey they declined by as much as 20 per cent between 1925 and 1929 (Keyder, 1981, 82–3). These unfavourable trends were responsible for the trade deficits in Hungary and the Balkans in 1928–9.

At the same time, these countries were faced by rising debt burdens. During the latter half of the 1920s, many of the debtor countries of Europe relied heavily on capital imports to plug the gap in their external accounts. Of the total flow of funds, both long- and short-term, into Hungary, Poland, Bulgaria and Yugoslavia between 1924 and 1928, half went to cover an import surplus in goods and services, while most of the remainder was earmarked for servicing foreign debts, so that only a small proportion of the borrowed capital found its way into productive activity (Ellis, 1941, 74; Political and Economic Planning, 1945, 110). By 1929, capital inflows were barely sufficient to cover interest and dividends on existing debts, while debt servicing was absorbing an increasing proportion of export earnings (Nötel, 1974, 84–5; 1984, 182–3).

Germany also became a heavy debtor in this period, though her position was somewhat different from that of other European debtors. The sums involved were much larger and her position was complicated by large reparations payments. Furthermore, she was not dependent on primary commodities for exchange earnings like her eastern neighbours. But because of the shortage of domestic savings following the great inflation, banks, businesses and public institutions resorted to massive borrowing 'to patch up a temporary stability at the expense of the future' (Royal Institute of International Affairs, 1933, 11).

There has been much debate about the alleged misuse of foreign capital. No doubt some of it was squandered on frivolous projects and on financing domestic consumption, but not all of it was used wastefully. However, what matters is that Germany, like her eastern neighbours, was living beyond her means and hence debt burdens rose. Thus by the end of the decade the financial position of a good part of Europe was becoming critical. The increasing burden of Europe's payments on account of private loans, war debts and reparations, at a time of weakening commodity prices and trade deficits, coincided with the suction of funds back to New York as a result of the American stock market boom, all of which served to intensify Europe's dollar shortage and threatened the collapse of the international financial system (Costigliola, 1976, 499).

The first sign of trouble appeared sooner than anticipated, as a result of the cutback of American lending from mid-1928 onwards. Between 1928 and 1930, capital inflows into Hungary, Poland and the Balkans were virtually wiped out, while those into Germany were almost halved in 1928–9 and fell to negligible amounts in the following year (United Nations, 1949, 11–12). It has been argued that the movements in the volume of long-term lending were sufficiently large and unstable to impart a major deflationary impact to the international economy in the late 1920s and early 1930s, and that many of the events which subsequently occurred between 1930 and 1933 can be attributed to the initial contraction in overseas lending (Fleisig, 1975, 5–6, 17–18, 54–5). The sharp contraction in US lending, and the accompanying tightening of monetary policy to control the stock market boom, resulted in tighter credit conditions and a check to investment and incomes in debtor countries, which then reacted back through reduced imports onto the metropolitan industrial economies.

The thesis is a suggestive one, but it is sometimes difficult to reconcile the precise order of events, such was 'the rush of disasters, tumbling one upon another' that subsequently occurred (Landes, 1969, 372). There is certainly some evidence that the reduction in lending caused a check to economic activity and investment in eastern Europe (Williams, 1963, 98; Ranki, 1983, 50). The German case is more equivocal. Both Schuker (1988, 123) and Fleisig (1975, 35) reckon that Germany was very vulnerable to a reversal of the capital inflow which accounted for some 10 per cent or more of the country's net capital formation. Temin (1971), on the other hand, has argued that the main problem initially in Germany was the decline in inventory investment, while Balderston (1983) rejects exogenous forces as the main deflationary force and explains the check to investment in terms of the inherent instability and structural weaknesses of the German economy, especially the deteriorating capital market conditions which were 'closing like a vice upon economic activity' (Balderston, 1983, 397, 415; cf. James, 1986, 136–7). But if, as he has shown elsewhere (Balderston, 1982), the malfunctioning of the economy had its origins in the inflationary experience and forced the Reichsbank to follow a tight monetary policy to maintain stable exchanges in the face of wage pressures, which in turn induced a large inflow of short-term credits, it can be argued that the German economy was highly vulnerable to shifts in foreign sentiment, a point recently confirmed by Ritschl (1998, 53) who, using a Keynesian framework, argues that 'a major force driving the German economy into depression in the early 1930s was the halt to foreign borrowing introduced by the Young Plan'.

Though there has been heated debate about the origins of Germany's economic downturn and the subsequent failure of democracy, there is fairly general agreement that the Weimar Republic was anything but robust. On both the economic and the political front conditions were very fragile and it did not require much to tip the balance. The economic and social pressures, especially with regard to the distributional conflicts over income shares, could not easily be accommodated, let alone contained, within a political system which itself was fragmented and hopelessly divided. As Kershaw (1990, 21) summed up the situation: 'When the depression set in, the fabric of the political system was too weak to hold and its remnants of legitimacy fell apart in shreds' (see also Voth 1993; 1995).

Outside Europe the decline in American lending was inflicting balance of payments problems on many primary producing countries from late 1928 onwards, which in turn had an adverse impact on their demand for imports from the industrial economies. Britain, for example, experienced a deterioration in her trade position with low-income countries at an early date (Corner, 1956; Solomou, 1996, 95). This was soon to be followed by a weakening demand in Europe for primary commodities which, in conjunction with rising stock levels, activated a serious decline in primary prices. As a result, the export revenues of Asia, Africa, South America, Oceania and Canada declined by around one-quarter on average in 1930 (Fleisig, 1975, 47).

It was therefore through the balance of payments mechanism that debtors first felt the main impact, since these countries had been dependent on capital inflows to close the gaps in their balance of payments. Once capital imports were curtailed, the only way to square their external accounts was to draw upon their limited reserves of gold and foreign exchange to cushion the impact. Thus the reserves of many debtors along the periphery and in Europe began to seep away during the period 1929–30 (League of Nations, 1943d, 23). But this could only provide a temporary solution to the problem; it could not cope with the subsequent course of events, namely a permanent reduction in capital imports, the collapse of primary commodity prices and the downturn of the American economy. The latter was followed by a further decline in lending and a cut in American imports, reinforced in 1930 by the new tariff legislation, which severely reduced the flow of dollars to Europe and the rest of the world (Meltzer, 1976, 460). The process of attrition in debtor countries was completed as commodity prices plummeted by 50 per cent or more through the course of the depression. As a result, many primary producing countries faced a severe and prolonged deterioration in their terms of trade and in their trade balances as export earnings fell faster than import values, while their external debt obligations, which were fixed in terms of gold, rose sharply as a percentage of export receipts. The dramatic rise in the debt servicing burden can be seen from the data for a selection of countries in Table 4.2.

Table 4.2 Debt servicing as a percentage of export earnings 1926–32

Country	1926	1928/29	1931/32
Argentina	10.0	10.4	27.6
Australia	25.0	28.0	47.0
Bolivia	7.3	7.8	50.0
Brazil	13.1	16.7	40.4
Bulgaria	–	12.3	22.0
Canada	16.6	22.2	53.5
Chile	5.5	9.2	102.6
Colombia	2.7	11.9	21.8
Greece	–	32.0	44.0
Hungary	–	17.9	48.0
Peru	2.6	7.4	21.4
Poland	–	11.3	27.0
Romania	–	14.6	36.0
Yugoslavia	–	18.1	36.0

Sources: Drabek (1985, 425), Nötel (1986, 223), Mazower (1991, 112, 202), Jorgensen and Sachs (1989, 58), Cardosa and Dornbusch (1989, 119), Urquhart and Buckley (1965, 160–61).

Thus with dwindling reserves and an inability to borrow further, debtor countries in Europe and overseas were forced to take drastic action. The way out of the impasse was sought through deflation, devaluation, default on debts and restrictive commercial policies. Once started, the deflationary forces were quickly transmitted through the links forged by the fixed exchange rates of the gold standard, as countries sought to protect their currencies with internal deflation. As Temin (1993, 92) noted: 'The single best predictor of how severe the Depression was in different countries is how long they stayed on gold. The gold standard was a Midas touch that paralysed the world economy.' But if policy makers found themselves boxed in by the constraints of defending the gold standard, some countries recognized early on that it was a futile exercise, especially as it would involve politically intolerable levels of compression. It was far easier to jettison the straitjacket imposed by the exchange rate mechanism, which Australia, New Zealand and several Latin American countries did in 1929–30.

This was the first chink in the gold standard armour, but it imposed a greater strain on the countries still on gold and thereby helped to intensify the depression. The real assault on the gold standard had to await the financial crisis of 1931, which finally brought its disintegration. Given the constraints it imposed, it is surprising that it lasted as long as it did. The severity of the depression and the massive rise in real interest rates, coupled with the deflationary policies required to defend the system, would seem to indicate that an alternative course of action would have been desirable (Grossman, 1994, 667–9; Virén, 1994, 121, 129). But at the time fears about the possible inflationary consequences of abandoning the standard, and concerns about the state of public finances, were important considerations in holding the status quo. This was especially the case in Germany where fiscal problems, arising out of the Reich's debt repudiation following the inflationary episode, exerted a powerful constraint on counter-cyclical action to combat depression (Balderston, 1982, 512–13).

In any case, for a time it was hoped that the crisis along the periphery could be contained. In fact, had creditor countries been more willing to come to the rescue of the debtors before the depression and financial crisis in Europe raised the issue of world liquidity to a completely different order of magnitude, the situation might have been eased. Unfortunately, the two strongest creditors, the United States and France, were unwilling to do this, and for much of 1929 they were draining funds from Europe and putting pressure on London's reserves. A partial revival of American lending in the first half of 1930 offered some hope, but it proved a false dawn. The sharp decline in activity worldwide and concerns about the state of financial institutions in both America and France further undermined confidence and resulted in a new scramble for liquidity. Though the final phase of the financial crisis was not played out until the spring and summer of 1931, there were signs that the international financial situation was becoming precarious well before the collapse of the Credit-Anstalt in May 1931 triggered off repercussions throughout Europe. The financial situation in central/east Europe was known to be parlous, partly because of injudicious banking practices, the widespread foreign ownership of national bank deposits and the large volume of short-term credits on capital account in the European banking system which were vulnerable to any crisis of confidence. Furthermore, uncertainty regarding public sector deficits also played a role in undermining confidence and stability in the international financial system. Thus, throughout 1930–31, the international financial situation was steadily deteriorating and it was only a matter of time before it collapsed.

The situation was brought to a head by the Credit-Anstalt's collapse which rocked the whole financial structure of the continent and had severe repercussions on the banking systems of many European countries (Schubert, 1991, 4). It alerted creditors to the inherent dangers in countries dependent on short-term credits and the implications this could have for currency convertibility, especially in those countries that had experienced serious inflation in the previous decade (Balderston, 1994, 64; Schubert, 1991, 170). It put severe pressure on many continental banks, resulting in the large-scale withdrawal of short-term funds, by both nationals and foreigners, through the early summer of 1931 until brought to a halt by the imposition of exchange control (Ellis, 1941, 74; James, 1986, 398; Ranki, 1985, 71; Nötel, 1986, 227). In the case of Germany, for example, some 30 per cent of its foreign short-term assets were withdrawn prior to the imposition of exchange control in the middle of July (Fleisig, 1975, 148). The gold and foreign exchange reserves of 18 European debtor countries fell by nearly a half between 1928 and 1931, with most of the loss taking place in 1930–31 (League of Nations, 1944, 40–41).

The scramble for liquidity reached panic proportions in the summer of 1931 and eventually the heat was switched to London, which bore the brunt of the final phase. The rapid withdrawal of sterling balances and loss of gold reserves between July and September, despite assistance from New York and Paris, were partly occasioned by doubts as to Britain's own financial viability (Hamilton, 1988, 74). On 21 September, Britain was forced to relinquish the gold standard, which finally signalled the end of the old economic order. Many countries followed Britain's example, while nearly all countries in quick succession took defensive action to protect their economies.

Though dramatic, it is important to place the crisis in proper perspective. The short-term liquidity problems of 1931 did not initiate the process of disintegration, 'they served rather to deliver the economic coup de grâce' (Fleisig, 1975, 103). The initial deflationary force was the collapse in long-term lending at a time when Europe was extremely vulnerable. The short-term liquidity crisis was partly a consequence of that event and the repercussions which followed from the dramatic downturn in prices and economic activity. The problem in 1931 was not so much the scale and volatility of short-term capital flows or the negative implications for the real economy, but the fact that it proved impossible to muster sufficient credit lines to stem the panic as it spread from one country to another. Several factors explain this failure: fears of exchange losses through currency depreciation, exchange control and the possible collapse of financial institutions; political motives, such as Germany's refusal of French assistance in July 1931 because it was made conditional on dropping the proposed union with Austria; and the absence of collaborative action to provide lender of last resort facilities.

THE LEGACY OF DEPRESSION

The immediate effects for the crises of the early 1930s are well-known and need not be detailed here. What is important is the longer term consequences for the future of Europe. There were both economic and political dimensions in this regard. The door was finally closed on the old liberal economic order. Economies became more autarkic and state-centred during the 1930s as countries attempted to insulate themselves from depression, while nationalistic forces in the less developed regions worked in the same direction. Trade relationships became more polarized into regional groupings, and bilateral trade relationships became more common. Despite this, however, Europe's relative economic decline (measured in world terms) tended to stabilize in this period, partly because of the sluggishness of the American economy.

The political consequences were also serious. Things deteriorated on both the domestic and international fronts. The depression gave a serious jolt to liberal bourgeois values and parliamentary democracy, which finally became discredited, and there was a shift towards authoritarian regimes. As Palmer (1970, 207) described the situation in the lands between (east-central Europe): 'Cancerous cells, already diagnosed in the political body, throve on its depredations. In the end it claimed the very concept of a liberal society as its victim and the soul of Europe lay exposed to new ideologies of violence and inhumanity.' Germany's blatant rejection of liberal values served as an example to many peoples shaken by uncertainty and who now questioned the virtues of bourgeois democracy. According to Rothschild (1974, 23), political radicalization was the product of economic despair and, when this was combined with the drive for hegemony in the region, the whole economic and political future of eastern Europe was thrown into the melting pot. However, one should bear in mind that political instability was common throughout the 1920s and that democratic institutions had never taken firm root in the successor states, or even in Germany for that matter. One by one, with the exception of Czechoslovakia, they fell prey to the forces of reaction. By the end of the 1930s, the majority of European nations were governed by some form of authoritarian regime (Lee, 1987, xi–xv). The reasons for parliamentary failure are varied and complex and have been discussed in some detail by Newman (1970), but there seems little doubt that the depression speeded up the forces of political disintegration.

Most of the new regimes were not unsympathetic to Germany's cause, which obviously made infiltration in eastern Europe that much easier. Meanwhile, Germany herself had been taking advantage of the course of events, especially the more sympathetic western attitude to her demands, while the waning of international collaboration among the Allied countries, most apparent in the failure of the London Economic Conference in the summer of 1933, encouraged her to press for more. Even before the assumption of power by the Nazis at the start of that year, Germany had been surreptitiously rearming (with clandestine assistance from the USSR for training purposes), while also loosening the restrictions imposed by Versailles. Once the Nazis were in power, the process was speeded up, overt rearmament was commenced and, by the mid-1930s, with the reoccupation of the Rhineland, Hitler had a clean slate on which to embark on the conquest of Europe.

The economic situation worked in Germany's favour during this period. It saw the collapse of the old economic order, along with the cherished gold standard. In its place more autarkic economic systems arose, with greater emphasis on state intervention and control, and above all restrictive commercial policies. Again such policies were not entirely new, since the 1920s had seen their forerunner in the nationalist measures taken by some of the successor states. But these were modest in comparison with the harsh policy reactions to the crisis of the early 1930s. The most dramatic changes were those on the external side. Though the collapse of the gold standard and the concomitant depreciation of currencies in some countries allowed them more room for manoeuvre in macroeconomic policy to stimulate recovery, the move to extensive trade regulation and exchange control elsewhere had the opposite effect: 'By 1935 Europe had descended to a historical nadir in trade and commercial policy.' (Friedman, 1978, 158). The majority of countries in Europe were by then using every conceivable form of trade and payments restrictions to a greater or lesser degree, including tariffs, import quotas, exchange controls, bilateral clearing agreements and controls on the movement of capital – everything, in fact, except formal economic blockade.

Such policies were partly a pragmatic response to adverse trade balances and capital flight, and partly designed to foster the process of import substitution for the benefit of domestic activity. They had a mixed aspect in the latter respect, but they did result in a general improvement in trade balances. During the period 1928–35, the majority of European countries improved their trade accounts and in aggregate Europe turned a large deficit into a significant surplus. However, this was at the expense of both trade and incomes. By 1935, European trade values (exports and imports) were about two-thirds down on their pre-crisis levels, in volume about one-third lower, and even at the peak of the cycle in 1937 they still fell short by a good margin. Friedman (1974, 98, 106) calculates that there were sizeable income reactions to trade losses arising from commercial restrictions. But for those countries devaluing after leaving gold, these were partly offset by trade and income gains through increased competitiveness and more relaxed monetary and fiscal policies.

One notable feature of the commercial world in the 1930s was the emergence of trade blocs and currency zones such that 'the pattern of multilateral settlements was submerged beneath a web of bilateral and regional commercial and monetary arrangements' (Eichengreen and Irwin, 1995, 8). These included the groupings centred on France, Belgium, the Netherlands, Italy and Portugal with their respective colonies, the British Commonwealth and colonies along with other sterling area countries, Japan with Formosa, Kwantung and Manchuria, and Germany with south-east Europe. Trade within the blocs tended to increase proportionately but, except in the case of the sterling area countries, it is unlikely that there were any significant gains in trade volumes. Some indication of the disintegration of world multilateral trade can be seen from the growing importance of trade within the main power blocs in Table 4.3.

Following the general abandonment of gold, managed currencies became the order of the day during the 1930s. More or less simultaneously,

Table 4.3 Great power trade blocs (as % of the core country trade)

	Imports from bloc		Exports to bloc	
	1929	1938	1929	1938
UK: Empire	30	42	44	50
UK: Other sterling bloc	12	13	7	12
France: Empire	12	27	19	27
Italy: Colonies and Ethiopia	0.5	2	2	23
Japan: Korea, Formosa, Kwantung, Manchuria	20	41	24	55
Germany: Balkans	4.5	12	5	13
Germany: Latin America	12	16	8	11.5

Source: Derived from Hillman (1952, 486).

a number of loosely drawn currency zones developed, including the sterling area which was more or less coterminous with the British/Commonwealth trade bloc, the gold bloc principally composed of west European countries until its demise in September 1936, when France, the Netherlands and Switzerland gave it up, the yen zone covering part of East Asia, and the Reichsmark bloc. The last of these was the most distinctive and also the most significant in the context of Europe's future. It included the Balkan countries (Bulgaria, Greece. Romania and Yugoslavia), Hungary, Turkey and, of course, Germany. The close affinity that developed among these exchange control countries, which retained their former parities, was based on mutual necessity. The smaller countries had overvalued exchange rates and depended heavily for their exchange earnings on the export of primary products, especially agricultural commodities, for which the world market was weak. Germany, on the other hand, was anxious to gain access to more supplies of food and raw materials, especially when sustained rearmament was put in train from the mid-1930s, and hence was prepared to offer these countries a guaranteed market (Overy, 1989, 53–4).

An important feature of this bloc's trading operations was the widespread use of bilateral clearing agreements. Though clearing agreements only accounted for about 12 per cent of world trade in 1937, over half of the trade of Hungary, the Balkan countries and Turkey passed through clearing, and no less than 80 per cent in the case of Germany (League of Nations, 1939, 186; 1942a, 70–72). Briefly, clearing agreements entailed the bilateral balancing of claims between exchange control countries, thereby eliminating the use of official reserves for transaction purposes. They were therefore a useful device for minimizing the use of free foreign exchange.

The costs and benefits for the respective parties have been much debated. The orthodox view – and one held by many in the 1930s – is that Germany exploited the region for her own benefit; that she acquired, on favourable terms, access to raw materials and foodstuffs in exchange for highly-priced manufactured products, including the practice of dumping goods such as aspirins and cuckoo clocks which her customers could well have done without (see Einzig, 1938, 26; Jones, 1937, 76–7). At the same time, Germany piled up large, unrequited import surpluses with these countries, the Reichsmark balances from which could only be used to buy goods from Germany. Germany was therefore accused of financing her rearmament at the expense of the weaker eastern countries.

There is undoubtedly an element of truth in all these allegations, even if they are somewhat exaggerated (Kindleberger, 1973, 240–1). However, the benefits were certainly not all one way. It should be emphasized that the east European countries were able to gain a reasonably secure market for their primary products at a time when there were few other outlets available. Macartney (1942, 140–43) felt that Germany's trade drive saved the agrarian countries from ruin. Moreover, Germany did not exploit her monopsonist power to turn the terms of trade in her favour (Bonnell, 1940, 111; Kaiser, 1980, 160; Royal Institute of International Affairs, 1939, 119). In fact, Germany paid above world prices for the products of the region – on average by as much as 30 per cent – thus helping to raise the incomes of the countries in question (Neal, 1979, 392–5; James, 1993, 86). The evidence also suggests that these countries received more than ephemeral goods in return, since they were able to acquire a large part of their machinery and arms supplies, as well as some consumer goods, from Germany, though sometimes at prices well above those offered by Germany's competitors (Basch, 1944, 179; Momtchiloff, 1944, 56, appendices 1–4; Rothschild, 1974, 22; Overy, 1984, 118).

On the other hand, trade relationships with Germany could be very unpredictable, and the large blocked mark balances, though reduced in time, could serve as a means of exerting economic and political pressure on these countries, especially when world market conditions deteriorated later in the decade (Friedman, 1974, 34–6). When it suited her purpose, Germany had no compunction about cancelling contracts, as occurred in the case of the bumper Yugoslav plum harvest in 1939 (Hoptner, 1962, 103). It is also probably true that increasing trade dependence on a dominant partner slowed down structural diversification and the reintegration of the region into the world economy (Basch, 1944, 183). Germany was not prepared to countenance industrial diversification of the region which conflicted with her own export interests, except, significantly, defence requirements (Calic, 1994, 418). According to Einzig (1941, 15), Hungary and Romania were prevented from developing their fruit-canning and meat-processing industries in order to enable Germany to purchase the raw products.

In the light of the subsequent course of history, the main point of issue is how important the Reichsmark bloc was in terms of Germany's political and economic influence in the region. Contemporary and some later writers stressed the increasing dependency of the region on Germany which helped to pave the way for that country's subsequent domination (Munk, 1940, 151; Jones, 1937; Condliffe, 1941, 260-62; Friedman, 1974, 34–5; Calic, 1994, 418). Friedman (1974, 34–5) in fact refers to Germany's dominant economic position in the region and the 'colonization' of east European countries, and quotes a large chunk of text from Condliffe which is very critical of Germany's totalitarian methods of trade control. The blocked mark accounts and clearing agreements have also been seen as laying the foundations of the wartime system of exploitation (Harvey, 1954a, 267). Milward (1985, 354–9), on the other hand, is sceptical both of the charge of exploitation and of the notion that the bloc became a positive component of German foreign policy.

As far as intra-bloc trade is concerned, there was a marked increase among member countries which raised the combined share of intra-European trade, but this was largely due to the increased trade with the centre country. Eastern Europe's share of world trade declined, however, largely as a result of the contraction of the region's trade in primary products with the outside world. Trade dependency on Germany steadily increased in the course of the 1930s for Hungary and the Balkans, so that by the end of the decade Germany's shares in the exports and imports of these countries was running at 40 per cent or more (Aldcroft and Morewood, 1995, 67). For Germany, trade with the region was of relatively slight significance and she was still dependent on the rest of Europe for some 40 per cent of her import requirements by the end of the period (Griffiths, 1989, 27; League of Nations, 1939, 186; Hiden, 1977, 173; Kaiser, 1980, 325–6). On the other hand, German foreign investment in the region remained relatively small compared with that of Britain and France. Moreover, there is no close correlation between the region and the Nazis' immediate ambitions of acquiring living space in the east. In fact, according to Hitler's foreign policy, Czechoslovakia, Poland and the USSR were to be the main targets for territorial conquest (Milward, 1985, 342, 353).

Yet, these facts notwithstanding, there is evidence to suggest that Germany used her trade connections with south-east Europe for political purposes to infiltrate Nazi agents to spread political propaganda. Under commercial disguise, political agents were said to be widely employed throughout the region: Munk (1940, 151) refers to these countries being 'honeycombed with Nazi agents'. (There were also, it should be noted, more than a few communist agents in the region.) In Romania, the Germans set up a soya bean factory employing no less than 3000 commercial agents to spread the national gospel, while, in the case of Bulgaria, Germany military experts were said to dominate the army (Jones, 1937, 64, 72). Whether such agents were as thick on the ground as some contemporary accounts suggest is an open question, but there is little doubt that these countries were being sucked into the German political and economic sphere (Polonsky, 1975, 24, 130–31). By 1939, Germany's influence in the region was certainly more felt than in 1913 and, according to Rothschild (1974, 23–4), 'the combination of Nazi Germany's ideological, diplomatic, political and economic drives paved the way for her military conquests'. One by one, all the states in central-east Europe succumbed to her offensives: Albania, Austria, Bulgaria, Czechoslovakia, Greece, Hungary, Poland, Romania, Yugoslavia. On one thing at least most writers are agreed: that Germany's increasing domination of the region was facilitated by the fact that the western powers abandoned or withdrew their support at the crucial hour (Rothschild, 1989, 7; Overy, 1984, 118; Seton-Watson, 1945, 412).

THE NAZI SOLUTION FOR EUROPE:
THE NEW ORDER

In the summer of 1939, despite ominous signs of Hitler's intentions, the situation in Europe was still fluid. 'Europe was a cauldron of distrusts, deceit and double-dealing', as 'on all sides nation was dealing behind the back of nation, each mouthing platitudes of sincerity or uttering threats' (Toland, 1997, 542). By the end of 1941, all that had changed. Through conquest and satellite dependencies, Germany controlled a land mass that was almost synonymous with continental Europe. It stretched from Brittany in the west to the mountains of the Caucasus in the east, and from the Arctic tip of Norway to the shores of the Mediterranean. Only a few countries managed to retain their independence, notably Portugal, Spain, Eire, Switzerland and Sweden, none of which could be said to be wholly unsympathetic to the Nazi regime.

At the beginning of the Second World War, the prospects of a new order for Europe emerging out of the ruins of the Versailles settlement seemed a distinct possibility, and one which was initially greeted with a degree of approval by some non-fascist countries. The concept was a much-discussed topic in establishment circles in the early years, though it is doubtful if any formal plan was ever drawn up. The nearest thing to an official statement on the issue was that released on 25 July 1940 by Walther Funk, Reich Minister of Economics, who was entrusted by Goering to formalize arrangements for the New Order. The wider political aspects were given more concrete substance by the signing of the Tripartite Pact on 27 September 1940 between Germany, Italy and Japan, which delineated spheres of influence in the Euro-Afro-Asian hemisphere (Child, 1954, 47–8; Harvey, 1954b, 166). From these and other official statements made by various ministers and also by Hitler himself, it is possible to piece together the main outlines of the Nazi plans for Europe.

While the concept might be said to have borne some passing resemblance to the Austro-Hungarian Empire and the European Common Market insofar as it envisaged a single economic community, tariff-free zones, full employment and cross-border movement of resources, closer inspection suggests some important differences. The degree of freedom allowed was to be very limited. Production, trade and the exchanges were to be rigorously controlled, the main aim being to make Europe fairly self-sufficient *vis-à-vis* the rest of the world (Mazower, 1996, 37; Cameron and Stevens, 1973, 41–2, 72–4). Extensive state control and state ownership were also contemplated. Industry throughout Europe was to be extensively restructured and plans for the post-war rationalization and integration of various industries, including textiles, iron and steel, chemicals and oil were being prepared by Goering's staff between 1940 and 1942 (Overy, 1984, 121–2). It is also clear that the scheme was not to involve an equal partnership of nations. Indeed, Hitler's ultimate aim was to transform Europe into a German Empire, a unified Europe but one dominated by Germany in which the outlier territories would service the needs of the German people (Guillebaud, 1940, 454–5; Toland, 1997, 770–71). Thus for much of western Europe a tariff-free zone was planned together with the integration of the manufacturing interests with those of the central zone of manufacturing located in the Reich itself (Milward, 1979, 162). For the less developed regions to the east, partial deindustrialization was prescribed so that they could concentrate on supplying the Reich with foodstuffs and raw materials. Funk himself acknowledged that he was essentially interested in the economic exploitation of Europe (Child, 1954, 47), though the question of how the need for more living space and the overpopulation problem in south-east Europe would be reconciled was never explained.

No systematic plan was ever drawn up for the administration of the conquered territories; structures were imposed somewhat on a trial-and-error basis, with considerable variations in the type of control. Nevertheless, there was some attempt to allot to each country or region a form of control suitable to its perceived final status in the Nazi conception of the New Order, which envisaged a single economic community for the whole continent working under German direction and with the Reich as the industrial hub of the system. Three broad categories of control may be distinguished. The central industrial core based on Germany was to be brought under unified control by incorporating into the Reich the following territories: Alsace-Lorraine, Luxembourg, the Protectorate of Bohemia and Moravia, Polish Upper Silesia and Austria. These were regions primarily of heavy industry essential both to the German war effort and to the fulfilment of the long-term objective of making Germany the industrial heart of Europe. The second group comprised what were termed the 'colonial' territories: the General Government of Poland, the Baltic States and the occupied parts of the USSR and south-eastern Europe. Direct control of economic activity in these regions was imposed by Germany to ensure that the best possible use was made of their resources and that they produced what the Reich required. The third group of countries, not destined for either incorporation or colonization, included most of the advanced nations of the west, that is Norway, Denmark, Belgium, the Netherlands, France (after complete occupation, from November 1942) and northern Italy (after September 1943). For the most part, the general administration of economic life was left in the hands of the native inhabitants, but Germany exercised considerable influence over what should be produced.

Though long-term plans for the restructuring of Europe, however vaguely conceived, were never abandoned, the New Order failed to take concrete shape during the course of the war. More pressing problems eventually took precedence, though in part some of these, such as the exploitation of non-German territories, might be seen in terms of their eventual place in the new Europe. Thus, apart from the centralization of financial transactions in Berlin and the use of the German Reichsmark as the main unit of settlement within the German-dominated territories, little further progress was made towards the New Order. It retained a shadowy existence, but propaganda on the subject steadily diminished and, by the winter of 1942–3, the German media had lapsed into silence on the subject. This was despite the fact that the new German Empire was far from being a coherent and efficient political and economic machine, consisting as it did of a motley collection of territories acquired in a very unsystematic manner and ruled in different ways. Why therefore did Germany fail to consolidate the hegemony so rapidly achieved between 1938 and 1941 and realize the ambition of a more united and integrated Europe?

There are several possible explanations. For a start, the Nazis never had a very clear idea of what the New Order involved. No complete and comprehensive plan for the restructuring of Europe was ever published, so that the concept remained vague and confused, being based largely on the somewhat conflicting statements of Reich ministers from time to time. Hitler himself was very unclear as to what was involved in creating a new structure for Europe and by the latter half of 1941, with Russia still undefeated and Britain holding out, he felt that the matter should be left in abeyance until the domination of Europe had been completed (Cameron and Stevens, 1973, 41–2, 72–4). Although he envisaged a more self-sufficient Europe after the war, it is doubtful whether his concept of a new Europe ever got much beyond the stage of German domination and ethnic cleansing, that is, ridding Europe of Jews and other undesirables.

Secondly, the speed and success of military conquest outran the regime's plan for a new Europe. As a result of the rapid acquisition of new territories, the Nazi regime became preoccupied by the more immediate task of controlling and administering them. By the time the Reich was in a position to give more thought to the idea of a new Europe, the tide had begun to turn on the battle front. The Russian giant proved more resilient than anticipated and the entry of the United States into the war in 1941 considerably altered the balance of forces. Hitler was now faced with a long war of attrition requiring total mobilization and the full exploitation of European resources. This meant a struggle for survival involving a shift to more immediate objectives and abandonment of long-term planning for the future of Europe.

Thus, once the war turned against Hitler and Germany was faced with a long and costly war, the focus of attention inevitably turned towards making the most of her conquests to service the war machine, and so the question of the New Order naturally faded into the background. The urgency was all the more acute given the fact that Germany's domestic economy was performing badly under Goering (Overy, 1984, 138). The lack of coordinated planning, the multiplication of controlling agencies and frequent quarrels and boundary disputes between different agencies and between party and state were not the only factors explaining the failure of the economy to produce in quantity during the period 1939–42 (Kaldor, 1945–6, 33–4, 52). The fact is that Hitler had not anticipated a full-scale war until much later and hence, while the economy could service the successive lightning campaigns, it was not in a position to produce enough to defeat either Britain or the USSR (Overy, 1982, 273, 280–90; Harrison, 1988, 173). Furthermore, Hitler's reluctance to contemplate a drastic cut in domestic consumption and his prevarication over sanctioning total mobilization, at least until the winter of 1942–43, added further pressure to complement domestic resources from outside Germany. By then, the German war economy and major cities were the subject of disruptive and destructive Allied bomber raids. Accordingly, the exploitation of the resources of the occupied territories became a matter of high priority once the Blitzkrieg economy was found to be wanting. They were to be plundered mercilessly and inefficiently, to the detriment of their citizens: 'Like a gigantic pump, the German Reich sucked in Europe's resources and working population' (Kulischer, 1948, 264). There was no systematic plan of extraction; it was more like a 'gigantic looting operation' with 'little that was new and less that was orderly in the "New Order"' (Milward, 1965, 48–9, 52).

While the exploitation of the occupied territories may have been inefficient and inhumane, it did nevertheless yield substantial increments to Germany's domestic resource base. In fact, after 1939, much of the increase in the product available to Germany came from foreign contributions, including foreign labour in Germany which accounted for about a fifth of the civilian labour force in the later stages of the war – a total of some 8 million foreign workers (excluding Alsace-Lorraine and the Sudetenland) at the peak in 1944 (Kulischer, 1948, 264). Foreign contributions and levies accounted for about 14 per cent of Germany's domestic product between 1940 and 1944, and if we include the contribution of foreign labour the total addition to domestic resources was around one-quarter. Albert Speer reckoned that, through to the summer of 1944, some 25–30 per cent of Germany's war production was provided by the occupied territories, including Italy, though it is more than likely that he overestimated the latter's contribution.

Finally, racial priorities intervened to cloud the issue. As Mazower (1996, 51) notes, 'racial ideology prevailed over economic rationality'. Even so, though the New Order failed to take clear shape, it may have provided a convenient smokescreen for 'legitimizing' the more extreme ideological beliefs of the Nazi regime, possibly to its own detriment since it ultimately alienated so many peoples (Rothschild, 1989, 26). That apart, much time and energy went into running the gigantic ethnic cleansing programme involving the movement, resettlement and extermination of millions of people, together with the construction of a vast network of concentration and extermination camps, work camps and other ghettos of one sort or another throughout Europe.

Had the Third Reich survived, it is doubtful whether the contemplated post-war New Order for Europe would have produced an integrated Europe on the basis of an equality of nations. From all the statements made on the subject, it seems clear that the main objective was to restructure Europe in the interests of Germany. However, the question is an academic one. During hostilities the New Order fell foul of practical necessity and racial idealism. Instead of creating a new Europe, Hitler eventually left the continent in ruins, bombed, pillaged, exploited, destitute and divided, with output in 1945 but a fraction of that before the war, weaker than it had been in 1918, and at the mercy of two superpowers. The post-war outlook appeared bleak but, as we shall see in the next chapter, the outcome was far different.

FIN DE SIÈCLE

Though it may be convenient to explain the disintegration of Europe as essentially the product of war, depression and the machinations of a power-mad German, it is tempting to speculate what would have happened had these events not occurred. Almost certainly, things would not have remained the same. Europe could not have maintained her nineteenth-century predominance indefinitely. Towards the end of the century, changes were taking place in Europe and the wider world which could only betoken a shift in the distribution of power. Perceptive eyes could detect the winds of change. As noted earlier, Sir John Seeley (1883, 87–8, 181, 334, 349–50) had foreshadowed the eventual decline of Europe west of the Pripet Marshes and the rise of the two superpowers, the United States and Russia. Two decades later, Cunningham (1904, 228) was musing on the implications of the spread of industrialization across the globe.

All this was heady stuff at a time when Europe's world status still seemed impregnable and when the stability of the European system remained largely intact. But a little scratching under the surface reveals some disquieting features which suggest that Europe's political and economic future were far from secure.

To inter-war minds, the decades prior to 1914 could not fail to kindle nostalgia. Economically, it was a period of steady and stable growth in a world becoming ever more integrated under the banner of the gold standard, and which was less trammelled by restrictions on economic activity and intercourse than either before or since. It is not surprising, therefore, that after 1918 there was every hope of resurrecting the old economic order. In fact, however, the pre-war international economic system was far less robust and stable than many imagined. As Keynes (1920, 1) explained:

> Very few of us realise with conviction the intensely unusual, unstable, complicated, unreliable, temporary nature of the economic organization by which Western Europe has lived for the last half century. We assume some of the most peculiar and temporary of our late advantages as natural, permanent, and to be depended on, and we lay our plans accordingly.

Even the great bastion of the liberal economic order, the gold standard, essentially a European creation, was far from perfect and contained inherent weaknesses. However sacrosanct it may have appeared to post-war statesmen, the fact is that even in its heyday it had never worked as smoothly or as automatically as many were wont to make out. But conventional wisdom apart, there is reason to believe that its foundations were becoming less secure before 1914. De Cecco (1984, 118–22) reckoned that it was being increasingly weakened by recurrent crises, by the declining ability of Britain to exercise hegemony in the international money markets because of the challenge of other financial centres, especially Paris and Berlin, and as a result of the scramble for gold by New York, Paris and Berlin to the detriment of the Bank of England, which had to make do with a very slender gold reserve. Similar sentiments have been expressed by Eichengreen (1996, 43) who doubts whether the system could have survived for many more years in its then form, given the challenges it had to face. These included the increasing prospects of a gold shortage, the weakening of Britain's role, political tensions which jeopardized international collaboration, pressure exerted on London by the American financial system, and increasing doubts as to how long a single-minded commitment to external stability and currency convertibility could survive as increasing electoral representation challenged the traditional policy orthodoxy.

Meanwhile, Europe's dominion was under threat well before the First World War. America obviously posed the most serious challenge, with Japan a longer-term threat in the eastern hemisphere. Incipient industrialization in many less developed lands along the periphery was also a potent reminder that they would not always be prepared to service the metropolitan economies. And for good measure, there was the development gap in Europe itself, between the advanced north-west, on the one hand, and the poorer countries to the south and east, on the other. This posed a threat to European unity as national aspirations grew stronger over time.

In fact, it was the latter which proved the most damaging to European integrity. There is reason to believe that Europe's political system would not have stood the test of time. The trust and collaboration among the great powers which had helped to maintain the balance of power in Europe were showing signs of strain by the turn of the century, while the growing disparity between the developed and underdeveloped regions of the continent was becoming increasingly apparent (Hinsley, 1967, 27). The weak link in the chain was the Austro-Hungarian Empire. This was probably more a political than an economic failure. In fact, Good (1984, 4, 256) makes the ingenious suggestion that political failure could well have stemmed from growing economic success. Political institutions were not adapted to accommodate the pressures and challenges thrown up by new social classes and interest groups arising from economic growth and change, with the result that the dual monarchy could not contain the forces of nationalism generated by the 'hodge-podge' of nationalities within the empire, whose combined populations exceeded that of the two principal components. The inability to satisfy the aspirations of diverse ethnic groups and to quell sectional conflict and national rivalry meant that it was only a matter of time before the empire was undermined from within. Hayes (1960, 107) describes the situation as follows:

> Each of the Empire's numerous peoples had come to cherish a distinctive cultural nationalism, which was supplemented and fortified by some degree of political nationalism. In the circumstances it seemed inevitable that sooner or later the empire must disintegrate and be replaced, as in western Europe, by a congeries of national states.

Domestic upheaval revealed the weaknesses of the monarchy and left it exposed on the external front *vis-à-vis* stronger foreign powers. By the turn of the century, the Austro-Hungarian Empire was taking over the mantle of the sick man of Europe and the subsequent Balkan wars effectively marked its eclipse as a great power (Taylor, 1948, 228–9; Kann, 1974, ch. 8).

CONCLUSION

During the transwar period Europe was eclipsed from her former dominant role in world development. She was no longer the bountiful provider of capital and people to the rest of the world, she could no longer lay claim to new territory across the globe, and she could no longer aspire to influence the course of international development in the way she once had at a time when she was fighting in a hostile world for her own survival. The once global champion became distinctly inward-looking, especially from the late 1920s onwards. When hostilities finally ceased in 1945, the continent was even more destitute than it had been at the end of the First World War and it looked as though closing time had finally come to the gardens of Europe. Few people at the time could have anticipated her dramatic recovery in the post-war years which are the subject of the next chapter.

BIBLIOGRAPHY

Aldcroft, D.H. and S. Morewood (1995), *Economic Change in Eastern Europe since 1918*, Aldershot: Edward Elgar.

Aldcroft, D. H. and M.J. Oliver, (1998), *Exchange Rate Regimes in the Twentieth Century*, Cheltenham, UK and Lyme, US: Edward Elgar.

Alesina, A. and A. Drazen (1991), 'Why are stabilizations delayed?', *American Economic Review*, 81.

Arndt, H. W. (1944), *The Economic Lessons of the Nineteen-thirties*, London: Oxford University Press.

Artaud, D. (1973), *La reconstruction de l'Europe (1919–1929)*, Paris: Presses Universitaires de France.

Balderston, T. (1982), 'The origins of economic instability in Germany 1924–1930: market forces versus economic policy', *Vierteljahrschrift für Sozial- und Wirtschaftsgeschichte*, 69.

Balderston, T. (1983), 'The beginnings of the depression in Germany, 1927–33: investment and the capital market', *Economic History Review*, 36.

Balderston, T. (1994), 'The banks and the gold standard in the German financial crisis of 1931', *Financial History*, 1.

Barraclough, G. (1964), *An Introduction to Contemporary History*, London: C. A. Watts.

Basch, A. (1944), *The Danube Basin and the German Economic Sphere*, London: Kegan Paul, Trench, Trubner.

Bideleux, R. and I. Jeffries (1998), *A History of Eastern Europe: Crisis and Change*, London: Routledge.

Birdsall, P. (1941), *Versailles Twenty Years After*, London: Allen & Unwin.

Bonnell, A.T. (1940), *German Control over International Economic Relations 1930–1940*, Urbana, IL: University of Illinois Press.

Bordo, M.D. and H. Rockoff (1996), 'The gold standard as a "good housekeeping seal of approval"', *Journal of Economic History*, 56.

Boyce, R. (1989), 'World war, world depression: some economic origins of the Second World War', in R. Boyce and E.M. Robertson (eds), *Paths to War: New Essays on the Origins of the Second World War*, London: Macmillan.

Bretton, H.L. (1953), *Stresemann and the Revision of Versailles*, Stanford: Stanford University Press.

Bridge, F.R. and R. Bullen (1980), *The Great Powers and the European States System*, London: Longman.

Briggs, A. (1968), 'The world economy: interdependence and planning', in C. L. Mowat (ed.), *The Shifting Balance of World Forces 1898–1945*, Cambridge: Cambridge University Press.

Butler, H. (1941), *The Lost Peace: A Personal Impression*, London: Faber & Faber.

Calic, M.J. (1994), *Sozialgeschichte Serbiens 1815–1941*, Munich: R. Oldenbourg Verlag.

Cameron, N. and R.H. Stevens (eds) (1973), *Hitler's Table Talk 1941–1944: His Private Conversations*, London: Weidenfeld & Nicolson.

Cardosa. E.A. and R. Dornbusch (1989), 'Brazilian debt crises: past and present', in B. Eichengreen and P. Lindert (eds), *The International Debt Crisis in Historical Perspective*, Cambridge, MA: MIT Press.

Carr, E.H. (1942), *Conditions of Peace*, London: Macmillan.

Carr, E.H. (1947), *International Relations between the Two World Wars (1919–1939)*, London: Macmillan.

Carsten, F.L. (1986), *The First Austrian Republic 1918–1938: A Study Based on British and Austrian Documents*, Aldershot: Gower.

Child, C.J. (1954), 'The concept of the New Order', in A. Toynbee and V.M. Toynbee (eds), *Survey of International Affairs, 1939–1946*, London: Oxford University Press.

Cobban, A. (1944), *National Self-determination*, London: Oxford University Press.

Condliffe, J.B. (1941), *The Reconstruction of World Trade*, London: Allen & Unwin.

Corner, D.C. (1956), 'Exports and the British trade cycle: 1929', *The Manchester School*, 26.

Costigliola, F. (1976), 'The United States and the reconstruction of Germany in the 1920s', *Business History Review*, 50.

Cunningham (1904), *An Essay on Western Civilization in its Economic Aspects*, Cambridge: Cambridge University Press.

Dam, K.W. (1982), *The Rules of the Game: Reform and Evolution in the International Monetary System*, Chicago: University of Chicago Press.

Davies, N. (1997), *Europe: A History*, London: Pimlico.

De Cecco, M. (1984), *The International Gold Standard: Money and Empire*, London: Frances Pinter.

De Cecco (1995), 'Central bank cooperation in the interwar period: a view from the periphery', in J. Reis (ed.), *International Monetary Systems in Historical Perspective*, Basingstoke: Macmillan.

Drabek, Z. (1985), 'Foreign trade performance and policy', in M.C. Kaser and E.A. Radice (eds), *The Economic History of Eastern Europe, 1919–1975, Vol. I, Economic Structure and Performance between the Wars*, Oxford: Oxford University Press.

Eichengreen, B. (1989), 'Hegemonic stability theories of the international monetary system', in R.N. Cooper, B. Eichengreen, C.R. Henning, G. Holtham and R. Putnum (eds), *Can Nations Agree? Issues in International Economic Cooperation*, Washington, DC: The Brookings Institution.

Eichengreen, B. (1996), *Globalizing Capital: A History of the International Monetary System*, Princeton: Princeton University Press.

Eichengreen, B. and D.A, Irwin (1995), 'Trade blocs, currency blocs and the reorientation of world trade in the 1930s', *Journal of International Economics*, 38.

Einzig, P. (1938), *Bloodless Invasion: German Economic Penetration into the Danubian States and the Balkans*, London: Duckworth.

Einzig, P. (1941) 'Hitler's "New Order" in theory and practice', *Economic Journal*, 51.

Ellis, H.S. (1941), *Exchange Control in Central Europe*, Cambridge, MA: Havard University Press.

Ellsworth, P.T. (1964), *The International Economy*, 3rd edn, New York: Macmillan.

Fink, C. (1984), *The Genoa Conference: European Diplomacy 1921–1922*, Chapel Hill: University of North Carolina Press.

Fleisig, H.W. (1975), *Long-term Capital Flows and the Great Depression: The Role of the United States, 1927–1933*, New York: Arno Press.

Flood, C.B. (1989), *Hitler: The Path to Power*, Boston: Houghton Mifflin.

Foreman-Peck, J., A.G. Hallett and Y. Ma (1996), 'Optimum international policies for the world depression 1919–1933', *Economies et Sociétés*, 22.

Friedman, P. (1974), *Impact of Trade Destruction on National Incomes: A Study of Europe, 1924–1938*, Gainsville: University Presses of Florida.

Friedman, P. (1978), 'An econometric model of national income, commercial policy and the level of international trade: the open economies of Europe, 1924–1938', *Journal of Economic History*, 38.

Gathorne-Hardy, G.M. (1950), *A Short History of International Affairs, 1920–1939*, 4th edn, London: Oxford University Press.

Goldstein, E. (1997), 'The British official mind and Europe', *Diplomacy & Statecraft*, 8.

Good, D.F. (1984), *The Economic Rise of the Habsburg Empire, 1750–1914*, Berkeley, CA: University of California Press.

Griffiths, R.T. (1989), 'The economic disintegration of Europe: trade and protection in the 1930s', *European University Institute Colloquium Papers*, 138/89.

Grossman, R.S. (1994), 'The shoe that didn't drop: explaining banking stability during the Great Depression', *Journal of Economic History*, 54.

Guillebaud, G.W. (1940), 'Hitler's New Economic Order for Europe', *Economic Journal*, 40.

Hamilton, J. D. (1988), 'The role of the international gold standard in propagating the Great Depression', *Contemporary Policy Issues*, 6.

Harrison, M. (1988), 'Resource mobilisation for World War II: the USA, UK, USSR, and Germany, 1938–1945', *Economic History Review*, 41.

Harvey, P. (1954a), 'Finance', in A. Toynbee and V. M. Toynbee (eds), *Survey of International Affairs, 1939–1946*, London: Oxford University Press.

Harvey, P. (1954b), 'The planning of the New Order in Europe', in A. Toynbee and V.M. Toynbee (eds), *Survey of International Affairs, 1939–1946*, London: Oxford University Press.

Hayes, C.J.H. (1960), *Nationalism: A Religion*, New York: Macmillan.

Henig, R. (ed.) (1973), *The League of Nations*, Edinburgh: Oliver & Boyd.

Henig, R. (1995), *Versailles and After 1919–1933*, London: Routledge.

Hiden, J. (1977), *Germany and Europe 1919–1939*, London: Longman.

Hillman, H.C. (1952), 'Comparative strength of the great powers', in A. Toynbee and F.T. Ashton-Gwatkin (eds), *Survey of International Affairs 1939–1946: The World in March 1939*, London: Oxford University Press.

Hinsley, F.H. (1967), *Power and the Pursuit of Peace*, Cambridge: Cambridge University Press.

Hobsbawm, E. (1994), *Age of Extremes: The Short Twentieth Century 1914–1991*, London: Michael Joseph.

Hofman, J. (1977), *Economic Nationalism and Development: Central and Eastern Europe between the Two World Wars*, Boulder, CO: Westview Press.

Hogan, M.J. (1975), 'The United States and the problem of international economic control: American attitudes toward European reconstruction, 1918–1920', *Pacific Historical Review*, 44.

Hoptner, J.B. (1962), *Yugoslavia in Crisis, 1934–1941*, New York: Columbia University Press.

Jacobson, J. (1983), 'Is there a new international history of the 1920s?', *American Historical Review*, 88.

James, H. (1986), *The German Slump: Politics and Economics 1924–1936*, Oxford: Clarendon Press.

James, H. (1993), 'Innovation and conservatism in economic recovery: the alleged Nazi recovery of the 1930s', in W.R. Garside (ed.), *Capitalism in Crisis: International Responses to the Great Depression*, London: Pinter Publishers.

Jones, F. Elwyn (1937), *Hitler's Drive to the East*, London: Gollancz.

Jordan, W.M. (1943), *Great Britain, France and the German Problem, 1918–1939*, London: Oxford University Press.

Jorgensen, E. and J. Sachs (1989), 'Default and renegotiation of Latin American bonds in the interwar period', in B. Eichengreen and P. Lindert (eds), *The International Debt Crisis in Historical Perspective*, Cambridge, MA: MIT Press.

Kaiser, D.E. (1980), *Economic Diplomacy and the Origins of the Second World War: Germany, Britain, France and Eastern Europe, 1930–1939*, Princeton: Princeton University Press.

Kaldor, N. (1945–6), 'The German war economy', *The Review of Economic Studies*, 13.

Kann, R.A. (1974), *A History of the Habsburg Empire 1526–1918*, Berkeley: University of California Press.

Kemmerer, E.W. (1944), *Gold and the Gold Standard*, New York: McGraw-Hill Book Company.

Kennedy, P. (1988), *The Rise and Fall of the Great Powers: Economic Change and Military Conflict 1500 to 2000*, London: Unwin Hyman.

Kershaw, I. (ed.) (1990), *Weimar: Why did Germany Democracy Fail?*, London: Weidenfeld & Nicolson.

Keyder, C. (1981), *The Definition of a Peripheral Economy: Turkey 1923–29*, Cambridge: Cambridge University Press.

Keynes, J.M. (1920), *The Economic Consequences of the Peace*, London: Macmillan.

Killick, J. (1997), *The United States and European Reconstruction 1945–1960*, Edinburgh: Keele University Press.

Kindleberger, C.P. (1973), *The World in Depression 1929–1939*, London: Allen Lane, The Penguin Press.

Kiraly, B.K., P. Pastor and I. Sanders (eds) (1982), *War and Society in East Central Europe, Vol. VI, Essays on World War I: Total War and Peacemaking, a Case Study of Trianon*, New York: Brooklyn College Press.

Klein-Ahlbrandt, W.L. (1995), *The Burden of Victory: France, Britain and the Enforcement of the Versailles Peace, 1919–1925*, New York: University Press of America.

Kooker, J. (1976), 'French financial diplomacy: the interwar years', in B.M. Rowland (ed.), *Balance of Power or Hegemony: The Interwar Monetary System*, New York: New York University Press.

Kulischer, E.M. (1948), *Europe on the Move: War and Population Changes, 1917–1947*, New York: Columbia University Press.

Landes, D.S. (1969), *The Unbound Prometheus: Technological Change and Industrial Development in Western Europe from 1750 to the Present*, Cambridge: Cambridge University Press.

League of Nations (1939), *World Economic Survey 1938/39*, Geneva: League of Nations.

League of Nations (1942a), *Commercial Policy in the Inter-war Period*, Geneva: League of Nations.

League of Nations (1942b), *The Network of World Trade*, Geneva: League of Nations.

League of Nations (1943a), *Agricultural Production in Continental Europe during the 1914–18 War and the Reconstruction Period*, Geneva: League of Nations.

League of Nations (1943b), *Europe's Overseas Needs 1919–1920 and How They Were Met*, Geneva: League of Nations.

League of Nations (1943c), *Relief Deliveries and Relief Loans 1919–1923*, Geneva: League of Nations.

League of Nations (1943d), *The Transition from War to Peace Economy: Report of the Delegation on Economic Depressions*, Part I, Geneva: League of Nations.

League of Nations (1944), *International Currency Experience: Lessons of the Inter-war Period*, Geneva: League of Nations.

League of Nations (1945), *Industrialization and Foreign Trade*, Geneva: League of Nations

League of Nations (1946a), *Raw Material Problems and Policies*, Geneva: League of Nations.

League of Nations (1946b), *The Course and Control of Inflation: A Review of Monetary Experience in Europe after the First World War*, Geneva: League of Nations.

Lee, S.J. (1987), *The European Dictatorships 1918–1945*, London: Methuen.

Leffler, M.P. (1979), *The Elusive Quest: America's Pursuit of European Stability and French Security, 1919–1933*, Chapel Hill: University of North Carolina Press.

Lentin, A. (1991), *The Versailles Peace Settlement: Peacemaking with Germany*, London: The Historical Association.

Llewellyn, D.T. and J.R. Presley (1995), 'The role of hegemonic arrangements in the evolution of the international monetary system', in J. Reis (ed.), *International Monetary Systems in Historical Perspective*, Basingstoke: Macmillan.

Loveday, A. (1931), *Britain and World Trade*, London: Longmans, Green.

Macartney, C.A. (1939), *The Danube Basin*, Oxford: The Clarendon Press.

Macartney, C.A. (1942), *Problems of the Danube Basin*, Cambridge: Cambridge University Press.

Mantoux, E. (1946), *The Carthaginian Peace or the Economic Consequences of Mr Keynes*, London: Oxford University Press.

Marks, S. (1976), *The Illusion of Peace: International Relations in Europe 1918–1933*, London: Macmillan.

Mazower, M. (1991), *Greece and the Interwar Economic Crisis*, Oxford: Oxford University Press.

Mazower, M. (1996), 'Hitler's New Order', *Diplomacy and Statecraft*, 7.

McDougall, W.A. (1979), 'Political economy versus national sovereignty: French structures for German integration after Versailles', *Journal of Modern History*, 51.

McKinnon, R. 1. (1996), *The Rules of the Game: International Money and Exchange Rates*, Cambridge, MA: MIT Press.

Meltzer, A.H. (1976), 'Monetary and other explanations of the start of the Great Depression', *Journal of Monetary Economics*, 2.

Milward, A.S. (1965), *The German Economy at War*, London: The Athlone Press.

Milward, A.S. (1970), *The New Order and the French Economy*, Oxford: Oxford University Press.

Milward, A.S. (1979), *War, Economy and Society 1939–1945*, Berkeley: University of California Press.

Milward, A.S. (1985), 'The Reichsmark bloc and the international economy', in H.W. Koch (ed.), *Aspects of the Third Reich*, London: Macmillan.

Moggridge, D.E. (1992), *Maynard Keynes; An Economist's Biography*, London: Routledge.

Momtchiloff, N. (1944), *Ten Years of Controlled Trade in South-eastern Europe*, Cambridge: Cambridge University Press.

Mouré, K. (1992), 'The limits to central bank cooperation 1916–36', *Contemporary European History*, 2.

Mowat, R.B. (1923), *The European States System*, London: Oxford University Press.

Munk, F. (1940), *The Economics of Force*, New York: George W. Stewart.

Neal, L. (1979), 'The economics and finance of bilateral clearing agreements: Germany, 1934–8', *Economic History Review*, 32.

Newman, K.J. (1970), *European Democracy between the Wars*, London: Allen & Unwin.

Newman, W.J. (1968), *The Balance of Power in the Interwar Years, 1919–1939*, New York: Random House.

Northedge, F.S. and M.J. Grieve (1971), *A Hundred Years of International Relations*, London: Duckworth.

Nötel, R. (1974), 'International capital movements and finance in Eastern Europe, 1919–1949', *Vierteljahrschrift für Sozial-und Wirtschaftsgeschichte*, 61.

Nötel, R. (1984), 'Money, banking and industry in interwar Austria and Hungary', *Journal of European Economic History*, 13.

Nötel, R. (1986), 'International credit and finance', in M.C. Kaser and E.A. Radice (eds), *The Economic History of Eastern Europe 1919–1975, Vol. II, Interwar Policy, the War and Reconstruction*, Oxford: Oxford University Press.

Orde, A. (1978), *Great Britain and International Security 1920–1926*, London: Royal Historical Society.

Orde, A. (1990), *British Policy and European Reconstruction after the First World War*, Cambridge: Cambridge University Press.

Overy, R.J. (1982), 'Hitler's war and the German economy: a reinterpretation', *Economic History Review*, 35.

Overy, R.J. (1984), *Goering: The 'Iron Man'*, London: Routledge & Kegan Paul.

Overy, R.J. (1989), *The Road to War*, London: Macmillan.

Overy, R.J. (1995), *Why the Allies Won*, London: Jonathan Cape.

Palmer, A. (1970), *The Lands Between: A History of East-Central Europe since the Congress of Vienna*, London: Weidenfeld & Nicolson.

Parker, R.A.C. (1969), *Europe 1919–45*, London: Weidenfeld & Nicolson.

Perman, D. (1962), *The Shaping of the Czechoslovak State: Diplomatic History of the Boundaries of Czechoslovakia 1914–1920*, Leiden: E.J. Brill.

Pigou, A.C. (1920), *Memorandum on Credit, Currency and Exchange Fluctuations*, (paper prepared in connection with the Brussels International Conference at the request of the Secretariat of the League of Nations), Geneva: League of Nations.

Political and Economic Planning (1945), *Economic Development in S.E. Europe*, London: Political and Economic Planning.

Polonsky, A. (1975), *The Little Dictators: The History of Eastern Europe since 1918*, London: Routledge & Kegan Paul.

Ranki, G. (1983), *Economic and Foreign Policy: The Struggle of the Great Powers for the Hegemony of the Danube Valley 1919–1939*, New York: Columbia University Press.

Ranki, G. (1985), 'Problems of southern European economic development (1918–38)', in G. Arrighi (ed.), *Semiperipheral Development: The Politics of Southern Europe in the Twentieth Century*, Beverly Hills, CA: Sage Publications.

Ritschl, A. (1998), 'Reparations transfers, the Borchardt hypothesis and the Great Depression in Germany, 1929–32: a guided tour for hard-headed Keynesians', *European Review of Economic History*, 2.

Ross, G. (1983), *The Great Powers and the Decline of the European States System 1914–1945*, London: Longman.

Rothschild, J. (1974), *East Central Europe between the Two World Wars*, Seattle: University of Washington Press.

Rothschild, J. (1989), *Return to Diversity. A Political History of East Central Europe since World War II*, Oxford: Oxford University Press.

Royal Institute of International Affairs (1933), *Monetary Policy and the Depression*, London: Oxford University Press.

Royal Institute of International Affairs (1939), *South Eastern Europe: A Political and Economic Survey*, London: Oxford University Press.

Sayers, R.S. (1976), *The Bank of England 1891–1944*, 2 vols, Cambridge: Cambridge University Press.

Schlesinger, R. (1945), *Federalism in Central and Eastern Europe*, London: Kegan Paul, Trench, Trubner.

Schubert, A. (1991), *The Credit-Anstalt Crisis of 1931*, Cambridge: Cambridge University Press.

Schuker, S. A. (1988), *American Reparations to Germany 1919–33: Implications for the Third World Debt Crisis*, Princeton: Princeton University Press.

Seeley, J.R. (1883), *The Expansion of England*, London: Macmillan.

Seton-Watson, H. (1945), *Eastern Europe between the Wars 1918–1941*, Cambridge: Cambridge University Press.

Sharp, A. (1991), *The Versailles Settlement: Peacemakers in Paris, 1919*, Basingstoke: Macmillan.

Silverman, D.P. (1982), *Reconstructing Europe after the Great War*, Cambridge: MA: Harvard University Press.

Solomou, S. (1996), *Themes in Macroeconomic History: The UK Economy, 1919–1939*, Cambridge: Cambridge University Press.

Summers, A. and T. Mangold (1987), *The File on the Tsar*, paperback edn, London: Gollancz.

Taylor, A.J.P. (1948), *The Habsburg Monarchy 1809–1918*, London: Hamish Hamilton.

Temin, P. (1971), 'The beginning of the depression in Germany', *Economic History Review*, 24.

Temin, P. (1993), 'Transmission of the Great Depression', *Journal of Economic Perspectives*, 7.

Thomson, D. (1966), *Europe since Napoleon*, Harmondsworth: Penguin.

Toland, J. (1997), *Adolf Hitler*, Ware, Hertfordshire: Wordsworth Editions.

United Nations (1949), *International Capital Movements during the Inter-war Period*, New York: United Nations.

Urquhart, M.C. and K.A.H. Buckley (1965), *Historical Statistics of Canada*, Cambridge: Cambridge University Press.

Virén, M. (1994), 'A note on interest rate policy during the Great Depression', *Journal of European Economic History*, 23.

Voth, H.-J. (1993), 'Wages, investment, and the fate of the Weimar Republic: a long-term perspective', *German History*, 11.

Voth, H.-J. (1995), 'Did high wages or high interest rates bring down the Weimar Republic? A cointegration model of investment in Germany, 1925–1930', *Journal of Economic History*, 55.

Weinberg, G. L. (1969), 'The defeat of Germany in 1918 and the European balance of power', *Central European History*, 2.

Williams, D. (1963), 'The 1931 financial crisis', *Yorkshire Bulletin of Economic and Social Research*, 15.

Woytinsky, W.S. and E.S. Woytinsky (1955), *World Commerce and Governments: Trends and Outlook*, New York: Twentieth Century Fund.

Yates, P.L. (1959), *Forty Years of Foreign Trade*, London: Allen & Unwin.

Young, J. W. (1997), *Britain and the World in the Twentieth Century*, London: Arnold.

Zimmerman, L. J. (1962), 'The distribution of world income, 1860–1960', in E. de Vries (ed.), *Essays on Unbalanced Growth*, The Hague: Mouton.

5. Cold War and Common Market: Europe 1945–1973

Anthony Sutcliffe

APPROACHES TO REVIVAL IN A DIVIDED EUROPE

In 1945, Europe entered on its second post-war revival process in less than 30 years. The main difference from the lengthy and intermittent revival after 1918 was one of political and strategic context. The Europe of Versailles was one of independent countries, which were expected to cooperate through the League of Nations and other international bodies, rather than through military alliances. Post-1945 Europe was divided into two competing groups of countries, alliances in all but name, one dominated by the Soviet Union and its communist (Marxist–Leninist) ideology, and the other influenced by the United States and the free-market theories of capitalism. As early as 1946, Winston Churchill spoke, in a famous speech at Fulton, Missouri, of the coming division of Europe by an 'Iron Curtain'. In 1948, the division was confirmed by the Berlin airlift, the Soviet refusal of Marshall aid and the final creation by the Soviet Union of the Iron Curtain as a fortified barrier to the movement of people and goods between the two opposing camps.

As a result, the economies of the eastern European 'satellite states' – as they soon came to be known – were trapped in the huge but inefficient economic system overseen by the Soviet Union. The main aim of this juggernaut was to build up the strategic strength of the great association of countries now governed or guided from Moscow. Stalin's industrialization and collectivization policy, which began in the Soviet Union in 1928, was applied where appropriate to the satellite countries after 1945. Most were spared full collectivization thanks to Soviet recognition that their peasant agriculture was more productive than Russia's had been, and that peasant opposition would be hard to overcome. Industrialization, however, appealed to all the satellite regimes and provided a firm basis for the indoctrination of the workforce and a modernization strategy designed to create a new 'socialist man'. Heavy industry was stressed, mainly in the interests of strategic strength, and some of the satellites acquired unbalanced economies which became partly dependent on the Soviet Union. At the same time, the emphasis on self-sufficiency in Marxist–Leninist doctrine, as still formally acknowledged in the USSR after 1945, had some influence on development in the eastern satellites and was often an obstacle to economic efficiency.

In 1949, Stalin founded COMECON (Council for Mutual Economic Assistance) which purported to associate the communist economies on equal terms, but in practice it was dominated by the Soviet Union. Notwithstanding the implications of its title, COMECON did little or no planning or coordination for the socialist productive system, except in science, bulk transport networks, the clearing of payments and a few other areas (Pollard, 1997, 100). In general, it provided a helpful environment for the negotiation of bilateral trading agreements between the socialist countries (Reynolds, 1971, 89–90). There was no equivalent of the great array of reconstruction and coordinating institutions which emerged in western Europe after the war, initially and largely under American guidance (see Richards, 1970). COMECON never developed into a socialist equivalent of the European Economic Community (EEC). Eastern economic policies acted mainly to reinforce the military strategy of the Iron Curtain era. Communist Europe did little trade with western Europe and until the late 1960s almost no investment was directed there from the west. Migration and temporary movement across the Iron Curtain, in both directions, was virtually eliminated from 1948. Rates of growth in trade, together with economic growth as a whole, were high in the Soviet system, with the Soviet Union averaging 5 per cent growth in real GDP between 1950 and 1973 (Maddison, 1989, 36). However, the Soviet system had begun from a very low level, and called on massive natural resources which were cheaply available (see Maddison, 1969, 108–30). Labour could be directed much more easily than in western Europe, so that Siberia and other remote areas could be quickly exploited, often at heavy human cost. The rights of the individual were sacrificed and both the standard of living and the quality of life were much lower than in the west throughout our period. Per capita output, meanwhile, would also lag behind that of western Europe. Trade figures were impressive but they were achieved mainly by international exchange within the Soviet system.

Western Europe, meanwhile, secured a strong position within the world of increasingly unrestricted trade and movement created during and after the war by the United States, Britain and their allies (Sutcliffe, 1996, 6–23). The United States, in particular, wanted to avoid the mistakes of the inter-war years and one of its biggest goals was the achievement of high output and full employment on a world scale. Trade, specialization, and a reliable world currency system were fundamental to these objectives. Europe was a crucial participant as the world's biggest continental importer of primary products and an industrialised region second only to the United States. It was a major US aim to integrate the countries of western Europe (and, if possible, eastern Europe too) through trade, investment and, possibly, political institutions, and to help them to expand their trade with America and the rest of the world (Killick, 1997, 180). The phrase 'United Nations', first coined in the United States to describe China and other struggling early victims of Fascism, came to describe all the fighting anti-Axis countries by the end of the war. It was used to suggest a natural transition from strenuous belligerence to peacetime cooperation on a world scale. American organizations brought aid directly to Europe early on, including the United Nations Relief and Rehabilitation Administration (UNRRA), set up as early as 1943, and Government and Relief in Occupied Areas (GARIOA), set up in 1946. Western European states then readily joined the Food and Agriculture Organisation of the United Nations (1944), the International Monetary Fund (1945), the World Bank (1945), the United Nations Organisation (1946) and the 1947 General Agreement on Tariffs and Trade (GATT) (Sutcliffe, 1996, 10–12). Although some of these bodies were more active than others, they created a western European involvement in the organization of the world economy which no country could later give up, or indeed would want to give up.

Although western Europe welcomed this role, which gave it access to the prosperous dollar area, it had to struggle to compete economically with member countries of the dollar area, especially in the early post-war years. The United States and Canada, especially, were economically and technically even more advanced by the end of the war than they had been in 1939, owing to European concentration on armaments production while the United States, thanks to the great size of its economy, had been able to move ahead in the development of consumer goods and other non-war production, much of which had spread to Canada. On the other hand, western Europe had the advantage of trading within a dollar-based capitalist world economy in which industrialization, accelerated by the war, was spreading still further, to countries such as Japan, Australia and Taiwan, while the structure of world trade was being reinforced (Maddison, 1964, 25–7; Stearns, 1993, 87). Crude oil from the Middle East, for instance, was available to western Europe as readily as it was to the United States because British and Dutch oil companies traded there alongside the big American concerns. More generally, the colonial interests of several western European countries helped them to expand their overseas economic links even when their formal colonies began to obtain independence, from the later 1940s. The growth of large business organizations on a world scale, while driven mainly from the United States and the United Kingdom, incorporated western Europe and boosted efficiency there (Stearns, 1993, 87).

Table 5.1 reflects the difficulties faced by western Europe in returning to a peacetime economic footing. The base year of 1938, as the last year of peace, is the one normally adopted for this exercise, even though the continuing effects of the depression still affected output in that year in every country except Germany.

Table 5.1 Manufacturing production in the leading western European countries 1947–50 (100 = 1938)

	1947	1948	1949	1950
UK	115	129	137	151
France	95	108	118	121
Germany	33	50	75	95
Italy	93	96	101	115
Belgium	105	121	122	125
Netherlands	104	113	126	139

Source: Sutcliffe (1996, 24).

Britain was the most powerful economy to emerge from the war in western Europe. Britain's relative lack of damage, US aid, the government-backed export drive and full employment policies produced a relatively smooth transition to a peacetime economy with industrial output over one-half larger than in 1938 by 1950. In 1950, Britain's exports in manufactures made up 24.6 per cent of the world total, only slightly less than the US share of 26.6 per cent (Alford, 1996, 173). At the other end of the scale, West Germany's destruction, disruption and Allied disindustrialization policies meant that a return to 1938 levels of industrial output had not been achieved by 1950, despite a degree of revival, including the beginning of an export drive and the creation of a new currency, from 1948. West Germany's share of world manufactured exports was still only 7.0 per cent in 1950 (ibid.). As potentially the biggest economy in Europe, West Germany's serious disruption was bound to slow down the west European revival. The answer was likely to be extended US help, and/or cooperation among the European countries. The United States, in particular, was concerned about the economic and political implications of the German plight, which were likely to weaken the west European stance in the Cold War. Britain, and even more France, were less concerned, with France even looking forward to absorbing its occupation zone into an enlarged France and in controlling Ruhr output. The United States, for its part, was already looking forward to the day when Western Germany would become the leader of western Europe.

However, in any industrial revival, western Europe had the advantage that it could readily adopt the advanced production methods in the civil sector which had been developed in the United States during the war. The US economy had been big enough to maintain civil consumption at a high level while pursuing the wars against Japan, Germany and Italy, and the US encouragement of western Europe after the war meant that these new techniques were easily made available. The western European countries were able to incorporate many of these advanced American techniques and products, with Marshall aid (see below) acting powerfully to achieve this end between 1948 and 1952. In fact, during these years western Europe set out on a path of technological progress which allowed it progressively to catch up a United States which had constantly outshone it between 1864 and 1945 (Toniolo, 1998, 264–5).

By the early 1950s, most countries in western Europe were moving towards various forms of economic cooperation which would strengthen their trading position, especially in relation to the dollar area. The United States encouraged these moves, notably through its Marshall Plan aid programme (1948–52), partly because it wanted western Europe to develop as a bulwark against the Soviet Union. This bulwark took both military and economic forms. With even Germany transformed from a disarmed, guilty pariah to an informal anti-Soviet barrier from 1948, and a rearmed power from 1955, western Europe took on a world strategic role. NATO, created in 1949, was in effect a west European anti-communist alliance backed by the United States and Canada. This military effort was linked to trade and investment, and also to arms sales, especially by Britain, France and even neutral Sweden. Western European dominions, colonies and bases overseas, notably those of Britain and France, helped sustain this world role.

Western Europe's firm incorporation in the western, capitalist world was a major asset. It helped secure American support in a variety of attractive forms, including an international culture of consumerism and modernism and access to the dollar trading system. American aid, enterprise and investment helped it to move towards a high level of productivity and living standards (though always much lower than in the United States). At first, most of southern Europe lay outside this charmed circle, but by 1973 the region was making good progress in industrialization (except for Greece and Portugal) (Sutcliffe, 1996, 81–96). Nordic

Europe, with its high initial living standards but dependence on primary production, also moved strongly into industrialization (ibid., 75–80).

Inheriting a powerful economic structure from pre-war days, the industrial countries of western Europe, together with the Nordic region, enjoyed the highest living standards in the world after North America and Australia, once the immediate post-war problems had been overcome. Led by Britain and Germany, western Europe became strongly committed to exporting outside Europe from the later 1940s, thus strengthening its national currencies against the US dollar. The main industrial powers (the United Kingdom, West Germany and Belgium), which were joined by France in the 1950s, encouraged development in the rest of western Europe. Germany, in particular, drew in imports of food and consumer goods from elsewhere in western Europe in order to finance its European exports, which were mainly of producer goods. Italian textiles and Danish eggs were among the products which benefited from this exchange, with Italian motors and electrical products encouraged in their turn by the late 1950s. The export of manufactured goods from Italy to the other countries of the south boosted industrialization there in the 1960s. These diffusion processes had been normal in Europe in the nineteenth century (see Pollard, 1981), but had been partially interrupted after 1914. In the new western Europe, with the additional factor of American support, their operation resumed with a continental effect never seen before.

In 1950, western Europe was divided into three great economic regions. The countries with the greatest degree of industrialization were grouped in the north-west: the United Kingdom, West Germany and Belgium. Their industrial prosperity had been based since the nineteenth century on the great swathe of coal reserves which stretched across northern Europe from Ireland to Saxony. The United Kingdom and Belgium, with 47 per cent of their workforces respectively employed in industry, stood out as Europe's (and the world's) most strongly industrialized countries, but western Germany (43 per cent) was in the same class (Maddison, 1989, 134). If national boundaries are set aside, however, we can see that northern France formed part of this north-western industrialised region, while southern Germany was largely excluded from it. Meanwhile, two great bands of countries, to the north and south of western Europe, had economies in which primary production and primary-related services predominated. The Nordic countries (Sweden, Denmark, Norway and Finland), which formed the northern group, enjoyed high living standards in western European terms, mainly because their small populations were sustained by rich natural resources, both on land and in the sea. The southern band of countries (Italy, Spain,

Portugal and Greece), restricted by a poor soil, lack of minerals and a dry climate, suffered low living standards in western European terms. These conditions were in both cases historic, with both groups of countries declining to peripheral status in western Europe since the rise of the North German Hansa in about 1400 and the decline of Italy and Spain from around 1600.

After the war, US dollar trade was even more important to most of these fringe countries than it was to the industrial core. The Nordic countries were less threatened because they did a good deal of trade among themselves and exported a number of primary products such as fish, wood and iron, mainly to the industrial countries of northern Europe. Industrialization in the Nordic countries had accelerated during the war as they supplied Germany and replaced goods normally exported to them by the belligerent countries. After 1945, their links with the big economies of Britain and Germany were a stimulus. In the south, modernization was slow until the 1960s, except in northern Italy. However, the early growth of EEC trade favoured the south as the EEC wanted to bring backward countries there up to European standards.

Eastern Europe, meanwhile, industrialized powerfully under Soviet guidance, but its products were little traded outside the socialist system. Wartime devastation, especially in the German-occupied countries of Czechoslovakia and Poland, took years to repair. Economic recovery of the Soviet system was apparently slower into the 1950s than in the west (allowing for different methods of national accounting in the socialist countries) (Aldcroft, 1993, 172). The loss of population from the German Democratic Republic (DDR) and the slow rate of natural increase there, together with the heavy reparations exacted by the Soviet Union, led to a low rate of economic growth in one of the most industrialized regions of the east, and COMECON's main machinery exporter. There was no big technology gap with the USSR, so that there was little scope in the satellite countries for borrowed productivity gains, and consumer goods production especially was backward. There was also little sign of technology transfers from the west until the end of the 1960s (Aldcroft, 1993, 185). The low level of trade with the west (about one-quarter of the trade of the socialist system was with the west in 1970 (Reynolds, 1971, 881) was probably responsible for this result in large measure, together with the absence of the multinationals which did so much to diffuse innovation in the west. Reforms in the 1960s, designed to promote closer contacts between producers and their export markets, did not apply to the Soviet Union (Pryor, 1973, 245).

This large eastern bloc was almost entirely self-sufficient in goods and services, including oil. Most of its trade took the form of foodstuffs and raw materials traded against machinery and finished consumer goods (Reynolds, 1971, 88). However, its need for hard currency led it to negotiate export agreements with the west which, in the broader context of political and economic strategy, and ideological change, were to the advantage of NATO. Western Europe took some raw materials and a range of cheap consumer imports from the east under these agreements, but their quality was generally low, reflecting the structure of consumption which eastern Europe could sustain in its home markets. A case in point was the bulky, crude 'Leningrad' light meter, which no serious photographer in the west would dream of using until, from the 1970s, it became almost the only independent light meter on the western European market after nearly all western and Japanese cameras had switched to integral metering. Only the Russian television set, and its high-quality programmes, designed as they were to educate, and to while away the long winter hours, surpassed western standards, but there was little export potential, even for television programmes, outside the Soviet system.

Some specialization in advanced technology products, such as East Germany's cameras and Romania's diesel railway engines, was generated within individual countries, but even these products could not compete in modernity and quality outside the Soviet bloc. The rejection of almost all of East German industry by western firms in 1989–91, and Skoda's complete reconstruction by Volkswagen, would later provide embarrassing proof of the weakness of the satellite countries. The standard Wartburg car's three-cylinder engine and rusting bodywork meant that this leading East German producer had trouble selling its quotas when it launched an export drive in the west in the mid-1960s. Within a few years, Wartburg had withdrawn from most of western Europe. The later mass car of the 1970s and 1980s, the Trabant, was scarcely marketed outside East Germany, even in the Soviet system. Inferior technology, lower efficiency and unsophisticated consumers meant that living standards – including even the newest housing built to Stalin and later Khrushchev standards in the 1950s and 1960s – were much lower than in western Europe (Aldcroft, 1993, 184), while barriers to emigration after 1948 discouraged the efficient use of labour. The socialist approach to international trade and payments, even within the Soviet system, made it necessary to build up clumsy systems of bilateral agreements and clearing arrangements (Reynolds, 1971, 85–6). Wasteful use of resources (combined with serious shortages generated by the easy assumptions of the national plans) was endemic in the socialist system and state control over the direction of labour often allowed big increases in output without any productivity gains, or even demand in many cases. Though the most advanced region in the socialist system, the east European satellite group, was not a big exporter, at any rate not until the later 1960s, when it started to seek more hard currency and western investment. Apart from Cuba and the Third World (to which the Soviet system directed 10 per cent of its total exports by 1970 (Reynolds, 1971, 88), little of the world saw much of its products. As Lloyd Reynolds pointed out in 1971, Communist China's trade with the non-socialist countries had expanded by 1970 to two-thirds of its total trade in the aftermath of the 'Sino-Soviet split' a decade earlier (ibid.). This striking proportion hints at the scale of the opportunity which the Soviet system chose to miss.

However, the distorted pattern of east–west trade which built up from the 1950s did something to strengthen links between the two parts of Europe. East European goods which, while usually of a poor quality, were very cheap, could be made subject to import quotas so that they did not undermine western products in their home markets. Imported into western Europe, these goods earned much-needed hard currency for the east. The eastern countries also worked hard from the early 1950s to attract western tourists and their currency (Progressive Tours). Black market trade, which flourished at the end of the war throughout Europe but disappeared in the west in the 1950s, carried on in the east and even expanded there in the 1960s. It was strongest in the communist countries which bordered the Iron Curtain as hard currency was more easily obtained there, and the authorities generally tolerated it.

In the later 1960s, a slight dissolution of the links binding the European communist countries occurred when some of the satellites started to seek loans and trade with western Europe. Most of eastern Europe was now industrialized (see Morewood, Chapter 6 of the present volume). Imports from the west increased, with the encouragement of the Soviet Union from 1971. Poland, which wanted to develop a wider range of industries and modernize traditional ones such as shipbuilding, incurred big western loans and liberalized its society. Western banks saw this as a means of developing the east as a field of investment after the two decades of growth had created a strong economy in the west and a capital surplus. These developments were to mark the beginning of the dissolution of the Soviet system which would culminate in the 1990s as the post-war barriers between the two parts of Europe collapsed. However, from the early 1970s the eastern countries were embarrassed by the decline in the growth rate in the western world and loan repayments caused problems, especially in Poland. The oil crisis in 1973 made these difficulties more acute and the beginnings of the effective integration of east and west were largely postponed into the 1980s.

COOPERATION, INTEGRATION AND PLANNING IN WESTERN EUROPE

The post-war structure and progress of the western world had been the product of careful discussions and planning, with Europe taken fully into account (see Penrose, 1953). As early as 1942, the United States and Britain started to confer about the shape of the post-war world. Britain played a big part as the only western European ally of the United States (apart from the Free French) and the leader of the British Empire and the sterling trading area. Europe was seen as fundamental to this new world, and as the key counterpart of the United States in world affairs. Representatives of the European countries, including those with governments in exile, took part in the creation of the new trading policies and institutions finalized from 1944. The American vision was based on a world of free trade, with the US dollar as the main international currency. The pound sterling was made a reserve currency. The other European currencies did not enjoy reserve status, but Europe was recognized as the main US trading partner and an essential component in the success of the new world system. It was hoped that the new structure would prevent the recurrence of slumps like that of 1929–32, and the generation of political extremism whether of the fascist or the communist variety. Full employment, for instance, was seen as an important means of warding off Soviet propaganda, which always stressed the absence of unemployment under communism. Until 1948 at least, the danger of a communist takeover in western Europe could not be discounted. Fortunately, the danger of a revival of fascism in Germany and Italy quickly proved to be of little consequence, but the communist leadership of the anti-fascist resistance in France, Italy and Greece put the party in a strong position to campaign for reforms after the war (Sutcliffe, 1996, 42).

The revival of the western European economy after the summer of 1945 was a predictable result of the end of hostilities and by 1947 most European countries were absorbing their returnees and generating higher production. However, a growing problem was arising by 1947 from the incorporation of western Europe into the dollar system at a time when most European economies found it hard to earn enough US dollars to pay for the American goods and services which they needed (Sutcliffe, 1996, 15). The total overseas trade deficit of the western European countries in 1947 was 7.4 billion dollars (Aldcroft, 1993, 124). The United States became concerned about a series of dollar crises which would undermine the economy over much of Europe, and possibly set off a political protest which would favour the communists. Their solution, developed by the Secretary of State, George C. Marshall, was to set up a

massive aid programme providing large amounts of US dollars to participating European countries (Killick, 1997, 2–13, 94–103). The first funds
arrived in 1948. It was planned that, by the end of the programme,
member countries would have built up strong economies which no longer
generated dollar deficits.

As most Marshall funds were outright gifts, the normal controls on
repayment could not be used. However, the United States wanted to
make sure that the Marshall money was used effectively to make the
European countries powerful trading partners within the post-war
system. This meant modernizing them so that they could progress
towards US standards. To these ends, the United States required the participating countries to cooperate in planning the distribution and use of
the funds. The main body set up for this purpose was the OEEC
(Organisation of European Economic Cooperation), the coordinating
committee of the countries taking part in the Marshall Plan, which was
founded in 1947. The incorporation of Germany as a full member of the
OEEC encouraged western Europe to look forward to an era of economic cooperation, under American guidance, which would contrast with
the reparation-oriented atmosphere which had done so much harm after
the First World War.

As these arrangements developed in 1947 and 1948, the inclusion of
eastern Europe in the Marshall scheme, which the United States had originally offered, and which some of the eastern satellite countries had
welcomed, was rejected by the Soviet Union. The Russians knew that
American funds and advice would complicate their efforts to create
socialist economies in the newly liberated countries of the east and would
put the creation of the Iron Curtain into reverse. On the contrary, the
limitation of the Marshall Plan to western Europe encouraged the final
closing of the eastern frontier, with the main effect that immigration from
east to west, especially through the divided Germany, came to a virtual
halt. Western investment in eastern Europe came virtually to an end for
many years. In retrospect, the US promotion of the Marshall Plan in
relation to eastern Europe can be seen as an indirect feature of their own
Cold War policy, with Stalin's cooperation never seriously envisaged, but
Stalin at this time was the great negative force, rather than the Americans.
Whatever the line of causation, the exclusion of Marshall funds from
eastern Europe was one of the great milestones in the recent economic
history of Europe, with the communist sector firmly driven onto a stony
path which it would not leave until the late 1980s and early 1990s.

The effect of this separation of eastern and western Europe remains
controversial. If the United States had diverted a generous proportion of
Marshall funds to eastern Europe, the benefits in the west would have

been reduced. It would have been more difficult to achieve an effective concentration of investment funds in the west and cooperative planning would have been weakened. The US Congress would have been unlikely to vote additional funds to replace those directed to the communist countries. As it was, western Europe recognized that there were now no big markets for it in the east, and so turned with even greater vigour to export markets outside Europe, even though it had to face American competition there. Germany, in particular, benefited from this recognition. Focusing its efforts on southern Europe in the early years, it went on to develop world markets in the 1950s. Gradually, Germany, together with Britain's trade with its Commonwealth, drew the whole of western Europe into world exporting. By 1970, many of its products were competing with those of the United States on both price and quality.

The post-war technology gap with the United States proved an advantage to western Europe. With American encouragement, European firms could adopt perfected US processes, together with marketing information which virtually guaranteed their success in Europe. Refrigerators, vacuum cleaners and washing machines, available in the United States but virtually unknown in Europe before the war, now became a universal aspiration. Television, perfected by American engineers between the late 1930s and 1945, quickly spread across most of western Europe in the later 1940s and early 1950s (Sutcliffe, 1996, 147–8). Canned goods also became more common than before the war, allowing tastes for non-European fruits to expand. Coca Cola became the favoured drink of the young after 1945. These transfers from the United States, encouraged by American firms trading in Europe, continued into the 1960s, with frozen foods now more common as Europeans acquired freezers.

The big growth of the west European economy from the early 1950s soon overcame the US dollar shortage, and in this respect the aims of the Marshall Plan were achieved. All the Marshall member countries benefited to some degree from the improved US technology and management techniques which accompanied Marshall aid. By the end of the Marshall programme in 1952, most countries would be well on the way to full employment. Britain and the Nordic countries were even able to combine full employment and generous welfare policies. Germany was well on the way to becoming Europe's leading exporter. Dollars could be earned in trade between the European countries but exporters were encouraged by their governments to aim at the dollar area. The resulting advanced and high-quality products were usually competitive in Europe and could be readily sold in the non-dollar world. Less industrialized countries such as the Netherlands thus became major exporters in advanced products such as chemicals, refined oils and electronics. By the later 1960s, the EEC currencies had become stronger than the US dollar and by 1973 the Bretton Woods system had been undermined. However, the main implications of the decline of the dollar trading system would not become clear until after the first 'oil shock' of 1973. Until then, western Europe continued to produce and trade within the stable world system set up by the United States at the end of the war, and from which it benefited more than any other major region.

GROWING PRODUCTIVITY AND EMPLOYMENT: THE 1950s

These general features and tendencies, however, must not obscure regional variations within western Europe and processes of change through time. The 1950s stand out as the period in which output in western Europe made clear advances over the levels achieved in the late 1930s. At the same time, industrialization remained mainly concentrated in northern Europe, in the coalfield regions where it had come to be located by 1900. Some southward tendency of industrial development was visible by 1960, including parts of southern Germany, France and northern Italy, but the full economic potential of western Europe was far from being fully tapped in spatial terms. In the 1950s, therefore, the economic history of western Europe centres on the established industrial countries.

The leading industrial countries advanced on different growth paths, mainly because they had to react, from very different bases, to the general return to normal trading conditions. However, far from diverging after the war, Britain, Germany and France came to function as fully industrialized countries, with comparable living standards and social services, and a big export sector. This convergence was clearly visible by 1960, but it had progressed further by 1973, with only the relative decline of industrial Britain to detract from it by that time.

Changes through time were also marked by continuity rather than discontinuity and interruptions. Whereas economic shocks and fluctuations in the 1920s and 1930s had prolonged the effects of the First World War, recovery through the late 1940s and growth in the 1950s proceeded on a smooth path. The fluctuations of the business cycle were still detectable but it produced no absolute contractions, and growth proceeded at rates unknown before the war (Table 5.2).

The biggest shock, the outbreak of the Korean War in 1950, proved to be less disturbing than was at first feared, with the European industrial countries able to export military and military-related goods to the United States and other western belligerents such as Britain. Western Europe's

Table 5.2 Annual percentage compound growth rate in GDP 1950–64

	1950–55	1955–60	1960–64
UK	2.9	2.5	3.1
France	4.4	4.8	6.0
Germany	9.1	6.4	5.1
Italy	6.3	5.4	5.5

Source: Alford (1988, 14).

general participation in the Cold War, with Britain as western Europe's biggest military power and West Germany rearming from 1955 at the request of the United States, may have retarded economic growth in the long term, but in the short term it helped secure full employment and encouraged technology in areas such as electronics, fuel controls and jet engines. A trained workforce expanded and the prospect of steady employment increased confidence and security. At constant 1978 prices and exchange rates, the European NATO countries spent a total of US$26 614 million in 1950, and US$71 231 million in 1975, for military purposes (Thee, 1981, 424). This figure tended to fluctuate over the years at between one-half and two-thirds of total US military expenditure. This impressive outlay reinforced western Europe's involvement in world affairs and opened up markets to its armaments. France, which had developed nuclear weapons by 1960 and withdrew from the NATO command structure in 1966, went on to pursue a different path, expanding its exports in arms on the basis that they were independent of US technology. Much valued by neutral and Third World countries, these French weapons exports were linked to an independent overseas policy which secured for France – and indirectly for western Europe – an international respect which echoed that secured by West Germany in the 1950s. However, its anti-American character was something new, suggesting that western Europe might develop as an independent political and strategic force, armed with French and British nuclear weapons. This prospect would be clouded by the resignation of Charles De Gaulle from the presidency of France in 1969, and dispelled by the OPEC (Organization of Petroleum-Exporting Countries) intervention of 1973.

By the mid-1950s, western Europe, having passed through the Korean War, which ended in 1953, was approaching full employment and was beginning to enjoy rising living standards. By this time, post-war fears of a depression similar to that of 1921–2 had largely been dispelled and confidence had grown in the economic control policies linked to John

Maynard Keynes and promoted by the United States since the end of the war. Western European trade with the rest of the world had exceeded pre-war levels by as early as the mid-1950s. The strength and stability of the American economy and the positive effects of the Cold War in terms of its maintenance of European economic cohesion helped to create a feeling of confidence in western Europe.

Germany

The most important economies in the 1950s, as before the war, were West Germany and Britain. The two countries were very similar, as were their economies. West Germany emerged from its post-war readjustments as a country that was slightly smaller than Britain in terms of population (1950: 49 983 000 as against 50 363 000), with a similar area. West Germany, mainly at the demand of the Soviet Union, lost a good deal of territory after the war and German refugees (*Volksdeutsche*) from these lands flooded into the four Allied zones which made up the new Germany. It soon became clear, however, that the Soviet zone, to the east, would develop under communist control, so that the German territorial presence in western Europe would be limited to about half its pre-war area, at about 250 000 square kilometres. The economic effect of these changes was, however, much less disastrous than might have appeared likely in 1945. Most of the German refugees selected West Germany between 1945 and 1948, rather than the Soviet zone. By 1948, they totalled 10 million. With little work available in the cities, many went to live on farms, offering labour in return for lodging until the economy began to expand from 1948. Most of the refugees were young and their high birth rate increased demand and then began to enhance the labour force from around 1960. When they moved into the factories they proved hard-working and easy to train.

Existing industrial workers proved equally cooperative. They looked to established local firms to provide them with work. If the firms could meet their needs, they were willing to work long hours for low wages. The Allied reform of German trade unions in the late-1940s reinforced this attitude, with the new industry-wide unions encouraging cooperation between the employers and the workers (Eichengreen, 1993, 27–32). The German educational system, which had flourished during the war as many young people tried to avoid military service by enrolling on courses, attracted numerous students after 1945 owing to high unemployment. Women were numerous among the intake. Linked to industrial training, the schools and colleges produced large numbers of partly qualified people who took jobs as soon as they could.

The German industrial structure, as early as 1900, had leaned towards producer goods which at that time were used to develop domestic manufacturing or were exported largely to eastern Europe. Two wars had strengthened the trend. With great supplies of coal, iron and steel, especially in the Ruhr, Germany was well fitted to turn out the producer goods which most of Europe needed in order to reconstruct, or to expand its own industries. Able to produce very cheaply, Western Germany started to build up big exports to the rest of Europe in areas like railway equipment, tubes, girders and machine tools. In return, Western Germany imported consumer goods, especially from southern Europe. The quality of German producer goods in terms of design and production was so high that Germany created secure markets in Europe. From around 1950, Western Germany started to export powerfully outside Europe. It built up big reserves of sterling and US dollars. This helped it to maintain the value of the Deutschmark, which the Allies had helped create in 1948. With low inflation as a result, Germany was able to increase its exports at a time when Britain, in the later 1950s, was beginning to struggle with the problem of uncompetitive export prices. West Germany's continuing commitment to exports, which became the foundation and the inspiration of its whole economy and national life, meant that over the years 1950–73 its export volume increased at an annual average rate of 12.4 per cent (Maddison, 1989, p. 67). This was the highest rate of any major industrial country in western Europe. Meanwhile, West German living standards overtook those of Britain around 1960, with Germans enjoying a unique product of the war – new housing and bright, new cities.

Britain

Britain – with its allies – had won the war and it suffered much less physical and human damage than Germany. The serious reduction of German output after the war allowed Britain to begin the early years of peace as the leading European economy. With its connections with the United States and the British Empire, its new reputation in Europe as a great liberator and source of democratic ideas, its Bank of England, Lloyds and the Stock Exchange, Britain provided the strongest link between western Europe and the world economy. These connections were not, however, purely economic. Between 1941 and 1945, a special association had existed between the United States and the British Empire, a great maritime alliance linking the Pacific, Atlantic and Indian oceans. In 1945, Britain still had more military bases worldwide than the United States and its developing nuclear capacity seemed likely to make it a continuing world power. With the growing strategic threat of the Soviet Union, Britain could offer the United States its major European foothold, much as it had in the struggle against Hitler. However, all of this effort required heavy outlay. During the war American support had been provided directly by Lend Lease and other schemes. Britain's Lend Lease debt had been written off in 1945, in recognition of its key part in the victory. In peacetime, however, and with a number of NATO states rearming from 1949, Britain did not merit direct US financial support. This meant that Britain's special world role had to be financed out of the vigour of the British economy. But so did the social reforms, often referred to as the 'Welfare State', which were Britain's main social example to the post-war world.

This effort created serious problems. Industrial exports had to be maximized to secure US dollars. At the same time, domestic production, including agriculture, had to be expanded to reduce imports. All this had to be achieved at a time when the British people were seen to need a reward for their wartime efforts. Between 1945 and 1950, the new Labour government managed to achieve the targets which the new strategy required, but in 1951 the new Conservative government reduced Labour's controls in the hope that economic growth would generate the necessary funds. This end was achieved only in part, and at the expense of a higher rate of inflation, and by 1960 Britain was losing competitiveness in relation to many other European countries. Investment was held back and many firms struggled on with old equipment and inflated workforces. With the government still aiming for full employment, wages were much higher than on the continent, and the trade unions were powerful enough to prevent technical innovations unless they were compensated by increases in wages and bonuses, or shorter hours. These problems were reflected in a very low British growth rate: British GDP increased at a rate of only 2.9 per cent between 1950 and 1955, and 2.5 per cent between 1955 and 1960. Throughout these years, Germany and France grew much faster than Britain (Alford, 1988, 14).

Britain, as the world's first industrializer from the mid-eighteenth century, seemed to be moving on to a further stage of maturity in which business enterprise and hard, manual work were no longer the ideal for many people. Most of the best careers were seen to be in the tertiary sector and industry did not attract people of advanced education, whose numbers were being increased by the expansion of education since the Education Act of 1944. Workers were not as grateful for a job as they were in Germany and individual effort was less, with shorter hours worked and task flexibility discouraged by trade union demarcation and craft practices. With a buoyant home market, producers did not always see the need to secure foreign markets, and many of their products such as cars and electrical products were less and less competitive abroad. The

Commonwealth was an easy market and also a conservative one, so some British products survived there long after they were driven out of other foreign markets. This loyalty lasted until non-British products, especially from Germany and Japan, began to penetrate the Commonwealth in the later 1950s.

Few in Britain, however, were fully aware of these threats. In 1960, British living standards were still the highest in Europe (though about to be overtaken by Germany). Britain's consumer boom and leisure culture suggested that all was well. Britain's overseas tertiary activities remained very active and government policy to some extent favoured these activities at the expense of the rest of the economy, for instance by defending the value of the pound sterling. Britain's shipping, insurance, banking, Stock Exchange, cultural output and legal work, in particular, put it ahead of France and Germany (see Cassis, 1997). At the same time, Britain shunned the European trading area which was taking formal shape through the European Coal and Steel Community (ECSC) and the EEC. Some of the effects of these policies would become clearer in the 1960s, and Britain's application to join the EEC in 1961 would begin a long process of reassessment and readjustment culminating in Britain's final admission to the EEC in 1973. Throughout these years, however, the British economy would go through a process of relative decline which reduced her role and influence both in Europe and in relation to the United States.

France

France was one of the countries to benefit from the southward movement of industrialization in western Europe. Here, however, the nationwide potential for industrialization was much greater than in countries such as Italy, owing to the industrial foundations laid there since the nineteenth century. French defence of a strong franc, pursued between the wars at the expense of industrial growth, had led to a widespread national perception during the war that France was economically weak and backward in comparison with Germany, and when Charles De Gaulle both liberated and assumed authority over France in 1944, he moved towards a modernization strategy which would survive all the political fluctuations of the later 1940s and promote a successful industrialization movement from the 1950s. A new German attack was feared more by France than by any other European country except Poland, and modernization, though little visible to the people of France at first, was pushed ahead by civil servants in cooperation with a number of big firms. The leading civil servant was Jean Monnet, a member of De Gaulle's government-in-exile in London during the war. Prompted by De Gaulle, he introduced a directive national plan (Plan Monnet) in 1946 at a time when no other western European country had such a plan or was even seriously considering one.

The Monnet plan sought to coordinate basic production and infrastructural investment by drawing management, government and labour into membership of a number of committees. The result was a series of five-year targets, fixed by the committees in agreement with other committees and Monnet's central secretariat, which could clearly be met, allowing investment and workforce training to proceed in confidence. The first Monnet (four-year) plan was succeeded by others, and economic growth proceeded rapidly. Planned improvement in transport and power networks extended the scope for industrialization to remote areas. With a big surplus of labour on the land, employment could be created right across France's dense network of urban centres. The low birth rate of pre-war days was replaced after 1945 by one of the highest in Europe and it lasted through the 1950s and the 1960s. The national emphasis on conservatism and protection was replaced by a more entrepreneurial attitude. The French colonial empire, with its big native French population, provided a growing market for French exports without generating the commercial complacency seen in Britain. The French drew the native peoples into their own lifestyle so that they were a ready market for French products. The advertising of the ubiquitous French breakfast drink, Banania (slogan: 'ya bon Banania!'), crossed and recrossed so many racial and cultural boundaries that its actual provenance and clientele were completely obscured. In Algeria, substantial oil reserves were developed from the 1950s, to compensate in part for France's lack of coal. To the same end, a nuclear power programme was developed in France. This modernization process was not yet complete by 1960 but France was well on the way to becoming the third great industrial power of western Europe.

Italy

While France moved into a national process of modernization, southern Europe remained largely untouched in the 1950s. The exception was Italy, which went into a partial modernization process affecting the north of the country in the 1950s. Deprived of its colonies by the Allies at the end of the war, it was helped by the United States because of its strategic position in the Mediterranean and the danger of the spread of communism (Sutcliffe, 1996, 84–5). With Britain and France (which traditionally had an interest in Italy) impoverished by the war and unable to pump funds and expertise into the country, the United States became the main modernizing force, as they had been in the US Zone in Germany and as they would be in Greece. At first, however, the United States found it hard to divert funds for economic modernization to Italy owing to the unexpected British withdrawal from that area, and they were disturbed by the Italian inability to develop mass markets and to develop exports, even in their traditional area of cotton textiles. However, the United States was able to develop political stability in a country in some disorder after the war, and Italy had a chance to develop modernization policies in which civil servants played a part, much as in France. State intervention in industry, even using fascist institutions, policies and attitudes, was retained in the interests of directing effort into dollar-earning export industries, of which cotton textiles was at first the main example. Eventually, its low production costs, and its emphasis on consumer goods using methods and equipment derived largely from the American example, allowed it to build up a big export trade (Harper, 1986, 1, 8–9).

By 1948, worried by the Cold War, the United States at last decided to allocate funds to promote the Italian economy and especially to develop export industries. Some of these earned US dollars directly, while other exports, to Europe, could also be paid for partly in US dollars by countries which exported to the dollar area. Marshall aid was only part of this process. However, Marshall aid made a bigger impact on industry in Italy from 1948 than in any other European country. Some of it was used to promote social education policies, especially in rural areas, which undermined the negative forces of tradition and encouraged people to look outward and forward. Elections in 1948 produced a centrist government, favourable to reform and the American connection, and governments of this tendency would last until the early 1960s. The government reduced price controls and other controls over the economy inherited from the fascist and war years. However, this modernization was largely limited to the north of Italy. The Mezzogiorno, south of Naples, remained a backward, rural area. Nevertheless, the reforms drew Italy into the developing European structures such as NATO and the ECSC. This transition from Mare Nostra to European integration at a time of rapid development was an outstanding formula for progress. Italy's success would be an example for the modernization of the whole of southern Europe by the 1960s.

Much of the growth of output in Italy was caused by domestic consumption. Italians were traditionally reluctant to buy products which they could make for themselves, repair, or do without. Government plans encouraged these home market products at the same time as they boosted exports. It was partly a question of encouraging firms to produce the right products, many of which were aimed at housewives (for example, refrigerators) and young men (for example, motor scooters), but it transpired that, once developed to an easily serviceable standard, these could be exported, not to the United States, where standards were much higher, but elsewhere in Europe, especially to the rest of the south.

The South

Meanwhile, Spain, Portugal and Greece saw very little development in the 1950s. Portugal, which had retained a colonial empire, tried to draw on it for economic strength, but the effect of this policy was to weaken its efforts at home. Unlike the French Empire, it did not contribute to European economic growth and it did not foster democracy and enterprise in the colonies. Spain, still under Fascist control, pursued development along Italian lines with big national companies and development institutes but these made only pinpricks in an economy held down by a small-scale, unproductive agriculture. Greece, the main European victim of the spread of communism, was paralysed by a civil war between 1947 and 1949, while its unproductive terrain and shortage of large cities discouraged development in the 1950s. However, some of the foundations were being laid through cultural change for development in the 1960s.

DECOLONIZATION AND IMMIGRATION

As western Europe became part of a single western alliance, its role as an imperial modernizer of some of the more backward parts of the world came largely to an end. Japan's colonial aspirations in the Pacific and the Indies had been aroused by the presence there of the Americans, the British and the Dutch. The United States knew that the British and the Dutch, at least, could not revive their colonies adequately after the war and that their presence would weaken the Allied presence in the Third World. They therefore advised the European imperial countries to liberate their non-European colonies. Apart from France, which declined to act immediately, progress towards independence was made quickly. The European countries soon found that they could maintain and enhance their economic links with their former colonies, which weakened any reluctance which they might have had in ceding independence. Japanese overseas territories, meanwhile, including those of long standing like Korea, were liberated and any influence on them came from the United States and, later, Japan itself, not Europe.

Western Europe's role in the world economy was not greatly affected by decolonization, at any rate in the 1950s and 1960s. The trading links of the ex-colonies remained focused on the colonizing countries and investment still came mainly from Europe. Where the newly independent colonies were successful economically, as was the case at first in Ghana, the home countries benefited. France, which had always sought to turn its colonies into cultural extensions of the homeland, made an even greater effort after 1945, to prove to the the United States that its defeat by Germany had made a case for integrated overseas territories, capable of keeping France going worldwide in a future war. French investment, and the emigration of qualified and business people from the homeland, helped build up a French overseas trading network in Africa, the Caribbean and the Far East. Young colonial residents were encouraged to study in France, and they took home tastes and practices which helped French exports. The surviving French Empire, which was not decolonized until 1958 and after, thus retained even closer links with Europe than the ex-colonial empires.

There was a price to pay, however. France was involved in two big colonial wars, first in Indochina where the French were finally expelled in 1954, and then in Algeria, which gained independence in 1962. The war in Algeria, which France had been treating as a home territory, slowed down economic development there. However, by the later 1960s, Algeria was closely linked to France, owing especially to the exploitation of Algerian oil by the French ELF company. Indeed, by 1973, across all the former empires, European and world economic growth had helped most of the former colonies to develop and their links with Europe had expanded.

One condition of the decolonization process after 1945 was that the ex-colonial people should be allowed to live and work in their 'home' country in Europe. This condition was designed to allay fears that the departure of the colonial power might lead to a slump in the ex-colony. With the United States still taking few European immigrants, as before the war, the nineteenth-century pattern of heavy emigration from Europe was now replaced by an inward movement of non-European people. This flow became pronounced in industrial Europe in the mid-1950s (see Van der Wee, 1987, 160–62). Underpopulated dominions such as Britain's Australia still attracted white immigrants but the net flow, beginning in Britain as early as the late 1940s, was towards western Europe. With so few Europeans crossing the Iron Curtain from the east after 1948, the composition of the industrial population in northern Europe was moving towards a significant non-white, non-European basis by the 1960s.

In the nineteenth century, mothers, sweethearts and siblings had written letters to their friends and relations in the empires. From the 1950s, post offices in the overcrowded city districts favoured by the non-white immigrants were blocked by queues of people waiting to send letters, packets and postal orders to their 'home' in the Third World. Meanwhile, European governments found that their dealings with the newly independent territories, which were enhanced by aid and efforts to secure trade advantages, formed a large part of their links with the international economy.

Germany, with no empire of recent vintage or great size, and its sources of labour in eastern Europe blocked off, began in the 1950s to import labour on a large scale. At first it drew on southern Europe – especially Spain, Italy and, later, Greece – workers for who could travel independently, were happy to return home at the end of their contracts, and posed few problems of cultural assimilation. In the 1960s, however, it started to draw heavily on Turkey and Iran. Table 5.3 shows the uninterrupted progress in the number of foreigners with jobs in Germany.

Table 5.3 Total foreign workers in West Germany, and percentage of the total workforce 1954–71

Year	Total	Percentage
1954	72 906	0.4
1960	279 390	1.3
1965	1 164 364	5.5
1970	1 838 859	8.5
1971	2 163 766	10.0

Source: Sutcliffe (1966, 188).

The Moslem workers from Turkey and Iran were especially difficult to absorb. In the 1960s, many of them were offered unlimited residence or were allowed to bring their families into Germany, together with other non-European workers. Germany thus became an extreme example of the Third World transplant experienced by the industrial nations of northern Europe.

The influx raised problems of integration and social conditions. Most immigrants were uneducated and unskilled and could secure only unskilled manual jobs. Their low pay limited them to degraded housing in the older, crowded areas of the cities. In France, the multiple hostilities generated by the Algerian war produced a disaffected group of *pieds noirs* (repatriated white settlers from Algeria) and a sullen influx of Arab immigrants to France, seeking work. The Algerians, who came from the land and lacked experience of cities, aroused especial hostility among indigenous French people (Noin and White, 1997, 9). In Germany, the big Moslem influx from the 1960s created a large minority with a Moslem lifestyle and attitudes. Like the Algerians in France, the Moslem workers and their families antagonized the native Germans on cultural grounds. Opposition from white residents created tensions and in the 1960s they began to organize politically.

Europe's international involvement thus came to include a non-European presence which created divisions within European society. If the Soviets and the satellites had allowed immigration into western Europe from the east, many of these cultural and political problems would not have emerged. As it was, Europe acquired a new racial structure which in theory linked it to the non-European world, but in practice the immigrants generated very little foreign trade, even before 1973, as they were so poor. As a low-paid industrial workforce, they helped sustain European growth, but they remained an isolated social force which had done little to broaden western Europe's world social perspective by 1973.

THE EEC AND ITS WIDER IMPLICATIONS

When the Treaty of Rome was signed by 'the Six' – Germany, France, Italy and the three Benelux countries (Belgium, the Netherlands and Luxembourg) – in 1957, one of Europe's greatest historic milestones was set up. It recalled the year 800, when Charlemagne was crowned Holy Roman Emperor. This event, which also took place in Rome, had created an earlier potential for European integration, and the significance of the parallel was not lost on the founders of the EEC. Of course, Charlemagne's physical empire had declined and fragmented after his death in 814, with the idea of a united, Catholic Europe living on mainly in spiritual terms. In 1957, it was by no means clear whether the EEC would develop into an effective European organization, or whether it would stagnate or even decline.

At any rate, the EEC was not expected by its founders to offer rapid development, and this patience was one of its strengths. It was located within a continuum which had begun towards the end of the Second World War, and which had already created a firm basis for economic and political integration through a number of organizations and the confidence of a variety of leading individuals, Jean Monnet, the French civil servant, being the best known to history. Many of these people were fired not so much by economic hopes but by their determination to avoid another war in Europe. Economic cooperation at first was seen as only one way to this end, but by the mid-1950s it was generally seen as the most effective.

The value of economic cooperation lay in the concept of equilibrium and interdependence which could prevent large and powerful countries taking control of others. These ideas went back to the campaigning days of Norman Angell before and after the First World War, when his short book, eventually entitled *The Great Illusion*, was read by internationalists and pacifists throughout the world. Angell claimed that wars between advanced countries could not occur because they were dependent on one another for the means to make war. The First World War did not bear out these hopes, but the idea of economic cooperation survived into the 1920s and was still present in the 1940s.

These partly discredited ideas might well not have achieved more practical influence than they had between the wars. However, their strength was linked to the great growth of the West European economy after the war. From Jean Monnet's French national plan (1946) onwards, the assumption was widely made that there could be a long-term trend towards economic development. By the mid-1950s, this hope seemed well on the way to being fulfilled. The European Coal and Steel Community (ECSC), founded by treaty in 1951 by Germany, France, Italy, Belgium, Luxembourg and the Netherlands, was the direct antecedent of the EEC. It created a large trading area for strategic products, and quickly moved towards the formulation of economic and social policies. Armaments were becoming more burdensome for the NATO countries, and legal and political institutions like the Council of Europe were for the most part bogged down, but an international economic system would, it was increasingly felt by many European integrationists, tend to generate its own development as trade expanded and the more remote parts of Europe were developed.

This theoretical basis was more a feature of the EEC than of the other European organizations. It meant that progress was seen from the start as a long-term process with cooperation spreading gradually into new areas of activity, and across western Europe from the original core members, the Six. Political aims were there from the start but they were not overly emphasized, as they awaited prior economic and social progress. This was made easier by the leading role allotted to civil servants in the running of the EEC. They sought practical progress, very much on the lines of the ECSC. The EEC recognized that early achievements would be unspectacular, and later progress quite slow, but they felt that they could look forward confidently to at least 30 years of sustained achievement.

Looking back from the century's end, we can see that this is exactly what they achieved, with a largely integrated, prosperous Europe as a result. Total exports of the countries which would form the EEC in 1971, for instance, rose 9.3 times between 1948 and 1971, compared to a growth of 5.7 times in total world exports (United Nations, 1973, xx–xxi). Meanwhile, trade between the countries of the Six, which had made up 32 per cent of their total exports in 1958, had risen to 48 per cent in 1969 (Van der Wee, 1987, 377). Foreign investment in the EEC, originating particularly in the United States, stimulated growth in western Europe and allowed the import of more American technology. American aid to under-developed countries financed the export of some European development goods to the Third World. At the same time, however, the EEC's high external tariff and, later, the Common Agricultural Policy (see below), discouraged imports and to some degree cut off the EEC from the world economy (ibid., 378). Rapid economic growth in the 1960s progressively mollified these effects, however. New tariff barriers and quotas would spring up everywhere in the OPEC era after 1973, but the EEC had little choice but to participate at that time. The EEC was always a supporter of world trade and its policies, taken as a whole, were not isolationist.

The EEC was an outstanding achievement, not only in European but also in historical world terms. There had been a number of international integrating systems before 1939, but these were mainly the great European and American empires in which the terms of exchange were often distorted. A number of regional economic groupings were set up after the war, with a big surge in the 1960s, but their achievements were limited (Pollard, 1997, 100). South America, for instance, achieved little in the way of economic cooperation after the war and the Caribbean trade association, CARIFTA, was a disappointment. Africa's numerous countries were for the most part too backward and variegated to achieve any union. The Soviet Union and its satellites have already been discussed. In the later 1960s, some of the satellites, notably Poland, pursued more independent economic policies within the Soviet system, but these in any case tended to draw them towards the EEC, with early hopes building up of joining the EEC in due course. Meanwhile, West Germany, with Willy Brandt's *Ostpolitik*, and France under De Gaulle and, later, Pompidou, worked to develop trade links with the east, partly as a means of gaining independence from the United States. This confirmed the success and the strength of the EEC and the cumulative integration of western Europe. When, in the 1990s, a number of former Soviet satellites began negotiations to join the EEC, they would demonstrate not so much the failure of the Soviet system as the successful completion of European industrialization in the east under Russian guidance (see Maddison, 1969, 108–30). Even the eastern trade performance, whatever the limitations of the COMECON system, indicated a considerable degree of economic development within a generally effective system of exchange. The exports of the socialist economies of eastern Europe and the USSR increased 10.4 times between 1948 and 1971, albeit from a base five times lower in aggregate value terms than western Europe's (United Nations, 1973, xxii–xxiii).

The countries of western Europe also joined in the two big American currency and trade agreements. These were the Bretton Woods system of currency exchange, launched at a conference in the United States in 1944 and confirmed by the US Bretton Woods Act (1945), and the General Agreement on Tariffs and Trade (GATT), signed at Geneva in 1947. European thinkers and politicians, led by the British economist, John Maynard Keynes, played a large part in the creation of these systems, acutely aware of the need to avoid the problems which had followed the First World War (Killick, 1997, 23–31). These structures met their difficulties, largely because of the relative strength of the American economy, and therefore of the US dollar, after the war, but it was difficult for a western European country to refuse to take part in them given the benefits in terms of stability and potential growth which membership offered. Only the International Trade Organisation (ITO), a rapid American route to world free trade, failed to materialize in 1947–8, mainly because the underdeveloped countries believed that they could not compete with the industrial world. As recovery from the war proceeded, in the context of the wide range of American structures and ideologies, it eventually proved possible to meet the requirements of these institutions.

The most ambitious post-war task was the achievement of full world currency convertibility between the US dollar and the other currencies. This aim was designed to achieve international currency stability on the basis of the US dollar, replacing the gold standard of pre-war years. In practice, quick progress was impossible. Britain, as the most mature industrial nation of the early post-war years after the United States, was persuaded to move towards full dollar convertibility in 1946–7 with the backing of a huge US dollar loan ($5650 million) conceded by the United States and Canada in 1945. When full convertibility was reached in July 1947, holders of sterling rushed to buy dollars and the experiment ended ignominiously after a further six weeks. Full dollar convertibility, the key aim of Bretton Woods, was not achieved worldwide until 1959. However, the western European countries, with their maturing economies, played a key part in world progress towards convertibility. In fact, they developed in some respects into European versions of the North American economies and so provided a firm basis for the achievement of the Bretton Woods aims.

Progress towards the liberalization of trade was started by GATT reductions in quotas and tariffs from the later 1940s, OEEC reductions in quotas in the context of the Marshall Plan and the reduction of quantitative restrictions and tariffs under the guidance of the EEC from 1958. Tariff reductions in western Europe were greatly encouraged by West Germany's move towards GATT. This began in 1949, when the new republic was invited to attend the GATT conference at Torquay. This tribute to its new status as an independent country was welcomed in Germany, much as the invitation to join the OEEC in 1948, when Germany had decided to cooperate fully in an international organization rather than to press its own interests. Since the later nineteenth century, Germany had been strongly protectionist and these policies had been seen as serving it well. The German autarky policy under the Third Reich had raised the tariff barriers even higher. After 1945, the greatly reduced German national area had made these tariffs much less realistic, but in the parlous state of the German economy and the absence of a national state, nothing could be done. At Torquay, however, having sensed the atmosphere of free trade in Europe, Germany accepted the principle of free trade and went on to prepare a new tariff system which it introduced in 1950–1. In 1951, Germany signed the GATT agreement and secured a wide range of tariff reductions from other GATT members.

GATT progress in western Europe now accelerated as the increasing volume of trade encouraged tariff reductions. The OEEC started to remove quantitative tariffs from 1955, in association with GATT. Indeed, by the time the EEC started work in 1958, most tariffs had been reduced to low levels, and it would become increasingly difficult in real terms to distinguish between GATT reductions and the work of the EEC. Often neglected by the general public because of its intermittent meetings ('rounds') and technical proceedings, GATT linked western Europe to a worldwide process of trade reform which reduced its tendency towards self-centred perspectives.

Europe's willing participation in world associations led by the United States influenced the range of bodies which were uniquely or principally European in membership or identity. The Marshall Plan and the OEEC, discussed above, both assumed that the external trade of European countries would be encouraged, on the basis of cooperation within Europe. The European Payments Union (EPU), set up by the OEEC states in 1950 to overcome currency shortages suffered by states paying for imports or settling foreign debts, was an indirect product of the Marshall Plan, whose dollar payments had been designed to help towards this aim, but which were to come to an end in 1952. Designed to ensure that trading countries had a ready supply of foreign currency, including US dollars, and to smooth out bilateral imbalances in trade, it helped encourage trade between Europe and the rest of the world as well as within Europe. Germany, in particular, was helped by the EPU to develop its trade with Europe and, increasingly, the rest of the world, during its crucial growth years in the early and mid-1950s. The essence of the scheme was that member countries agreed to accept the currency of *any* other member country in payment for their exports. Members contributed to a currency fund which was used to cover individual national deficits, provided that the countries took action to cover the deficits by import substitution or expanded exports. Very much a continuation of the

Marshall Plan approach, this strategy produced rapid results in terms of national specialization and the growth of exports. Trade within Europe was especially favoured, with intra-European trade growing from 10 billion dollars in 1950 to 23 billion dollars in 1959 (Sutcliffe, 1996, 109), but supplies of US dollars were increased by the growing exports to the United States which occurred from the early 1950s, especially from Germany and Britain (Killick, 1997, 14–22). Member countries were advised to reduce trade barriers in Europe to allow deficit countries to export more. Exchange rates stabilized as countries resolved their deficits. In 1958, the EPU wound up its work as the European countries prepared to make their currencies fully convertible in 1959.

However, economic links with the rest of the world were to be a cause of contention, especially in connection with the creation of the EEC from 1958. The reinforcement of the economy of western Europe and growing internal trade offered the possibility of a partly autarkic economy. Agriculture was the main candidate for protection, given that North America, the British Empire and South America could produce large quantities of primary products more cheaply than could western Europe. With most of western Europe still based on a peasant agricultural system, the collapse of its agricultural structure was bound to produce social chaos, owing principally to the overcrowding of the cities by unemployed people. A right-wing political reaction might well occur, with a possible revival of Fascism. The founders of the EEC were aware of the need to protect western European agriculture and they looked forward to high tariffs on farm products entering western Europe. The danger of this was that western Europe's industrial links with the rest of the world would be limited because it would be impossible to agree the necessary tariffs or quotas in the context of European agricultural protection. However, these protectionist inclinations came up against a very strong momentum of cooperation within Europe and the history of the EEC and its predecessors would manifest an overall tendency towards internationalism, and on a world scale as well as a European scale.

The beginnings of discussions on European cooperation had taken place during the Second World War. The governments in exile began to talk in London, while the Allied countries involved Europe in their plans for worldwide systems. The three 'Benelux' countries – Belgium, the Netherlands and Luxembourg – created a customs union in 1948 in execution of wartime understandings. This move, by adjoining countries with obvious common interests and potential, proved easier to achieve than integrationist structures for western Europe as a whole. At first, the federalist movements in the various western European countries made some progress towards a new structure, but national opposition was widespread. In 1949, the Council of Europe was set up as a compromise in order to keep the federalist idea alive, but it was so weak that European federalism seemed to have lost its potential.

The Korean War helped generate the idea of a European army but, here again, national objections outweighed the support of the United States. Discussions came to an end in 1954, when the French assembly voted the idea down. This meant that economic cooperation alone could now generate western European cooperation. Some progress had already been made here by the European Coal and Steel Community, an extension of the Benelux association, which had started work in 1952. The most striking beneficiary of the ECSC was Italy, which at that time produced little steel but which strove to secure a stronger basis for its industries. Using 'minimills' making steel from scrap, Italy was promised a secure market from the other ECSC countries. Such encouragement of new industries in an aspiring country by consortia of European states, heralded by the Marshall Plan, now looked forward to the creation of a balanced European economy in the interests of all members. Intended partly to reduce the causes of dangerous disagreements between Germany and France in the field of strategic products, the ECSC nevertheless aspired to cooperation over a broad area of production, and to the coordination of social policy. In 1955, the ECSC invited the western European states to a conference on western European coordination, but the ECSC member countries were the only ones to attend. For two years they worked hard on the creation of of a full economic and social union of the six countries. When they signed their foundation document, the Treaty of Rome, in 1957, they made clear that other countries could apply to join when they wished.

This union, encouraged by the United States, was soon so powerful and influential that it was clearly bound to form the core of an integrated western Europe. Britain, though still Europe's biggest foreign trader, nevertheless declined to join. Confident in its huge Commonwealth and its ability to bring Europe's non-EEC countries together in a free trade unit, Britain set up its own association, the European Free Trade Association (EFTA), with seven member countries, in 1960, but this was much smaller in population and GDP and was never intended to develop proactive economic policies (Steininger, 1997, 535–40). On the other hand, its support for free trade principles made it more open to the rest of the world than the EEC was, while the Sterling Area and Britain's pretensions to a world strategic role alongside the United States gave it perspectives which stretched beyond Europe. Moreover, EFTA's free trade character was intended mainly to preserve trading links with the British Commonwealth and its total trading turnover was too small to rival the EEC.

The EEC sought from the start to develop institutions which new members could readily join and to discuss a possible basis and timing for joining. Ludwig Erhard, the West German Finance Minister, told an audience in Lisbon in 1961 that, without a combination of the EEC and EFTA, Europe would be so weakened that it would fall into the lap of the Russians (ibid., 536). However, EFTA was not seen as the leading force in this combination. Non-European countries and world institutions increasingly looked to the EEC as the chief western European negotiator.

The central position of the EEC in western Europe was made very clear by the British decision, in 1961, to apply to join the EEC. Although Britain wanted to retain its links with the Commonwealth, EFTA and the United States, and saw no reason why the promotion of free trade should not allow it to do so, it soon encountered national views within the EEC, and especially in the case of France, which questioned close links with the United States and access to products from outside Europe which could undermine European production. In the British case, the impact of cheap primary products from the Commonwealth was questioned. When President De Gaulle of France vetoed the British application in 1963, effectively excluding EFTA as well, the EEC moved away from the free trade concept which Britain had hoped to develop, and towards the customs union with political implications which had never been absent from discussions on European integration and which had moved forward from the ECSC into the EEC. Most EEC members would have been prepared to admit Britain, and later EFTA, on very much its own terms, in the interests of European unity. The French intervention (which lay entirely within the rules of the EEC) pushed the EEC into a more embattled stance which France used to promote its own interests, especially in the protection of its agriculture.

These episodes, and the continuing influence of De Gaulle's aspirations, slowed down all progress towards the creation of integrative European institutions until De Gaulle resigned from the French presidency in 1969. Until the later 1960s, for instance, the EEC did not seriously study the creation of a single currency. Meanwhile, in the early part of the decade the US dollar was still strong enough to provide the stability and confidence which the European countries required. The weakness of the dollar in the later 1960s led western Europe to discuss the creation of an exchange system which would impose order on the various national currencies. The creation of the currency 'snake' in 1972 was the first step towards the Euro of the year 2000. However, in 1973, the conditions of a single currency were still far away. There was no doubt that the EEC would remain the main pacesetter of European integration, but much remained to be done. When Britain and Denmark were at last allowed to join the EEC in 1973, the prospect of further extensions of membership became clearer, but the creation of a full range of institutions, policies and a truly continental membership was clearly some years away. At the same time, the EEC had retained its integrationist perspectives and its relationship to the rest of the world remained open and creative under the leadership of Germany and France.

GROWTH AND RISING LIVING STANDARDS IN THE 1960s

The 1960s in western Europe were marked by the developing presence of the EEC and the interest of other countries in signing the Treaty of Rome in their turn. The progress of economic development followed much the same course as it had in the 1950s, though with a tendency to deceleration in Germany. Southern Europe, in particular, continued to modernize, but much more quickly than it had in the 1950s. Now beginning to follow the example of northern Italy, the Italian south produced a growing quantity and variety of consumer goods, drawing on government support in training and capital in some cases. The other southern countries began to generate more industrial employment and their birth rates declined. Labour migration from the south to northern Europe now slowed down as more and more southerners found employment in their own region, leading the northern industrial countries to admit more labour from outside Europe (though the flow from Greece to Germany continued much as before, reflecting the very slow economic progress in Greece).

The labour shortage in northern Europe and the limited skills of most of the new migrants contributed to a general slowdown in the rate of growth there from the early 1960s. Wages and salaries, however, rose sharply, reflecting the labour shortage. During the 1960s, western European living standards reached new levels even in the countries of slow growth like Britain. This meant that further economic growth had to be achieved mainly by the development of new products or new methods. The northern countries were well equipped to achieve these, but they no longer had the advantages which they had enjoyed in the late 1940s and 1950s of drawing on accumulated American technology.

The most industrialized countries tended to be the most affected. The West German growth rate fell from 6.5 per cent in 1955–60 to 4.5 per cent in 1965–70 (Sutcliffe, 1996, 214). Belgium, which faced serious political and ethnic problems, increased its growth rate in the 1960s on the basis of heavy investment under a national plan, but the influence of organized labour remained a serious obstacle. Britain, whose low post-war growth rate had in part been due to its very high level of industrialization by the end of the war, tried to increase productivity through state incentive schemes and indicative national planning from 1964 on the lines of the French plans of the Monnet type. After some success in the early and mid-1960s, with British GDP growth increasing to 3.1 per cent per annum between 1960 and 1964, compared with 5.1 per cent in a now less successful Germany (Alford, 1988, 14), the need to defend Britain's weak pound sterling in the interests of the country's ambitious world role reduced the level of domestic investment and by the end of the decade Britain's growth rate was still among the lowest in Europe.

The Conservative government of 1970–4 tried to modernize the economy by applying to join the EEC, following the example of Macmillan's Conservative government in 1961, and by creating inflationary conditions in 1972–3. The EEC negotiations were successful in 1973, drawing Britain further away from the Commonwealth, but the 'Barber boom' soon slowed down as the balance of payments worsened. The return of a Labour government in 1974, in part a product of the oil crisis and the damaging miners' strike of 1973, and the even greater weakness of the pound, created a tangle of short-term policies backed by much verbiage. Britain's fundamental economic difficulties would not be tackled until the 1980s, when Britain's own output of high-quality oil allowed it to finance its high unemployment without foreign borrowing.

France was able to defend its growth rate. Having modernized very quickly from a low base, France still had much potential for growth and in the later 1960s it still had a higher growth rate than most of Europe. Planning and state investment sustained the momentum and a very high birth rate continued to boost demand. Growth in the south continued at a high rate. The confidence engendered by the enterprising De Gaulle regime and its numerous economic and social reforms made a big contribution to growth, with an ambitious modernization programme recalling the era of Emperor Napoleon III a century before. This rapid completion of the industrialization of France created a powerful, modern economic unit close to the existing industrial countries of Britain, Germany and the Benelux, and further encouraged journalistic promotion of the 'Golden Triangle' concept in north-west Europe.

The 1960s saw the European fringes and isolated regions like the Massif Central move substantially towards industrialization, producing an almost fully exploited land mass. The south, though as a whole still much the most backward part of western Europe, made more progress in the 1960s than in the 1950s. At the same time, the industrialization of southern Europe began to extend to southern Italy and to Spain. Portugal and Greece remained more backward, but Italy's emergence as an industrial power allowed it to play a bigger part in supplying the rest of the south and in contributing technology and investment to its industries. Slow growth in Britain and Germany could now be seen partly as a function of the general catching up in the south within a single Europe.

The Nordic countries now reached their optimum balance between industry and primary production. Their high living standards, which derived from their rich primary resources and low populations, led to high wage costs, but this proved to be no obstacle to industrialization as the Nordic countries developed advanced industries with a big export potential. Lavish investment produced good working conditions. Training was fully developed and social services and education produced a healthy and happy workforce.

The Nordic countries had a strong tradition of trading among themselves. This was reflected in their easy adhesion to EFTA, which they saw as a useful extension of their existing arrangements. By the 1960s, Nordic exports were creating links with the whole world, much as Germany had achieved in the 1950s. By 1960, Swedish and Norwegian shipyards had overtaken Britain and in 1965 the Nordic countries built 16 per cent of world shipping (Sutcliffe, 1996, 272). Saab aircraft, originally built after the war to defend Swedish neutrality, were widely exported in the 1960s, allowing Sweden to create links with the Third World and a number of small countries, as Germany had done in the 1950s. Sweden, in particular, became a widely respected arbiter of world affairs.

Britain's rejection by the EEC in 1963 did not greatly disturb the Nordic countries. EFTA had reinforced their existing mutual trading links and there was no question of this informal association breaking up. Their valuable primary products and the special character of their industries allowed them to develop specific agreements with the EEC. When Britain and Denmark were allowed to join the EEC in 1973, the adhesion of the other Nordic countries to the EEC was brought closer, but their enlightened and generous approach to international links remained of great value. In particular, Sweden's encouragement of foreign workers and the comfortable living which they enjoyed in Sweden further enhanced Sweden's international reputation.

At the end of the 1960s, western Europe retained the vision of modernity and change which had been building up since around 1950. The influx of American technology after the war, and a new European technology which emerged from the 1950s, combined with full employment and rising earnings, created confidence in an industrial civilization of the future. Education, which had given western Europe an economic advantage over most of the world from as early as the nineteenth century, had further expanded and improved, with new universities and technical colleges opening up advanced education and training to a broader clientele in almost every country. Only the United States, Canada, Australia and New Zealand could offer a better human environment, and in world terms western Europe enjoyed a considerable advantage in respect of workforce, enterprise and employment mentality (see Aldcroft, 1998, 235–54). Leisure prospects were clearly going to develop. Social problems would die out. Planning would secure the future. This was the product of the post-war years, a product which would fade away in the 1970s. In 1973, however, western Europe was still at the peak of its confidence – at any rate until OPEC intervened.

DECELERATION AND MONETARY PROBLEMS: THE LAST YEARS BEFORE THE OIL CRISIS

The rapid growth of the western European economy began to come to an end in the late 1960s, while inflation increased. Although this was partly a function of the investment cycle, long-term factors were at work. Just as the US economy and Britain experienced slow growth after the war owing to the completion of their industrialization processes, so western Europe's industrialization was approaching completion by 1970. Industrialization had meant land development, building, roads and other infrastructure, together with workers moving from low, rural wages to industrial wages in towns where there was more to spend the wages on. This revolutionary process tended to generate high growth rates, with increased demand spilling into production in nearby regions. Once the process was complete, however, either in a region or even more in a country, it was very difficult to maintain the growth rate without a spate of new processes. In the north, the rich supply of American industrial technology which had become available after the war was largely used up by the 1960s. Agriculture was now profitable almost everywhere and further productivity gains were hard to achieve. In the south, the impact of industrialization had left only some large, but almost unexploitable, regions untouched. Western Europe's visible labour shortage, with inexperienced non-European workers and their families being imported in large numbers, confirmed the impression of an exhaustion of the supply of both land and labour. The application of more capital could in theory resolve these problems, but in the industrial north the 1960s saw growing demands by organized labour which discouraged or increased the cost of investment. Political pressure from the Left, especially in France, Italy and Germany in the late 1960s and early 1970s, made it more difficult for the state to play a directive role. Students and other youth, their aspira-

tions boosted by the post-war boom, turned against capitalism and western Europe's prevailing liberal democracy in the later 1960s. Their
opposition to US intervention in Vietnam, which spread to much of the
older population, including many people of conservative inclination,
threatened the European confidence in the United States on which post-
war reconstruction had been based. Student riots in Paris in 1968 spread
to most of western Europe by the following year. The post-war western
European consensus of internal and external cooperation was now under
serious threat, and the historian will wonder how much more damage
might have been done if the oil crisis of 1973 had not reminded western
Europe of its common interest. On the other hand, European problems
from 1965 would no doubt have been resolved and, without the oil crisis,
western Europe would probably have grown, at a slower but still
respectable rate, into the 1970s and through into the 1980s.

Significantly, as the largest economy in western Europe, Germany
recorded a relatively low growth rate from the early 1960s, owing mainly
to a labour shortage, relatively high wages, high social security costs, the
completion of the re-equipment of western Europe and progress in the
industrialization of southern Europe. As a big producer of high-quality
capital goods, Germany was bound to suffer from the continuing progress
of post-war western European industrialization, and not only because of
the spread of replacement production in other European countries. Many
other countries were affected by the German slowdown, both because
they, like Italy, exported consumer goods to Germany, or because they
exported materials or components for the production of producer goods
in Germany. Some foreign labour from southern Europe was encouraged
to return home from the later 1960s, where it created unemployment.
France's high growth rate continued into the 1960s under the dynamic
political leadership of De Gaulle and a wave of technological progress,
but by the end of the decade it was being affected by the European deceleration. Britain, affected by low productivity since the later 1950s, was
forced to concentrate on an export drive which was baulked by labour
problems, high costs and low investment. Spain, while on the path of
modernization, remained only partially industrialized and could not
develop a momentum of its own.

The irony of this situation was that the United States, which had done
so much to create European prosperity, was now too weak to revive western Europe again. The Europeans could no longer rely on the US dollar,
and began to create their own exchange system, beginning with the
'snake' in 1972. With Japan declining to take action to revive world trade,
the EEC moved somewhat towards an isolationist position. Meanwhile,
OPEC looked ahead to the moment when it would secure a better price

for its oil. In 1973, western Europe would prove to be one of the parts of the world most vulnerable to oil attack, owing ironically to its outstanding rate of economic growth since the war.

Western Europe continued to be a heavy user of coal (75 per cent of total energy resources in western Europe in 1955) (see Morewood, Chapter 6 of the present volume) but, in step with the growth of its manufactured exports, it imported oil in growing volumes, from the United States and the Middle East. This trend had begun just after the war when European coalmining was affected by labour problems, especially in the Ruhr. Oil was widely used in the new industries, especially in the south. In international terms, the growth of oil consumption drew western Europe into strategic issues in the Middle East as British and Dutch companies joined American companies in the discovery and exploitation of Middle East oil resources. Linked to the British and American leading role in the creation of the State of Israel in 1947, this extraction of Arab oil at low prices increasingly made western Europe subject to hostility in the Middle East. The anti-Western revolution, in Persia in 1951, and the nationalization of the Suez Canal in 1956, followed by the Franco-British invasion of the canal zone, saw western Europe increasingly involved in a major world region, very much at the time when imperial involvement elsewhere had been abandoned or reduced. This stored up trouble for western Europe in the future. Meanwhile, oil became progressively cheaper and western Europe became more and more dependent on it. As Morewood shows below (Chapter 6), dependence on non-European oil began to make western Europe vulnerable from the later 1960s, but this was not visible until the early 1970s, by which time oil provided some 60 per cent of western European energy and coal had sunk to around 20 per cent.

Nuclear power, with Britain the main leader after the war as a by-product of its independent nuclear weapons programme, came into use with the first nuclear power stations in Britain from around 1950. It spread to France within a few years and by the 1960s nuclear power stations were to be found in other countries of western Europe. Fears for the environmental implications were now being voiced, but a further expansion of nuclear power into the 1970s was still expected. The advantage of nuclear generation at this time was that it could replace coal, which was bound to become a relatively expensive source owing to rising wages and the gradual move towards difficult coalfields. The import of coal from outside Europe was not seen as a big possibility at this time. Nuclear progress did suggest, however, the coming of a clean, modern Europe in which the old Coketowns would at last be replaced by clean, modern communities. This vision would disappear in the 1970s, as OPEC oil policies dragged western Europe back towards international cooperation in the energy field.

THE 'GOLDEN AGE'

Economic historians love to discern unique eras, such as the two very different 'great depressions', but the concepts of a European 'golden age' or 'miracle' between the Second World War and the oil shocks of the 1970s are as much the products of journalism as of objective analysis (see Toniolo, 1998, 252). Moreover, they are almost always applied to western Europe alone. The huge, complex region of eastern Europe, which experienced massive development and growth rates comparable to, or higher than, those of western Europe – though at the expense of loss of human freedom and chronic pollution – is rarely portrayed as 'miraculous'. Indeed, its low living standards in comparison with western Europe ruled out all 'golden' concepts as seen from the west. Yet the big variations in living standards within western Europe, which would survive into the 1990s (Sutcliffe, 1996, 296), were rarely seen as detracting from the 'golden' vision, with aggregate growth rates, or growth rates in the leading industrial countries, normally perceived as the main criterion (Toniolo, 1998, 252–3).

What west and east most had in common after 1945 was their status as great trading blocs. Their internal links helped in their industrialization, with even backward regions 'taking off' and core areas becoming the dynamos for large regions. The main difference between them was that the west became a powerful participant in an expanding world trading system, while the east's trading was largely limited to the communist bloc and Third World countries sympathetic to communism. This feature was linked to widespread state ownership of the means of production in the east, which was largely complete by the early 1950s (Aldcroft, 1993, 170). In the eastern satellites, the extensive socialization of agriculture failed to lift productivity up to western levels. By the early 1960s, about 95 per cent of the aggregate national income of the east came from the state sector (ibid., 171). Eastern products increasingly conformed to the unique requirements of communist usage, while imports from the capitalist world were so limited that awareness of the best western practice was very restricted. These weaknesses were counteracted to some degree by the economic planning which exercised an uneven and intermittent influence in the east, but this was more suitable for growth and equipment than for the control of supply. In any case, the massive dominance of state producers, and the armed forces, especially in the Soviet Union, restricted the scope for comprehensive planning and limited the role of cooperatives, which had a degree of potential, especially in the satellite countries. In the west, France made a great success of a system of national plans between the 1940s and the 1970s but no other country followed the same path except in relation to short periods and partial aspects of planning. Nevertheless, the socialist bloc continued to grow faster than the west through the 1950s and the 1960s, according to its own somewhat idiosyncratic figures. According to figures recalculated by Aldcroft, per capita domestic growth rates in the east averaged 5.7 per cent over the two decades, compared to nearly 4 per cent in the west. Productivity growth was also rather greater in the east (ibid., 173). Of course, progress in the east was achieved on the basis of much lower per capita output levels, especially in agriculture, and in a context of much greenfield development in mining and manufacturing. Much workforce training was carried out *ab initio* and skills were restricted to those required for the job in hand. This did not compete with the economic success of the west. However, concentration on producer goods and the relative neglect of agriculture, combined with a high rate of population growth (except in East Germany), allowed the east to provide 30 per cent of the world's industrial output in 1970, compared to 18 per cent in the early 1950s (ibid., 183).

The happy experience of western Europe after 1945 showed the importance of trading, openly and generously, within the world economy. The rapid growth of the world economy after 1945, which must be attributed partly to US policy, provided an encouraging context for the European economies which, as we have seen, were directly helped and advised by the United States. The removal of trade restrictions within western Europe allowed each country to produce in areas where it had a comparative advantage. The need to export within the dollar area made all of Europe more competitive. The annual average compound growth rates as calculated by Maddison show how impressively western Europe advanced, between 1950 and 1976, in comparison with other trading nations and regional groups (see Table 5.4). Only the relative decline of Britain as an industrial nation from the 1950s detracted from this picture (see Landes, 1998, 453–64).

These figures should be compared with the world leaders in export performance: South Korea (20.3 per cent), Taiwan (16.3 per cent) and Japan (15.4 per cent), and certain leading countries in the industrialized world which did not register an outstanding export performance: Canada (7.0 per cent), the United States (6.3 per cent) and Australia (5.8 per cent). Western Europe stands out as a very successful group of exporting countries drawing on physical closeness and an industrial core which could easily expand to the very limits of the continent.

The resulting growth of output encouraged efficiency through scale economies within each country and across western Europe as a whole. Total exports increased 6.4 times in western Europe between 1948 and 1971, compared to 5.7 times in the world economy as a whole (United

Table 5.4 Annual average compound growth rate in export volume 1950–73 (per cent per annum)

Germany	12.4
Italy	11.7
Austria	10.8
Netherlands	10.3
Belgium	9.4
France	8.2
Switzerland	8.1
Norway	7.3
Sweden	7.0
Denmark	6.9
UK	3.9

Source: Maddison (1989, 67).

Nations, 1973, xxii–xxiii). EEC exports rose 9.3 times (ibid., xx–xxi). Western Europe took its chance to 'catch up' on the United States, restoring the position which it had lost at the end of the nineteenth century. Nearly all its growth after 1945 took place on a 'best-practice' basis, using American technology or developing competitive European technology and methods. The assurance of democracy and union rights created a contented, hard-working labour force. Even part of the labour force was attracted from outside Europe. Multinational companies, mainly an American and British phenomenon before 1939, but multiplying much faster after 1945, proliferated on the continent of Europe, reflecting the big expansion of European trade (see Table 5.5). With technology transfer from US firms carried out to a large extent via overseas subsidiary companies (Elliott and Wood, 1979, 7), multinationals played a big part in increasing productivity in western Europe.

Looking back on this productive period of Europe's history, we can see that western Europe's 'miracle' was based on a willing incorporation into the America-led world economy, and on cooperation between all the countries of the continental region. American leadership would start to flag in the late 1960s, leading to the fading of the 'miracle'. Western Europe's problems after 1970 would lead to the perception of a new era, which has generated its own names, such as 'post-oil shock', or 'post-industrial' (see McCormick, 1988). That new era will be the concern of the next chapter. However, the end of the 'miracle' in the 1970s as growth rates plummeted throughout western Europe must not obscure the post-war achievement of a continental region which was almost fully industrialized by 1973, except

Table 5.5 Total numbers of multinationals by country of origin in 1973

USA	2567
UK	1588
GFR	1222
Switzerland	765
France	565
Netherlands	467
Japan	211
Rest of world	2096
Total world	9481

Source: Pollard (1997, p.29).

for parts of southern Europe. The parallel advance of eastern Europe was based on state control, but cooperation between the component countries was an important feature of economic activity. The 'oil shock' did not affect the Soviet system directly, but the 1970s would begin a period of problems and adjustments which ultimately would have a bigger impact on eastern Europe than anything felt in the west. This very different 'new era' in the east will also figure in the next chapter.

BIBLIOGRAPHY

Abrams, R. *et al.* (1990), *The Impact of the European Community's Internal Market on the EFTA*, Washington: International Monetary Fund.

Aldcroft, D. (1993), *The European Economy 1914–1990*, 3rd edn, London: Routledge.

Aldcroft, D. (1998), 'Education and development: the experience of rich and poor nations', *History of Education*, 27.

Aldcroft, D. and S. Morewood (1995), *Economic Change in Eastern Europe since 1918*, Aldershot: Edward Elgar.

Alford, B. (1988), *British Economic Performance, 1945–75*, London: Macmillan.

Alford, B. (1996), *Britain in the World Economy since 1880*, Harlow: Longman.

Bairoch, P. (1976), 'Europe's gross national product, 1800–1975', *The Journal of European Economic History*, 5.

Balassa, B. (ed.) (1975), *European Economic Integration*, Amsterdam: North-Holland.

Barnouin, B. (1986), *The European Labour Movement and European Integration*, London: Frances Pinter.

Bideleux, R. and I. Jeffries (1998), *A History of Eastern Europe: Crisis and Change*, London: Routledge.

Boltho, A. (ed.) (1982), *The European Economy: Growth and Crisis*, Oxford: Oxford University Press.

Cameron, R. (1998), *A Concise Economic History of the World*, 3rd edn, Oxford: Oxford University Press.

Cassis, Y. (1997), *Big Business: The European Experience in the Twentieth Century*, Oxford: Oxford University Press.

Crafts, N. and G. Toniolo (eds) (1996), *Economic Growth in Europe since 1945*, Cambridge: Cambridge University Press.

Crouzet, F. (1970), *The European Renaissance since 1945*, London: Thames and Hudson.

Crouzet, F. (ed.) (1993), *The Economic Development of France since 1870*, Aldershot: Edward Elgar.

Deighton, A. (1993), *The Impossible Peace: Britain, the Division of Germany and the Origins of the Cold War*, Oxford: Oxford University Press.

Eichengreen, B. (1993), *Reconstructing Europe's Trade and Payments: The European Payments Union*, Manchester: Manchester University Press.

Eichengreen, B. (ed.) (1996), *The Reconstruction of the International Economy, 1945–1960*, Cheltenham, UK and Brookfield, US: Edward Elgar.

Elliott, R. and P. Wood (1979), *The International Transfer of Technology and Western European Integration*, Department of Political Economy, University of Aberdeen.

Federico, G. (ed.) (1994), *The Economic Development of Italy since 1870*, Aldershot: Edward Elgar.

Feinstein, C. *et al.* (1997), *The European Economy between the Wars*, Oxford: Oxford University Press.

Ferro, M. (1997), *Colonization: A Global History*, London: Routledge.

Foley, B. (1998), *European Economies since the Second World War*, London: Macmillan.

Foreman-Peck, J. (1983), *A History of the World Economy: International Economic Relations since 1850*, Totowa, New Jersey: Wheatsheaf Books.

Galassi, F. and J. Cohen (1991), 'The economics of tenancy in early twentieth century southern Italy', *Economic History Review*, 47.

Galbraith, J. (1994), *The World Economy since the Wars*, London: Sinclair-Stevenson.

George, S. (1996), *Politics and Policy in the European Union*, 3rd edn, Oxford: Oxford University Press.

Harper, J. (1986), *America and the Reconstruction of Italy, 1945–1948*, Cambridge: Cambridge University Press.

Harrison, J. (1985), *The Spanish Economy in the Twentieth Century*, Cambridge: Cambridge University Press.

Henig, S. (1997), *The Uniting of Europe: From Discord to Concord*, London: Routledge.

James, H. (1996), *International Monetary Cooperation since Bretton Woods*, Oxford: Oxford University Press.

Kenwood, A. and A. Lougheed (1992), *The Growth of the International Economy, 1820–1990*, London: Routledge.

Killick, J. (1997), *The United States and European Reconstruction, 1945–1960*, Edinburgh: Keele University Press.

Landes, D. (1998), *The Wealth and Poverty of Nations: Why Some Are Rich and Some Are Poor*, London: Little, Brown and Company.

Lee, S. (1982), *Aspects of European History 1789–1980*, London: Methuen.

Maddison, A. (1964), *Economic Growth in the West: Comparative Experience in Europe and North America*, London: Allen & Unwin.

Maddison, A. (1969), *Economic Growth in Japan and the USSR*, London: Allen & Unwin.

Maddison, A. (1989), *The World Economy in the Twentieth Century*, Paris: OECD.

McCormick, B. (1988), *The World Economy: Patterns of Growth and Change*, Oxford: Philip Allan.

Mitchell, B. (1980), *European Historical Statistics, 1750–1975*, London: Macmillan.

Noin, D. and P. White (1997), *Paris*, Chichester: John Wiley.

Penrose, E. (1953), *Economic Planning for the Peace*, Princeton, NJ: Princeton University Press.

Persson, K. (ed.) (1993), *The Economic Development of Denmark and Norway since 1870*, Aldershot: Edward Elgar.

Pollard, S. (1981), *Peaceful Conquest: The Industrialization of Europe, 1760–1970*, Oxford: Oxford University Press.

Pollard, S. (1997), *The International Economy since 1945*, London: Routledge.

Pryor, F. (1973), *Property and Industrial Organization in Communist and Capitalist Nations*, Bloomington and London: Indiana University Press.

Reynolds, L. (1971), *The Three Worlds of Economics*, New Haven and London: Yale University Press.

Richards, J. (1970), *International Economic Institutions*, London: Holt, Rinehart and Winston.

Rostow, W. (1985), 'The world economy since 1945', *Economic History Review*, 2nd series, 33.

Scammell, W. (1980), *The International Economy since 1945,* London: Macmillan.

Smith, A. (1983), *The Planned Economies of Eastern Europe,* London: Macmillan.

Stearns, P. (1993), *The Industrial Revolution in World History*, Boulder, CO: Westview Press.

Steininger, R. (1997), '1961: Europe "at sixes and sevens"; the European Free Trade Association, the neutrals and Great Britain's decision to join the EEC', *The Journal of European Economic History*, 26.

Stubbs, R. and G. Underhill (eds) (1994), *Political Economy and the Changing Global Order*, London: Macmillan.

Sutcliffe, A. (1996), *An Economic and Social History of Western Europe since 1945*, London: Longman.

Temin, P. (1997), 'The golden age of European growth: a review essay', *European Review of Economic History*, 1.

Thee, M. (1981), *Armaments, Arms Control and Disarmament*, Paris: UNESCO Press.

Toniolo, G. (1998), 'Europe's golden age, 1950–1973: speculations from a long-run perspective', *Economic History Review*, 51.

United Nations (1973), *Yearbook of International Trade Statistics, 1970–1971*, New York: United Nations.

Van der Wee, H. (1987), *Prosperity and Upheaval in the World Economy, 1945–1980*, London: Penguin.

Van Zanden, J. (ed.) (1996), *The Economic Development of the Netherlands since 1870*, Cheltenham, UK and Brookfield, US: Edward Elgar.

Von Tunzlemann, N. (1992), 'The main trends of European economic history since the Second World War', in D. Dyker (ed.), *The European Economy*, London: Longman.

6. Europe at the crossroads 1974–2000

Steven Morewood

After the era of supergrowth, in the final quarter of the twentieth century the optimism that Western Europe basked in during the 'Golden Age' gave way to a period of slowdown, moribund progress and uncertainty over the way forward. The 'long boom' began to falter in the late 1960s, tottered unsteadily by the early 1970s, and was finally rendered irretrievable by the disruption to energy supplies emanating from the first oil shock. Its demise revived some old ghosts from the past. Intolerable rates of inflation, last seen in the aftermath of the First World War, afflicted most continental economies, while mass unemployment, on a scale comparable with that of the turbulent 1930s, returned with a vengeance, engulfing even the powerhouse German economy by the early 1990s. The connection was not lost on its unemployed who, in February 1998, took to the streets, with posters revived from the great depression, which proclaimed 'Nehme jede Arbirt an' ('Any work accepted'). Indeed, Helmut Kohl, Germany's 'eternal chancellor', lost the September 1998 general election after 16 years in office, with his successor promising to tackle mass unemployment and to modernize the economy.

By the mid-1980s, European competitiveness in the global economy had been progressively eroded by competition from the rejuvenated American and Japanese economies and the emerging economies, not least the 'tigers' of Southeast Asia. Faced with such fierce multi-direction trading rivalry, the European Community (EC) decided that the key to a return to economic prosperity lay in achieving a true common market, the single market or 'Europe without frontiers'. Much hope was invested in this grandiose project, but when it faded to match initial expectations the emphasis switched to introducing a single currency, which could rival the dollar as a vehicle currency, to 'complete' the transformation.

This seminal period also saw the dramatic collapse of the Soviet bloc in eastern Europe, with the fall-out engendering profound implications for the region as a whole. The reintegration of the continent was beset with problems: how successfully former socialist command economics could transform themselves into free market models; the prospective membership of at least some, perhaps eventually all, former communist countries of

NATO and the European Union (EU), which carried strategic and budgetary implications; the chill wind of competition that would blow from east to west in low-tech products, reflecting the former socialist states' much cheaper labour costs in the short term; and the wisdom of extensive investment in eastern markets, with German banks in particular finding themselves exposed by the Russian economic collapse of the late 1990s.

In the final quarter of the twentieth century, western Europe increasingly looked inwards and aimed to regenerate itself, partly because of outside competitive pressures, but also through a desire to maximize the potential of the Community. Indeed, this period marked a reversal of the investment flows of the imperial era, with many former colonized powers, now industrialized, sending capital to Europe. Although the continent continued to seek an improved export performance in outside markets, in an era of global economic integration the emphasis was on the creation of the world's largest trading bloc. Other regional trading blocs emerged (principally the North American Free Trade Association (NAFTA) in North America and the Association of Southeast Asian Nations (ASEAN) in Asia), reflecting a trend for growing regional integration in the global economy. Within regions one power became dominant: near the end of the century, the EU, the United States and Japan were responsible for two-thirds of global output (at market prices). Beyond Europe, amicable trading relations continued with former colonies, but penetration of the booming Asian emerging markets was limited. In 1996, only 15 per cent of Europe's exports went to Asia. The United States' performance (18 per cent) was only marginally better. Neither could compete with the dominant regional power (Japan) which directed 42 per cent of its exports to the region (Wolf, 1998). At the same time, its success proved a double-edged sword, for while it benefited enormously while the boom lasted, when the Asian economic bubble finally burst in 1997–8, Japan was mired in recession. By comparison, apart from some turmoil in its financial markets, Europe generally escaped lightly (though, as the major recipient of inward investment from Southeast Asia, Britain felt the impact of the contraction more).

THE REASONS WHY: THE END OF THE 'LONG BOOM'

At the Paris summit of October 1972, the EC set itself an objective: 'to transform, before the end of this decade and in strict conformity with the treaties already concluded, all member states' relations into a European Union' which embraced an economic and monetary union (EMU). That these aims proved unattainable within this timeframe and were not firmly back on the agenda until the mid-1980s is testimony to the economic whirlwind (the worst since the 1930s) which swept through the continent in the interim. The optimism of 1972 was framed against a background of remarkable growth. Between 1960 and 1973, the EC economy grew at a faster rate than the United States' (4.6 per cent per annum against 4 per cent), but between 1973 and 1980 slowed down to 2.3 per cent (Ball and Albert, 1983, 10). The end of supergrowth was not confined to western Europe (see Table 6. 1) and affected all advanced economies.

Table 6.1 GDP per capita (% rates of growth)

Period	1973–89	1973–79	1979–89
Australia	1.7	1.5	1.8
Austria	2.4	3.0	2.0
Belgium	2.0	2.1	1.8
Canada	2.4	2.9	1.8
Denmark	1.7	1.6	1.8
France	1.9	2.2	1.6
Germany	2.0	2.5	1.9
Italy	2.7	3.0	2.3
Japan	2.9	2.4	3.1
Netherlands	1.5	1.9	1.3
Sweden	1.7	1.5	1.8
Switzerland	0.9	–0.1	1.7
United Kingdom	1.8	1.5	2.2
United States	1.6	1.6	1.5
Average	2.0	2.0	1.9
OECD	1.8	1.9	1.7
Euro (15)	2.0	2.1	2.0

Source: OECD (1997).

At the heart of explanations for the demise of the 'long boom' lies the immense resource shock of the 1973–4 oil crisis, which exacerbated an already inflationary environment. The cheapness of crude oil from the Middle East was unquestionably a major factor in the duration of the 'long boom'. In 1966, oil supplanted coal as western Europe's most significant energy source and by 1970 had achieved this position in every country except Britain. The continent's dependence on imported oil from the Middle East (see Table 6.2) was signified by refining centres that were

Table 6.2 Primary sources of energy in western Europe, 1955 and 1972 (%)

Use	1955	1972
Coal	75	23
Petroleum	22	60
Natural gas	1	9
Other	2	8
Produced in Europe	78	35
Imported from non-Europe, net	22	65

Source: Prodi and Clo (1976, 92).

established in Bavaria, eastern France and Switzerland, which were linked by pipeline to the southern ports of Marseilles, Genoa and Trieste, thereby minimizing the sea transportation required from the Persian Gulf, eastern Mediterranean and North Africa (Odell, 1986, 124-5).

Western Europe's dependence on imported oil dates from the immediate aftermath of the Second World War when, facing a coal production crisis, the continent turned to refineries in the United States, the Caribbean and the Middle East to meet a critical energy gap. At first, with no substantial refining capacity of its own, the continent imported oil products predominantly. Their expense led governments to encourage companies to establish their own refineries, a move which coincided with the development of supertankers, which reduced the expense of transporting crude oil over long distances. To meet its fuel oil requirements, western Europe therefore turned increasingly to the Middle East, a region which, from being of relative insignificance as an oil producer before 1939, gained the lion's share of internationally traded oil after 1945. Foreign oil companies struck black gold in Kuwait and Saudi Arabia while existing fields in Iran and Iraq were developed to their full potential. By 1973, these four producers combined were generating more than 750 million tons of oil annually, over half the American total for the same year (Odell, 1986, 89, 114–17).

In retrospect, the dangers inherent in overdependence on oil supplies from a region riven by antagonisms between Arabs and Jews and increasingly anti-western in outlook are clear to see. The prolonged closure of the Suez Canal (1967–75) during and after the Six Day War ought to have rung alarm bells. So, too, should the rise of the Organization of Petroleum Exporting Countries (OPEC), established in 1960, which in 1968 announced its intention of securing greater control over oil resources for its members, including the fixing of prices (Venn, 1986, 132). Instead, the continent's dependence grew to a point where, by 1972, oil met nearly two-thirds of western Europe's total energy consumption (Odell, 1986, 124). In France, for example, 72.5 per cent of its primary sources of energy were petroleum-based, while Italy (78.6 per cent) was even more exposed (Prodi and Clo, 1976, 95). As Aldcroft (1993, 202) observes, the bargain price of energy and abundant supplies encouraged 'the rapid development of energy-intensive sectors, not only in terms of the most obvious mass penetration of cars, consumer durables and chemical products throughout the income ranges, but also in terms of the intensive use of petroleum as a fuel of heat in industry and for domestic purposes'. The scene was set for a catastrophe.

On 16 October 1973, as war raged once more between Israel and her Arab neighbours, OPEC doubled crude oil prices and the following day imposed an oil embargo. Thus began the 'oil decade' (1973–82) when the political clout and economic influence of the oil states reached their peak. At this time, foreign companies, which had hitherto enjoyed exclusive rights to oilfields through concessions dating from the 1920s, were replaced by national companies (Gilbar, 1997, 27–8). As a supporter of Israel, the Netherlands was singled out for punitive treatment. Following the Vienna summit on 6 November 1973, when the Common Market judiciously backed the Arab demand that Israel withdraw to its pre-1967 borders, OPEC exempted its members (bar the Netherlands) from a 5 per cent reduction in production in December. But the respite was momentary, with the cutback resumed in January. Not only that, the shortfall in supply was doubled. Worse still, on 23 December the Gulf OPEC ministers sanctioned a further price increase, to $11.65 a barrel, making a more than 400 per cent rise compared to the pre-crisis price of $2.59. Not until March 1974, following the Israeli–Egyptian separation of forces agreement, was the embargo effectively ended when seven producers, headed by Saudi Arabia, broke ranks (Shwadran, 1986, 47–51).

The economic reverberations of the oil shock, however, remained in the system much longer. During the 1970s, with oil shocks at either end of the decade, oil prices increased tenfold. The EC rate of inflation shot up to 17.5 per cent after the first oil shock and remained at 13.5 per cent between 1975 and 1978, before receiving a further fillip with the second oil shock (Ball and Albert 1983, 14). Containing the inflationary effects of the steep increase in oil prices, energy conservation and efficiency became obligatory key themes on the agendas of western governments. The energy crisis carried with it a multitude of economic sins: an increased demand for money, the phenomenon of inflation and unemployment rising in tandem (stagflation), a fall in tax receipts, balance of payments problems, public sector deficits, plummeting rates of investment as orders fell, interest rates rose and jobless figures shot up, and declining living standards.

The macroeconomic responses to this cocktail of problems varied, although the tide of events galvanized governments, however reluctantly, away from full employment demand management policies and towards the control of inflation, which became their number one priority. Monetarism came into fashion and for a time the control of the money supply was seen as an effective way of checking inflation. With the events of 1923 and 1948 in mind, West Germany was quickest to grasp the nettle, stamping down on rising prices and pursuing policies designed to strengthen the Deutschmark to reduce the cost of imported oil as a means of cushioning the effects of the supply shock. Across the continent, governments sought to restrict private consumption and alleviate the impact on industry. In fact, the reduction in the availability of petroleum was contained remarkably well across the community over the fortuitously mild winter of 1973–4, when oil product reserves never fell below 80 days' consumption. The contraction in demand was therefore attributable to a combination of exorbitant price increases, the greater utilization of other energy sources and restrictive government measures, such as banning Sunday driving and imposing stricter speed limits on motor vehicles. Moreover, the oil shock halted the growth of energy-intensive sectors and, by transferring wealth to OPEC countries with a relatively weak demand for industrial imports, created substantial balance of payments deficits in OECD countries (Aldcroft, 1993, 203).

Growing concern at the finite nature of mineral resources predated the first oil shock when the Club of Rome's report, *The Limits of Growth*, appeared, with its doomsday scenario of the exhaustion of the world's natural resources unless remedial action was taken (Meadows *et al.*, 1972). Environmental groups, which emerged in the late 1960s, enjoyed growing popular support, making western governments sit up and take notice, especially in West Germany and Holland, where environmentalists threatened government majorities. Although the Club of Rome's Malthusian prose somewhat overstated the case (assuming that super-growth was sustainable, causing the exhaustion of some minerals within half a century, it ignored the possibilities of fresh discoveries, recycling and new energy technology), the EC was galvanized into action, leading to the unveiling of its first environmental programme (1973–8) in November 1973, just as the tidal waves of the first oil shock were breaching the last redoubts of the faltering 'long boom'.

Reducing import dependence became a key theme of energy policies. After the second oil shock underlined the continued vulnerability of Europe to major disruptions of Middle East oil sources, strategic stocks were built up to withstand all but the most prolonged of oil disasters. The 1990–91 Gulf crisis, therefore, while it caused some temporary price dislocation, was but a minor blip. By December 1993, OECD governments could call on over one billion barrels of stock which, with International Energy Authority, EC and industry stockpiles, provided insurance for over three months' projected forward demand. The government-controlled stocks alone were sufficient to weather a 12 per cent shortfall of world supply for 130 days. Europe's oil dependency on Middle East supplies has in fact declined significantly: net oil imports represented less than 10 per cent by value of all EC imports in 1992, compared with 26 per cent in 1980 (Mitchell, 1994, 57, 62). As well as energy efficiency, the growth in the natural gas market, from small beginnings in northern Italy and southern France, to multi-source availability (Holland, the North Sea, Alaska, North Africa, the Soviet Union and its successors), partly helps explain the decline (Odell, 1986, 129–35). The North Sea oil bonanza led to sterling becoming a petro-currency at the peak of production in the early 1980s, while by the late 1990s Norway was the world's second largest oil producer. Moreover, technical developments in production technology near the end of the century were such as to persuade Elf-Aquitaine, a French developer, to contemplate developing a massive new field discovered in 1400 feet of water off Angola (Corzine, 1998, 30).

Although the first oil shock is often seen as the principal factor in terminating the 'long boom', in fact it was preceded by a number of worrying developments which cumulatively threatened to end western Europe's period of greatest prosperity, albeit at a later date. The precise reasons for the European economic downturn are complex, but of key importance was the conjuncture of five predominant features: the collapse of Bretton Woods and return to free floating currencies; labour market constraints; the exhaustion of the catch-up effect and the end of the mass consumption goods phase; the emergence of highly competitive Newly Industrializing Countries (NICs); and the rise in the cost of primary products, culminating in the *coup de grâce* of the oil shock. Added to this, often misguided government policies worsened the situation: the introduction of floating exchange rates which removed external constraints, combined with the availability of large international reserves, led to an unfortunate final push on the accelerator by several governments concerned to combat rising levels of unemployment (Aldcroft, 1993, 205).

The 'golden age' may have ended on a high note with a last gasp mini-boom (1972–3), but it was one with decidedly shaky foundations. The British 'dash for growth' (Barber boom) was the worst case: although the immediate impact of reflation was to push the rate of growth to 1.5 percentage points above the OECD average for 1973, this was only achieved through incurring an external deficit nearly 4 per cent greater than the OECD average by the following year, leading ultimately to a lower growth rate than the norm by 1978 (Ball and Albert, 1983, 34–5). The beginning of 1973, as much as its oil-dominated ending, delineated a turning point for the worse. The Bundesbank then became so concerned with German inflation that it began applying the brakes through a credit squeeze. The Italians, who experienced a $5 billion negative swing in their current account between 1969 and 1973, as the lira appreciated to an uncompetitive level *vis-à-vis* the weakened dollar, resorted to devaluation in a doomed attempt to revive their flagging exports (Boltho, 1982, 493, 519).

It can be argued that the economic slowdown after 1973 marked a return to average growth rates following the exceptional and unrepeatable features of the 'golden age' (Aldcroft, 1993, 195; Crafts and Toniolo, 1996, 25). By the late 1960s, growth trends had already turned downwards in Britain and France. In the former case, the Labour government's economic growth targets were swept off course by its avowed refusal to devalue sterling until there was no other choice. In the latter case, planning targets were met more and more infrequently, with civil servants and the managers of big business and their respective trade unions being accused of favouritism by their smaller counterparts, an acrimonious position which turned planning into an impediment to expansion. This irregular growth was to become more generalized throughout western Europe by the end of the 1970s.

A wages explosion introduced another destabilizing factor: rising per capita incomes became the norm and the expectation; labour markets tightened as agricultural labour reserves were depleted; improved conditions of work, shorter hours, more holidays and higher pay were the constant mantras of trade unions throughout the continent. Such attitudes marked a decisive shift, with labour now no longer willing to bear the brunt of the consequences of a downturn as it had been during the Korean War period. Most governments attempted to deploy some form of incomes policy to contain escalating labour costs but, with the exceptions of Austria and West Germany, these proved unsuccessful. Moreover, the narrowing technological gap between the United States and western Europe meant there was limited scope for substituting capital for labour, at least in the short term. As a consequence, this period produced a rise in real wages which ran ahead of productivity increases (a problem which afflicted Britain in the early 1960s, but now became contagious), contributing to falling profit levels. Employers often responded by raising their prices to protect profit margins (Lloyd-Jones and Lewis, 1998, 187). There was, too, the constraint of restrictive practices, especially evident in Britain and France, which accentuated rigidities in the labour market (Von Tunzlemann, 1992, 47).

As Temin (1997) notes, proponents of the new growth theory have thus far failed to come up with any satisfactory explanation for the termination of the 'golden age'. Supporters of the long wave school (see Barnett, 1998a; Lloyd-Jones and Lewis, 1998) suggest that the end of the 'long boom' marked a natural cut-off point. Based on the ideas of the Russian economist, Nikolai Kondratieff, the long wave theory posits an economic cycle of 45 to 60 years in duration. Joseph Schumpeter then embraced and refined the theory to incorporate clusters of strategic innovations, such as railways and electricity, which, on their introduction, drive growth forward until their impact lessens, when a recession/depression occurs until the next wave of innovations sweeps in. For the 'long boom', motor vehicles and consumer durables, such as television, refrigerators and transistors, which began to have a mass impact from the 1950s, are seen as constituting the innovatory engine of growth. Van der Wee (1991, 90) considers that 'the exhaustion of innovation potential in the leading industrial sectors of the western economy' was a key ingredient in the downturn. The 'catch-up' effect of the 'golden age', which began with a clear development gap between western Europe and the United States, had virtually exhausted itself by the 1970s. Indeed, the catching-up tendency encouraged massive overinvestment in traditional industries, leading to excess capacity. More equitable levels of income and a narrowing of the technology gap closed down further opportunities for supergrowth. These would now pass to the NICs, who stole a march on western Europe by focusing on similar relatively low-tech sectors (Van der Wee, 1991, 90). Finally, Rostow (1985) produced a variant of the Kondratieff long wave, couched in terms of a price cycle rather than an output cycle, measured over time by the terms of trade between manufacturing countries and primary producers. During much of the long post-war boom, these had favoured industrial producers. From the late 1960s, however, primary producers benefited from an upswing in international commodity prices that acted as the prelude to the oil shock.

Price inflation served to augment the economic crises experienced across western Europe and deepened the downturn already under way, resulting in inflation without growth. Trade union pressure made it difficult to reduce wages, adding to price inflation. In the 1960s, prices rose on average by 3 per cent annually, but the following decade the figure had nearly tripled. During the 'golden age', employment rose in tandem with manufacturing capacity. Mass unemployment, banished since the 1930s, returned with a vengeance. The jobless total across the EC had doubled within five years of the second oil shock of 1979. The European 'golden age' was no more, and by the end of the century was but a distant memory, an aberration that belied Europe's relative economic decline since 1914.

IMPORT-LED GROWTH IN EASTERN EUROPE: CAUSES AND CONSEQUENCES

By the late 1960s, all eastern Europe (bar Albania) could claim to be industrialized, but extensive growth, based on switching labour from agriculture to industry, from countryside to city, was nearing exhaustion. Planning reforms, introduced in the 1960s with the intention of sustaining economic momentum, essentially failed to render the command economies any more efficient. The 'Action Programme' of the Prague Spring of 1968 and unrest in Poland at the start of the 1970s were symptomatic of a growing restlessness among the caged populations of the Soviet bloc. It was clear that overemphasis on heavy industry starved light industry of resources, leading to a shortage of consumer goods and a distinct lack of choice. The Soviet Union gave the lead when, at the 24th party congress of March 1971, the new five-year plan accorded consumer goods priority for the first time. Moreover, a new technological age dawned in the 1970s with the invention of the microchip in California's Silicon Valley and innovative technology-driven methods of production. In the shadow of such developments, the Soviet bloc's technological backwardness was brought into sharp relief.

As east–west détente produced a thaw in the Cold War, so the opportunity arose to embark on an import-led growth strategy. This was to be based on high-tech western imports, which were coveted by East Europeans either because of their higher quality or, quite simply, because they themselves were incapable of producing particular technologies. American and European banks, lacking industrial customers as recession gripped their continents, and anxious to recycle 'petrodollars' deposited by Arab clients, proved more than willing to finance the inflow of western machinery and technology. Equally, east European governments were forced to turn to them for finance since their own currencies were non-convertible and free world exporters demanded hard currency. To pay for the loans, derivative manufactures would be produced and exported to the west and world markets. Success promised to turn command economies around, reinstate the spectacular growth rates of the 1950s and improve living standards sufficiently to ward off potential revolts by the population.

After negligible involvement in the free world economy arising from ideology and the height of the Cold War, 35.6 per cent of the Soviet bloc's total imports came from the west by 1975. Nor was this dangerous level of dependency adversely affected by the first oil shock, since the Soviet Union, for political–strategic reasons, provided its satellites with low-cost energy within the framework of the Council for Mutual Economic Assistance (CMEA). So, where the oil shock brought western economies to a shuddering halt, eastern Europe was let off the hook. But in the longer term, Moscow's calculated benevolence proved a mixed blessing. Bloc countries were not compelled to adopt conservation measures, so that energy-intensive industries continued unabated, with the worst offenders spewing out pollution on a scale that threatened the health of local inhabitants. More significant still was the fact that the inflationary consequences of the first oil shock were transmitted to eastern Europe through the conduct of ever more expensive technological imports which greatly increased the size of external debts. It would have been difficult to choose a more inopportune moment to become entangled with the free world economy, and in the 1970s were sown the seeds of destruction that culminated in the 1989 revolutions.

The situation was made all the worse by the spectacular failure of the import-led growth strategy. As Mikhail Gorbachev would discover to his cost, there was no middle way between capitalism and communism. The blunt truth was that centrally planned economies were unsuited to the effective utilization of western technologies. For one thing, money was squandered on fruitless projects. Poland was the worst example: 416 import licences were purchased between 1971 and 1980, but very few projects were completed and those that were often turned into white elephants, with output far below projections. In reality, as Bideleux and Jeffries (1998, 571) observe, 'East European regimes eagerly accepted Western loans, investments, joint ventures, industrial installations and "technology transfers" as a substitute for more fundamental reforms in their socio-economic systems.' Yet, without them, import-led growth was doomed to failure. Again, the absence of effective quality control ensured that the enormous gap in standards between east and west remained. Furthermore, central planners were woefully ignorant of market opportunities in the west. The misguided production of heavy luggage in Poland, when western consumers had moved on to light plastic and soft baggage, was a classic example of a wasted opportunity. Frequent failures to meet delivery deadlines also saddled east European manufacturers with poor reputations in the west. Even without these problems, it is doubtful whether export–import-led growth could have succeeded at this juncture (as it also failed for the military dictatorships in Argentina, Brazil and Chile). The world economy was in recession, 'which permitted only few successes to penetrate the protected and recessionary import markets in the west and the world generally' (Frank, 1994, 324–5). Compounding the mounting problems was endemic corruption. False accounting by export firms ensured that they received more imported components and specialist materials than their actual mediocre performance justified. And finally, the heavy industry lobby, aghast at losing its priority status, proved adept at redirecting much of the foreign lending to meet its own requirements (Drewnowski, 1982, 32; Smith 1983, 34–5).

By the end of the 1970s, eastern Europe's 'western strategy' was in tatters: it had palpably failed to deliver higher growth rates, improve productivity and production standards, or to modernize economies. Computers, for instance, were a rarity across the bloc and those that existed were certainly not IBM-compatible! In 1980, the number of telephone lines per 100 inhabitants, a good yardstick of progress, was only 7.7 for eastern Europe, compared to 28 for the EC and 79 in the United States. Although, as Frank remarks (1994, 324), eastern Europe was not unique in experiencing economic crises and falling living standards in the 1970s (Latin America and Africa also got into difficulties), what marked it out was 'an important deterioration and retrocession in its *relative* competitive standing and standards of living compared to Western Europe, and even to ... NICs in East Asia'. Poland had been the worst culprit in embarking on import-led growth, but the 'Polish disease' afflicted the whole region. Failure resulted in an enormous bill. By the end of the decade, debt repayment exceeded the inflow of western capital (Bideleux and Jeffries, 1998, 571). Loans from western banks, from a negligible $5.7 billion in 1971, stood at $74.7 billion by 1981 (Sirc, 1994, 104). It became increasingly difficult to borrow from western banks as international capital markets tightened and they demanded exorbitant double-digit rates of interest. Such was the plight of Poland and Romania that their debts needed to be rescheduled. In 1980, an independent trade union, Solidarity, rose in revolt in Poland. Eventually, under Soviet pressure, it was crushed, for the time being, by the Polish government through the imposition of martial law. It was a portent of things to come (Aldcroft and Morewood, 1995, ch. 9).

EUROSCLEROSIS AND DECLINING COMPETITIVENESS IN WESTERN EUROPE

Herbert Giersch coined the term 'Eurosclerosis' (see Giersch and Wolter, 1983; Giersch and Bertola, 1990). He argued that the welfare state inhibited economic adjustment. The overextended welfare state was reflected in the fact that in 1981 the EC devoted 30 per cent of its GDP to social expenditure, compared to 21 per cent in the United States and 18 per cent in Japan. What he considered to be overgenerous unemployment benefit provision had two negative effects: reducing the incentive for redundant workers to seek new jobs, and removing the pressure on employed workers to moderate their wage demands. In many countries real wages

increased above the trend rate of the 'long boom' in the 1970s, notwithstanding the recessionary environment. A variation of this argument was
put forward by Olson (1982; 1996), who suggested that the protracted
nature of the 'long boom' eventually nurtured the re-emergence of pressure groups whose 'sclerotic' influence had been broken by the Second
World War and the post-war settlement. Olson argued that long periods
of stability produce a multiplicity of organizations for collective action
that over time will impair economic efficiency and dynamism. Trade
union wage demands became impossible to resist and labour applied further pressure to extend the benefits system.

'Eurosclerosis', as a term, has also been applied to EC economies
which, by the mid-1980s, were deemed to be suffering from a range of
afflictions: industrial decline, falling productivity and a lack of competitiveness in world markets, as reflected by a continued rise in
unemployment and economic stagnation. Against the world's two leading
economies, the United States and Japan, gaps had widened in key areas:
trade, productivity, employment, investment and technology (Jones, 1996,
171). The emergence of NICs in the Third World (Brazil, South Korea
and so on) was a worrying trend which was reflected by increased import
penetration into western European markets and reduced export opportunities in NIC markets and third markets. It was in the 1960s that the first
wave of NICs transformed their economies, moving away from import
substitution to export-led growth strategies, with the 1970s seeing them
firmly established as serious competition in world markets, a position
they would consolidate in the 1980s. Their seemingly magic formula
included an education drive, government encouragement to home manufacturers in the form of export credits to trade overseas, and an
undervalued currency, together with a cheap and obedient workforce,
ready to work long hours for a pittance under often appalling conditions.
The NICs deprived European manufacturers of market share because the
latter were unable to compete in terms of cost.

In 1983, Malcolm Baldridge, the US Commerce Secretary, delivered a
speech in Venice in which he warmed to the Eurosclerosis theme. European
competitiveness, he suggested, was being eroded through a panoply of
restrictive measures. These included hefty government subsidies to sustain
inefficient state-owned industries; labour market rigidities deriving from a
desire to protect jobs rather than face competition; high overhead costs
from employing labour; and the deployment of a series of measures to
shield domestic manufacturers against imports. In short, Europe was living
beyond its means and apparently incapable of facing the hard choices
required to achieve the metamorphosis demanded to become, once more, a
formidable player in world markets (Welsh, 1998, 31).

That same year there appeared the Ball–Albert report on the costs of
'non-Europe' (see below). It arose from the growing unease within the
European Parliament at the lack of effective trade integration, a state of
affairs epitomized by lorry drivers being held up for hours in queues at
EC national borders while customs officials checked their documents and
cargoes to ensure compliance with national regulations. From this concern sprang *Kangaroo News*, an influential publication, whose title
alluded to support for hopping across frontiers – there was even a
'Kangaroo group' of Euro MPs! Widely circulated among large corporations, it catalogued the protection which member governments were
affording domestic producers. Parliament then commissioned two leading
economists, Professor James Ball, principal of the London Business
School, and Michel Albert, a former *Commissaire du Plan*, to investigate
the consequences of the lack of a true common market. Their findings
suggested the tantalizing possibility that as much as 2 per cent might be
added to the Community's GDP through the eradication of frontier
delays alone. The authors spelt out the dangers of the 'Balkanization' of
the European economy precluding companies from operating efficiently.

The report blamed Europe's dilatory recovery from the economic crises
of 1973–82 on the prevalence of 'non-Europe', a term employed by
Albert to denote the lack of intergovernmental cooperation and the effectiveness of common policies. The precipitous fall in manufacturing
investment that, in 1970, calculated as a percentage of GNP, was double
that in the United States, but by 1983 was only just above the American
level, gave cause for concern. So too did the dramatic rise in public expenditure as a percentage of GDP (see Table 6.3), which by 1982 topped
50 per cent, compared to approximately 35 per cent for the strongly
recovering United States and Japan. Two main causes were identified:
public corporations appeasing the demands of income earners determined to protect their 'golden age'-induced standard of living; and the
spectacular upsurge in social security expenditure. Social welfare costs
were in fact increasing twice as quickly as overall wealth, reflecting expensive medical advances in health care, resulting in ever-expanding numbers
of older people, which in turn inflated the state pensions bill.
Furthermore, rising unemployment reduced social security contributions
while unemployment benefits escalated. The 'long boom', and the full
employment that went with it, enabled west European regimes to court
popularity with the electorate through constructing ever more extensive
welfare systems for all. The enormous costs involved burdened both governments and employers, with the latter's social security contributions
increasing rapidly to sustain welfare programmes, thereby adding to
labour costs and helping to render European exports less competitive

Table 6.3 Public sector expenditure (as a percentage of GDP)

Country	1960	1967	1973	1980	1981	1982
USA	27.8	31.2	31.2	33.2	33.5	35.5
Japan	20.7	22.7	22.1	32.7	33.3	34.8
EEC	32.1	37.5	39.9	47.1	49.8	50.8
France	34.6	39.0	38.5	46.2	50.8	51.9
FRG	32.0	38.2	40.5	46.9	49.3	49.7
UK	32.6	38.5	41.1	44.3	45.3	46.2
Italy	30.1	33.7	37.8	45.6	53.0	54.9

Sources: OECD and Eurostat.

over the longer term (Ball and Albert, 1983, 14–16). The report was at pains to emphasize the detrimental impact of overextended welfare systems on competitiveness, with compulsory levies rising twice as fast in Europe as in the United States over the last ten years:

> This situation leads, by an invisible but inexorable process, to an increasing burden of compulsory contributions which gradually weakens the system of production itself. We are slowly killing the goose that lays the golden eggs. This is especially true in some countries, such as France or Italy, where industry has to bear the main brunt of social contributions. The inevitable result of this inflated growth of the welfare state is discouragement, the impoverishment of industry and the loss of enterprise. . . (Ibid., 25)

The authors equated EC unemployment, then running at 12 million, to a 'cancer' which spread protectionism and reduced investment to protect remaining jobs. In technological products, the community's record was lamentable (eight out of 10 personal computers sold were American and nine out of 10 video recorders came from Japan). In facing the third industrial revolution, Europe had '*suffered a veritable "technological shock" no less formidable than the "oil shock"*' (Ball and Albert, 1983, 30, original emphasis). Ball and Albert considered that the heart of the growth problem was the failure to adopt a collective approach, in keeping with the spirit and aims of the Treaty of Rome, in preference to selfish and restrictive national policies. The absence of monetary and exchange rate stability through floating until the arrival of the European Exchange Rate Mechanism (ERM) was seen as worsening the crisis. In key areas, like technology, only 'non-Europe' existed; resources were squandered and potential economies of scale wasted. In short, the common market existed in name only.

In response, the European Parliament established a temporary special Committee on European Economic Recovery to consider the report's findings. It conceded (European Parliament, 1984a, 6) that member governments had reacted to the external shocks of the 1970s 'in an uncoordinated fashion and, sacrificing the future to the present, failed to make the adjustments needed to sustain growth and employment at the right time'. In particular, European firms suffered a decline in competitiveness, not least because of the 'rigidity of wage costs, high financial and fiscal costs and inadequate research and innovation'; productive investments fell off, especially in new technology sectors; and public sector deficits spiralled through the need to sustain increasing numbers of unemployed and the extended universal welfare provisions, many of them introduced in this period.

Worse still, European governments addressed faltering growth in a ramshackle fashion rather than collectively, resulting in greater financial support for struggling sectors, increased frontier controls and extended protection for national markets, all of which negated the perceived advantages of a common market (specialization, economies of scale and the optimum allocation of factors of production). Added to unstable exchange rates and dispersed R&D, these tendencies acted to discourage investment in growth sectors. Moreover, apart from achieving some measure of monetary stability and budgetary adjustment, member states had been unable to nurture successful expansionist policies to restore demand and create jobs. The failure compromised the community's prospects of successfully adjusting to the new international trading environment and realizing the enormous potential from a market with a combined population of 270 million and 20 per cent of world trade. The committee considered that

> policies for reviving demand cannot have any lasting impact so long as the structural obstructive factors – a high rate of inflation, the compartmentalization of the markets, the instability of exchange rates, loss of ground in technological development, high taxation, the rigidities of the labour market and the capital market, the high cost of social welfare provisions and the over-indebtedness of the public authorities – have not been removed or attenuated. (European Parliament, 1984a, 7)

The committee viewed with envy economies that had managed to control inflation, which enjoyed flexible real wage costs and had realigned their industrial strategies to embrace growth sectors.

The problem was that Albert and Ball could not agree on solutions to revive the stricken European economies. While recognizing that a return to 'golden age' growth rates was unrealistic, the two authors offered conflicting diagnoses. Albert favoured investment at the community level in key areas such as R&D, growth industries, energy and the poorer countries and regions; Ball was rightly sceptical about his colleague's assumption that those in work would be willing to make sacrifices for the unemployed. Nevertheless, a degree of consensus was achieved on the way forward, centred on market reforms and exchange rate adjustment through a European monetary stability zone. What was clear was that 'go-it-alone' policies, based on a hefty increase in public sector spending, as pursued by Britain 1975–6 and France (1975–6, 1981–2), only led to revived inflation, balance of payments disequilibrium and exchange rate mayhem.

The committee's conclusions were in many ways the precursor of the subsequent legislative programme surrounding the single market. The committee's chairman was Jacques Moreau, a French trades unionist with close ties to Jacques Delors, then Minister of Finance in the Mitterrand government. Delors came along at a time when a head of steam was developing for a bold new initiative. A draft treaty on European union, initiated by Altero Spinelli, an Italian Euro MP, was approved by the European Parliament in February 1984. Four months later, the Fontainebleau summit of heads of government unjammed a number of contentious issues: milk quotas were deployed as a means of controlling farm spending; structural funds would be increased; the Spanish and Portuguese applications for membership became acceptable after much stalling; and the long-running dispute over Britain's budget contributions was resolved. From the deliberations emerged the Dooge committee whose report, published in March 1985, recommended a widening of community objectives, including a 'homogenous internal economic space' (Grant, 1994, 64–5).

Delors, who became President of the European Commission in January 1985, was all too aware that a 'big idea' was required to regenerate the community. He was convinced that the original Monnet-Schuman motive for creating the common market – 'never again war between us' – was out-of-date. Now nothing less than European union was required 'to guarantee survival' and prevent member economies from becoming 'museums for the Japanese and the Americans to visit'. Delors at first considered promoting a single currency but, faced with the prospect of stiff British opposition, opted to delay this option in favour of a single market. All 10 member states were keen on this idea, with the British, often portrayed as the sourpusses of the community, so enthused that they even provided the commissioner for the single market, Lord Cockfield, a Thatcherite and former British trade secretary. Here was a propitious moment to give birth to a new child, not least because the EC's annual growth rate, after bumping along the bottom at an average of just 1.6 per cent in the the years 1982–4, was on a rising trend, moving to 2.6 per cent over 1985–7 and 3.6 per cent between 1988–1990 (Grant, 1994, 66). There now seemed some light at the end of the tunnel and it was called 'the single European market'.

THE COMING OF THE SINGLE MARKET

In the Treaty of Rome, the founding members of the community committed themselves to creating a free trade area, with a common external tariff (a customs union) and envisaged the free movement of the factors of production. It was intended that the proposed 'common market' would be complete by 1969. In the event, by that date, only the customs union was in place and a truly integrated market was lacking. In 1982, Nicholas Kaldor considered the EC to be a 'preferential trading area' rather than a free trade area, since the removal of internal tariff barriers was accompanied by the erection of non-tariff barriers (Dyker, 1992, 52). These fell into three broad categories: physical barriers, like frontier and customs controls, which inflated the cost of intra-EC transactions; the absence of common technical standards, tending to enhance costs or hinder trade through the need to reconfigure, relabel and repackage goods to suit particular national markets; and the variations in indirect taxes (VAT and excise duty) which acted to distort trade.

The failure to implement fully the original intentions of the Treaty of Rome, that is the free movement of people, goods, capital and services, was seen as the heart of the problem. For example, only four member states (Britain, West Germany, the Netherlands and Denmark) allowed the full freedom of capital movement. The impediments to the single market had to be removed if the global playing field was to be levelled. National interests needed to be set aside. As Lord Cockfield remarked, 'Only on a European rather than a national basis can we hold our own in the world.' A study group was formed under Cockfield with a remit to ensure that the community fulfilled its full economic potential through the formulation of a legislative programme as a prelude to the launch of a single market. The outcome was the White Paper of 1985, which sought to identify the existing barriers preventing a truly common market. To achieve a Europe 'without frontiers', over 300 legislative proposals were drawn up, with 31 December 1992 selected as the completion date for the programme (European Commission, 1985).

At the Milan summit of June 1985 the European Council endorsed the legislative programme in a slightly scaled down form. The 12 member states were to form a single enlarged market based on the flexible utilization of human, material and financial resources, which would be chan-nelled by market forces where they were best used. The measures required were grouped into three categories: the elimination of physical barriers, such as customs posts; the removal of technical barriers, such as the lack of standardization and varying product regulations; and the elimination of fiscal barriers, such as differing approaches to indirect taxation, which produced price discrepancies and distorted competition. Cumulatively, these barriers resulted in a fragmented market with business and con-sumers paying the penalty (ibid.).

The importance of the single market was such that it inspired the con-vening of the first intergovernmental conference since 1957 to endorse the Single European Act (SEA), which came into force on 1 July 1987. This made the creation of the single market a top priority. To prevent Eurosclerosis through the use of national government vetoes, a qualified majority rule was introduced which applied to most areas of the legisla-tive programme, except tax, where unanimity was still needed. Once a policy had been agreed in principle, its implementation now only required a qualified majority. Delors suggested that the Single European Act had six key objectives: the creation of a single market without frontiers; the introduction of regional structural policies; promoting cooperation in research and technology; monetary policy cooperation; the consideration of social policy at every level; and the improvement of environmental policy. While the social side of Delors' agenda was anathema to the Thatcher government, there was broad support for the single market because the emphasis was on closer economic integration. As Margaret Thatcher put it in her famous Bruges speech of September 1988: 'By get-ting rid of barriers, by making it possible for companies to operate on a Europe-wide scale, we can best compete effectively with the United States, Japan and other new economic powers emerging in Asia and else-where.' Nevertheless, Delors recognized the political implications of the SEA, which represented a further shift of power away from national gov-ernments towards institutions (Grant, 1994, 70).

There were two principal perceived advantages of the Single European Market (SEM). Internally, it was expected that the consumer would bene-fit from greater specialization of production at company level and from falling prices through economies of scale. Externally, it would strengthen the EC against its major competitors. The European Commission insti-gated an investigation into the likely impact. Based on a survey of 11 000 firms, the resulting report was brimful of optimism, anticipating that the SEM would increase competition, encourage industrial rationalization and lower costs through the greater utilization of scale economies. The report was peppered with rose-tinted calculations. It predicted that, in its first five to six years, the SEM would create between 1.8 and 5 million new jobs, facilitate a marked fall in prices of between 4.5 and 6.1 per cent, bring greater choice to consumers at more competitive prices and lead to a rise in the Community's GDP of around 3 to 6 per cent (Cecchini, 1988).

The SEM was anticipated by preliminary investment over several years. One outcome was to increase the scale of inward investment in the EC, especially to Britain, which the Japanese and South Koreans favoured. Japanese direct investment in Europe rose from $8.8 billion (1970–84) to $74.6 billion (1985–93). Indeed, in 1992, the EU attracted 50 per cent of foreign direct investment (FDI) around the world (Monti, 1996, 85). The boom of the late 1980s was assisted by the lead-up to the SEM. Brussels estimated that 30 per cent of the potential benefits had arrived in advance of the official opening date, while cross-frontier mergers and acquisitions rose from 2190 in 1987 to 4553 in 1992. Preliminary measures included the removal of exchange controls. On 1 January 1993, three of the last four members to effect this change (Ireland, Spain and Portugal) carried it out, with only Greece to follow.

THE RECORD OF THE SINGLE MARKET

The opening of the SEM was ushered in by the lighting of bonfires that symbolized the realization of the four principal aim of the community's founders: the free movement of people, goods, capital and services. Originally comprising 12 countries and 344 million people, and representing 25 per cent of world economic output, the SEM was further extended in January 1995 to include most EFTA countries (Finland, Austria and Sweden), when it became known as the 'European Economic Area'. With this third enlargement the EC could boast the world's biggest single trading market, one-third larger than the American market, and greater than the NAFTA (United States, Canada and Mexico) in respect of GDP, population and share of world trade (Milner, 1994).

The creation of the SEM has been called 'a potential revolution'. Certainly, it rendered the common market much more transnational than before. National banks could open branches elsewhere in the SEM while students of one country could attend the universities of others as of right. An immediate effect was that lorry drivers, previously held up by endless form filling to cross national borders, could now take their goods from country to country without being troubled by customs officers and border police (Britain, Ireland and Denmark were the exceptions in still insisting on border checks). No fewer than 60 million customs forms per annum were averted, plus 85 per cent of red tape hitherto involved in border crossings. The pre-1992 system cost traders and road hauliers an estimated Ecu 7.5 billion a year, where the changes saved them around ECU 5 billion annually, equivalent to about 0.7 per cent of total trade turnover in the EU (Monti, 1996, 14–15).

The notion that 1 January 1993 would bring a 'Big Bang' overnight transformation of SEM participants' economies failed to recognize either the possibility that a recession would then be gripping the continent or the obstacles that remained. In the SEM's first year, EC GDP fell by 0.3 per cent and unemployment rose to 10.5 per cent of the workforce and went on rising. This was crucial in regressing the potential of the SEM, for when companies failed to galvanize consumers with price cuts and quality improvements, their enthusiasm waned and they refrained from expansion. At best, the SEM contained the recession, with estimates of its job creation effects ranging from 300 000 to 900 000 (ibid., 108), though this was a far cry from the heady optimism of the Cecchini Report. By 1997, it was claimed that the single market had increased GDP in the EU in the order of 1. 1 to 1. 5 percentage points and reduced inflation by 1 per cent (*EP News*, 1998, 4), a performance which was dwarfed by the American economic renaissance.

There was a mixed record in the removal of technical barriers. After the laborious process involved in requiring approval for the sale of new motor car models in each member state, a new 'whole type approval' directive was introduced covering the entire SEM, saving around 10 per cent in development costs. The scale of the task was such that an inevitable backlog sprang up, with regulators failing to keep up with legislation: the European Standardization Committee alone had 500 technical committees under its authority. The principle of mutual recognition, whereby members recognize that, since they all face the same product risks, their precautions and safeguards are generally acceptable, proved more problematical. Foodstuffs were a particularly sensitive area (witness the reaction to Britain's BSE crisis) in which to achieve harmonization (Monti, 1996, 24, 27– 8, 32).

Delays in the implementation of key segments of the SEM militated against maximizing its potential. There was no free trade in insurance until July 1994 and in investment services until January 1996; no liberalization of basic telephone services until 1998 and, for poorer countries, even later; until 1997, VAT was charged on goods in the country of destination rather than the country of origin, creating a mountain of paperwork surrounding charges and refunds; and duty-free shopping at airports and on ferries for pan-European travellers remained an anomaly until July 1999. Again, where the interests of domestic operators are threatened, governments have often proved dilatory in transposing SEM directives into national law. By 1996, just three members had properly implemented public procurement directives, with the rest providing 'a classic illustration of how governments, and companies, want to have their cake and eat it, happy to seize on opportunities in neighbouring markets but still keen to keep their own market off-limits to competitors' (ibid., 9). Similarly, although in principle the SEM liberalized air transport, in practice national carriers remained largely protected (for instance, in the allocation of prized landing slots at key airports). With a few exceptions, the cost of flying within Europe remained expensive when compared to transatlantic tariffs.

At York on 21 March 1998, the European Commission undertook to initiate a year-long investigation into the reasons for Europeans paying significantly higher prices than Americans for a majority of products and into the causes of continued substantial price differences across the EU. In justifying the move, the commission pointed to a number of examples. For instance, personal bank charges showed huge variation, with British rates half those of Germany and one-fifth the French level. British car buyers could expect to pay a substantial premium when buying continental models in Britain rather than in their country of origin. Even excluding tax, huge price differentials were evident: for compact discs, Americans paid 25 per cent less than the French and 9 per cent less than Britons. Different tax regimes meant that, unlike their American counterparts, British consumers failed to benefit from falling oil prices, with three-quarters of the price consumed by tax. On alcohol and tobacco, much steeper British excise duties fostered cross-Channel visits to northern France to benefit from comparatively cheap French beer, wines and cigarettes (Smith, 1998a). The wide disparities in VAT rates further militated against the creation of a level playing field.

The shortcomings of the SEM were highlighted in 1995, when the European Commission established the Competitive Advisory Group (CAG) to make recommendations to improve European competitiveness. Chaired by Carlo Ciampi and, later, Percy Barnevik, with prominent industrialists, trade unionists, politicians and academics to make recommendations, CAG offered a critical prognosis. Its reports pointed to several deficiencies, including the importance of encouraging small and medium-sized enterprises (SMEs), whose latent contribution was seen as vital for innovation and job creation; of the need to reduce state aid; and the need to render the European Company Statute user-friendly. CAG further recommended that telecommunications, electricity, natural gas and postal services be opened up to competition (Jacquemin and Pench, 1997).

Only a few years after its creation, a rounded evaluation of the effectiveness of the SEM is clearly not possible. Aside from the incompleteness of the single market programme, there are several imponderables to weigh in the balance. Somewhat ironically, there is the possibility that, contrary to its intentions, the SEM actually reduced growth because the increased competition it engendered discouraged some firms from investing in R&D, fearing that the high outlays demanded would not be recouped. Its establishment coincided with the accelerated liberalization of international trade, suggesting that there would have been some backwash from this in any event. Again the rise in the EU growth rate to 2.9 per cent in 1994 could be said to have had as much to do with the downfall of the ERM as with the arrival of the single market (Mills, 1998, 67). One irony was that non-European firms – Japanese carmakers and electronics companies and a plethora of American multinationals from IBM to McDonalds – were prominent among the main beneficiaries of the SEM. By the mid-1990s, over half of American FDI was in the EU (Monti, 1996, 85). Smaller European companies generally did not become as immersed in the SEM's opportunities for a combination of reasons, including exchange rate risk, cultural differences, language barriers and formidable legal complications.

What '1993' has not achieved is the introduction of a true single market, where duties, taxes and legal systems are harmonized across national boundaries. While it has clearly broken down barriers in some areas, the scale of the task remaining is reflected by the total number of regulations, directives and legal acts which rose inexorably, from 1947 in 1973 to 23 027 by 1996 (Szamuely and Jamieson, 1998, 52). It was also argued that the single market could not be complete without a single currency. The transaction costs involved in switching from one currency to another increased with the arrival of the SEM, in absolute terms, from Ecu 33.1 billion to Ecu 58.1 billion between 1986 and 1995. Moreover, currency differences were perceived as a barrier to the transparent prices intended within the SEM, allowing companies to obscure price mark-ups (Monti, 1996, 142). The removal of national controls over the movement of capital was an essential component of the SEM. It was also a natural step towards one currency but, as will be seen, concomitantly introduced a destabilizing factor.

THE ERM AND THE SINGLE CURRENCY

Created at a time when Bretton Woods and the dollar were in their heyday, the fledgling European Economic Community did not see the need for a single currency, and devaluations and revaluations of national currencies occurred within the international monetary system. By the late

1960s, however (see Chapter 5 of the present volume) Bretton Woods had become discredited, not least because of the undermining of the once almighty dollar through the United States' unfortunate involvement in the quagmire of Vietnam and the costs of the 'Great Society' programme. The Johnson government, fearing electoral defeat if it raised taxes to pay for war and social reform, resorted instead to heavy borrowing, thereby injecting inflation into the system. Increasingly, European governments became unhappy at holding depreciating dollars in their reserves and began casting around for an alternative. The Hague summit of December 1969 formally adopted EMU, but only as a long-term objective. The following October, the Werner Committee submitted a plan which suggested a stage-by-stage approach until 1980, by which time there could be either the irrevocable fixing of exchange rates or, preferably, the introduction of a single currency. Werner envisaged a community-wide central banking system with a common monetary policy (Werner, 1970).

Following the Smithsonian Agreement of December 1971, 'the snake in the tunnel' system was introduced in March 1972. Originally comprising the EC Six, it was soon extended to the three new members (Britain, Ireland and Denmark) and to Scandinavia (Norway and Sweden). The Smithsonian format ('the tunnel') allowed currencies to move 4.5 per cent against the dollar, but looking towards eventual monetary union the snake system restricted the divergence of member currencies from par value to 2.25 per cent ('the snake'). The system proved unworkable in the choppy economic waters of the 1970s. No sooner had Britain and Ireland joined the system than they were forced out by an exchange crisis. Subsequently, Italy and France met the same fate, leaving only Germany, Benelux, Norway and Denmark as viable members by 1979 (Sumner, 1992, 138).

The idea of a European monetary bloc was not revived until 1978 when, concerned at another precipitate weakening of the dollar, Helmut Schmidt, the German chancellor, persuaded Roy Jenkins, then President of the EC Commission, to back the proposal at the European Council meeting in Copenhagen. Jenkins, unlike the lukewarm British Labour government, was persuaded of the case for this leap in the dark:

> The era of violent currency fluctuations, which had set in with the end of the Bretton Woods system in 1971, had coincided with the worsening of Europe's relative economic performance. In the 1960s, with fixed exchange rates, the Europe of the Six had performed ... at least as well as America or Japan. In the mid-1970s, with oscillating rates, it had performed dismally. Nor was this surprising. For the other two main economies the fluctuations had been external, affecting only relationships across the oceans. For the Community they had been viscerally internal, with the French franc and the D-mark diverging from each other as much as either had done from the dollar or the yen. (Jenkins, 1994, 464)

In December 1978, the Brussels summit formally endorsed the creation of the European Monetary System (EMS), following a dramatic speech in its favour by Jenkins (ibid., chs 25–6).

The ERM was the most important component of the EMS. The successor to the snake, within it each member had a central rate, denominated in Ecus. (Introduced in 1975, the Ecu was a nominal currency of settlement made up of a weighted basket of EC currencies. It was not, however, legal tender and did not exist in note or coin form.) For the majority, the maximum fluctuation each side of the rate was 2.25 per cent, but in March 1979 Italy was allowed to join with a wider 6 per cent band. This set a precedent, later followed by Spain, Britain and Portugal. The intention was that these wider band members would eventually move to the narrower band, as Italy did in January 1990. For several years, following the second oil shock, inflation rates across the community had diverged markedly, ranging in 1978 from West Germany's exemplary 2.7 per cent to Italy's profligate 12.1 per cent. Now it was anticipated that the discipline imposed by the ERM would generate convergence around a lower mean level (Sumner, 1992, 144).

In theory, the ERM was not a system of permanently fixed parities. Although central banks were expected to intervene to maintain the value of a currency within the prescribed parameters, in practice some flexibility was allowed. Indeed, between 1979 and 1987, there were frequent adjustments, with the Deutschmark being revalued six times and other ERM currencies devalued. Given this flexibility, the ERM proved remarkably stable between 1987 and 1991. Currency realignments were smaller among members than between free-floating currencies over the period, a low inflation environment was created and, crucially, the ERM catered for differing economic performances.

In June 1988, the European Council established the Committee for the Study of EMU under Delors' chairmanship to consider whether the SEM could be bolstered by a single currency. Comprising 12 central bank governors and five independent experts, the committee's findings provided the framework for the Maastricht Treaty (see below). The Delors Report of 1989 contained some key differences compared to the Werner Report. Where the latter advised removing capital controls at the end of the EMU process, it was now recommended they be removed at the start. Werner envisioned a loose federation of central banks. The Delors Report wanted a European Central Bank to oversee a single monetary policy with national central banks becoming operating arms. Where the reports converged was in the goal of price stability.

The Delors Report suggested that EMU be achieved in three distinct stages. Stage One would see the removal of capital controls, the reduction of inflation and interest rate differentials and the increasing stability of intra-European exchange rates. Stage Two would witness the further convergence of national economic policies and the creation of a temporary entity, the European Monetary Institute (EMI), to plan for the final stage. In Stage Three, a European Central Bank would succeed the EMI as the exchange rates of qualifying members were irrevocably fixed as a prelude to the introduction of a single currency (Delors Committee, 1989).

Stage One, which commenced in July 1990, changed the nature of the ERM overnight into a mechanism leading up to a single currency. This new 'hard' ERM was one where EMU credibility was seen to rest on maintaining parities. Moreover, German interest rates had become the benchmark for ERM members. This was all very well when the Bundesbank set an appropriate rate for the rest to follow. Britain's belated entry in October 1990 was partly motivated by the need to bring down her double-digit base rate (at 15 per cent it was more than double her ERM partners) by shadowing the Bundesbank's renowned anti-inflation strategy. The apple cart was then upset when, in response to the fall-out from the huge costs involved in German reunification, the Bundesbank began raising interest rates at a time when many of its ERM brethren were in economic difficulty.

The German base rate represented an impenetrable floor (Britain got to within a quarter of a percentage point in August 1992). The British Chancellor, Norman Lamont, found the Bundesbank equally unmoved when he sought a reduction in German rates at the Bath ERM summit of September 1992. Four times he made the request; four times he was denied. The scene was set for a crisis. The markets sensed that slavishly following German interest rate moves and maintaining existing exchange rates were inappropriate to economies experiencing or facing recession. Further jitters were caused after the prospects for EMU dimmed when Denmark rejected the Maastricht Treaty and the imminent French referendum hung on a knife-edge. As Margaret Thatcher once famously remarked, 'You can't buck the market.' With exchange rates transparently out of line and governments failing to make the necessary adjustments, the outcome was a crushing attack on the system by speculators. The upshot was the forced exit of sterling and the lira from the ERM in September 1992 and, after five realignments and a further major crisis in July 1993, centred on five currencies, the ground rules had to be changed. On 2 August 1993 the normal fluctuation bands were widened from plus or minus 2.25 per cent to plus or minus 15 per cent for all ERM member currencies bar the Deutschmark and the guilder. The European Commission estimated that the currency turmoil of 1992–3 had led, by 1995, to a diminution in growth of between 0.25 and 0.5 percentage points (Jones, 1996, 184–7; Monti, 1996, 142).

Several views emerged from the ERM débâcle. The British felt that there were structural 'faultlines' in the system, stemming from the Bundesbank's dominance, which rendered precarious any return to the ERM. 'We want to be satisfied,' remarked Lamont, 'that the German policy that has produced many of the tensions in the ERM is going to have changes that will lead to a more stable environment.' The German chancellor derided these comments as 'inappropriate for a minister'. The general continental view was that the crises only served to underline the need for a single currency which was invulnerable to speculative attack (see Eichengreen, 1997, ch. 7). The French, in particular, drew the lesson that a European Central Bank was essential to emasculate the root cause of the crises – the dominance of the Bundesbank. Unlike the British, therefore, they decided to push forward with EMU.

THE ROAD TO MAASTRICHT AND BEYOND

Before the Maastricht Summit of December 1991, which concluded the Treaty on European Union, the ever sceptical British put forward a plan for a dual currency system comprising a 'hard Ecu' running parallel with national currencies. Maastricht endorsed the three-stage approach of the Delors Report, with Stage One to run from 1 July 1990 to 31 December 1993, when the single market came into effect; Stage Two from 1 January 1994; and Stage Three either in 1997 or, at the latest, 1 January 1999. In December 1995, again at Maastricht, the European Council endorsed the latter date, the former having proved wildly impractical. The idea of a definite start-up date emanated from the French and was designed to render EMU irreversible. Ever reluctant, the British and Danes negotiated opt-outs over joining the single currency.

The Maastricht Treaty established 'a European Union ... an ever closer Union among the peoples of Europe, where decisions are taken as closely as possible to the citizens'. The phrase was a political compromise to overcome British objections to federalism. In economic terms, the two achievements of Maastricht were the introduction of a Social Chapter and defining the gateway to EMU. The chapter established basic minimum standards in areas such as hourly pay, health and safety at work, working conditions and gender equality. The treaty laid down five basic entry criteria to qualify for EMU. First, price stability: an average rate of inflation no more than 1.5 percentage points above the three best performers. Second, exchange rate stability: sound performance without devaluation within the ERM for at least two years preceding entry to the single currency. Third, interest rate stability: long-term rates were not to exceed the three best performers by more than two percentage points. Fourth, sustainable public finances: the public deficit was to be at or near to 3 per cent of GDP unless there were exceptional and temporary mitigating circumstances. Last, the ratio of public debt to GDP must not exceed 60 per cent – although this condition was loosened by the acceptability of a diminishing ratio 'at a satisfactory pace' (Treaty on European Union, 1992).

The road to the single currency became increasingly strewn with obstacles as the start-up date grew nearer. Meeting the entry conditions did not prove easy. Government efforts to address the strict Maastricht convergence criteria meant budget cuts, falling subsidies and rising unemployment. The drive to EMU had economic consequences because of the mismatch of fiscal and monetary policies that only exacerbated the recession of the early to mid-1990s. Where the United States managed to achieve low real interest rates, in continental Europe they remained too high and, though more appropriate levels manifested themselves from 1996 onwards, it could be argued that the reduced inflationary risk and high unemployment justified even lower rates (Jacquet, 1998, 51). Indeed, seeking to qualify for EMU worsened the cyclical downturn, producing crisis levels of unemployment in Germany and France. By the start of 1998, French unemployment was at 12.4 per cent (six million), prompting protest marches, benefit office sit-ins and the like. French governments traditionally have caved in to radical protesters, such as farmers and truck drivers. Some concessions were made on this occasion to the benefit protesters by the socialist Jospin government (£100 million emergency assistance and a promised review of welfare hand-outs), but to concede the estimated £3 billion needed to meet their demands in full would have jeopardized French membership of EMU in the first wave (Henley, 1998, 4).

Two years away from the selection day (2 May 1998) Italy, as well as Greece, appeared a non-starter in the qualifying line-up, Spain and Portugal looked doubtful, while French and German participation was by no means assured. In fact, on an ultra-strict reading of the entry criteria only Luxembourg would have qualified! What each straggler then engaged in was a tightening of belts and a search for extra revenue to meet the public deficit target in 1997. They were assisted by the start of an economic upturn that saw the prospective euro-zone economy grow by 2.8 per cent in the final quarter of 1997 (Kuper, 1998, VI). Economic gymnastics were performed to qualify for the Maastricht entry conditions. France reduced its deficit through a multi-billion transfer from the France Telecom pension fund equivalent to 0.5 per cent of GDP; Italy introduced a special euro tax and raided the severance pay fund of public companies preparing for privatization; Belgium sold off some of its gold reserves to cut its debt as well as parting with several public buildings to boost its current account. As Mills (1998, 70) remarks, 'these transactions are "one off" and have nothing to do with complying with the underlying financial discipline which the Maastricht criteria are supposed to secure – yet another example of politics first and economics a long way second'.

By summer 1997, there were worrying signs of dissent between Germany and France, the prime movers in the drive towards the single currency. They could not agree over the policy objectives of the currency: for Germany it represented an external discipline of checks and balances to produce negligible inflation and stability, but France saw its role as creating employment and generating growth. Franco-German differences were also reflected in their views on the nature of EMU: the French would be content with a 'soft' euro while the Germans nailed their colours to a 'hard' euro which would hold its value against the dollar and play an equivalent role to that of the Deutschmark in suppressing inflation and buttressing sustained growth. At German insistence, a stability pact was introduced in December 1996 with the object of ensuring sustained convergence through continued fiscal discipline. Under this, participants were to keep their budget deficits under the 3 per cent Maastricht limit, or else face a fine of 0.1 per cent of GDP for each point above the ceiling. To appease the recalcitrant French, a growth element was added to the pact. The bickering continued on 2–3 May 1998 when the 11 first-wave euro entrants were confirmed. The preferred German candidate for the presidency of the ECB, Wim Duisenberg, boasted impeccable anti-inflationary credentials and came from a country (the Netherlands) which had pegged its currency to the Deutschmark since 1983. However, after prolonged dogfighting behind the scenes, the French got their way and it was announced that Duisenberg would only serve half his eight-year term when, for 'personal reasons', he would step down in favour of the current president of the French central bank. It was no wonder that, on hearing the news, journalists burst out into guffaws of incredulous laughter (Whitney, 1998).

In the end (see Table 6.4) through a mixture of sacrifice and statistical contortions, 11 countries were deemed to have met the Maastricht convergence criteria. Some doubts remained. Belgium and Italy, both with debt ratios double the Maastricht limit, only qualified through the back door since theirs were deemed to be sufficiently diminishing. Only in the price inflation category did the qualifiers comfortably meet the Maastricht criteria.

Table 6.4 Qualified success on convergence criteria

Targets	Budget deficit/GDP 3%	Debt/WP 60%	Price inflation 2.7%
EMU hopefuls			
Austria	2.5	66.1	1.2
Belgium	2.1	122.2	1.5
Finland	0.9	55.8	1.2
France	3.0	58.0	1.2
Germany	2.7	61.3	1.5
Ireland	−0.9	67.0	1.2
Italy	2.7	61.3	1.5
Luxembourg	−1.7	6.7	1.4
Netherlands	1.7	70.4	1.9
Portugal	2.5	62.0	1.9
Spain	2.6	68.3	1.9
Refuseniks			
Britain	1.9	53.4	1.9
Sweden	0.4	76.6	1.9
Denmark	−0.9	55.8	1.2
Rejected			
Greece	4.0	108.0	5.9

Source: *The European*, 2–8 March 1998.

THE CASE FOR A SINGLE CURRENCY

'Economic and monetary union,' suggested the European Commission in March 1998, 'will revitalise the European economy and the single market, foster investment, boost business competitiveness, benefit consumers and savers and make life easier for citizens where both work and travel are concerned' (Champion and Culp, 1998, 50). Helmut Kohl, Germany's 'Bismark in a cardigan', steadfastly believed that the euro would render Europe more competitive by compelling economies to become slimmer and more flexible. In this view, EMU is less a straitjacket than a *deus ex machina* which will introduce the changes which national governments, by themselves, have proved unable to face (Garton Ash, 1998, 5).

Perhaps the greatest argument in favour of EMU is the role it promises to play in promoting a more integrated single market through removing the uncertainties and costs engendered by unpredictable national exchange rates, enhanced capital mobility and transparent prices. The costs which euro-zone countries will experience, allowing direct comparisons to be made between the retail cost of goods, are viewed as a means of driving down prices through the market forces this should unleash. EMU is expected to cut costs by allowing companies to sell across the euro-zone in one currency. Daimler, a dominant multinational, anticipates annual savings of 100 million Deutschmarks in currency exchange costs (Nagorski and Thiel, 1998, 17).

One argument (Munchau, 1998, 11) is that the 11 start-up members, with a combined market of 288 million people, will for the first time enjoy the benefits of a true single market. It is also anticipated that the euro will promote investment outside home capital markets. In Germany, France and Italy, just 5 per cent of wealth was held abroad by 1997, a figure which optimists expect to rise as the anticipated low interest regime of the European Central Bank (ECB) reduces returns on government bonds and renders pan-European stock markets more enticing (Champion, 1998, 7).

The European Commission estimated that the transaction costs involved in converting currencies represented 0.33 per cent of EU GDP. By removing these charges, which large companies can absorb but which are a deterrent to SMEs, optimists expect the SEM to draw in far more smaller players. The example is often given of the apocryphal traveller who visits 10 EU states and, without spending anything, loses half the money through constantly changing currencies.

The collective pooling of national reserves into one vast war chest within the European Central Bank is expected to end the prospect of any repeat of the speculative attacks of ERM days, thereby saving vast sums hitherto required to defend individual currencies. Indeed, if the ECB exerts sufficient discipline, optimists predict that the euro-zone will be an area of monetary and price stability. In this scenario, EMU promises to introduce lower and less volatile rates of interest, creating a sustainable environment of low inflation, leading to higher growth. Moreover, the stability pact would preclude reckless government spending (see Eichengreen and Wyplosz, 1998).

In the long term, it is conceivable that EMU could collapse as certainly as the gold standard, Bretton Woods, German monetary union (1857–1918) and the Soviet system (1917–91). This would, however, require a political and economic catastrophe centred on EMU to persuade a majority of its members to seek to disengage themselves, a process which, even if agreed, would inevitably take some years to achieve, involving parliamentary sanction, referendums and the recreation of national currencies. Faced with such a protracted and unpredictable withdrawal process, it is far more likely that euro-zone members would choose to continue (Munchau, 1998b, III).

Again the argument that a soft euro will not hold its value against the dollar ignores the fact that only a small proportion of the euro-zone's GDP will comprise trade with outside nations utilizing other currencies. Furthermore, EU members remaining on the fringes of the euro-zone, whether by choice or otherwise, are still liable to conduct a good deal of their trade with the 11 in euros. Here the American example is instructive. Like the EU, the United States mainly trades with itself, for which reason the Federal Reserve, in recent years, has rarely attempted to manage the dollar when it has soared or dropped against other major currencies. Optimists believe that in time the euro will share the spotlight with the dollar as the world's reserve currency. There is an inevitability about this: the euro zone will be the world's largest exporter and importer (not including intra-EU trade), the second largest currency area and, if EMU is extended to all 15 EU members, it will become the world's largest economy. Moreover, the euro is liable to be used extensively by London, anxious to retain its status as Europe's leading finance centre, and countries in eastern Europe, and North Africa where local currencies were generally pegged to European currencies. And the euro-zone is running a substantial current account surplus where the United States labours under a heavy deficit. Given these factors, it is probably only a matter of when, and not if, the euro attains the status of a leading international currency (Barnett, 1998b; Portes and Rey, 1998; Bergsten, 1997).

THE CASE AGAINST A SINGLE CURRENCY

The kernel of the pessimists' case objecting to EMU resides in the euro's much deeper implications than as a simple addendum to crown the single market. Indeed, far from being an economic necessity, EMU's opponents suggest the process was driven by political considerations that sought greater integration. 'Entry into monetary union,' the Bundesbank warned, 'will have significant economic implications which must be given careful consideration when the decision is taken. The selection of the participants ultimately remains a political decision' (Champion and Culp, 1998, 50). As Hugo Young perceived, 'Economic and monetary union is essentially about politics – a species of political integration, unknowable in detail but axiomatic in principle – and only secondarily about economics' (Young, 1998, 13). Indeed, some critics suggest that without political union EMU is doomed to failure because without political support the pockets of high unemployment and high inflation, or both, which its policies threaten to unleash, will topple its carefully constructed edifice as certainly as the iceberg sank the seemingly unsinkable *Titanic*. Newt Gingrich, the Republican Speaker of the US House of Representatives, warned that Europe was engaging in the EMU process in 'reverse order', whereas the successful American model saw the states achieve political unity before merging their dollars into one entity: 'The last step was the emergence of … a unified currency and a unified national debt in a setting in which there was presumptively one national economy' (Gingrich, 1998).

Being part of EMU will severely limit individual government freedom in monetary policy and elsewhere. No longer can members resort to bank rate changes and manipulate their exchange rates to suit their national situations. The stability pact penalizes excessive budgetary deficits, thereby necessitating tight controls over public expenditure. The British have been especially sensitive to losing control over monetary instruments. As Jenkins recounted the objections of two successive prime ministers to British membership of the ERM:

> … Callaghan vehemently denied that he was staying out because of political difficulties at home … 'But,' he added, 'I am nervous of being locked in at too high a rate of exchange, which will prevent my dealing with unemployment.' … [Following her election, Mrs Thatcher] assured me that she was in principle in favour of full participation in the EMS but was 'nervous' of being locked in at too low a rate of exchange, which will prevent my dealing with inflation'. (Jenkins, 1994, 483–4)

It remains to be seen whether the elaborate decision-making process surrounding the coordination of economic policies (the European Central Bank, the Stability and Growth Pact, the Euro-X forum, the Euro-fed and Ecufin gatherings of finance ministers) will knock economies into shape or seek the lowest common denominator of acceptability.

There is the argument that EMU is only really appropriate to Germany, France, Austria and the Benelux countries which, since the 1980s, have had virtually the same monetary policy. Since this homogeneous group did not enjoy an economic renaissance as a consequence of its rectitude, it seems less likely that the far more disparate first wave of EMU members will perform otherwise. Chote (1998, 11) propounds the alarmist scenario:

> The largely unaccountable ECB is likely to run a tight monetary policy in its early years, to establish the 'credibility' to which every central bank aspires. Eventually, as unemployment rises and political extremism foments, fiscal prudence will crack. Unless, of course, the disciplines of the single currency have by then inspired the liberalising structural reforms that years of excessively tight monetary policy in France have so far failed to deliver.

Again, the suggestion that the single currency is invulnerable to speculative attack because it is indivisible only truly applies after the introductory three-year period (1999–2002) when national currencies will still be in circulation. Pessimists suggest that this represents an Achilles' heel of the system when speculators might use the window of opportunity to attack (Mills, 1998, 70–71).

The idea that EMU can be a panacea for European unemployment is as illusory as the belief that its causes spring entirely from monetary policy. 'There remain,' as Jacquet (1998, 55) points out, 'fundamental issues that nation states, individually but also collectively in Europe, need to address irrespective of EMU, or even more urgently within EMU. These include all aspects of structural reform, from the tax system to the labour market and the welfare state.'

The difficulties of achieving convergence going into a single currency suggest that maintaining it within the euro-zone will prove doubly difficult. France, for example, only just met the Maastricht criteria for the ratio of debt to GDP. Yet the trend is clearly against the sustainability of this condition, with French debt constituting 36 per cent of their GDP in 1991, rising to 58 per cent on the eve of entry (Graham, 1998, iv). The Bundesbank sounded a warning note (Champion and Culp, 1998, 51):

> In assessing the budgetary situation in Greece, Ireland, Portugal and Spain, it needs to be remembered that these countries are receiving substantial net payments from the EU budget. Pension insurance systems and other demographic trends are expected to drag on the financial positions of virtually all member states. In addition an excessive level of debt will restrict the future scope of fiscal policy action and will easily come into conflict with monetary policy – especially if short-term borrowing or borrowing at various rates of interest have a large share in financing.

The fear is that the 11 first tranche EMU members will suffer from a soft euro through the inclusion of Italy, Portugal, Spain and Belgium. In its early years, the euro could fluctuate wildly against the dollar and the yen, leading to a weak euro, and importing inflation. Equally, there is the possibility that the euro will be overvalued, creating problems for European competitiveness in world markets.

When the drive began for a single currency, Germany, as Europe's largest and strongest economy, was in the forefront. Reunification then intervened and became a monkey on the back with the costs representing between 3.5 and 4 per cent of GDP. What is unpredictable is how long it will take to bring the eastern sector up to the standard of the western half. Official forecasts suggest subsidies will be required until at least 2002, with expenditures tapering off after that (Richards, 1998, 7). Germany's other problem is its failure to imitate Thatcherite reforms in the 1980s, falling behind in the key areas of privatization, deregulation and trimming the welfare state. Its structural problems therefore remained, including an over-rigid labour market, the punitive costs to employers of welfare-related non-wage costs, a complex tax system reflecting too much red tape, and the largely untapped potential of its service sector. These supply-side inadequacies, by no means unique to Germany, helped persuade 155 economists, in February 1998, to urge the postponement of EMU (Norman, 1998, iv). Italy, the potential 'sick man' of the euro-zone, has been notorious in its reluctance to embrace privatization wholeheartedly. France was also averse to pursuing a Thatcherite agenda: in 1997 its public sector wages bill consumed 40 per cent of budget outlays. The Germans have at least made a start in freeing up their labour market, with trade unions endorsing flexibility clauses in labour contracts, but the French and Italians coveted the introduction of a 35-hour working week in the questionable belief that it would create more jobs (Munchau, 1997, i).

The big question in relation to an 'optimum currency area' (OCA) is, as its original proponent, Robert A.Mundell (1961), suggested, whether it can withstand asymmetric shocks. The likelihood of these occurring in future cannot be predicted with any certainty, but what is apparent is that, even if the general economic environment of EMU members is similar, their national reactions to shocks will differ because no one economy is the same. Moreover, EMU hardly meets Mundell's definition of an OCA because it lacks two essential characteristics of the United States' system: first, it lacks inter-state labour mobility, which acts as a central adjustment mechanism; second, as a political union, the United States permits and facilitates inter-state transfers in response to asymetric shocks (Jacquet, 1998, 59–60; Eichengreen, 1997, ch.3). On the first point, Obstfeld and Peri (1998) highlight the fact that, in comparison to the American model, the EU exhibits little interregional labour mobility, relying more on fiscal transfers between prosperous and struggling regions. Unless the stability pact is modified, they anticipate the creation of a European transfer union to help divert resources to euro economies in trouble, but the scale of its task might be such as to bankrupt EU finances.

The most frequently cited criticism of the single currency is that EU labour markets are not flexible enough to withstand asymmetric shocks which afflict particular regions. Wilhelm Nolling, a former member of the Bundesbank's central council, and a vocal critic of EMU, suggested that the only true convergence attained is towards greater unemployment and increased levels of public debt (Munchau, 1997, i). The common interest rate for all holds the danger that, while it may be appropriate for one or more countries, for another or others it will be singularly inapt. Inflation might be stoked up by too low a rate. Conversely, there are likely to be regions within the euro-zone where pockets of high unemployment develop which will remain since most of the jobless prefer to stay on benefit rather than move elsewhere in the EU and because individual states no longer have the weapons to alleviate localized recession, in particular the safety valve of devaluation. In such instances, high interest rates will be singularly inappropriate. If EMU multiplies regional disparities in the EU then the strains imposed on structural funds will be immense (Cook, 1998, 26, 30).

Finally, the optimists' blithe assumption that the euro's transition to a revered international currency that can match or even topple the dollar will be smooth and automatic ignores the realities of the situation. The dollar's entrenched position in the international finance system (see Table 6.5) was reflected by its standing in foreign exchange reserves, export invoicing and foreign exchange transactions. Caution also needs to be exercised because the euro-zone needs to establish a reputation for economic stability (not a given by any means). Moreover, with Britain absent in the first wave, Europe's capital markets, such as the domestic securities market, are no match for their considerably larger American counterparts. The absence of a central government bond issuer is also liable to handicap European fixed income markets (Barnett, 1998b). Bergsten (1997) has also warned that the introduction of the euro could increase exchange rate instability since both the EU and the United States have relatively closed economies – though clearly this is not true of all Community members (Britain and the Netherlands are two notable exceptions).

Table 6.5 The mighty dollar

	Share in world output (%)	Share in global reserve holdings (%)	Share in world export invoicing (% 1992 figures)
USA	27	56	48
EU	31	20	33
Japan	21	7	5

Note: 1995 figures unless stated.

Source: Barnett (1998b).

EAST MEETS WEST: THE INTEGRATION OF EUROPE

The sudden and dramatic collapse of the Soviet bloc in eastern Europe during 1989, as Moscow's former satellites fell one by one like a pack of cards, marked the beginning of the end of the Cold War. The east–west confrontation held its dangers, but also carried certain advantages. When communism was in its death throes, Gorbachev spoke optimistically in 1987 of 'a common European home'. From the vantage point of western Europe, the old bloc system held the attraction of excluding from the integration process laggard east European economies. Now the EU needed to confront the issue of increased trade with former Soviet bloc countries, which created policy dilemmas.

In metamorphosing themselves into viable free market economies, the new democracies were anxious to join the EU as soon as possible. The main benefits for them of a 'return to Europe' were joining an enormous free trade area, gaining access to grants and subsidies and, with NATO membership, the collective security which EU status would confer, as well as facilitating the reorientation of their trade westwards, away from former CMEA markets and their Soviet paymaster. East Europeans pointed to the precedent of the second enlargement, which allowed backward Mediterranean countries into the EC, but their admittance had as much to do with the Cold War as with economics.

Bruised by the experience, existing members were wary of admitting further net beneficiaries to the EU's already strained budget. There were also sensitive areas (agriculture, textiles and steel) to consider. On the other hand, the opening up of eastern Europe presented seemingly mouth-watering market opportunities for EU exporters, while Brussels was sensitive to the dangers of overt hostility which might derail emerging democracies and recreate old divisions.

The result, inevitably, was fudge and compromise. Thus, in December 1992, at the EU's Edinburgh summit, the prospect of extending membership eastwards was conceded but, crucially, no timetable was set. In the meantime, associate agreements were used as a double-edged sword. On the one hand, economic reforms were encouraged by the tantalizing prospect of eventual EU membership, but, on the other, the onerous terms of the agreements were deployed to discriminate against east European trade in sensitive areas. Czechoslovakia, Hungary and Poland concluded associate agreements in 1991, followed two years later by Bulgaria and Romania. At a time of rising unemployment, the EU was anxious to protect jobs. The fact that not all EU members ratified the initial agreements by the January 1993 deadline evidenced their concern at the prospect of being flooded with cheap imports from the east. Agriculture was a particularly touchy area, provoking French farmers to demonstrate against farm imports from eastern Europe. Accordingly, there was only very limited liberalization in agriculture under the agreements, with just a token number of quantitative restrictions abolished. Again the majority of food tariffs remained in place (Aldcroft and Morewood, 1995, 218–22).

The EU's stance was not entirely self-serving. There was a recognition that to confer preferential treatment to associates would only delay the economic transformation required for eventual full membership. For example, east European steel sectors were overdeveloped, brimful of outdated technology and too energy-intensive. Many of the EU's own steel sectors (the privatized British was a notable exception) already suffered from overcapacity and overmanning and it harboured no desire to reinforce these tendencies. Forcing restructuring to bring eastern plants up to world standards was therefore essential medicine for the patient. In the same vein, financial aid was extended via the PHARE (Poland and Hungary: Assistance for Restructuring the Economy) programme, which focused on restructuring key sectors of former command economies, by the European Bank for Reconstruction and Development (founded in 1991 specifically to assist economic development in eastern Europe) and the European Investment Bank, the EU's own long-term investing institution.

The desultory attitude of some members towards eastern enlargement sprang from a number of concerns. First was the nature of the transforming economies. Quite simply, they were generally too poor, too populous and too agricultural for early admission. Second was the vexed question of the Common Agricultural Policy (CAP). The French, in particular, were not keen to extend its benefits to the likes of Poland and Romania, where low-productivity farmers were thick on the ground, or to Hungary and Bulgaria, where the prominence of food exports reflected relatively efficient agricultural sectors (Bideleux and Jeffries, 1998, 632–3). Already the CAP consumed the largest part of the EU's budget. In 1994, it was estimated that to allow east European farmers access to its subsidies would lead to their receiving Ecu 58.1 billion, amounting to two-thirds of the current EU budget. Finally, there were the concerns of the Mediterranean countries that to allow in a galaxy of new, poorer members would lead to their regional aid being substantially reduced.

At Copenhagen in June 1993, the European Council decided the criteria for new members. It required that they should have stable institutions which guaranteed democracy, the rule of law, human rights and the protection of minorities; a functioning market economy able to cope with market pressures inside the EU; and the ability to assume the obligations of membership, including the goals of political, economic and monetary union (Bideleux and Jeffries, 1998, 600). On 16 July 1997, Jacques Santer, President of the European Commission, presented 'Agenda 2000' to the European Parliament which contained a detailed strategy for widening the EU in the early part of the twenty-first century, a prospect which he described as 'an historical opportunity'. The commission's pre-accession strategy addressed three specific problems: the need to reform EU policies to cope with enlargement while at the same time aiming to achieve sustainable growth, higher employment and better living standards; negotiating enlargement and preparing applicant countries for entry; and financial arrangements.

Of the 10 applicants from eastern and central Europe, the Commission judged that Hungary, Poland, Estonia, the Czech Republic and Slovenia were best placed to meet the Copenhagen entry criteria. In December 1997, the Luxembourg European Council endorsed this assessment, adding the non-Turkish half of Cyprus to the list. Negotiations with the favoured few commenced in May 1998, although 'Agenda 2000' assumed the earliest entry date as 2003. The remaining five (Bulgaria, Romania, Latvia, Lithuania and Slovakia) would be asked to enter into partnerships with the EU to help facilitate their eventual entry which, in view of their relative backwardness, might take a decade or more. Only Turkey, considered too dilatory in its economic and social reforms and unacceptable for its human rights record, was excluded as a prospective member.

'Agenda 2000' seeks to square the circle: to cap overall EU spending and yet prepare to accommodate new members, primarily in the east, by redirecting resources to them. As Santer recognized, 'We cannot think of pursuing agricultural reforms or the reform of structural policies without at the same time taking into account enlargement and the financial constraints.' The extra costs involved were estimated at Ecu 75 billion, a sum hailed by Santer as 'a veritable Marshall Plan for the countries of Central and Eastern Europe', which reflected the mammoth task involved in bringing applicants up to standard. Environmental protection, transport, energy, industrial restructuring and agricultural infrastructure are just some of the areas involved. The Commission was opposed to upgrading taking place within the EU, a requirement which, in itself, will ensure that imminent entry for the majority is ruled out (European Commission, 1997).

The assumption that the expenditure ceiling of 1.27 per cent of each member's GNP did not have to be raised to accommodate enlargement is questionable to say the least and rests on the success of key reforms. Some sacred cows need to be slaughtered: Britain's cherished annual budget rebate, the CAP in its present form, the distribution of aid favouring the poorer Mediterranean members. None of these prospective changes, while laudable in themselves, will be easy to achieve in practice.

The proposed reforms to the CAP, which consumed half of the EU budget, involved slashing guaranteed prices to bring them into line with world levels and moving from public subsidies to direct payments to farmers. As the EU's largest net contributor by far, Germany was keen to engineer for itself a less disproportionate share of the constitution of the annual EU budget. In Spring 1998, beleaguered Chancellor Kohl, facing potential defeat in the September elections, rattled his sabre and demanded that Britain's annual EU budget rebate of two-thirds of its net contribution (then running at £2 billion) be extended to other net contributors. Nor was this purely electoral posturing, for the EU's other principal paymasters (Austria, the Netherlands and Sweden) joined the campaign. Budgetary reform faces a veritable obstacle course: Britain holds its rebate status dear; the 'Club Med' members will resist change because of the impact on their aid programmes; France, which, despite its status as one of the EUs richest members, still contributes comparatively little to the budget, will want to maintain the status quo.

By 1998, the regional aid programme, established in 1973 at the behest of Britain to counter-balance excessive spending on the CAP and intended to bring living standards into line, was itself consuming up to one-third of the EU budget. Over two-thirds of that was directed to Objective 1 regions for road construction, industrial conversion and other upgrading projects. Local GDP had to be under 75 per cent of the EU average. To reduce the structural fund budget, the commission proposed that such expenditure be contained to a maximum of 0.46 per cent of EU GDP, which required a reduction in the eligible areas from 51 per cent of population to 38 per cent. Early casualties of this more vigorous approach to aid spending were several of Britain's 'poor regions' which no longer qualified for 'Objective 1' status under the tighter spending limits announced on 18 March 1998. All of Greece, the majority of Portuguese and Spanish regions and five Italian regions, together with seven regions of the former East Germany, one Austrian region, two British (Merseyside and South Yorkshire) and four French overseas departments still qualified. The southern members pressed for an increase in the overall EU budget, a desire that will be difficult to reconcile with the demands of net contributors for more equitable treatment (*The Economist*, 1998, 49–50).

Notwithstanding all the problems associated with the east–west trading relationship, a significant increase in trade developed in the post-communist period. This reflected the desire of former Soviet bloc countries to reorient their trade westwards and western exporters seeking to take advantage of new openings in the east. The EU increased its exports to the 14 new states of central and eastern Europe (including the

Baltic states, but excluding the former Soviet Union) on average by 25 per cent per annum between 1991 and 1995, to reach a value of $61.6 billion by the latter date. In percentage terms, this represented an increase from 4.2 per cent of EU exports to 8.4 per cent. In the other direction, EU imports from the ex-communist countries stood at over 7 per cent by 1995, reflecting an average annual growth rate of 20.8 per cent over five years. Indeed, trade with the former Soviet bloc was growing much faster than with any other regions of the world.

By 1995, Germany and Italy were the main exporters to the European east (accounting for almost 70 per cent of trade) while the leading transition economies in central Europe (Poland, Hungary and the Czech Republic) dominated trade with the EU (representing over 61 per cent of the total). Not surprisingly, manufactured goods formed the majority of EU exports, including industrial machines (the largest single category), motor cars and commercial vehicles and electrical machines and appliances. Although the EU registered trade deficits in clothing, iron and steel and furniture, in overall terms, as it took advantage of the opportunity to develop export markets with the region, its trade surplus rose substantially, from Ecu 1.5 billion in 1991 to Ecu 7.6 billion by 1995. Moreover, some western firms turned the cheaper labour costs in the European east to their advantage by relocating labour-intensive operations there (Done, 1996).

EUROPE IN THE WORLD ECONOMY

In the period under review, the international economy became more globalized and interdependent than ever before, as multinationals spread their operations even further afield in response to new markets opening up in Europe, Asia and South America. Indeed, trade has tended to grow faster than national economies with the total volume of world trade exceeding $4 trillion by the mid-1990s (Barnes, 1996, 3). Again capital controls were swept aside (as in Europe), facilitating the movement in and out of capital, which promoted investment in emerging markets. The liberalization of developing countries' economies was promoted by the World Bank and International Monetary Fund, which made loans and grants conditional on such measures. This period also saw a trend towards global free trade.

Globalization represented a double-edged sword for the industrialized countries: on the one hand, the opportunity to increase exports, on the other the emergence of vibrant competition from transition economies. The EU, ever sensitive to rising unemployment, has responded in two main ways to protect its position: first, by involving itself in new multilateral trade arrangements; second, by concluding bilateral agreements with trading partners. The Common Commercial Policy, established by Article 110 of the Treaty of Rome, provided the mechanism for the collective negotiation of trade agreements (although individual member states were not averse to taking national action where appropriate). In 1988, the European Commissioner for EU external trade suggested that, as the world's largest trading partner, 'we have a vital interest in the maintenance of a worldwide liberal trading system' (Owens and Dynes, 1990, 200). Such platitudes belied a more complex position. As Barnes (1996, 15) observes, Brussels 'is committed to trade liberalisation only to the extent that it improves the economies within the EU'. The single market generated fears of a closed shop, a 'Fortress Europe' to the EC's major trading partners. These concerns proved largely unfounded, partly because Europe is more heavily dependent on external trade than the United States. Indeed, the EU is the world's biggest trading group, enjoying over one-fifth of world trade in goods by the mid-1990s. As the world's largest exporter, the EU has an interest in open markets, but at the same time is wary of the need to afford some degree of protection to domestic producers.

Voluntary Export Restraints (VERs), which provide a means of regulating trade levels with individual countries, were pioneered in the EC during the 1970s and became the most important form of non-tariff barrier. There is in fact nothing 'voluntary' in such agreements beyond accepting a VER in preference to quotas, tariffs and technical barriers. By the early 1990s, VERs were evident in several important areas. In motor cars, Japan had VER arrangements with several EU countries to limit its market share, which were then supplanted by an EU-wide agreement. Although this was against the spirit and rules of GATT and the World Trade Organisation (WTO), the response of Brussels was that 'the transitional regime for automobiles is in no way official and represents an informal and voluntary agreement by both parties' (ibid., 8). Steel was another target of VERs: the Americans used them to control EU and Japanese imports, while the EU, in turn, deployed VERs to avoid being swamped by NIC output. VERs have not assisted economic growth because their impact generally has been to drive up the price of the commodity in the protected country, allowing inefficient domestic producers to survive. Anti-dumping measures also provided the EU with a means of protection, although in this respect the United States practised a more restrictive regime, having 306 instruments in force in 1994, against the EU's 157. The EU became sensitive to 'dumping' by South Korea and China and, with the arrival of transforming former communist economies on its doorstep, such concern was heightened. For example, between 1989 and 1991, the number of cheap Chinese bicycles sold in the EU shot up from 693 000 to 2.1 million, prompting Brussels to slap on a punitive 34.4 per cent anti-dumping duty (ibid., 9, 26).

Brussels established a flexible pecking order of trading privileges. In the mid-1990s, Norway, Iceland and Switzerland, all potential future members (and more importantly, net contributors) were at the top of the list, enjoying free trade in goods with the EU. Next came 70 states in Africa, the Caribbean and the Pacific, many of whom were former colonies of EU members. Although they enjoyed duty-free access to the EU (except, predictably, in agricultural products), there were restrictions governed by rules of origin. The Lomé Conventions, first signed in 1975, and renewed periodically thereafter, centred on a mix of trade and aid, and became progressively more favourable to the primary producers (see Mahler, 1994). Third came central and eastern Europe and the Mediterranean, whose trading was restricted by caveats centred on 'sensitive' goods, which cynics might transcribe to read 'uncompetitive'. Similar restrictions apply to the last group, the Less Developed Countries, whose access was governed by the General System of Preference (Barnes, 1996, 16–17).

Regional trade arrangements have become very much a part of the international landscape. The EU, United States and Japan – the so-called 'triad' – are the main trading blocs around which revolve the majority of world trade. By the early 1990s, Europe (the EU and EFTA) and North America (the United States, Canada and Mexico) accounted for around 65 per cent of world imports and almost half of developing country exports, while Japan and the emerging Pacific rim economies made up about 16 per cent of world trade.

The United States and Japan are easily the EC's largest trading partners. The nature and vicissitudes of the trilateral relationship provide an instructive means of examining European competitiveness. While the EC managed to achieve an overall current account trade surplus of almost 1 per cent of GNP between 1983 and 1990, this aggregate masked the fact that several members ran trade deficits and it was largely the persistent German surplus which kept the ship afloat. Notwithstanding the United States' consistent trade surplus with Europe, the converse of its trading position with Japan, the American–European economic relationship was often brittle. Washington was agitated by the continued protection of EU farmers and discrimination in public procurement while the EU, in turn, grew concerned at the rise in American anti-dumping legislation, the 'buy America' campaign, which effectively excluded foreign firms in public procurement, and (this particularly exercised the French) the dominant global position of American television programmes and films. In 1996, the New Transatlantic Agenda established an ambitious framework for driving forward EU–US trade relations. It bore fruit the following year with agreements on financial services, information technology and product testing. A further manifestation of the improved relationship was the Transatlantic Business Dialogue, directed towards lubricating the exchange of goods and services. These initiatives marked the American recognition that the EU is 'by far its largest commercial partner and its most important ally in developing and supporting the global trading system' (Lambert, 1998, 11).

The EU–Japan trading relationship also proved a difficult one. There was a conspicuous, albeit diminishing, EU trade deficit with Japan. While this partly reflected competitive differences there was also concern at the latter's restricted access. Brussels' deployment of VERs and anti-dumping duties was a halfway house response to the range of non-tariff barriers that presented an insuperable barrier to the effective penetration of Japanese markets. The 'Gateway to Japan' initiative, launched by the EU in February 1994, sought better trading relations with Tokyo but, as with the more bludgeoning American efforts to prise Japan open, only limited success was achieved (Barnes, 1996, 28–9).

By the early 1980s, deterioration in the international trade environment created the impetus for a new instalment of GATT negotiations. The Uruguay Round commenced in September 1986. Involving 105 governments, the difficulties of the negotiations were such that not until April 1994 was the round concluded at Marrakech, leading to the creation of the supervisory WTO in January 1995 which replaced the GATT. In the event, more substantial tariff cuts than those initially envisaged were finally agreed, with tariffs for industrialized nations falling from an average of 5 per cent to 3.5 per cent. The EU was to reduce its customs duties from 6.8 to 4.1 per cent, the United States from 6.6 to 3.4 per cent and over 40 per cent of EU imports would be tariff-free. The round also addressed non-technical barriers, aiming to slash red tape, thereby reducing delays and the extra costs involved in international trade. At the EU's insistence, services were included in the round for the first time, reflecting their increased importance within the modern 'dual economy' of manufacturing and services. The 1974 Multi-Fibre Arrangement to restrict textile imports to industrialized countries also came under scrutiny. Here, while the EU conceded that its existing barriers must be eradicated, this was only with the insistence on a prolonged phasing out process over 10 years (1995–2005).

Agriculture proved the most difficult area, reflecting the influence of farming communities and food exporters and importers in both the EU and United States. While insisting on maintaining financial props for its farmers, the EU blinked sufficiently to endorse a 20 per cent cut in aid. After much hectoring, there was a compromise agreement over the vexed issue of subsidized food exports, a practice long favoured by the Community. Developed countries agreed to cut the level of their export subsidies by 36 per cent and the volume of subsidized exports by 21 per cent. All these concessions would take effect over a six-year period. There was no movement, however, on the notorious set-aside scheme, which induced farmers to leave land fallow when there was no market for a crop. The EU also insisted on retaining a 14 per cent tariff on semiconductor components, which penalized non-European computer manufacturer exporters (European Commission, 1995; Barnes, 1996, 24). For all its achievements, the Uruguay Round signified the winning of a battle for free trade, but not the whole war. Apart from the absence of China and Russia from the system, several issues, such as services, agriculture and industrial tariffs, demand further liberalization and, together with social and environmental questions, will be the subject of a new round (the 'Millennium Round') starting at the turn of the century.

Global integration has raised living standards generally, but the expansion of world trade, especially between developed countries (the north) and developing countries (the south), has pushed up the jobless totals in the former. Traditional industries, such as coal mining, textiles, steel and shipbuilding, where once Europe was supreme, were established in the south (for instance, ship construction in South Korea and steel making in Egypt). The Europeans found themselves unable to compete in terms of price because of the low wages in the south. The result was an acceleration in deindustrialization, a natural corollary of which was increased unemployment as unskilled workers in the north lost their jobs, a situation compounded by the labour-intensive nature of many of these industries. So, in contrast to the 'golden age', unskilled workers have found themselves in much less demand.

The increase in unemployment in the north coincided with the greater export penetration of the south which started in the late 1960s. Western Europe suffered to a greater degree than the United States because institutional pressures causing relative wage rigidity were much stronger. Moreover, the persistence of high unemployment on the continent can partly be explained by the inability of the unskilled out-of-work to reorient themselves to the jobs market where, with technology and service industries predominating, they find themselves unable to find work. Thus the gap between the skilled and unskilled has widened over recent decades, as has the gulf separating their unemployment rates. While the United States and Europe have faced the same problem, in the former flexible wages led to a fall in the relative wages of the unskilled, where in the latter wage cuts have been stoutly resisted. This has meant that 'the demand shift has emerged largely as higher unemployment among unskilled workers' (Wood, 1994, 18, 22). The answer lies partially in improved education and training, but there is a finite limit to natural ability and a large residue of unskilled workers will persist.

At the start of the period under review, Europe appeared to have lost its impetus as a major force shaping the international economy, and the future seemed to belong to the emerging economies, with some optimists forecasting that the millennium would usher in 'the Asian century'. But just as western Europe was unable to sustain supergrowth rates, so it was with the developing countries. In mid-1997, Thailand faltered and within a year there had been a 'domino effect' engulfing Southeast Asia, Russia and Latin America. The crisis was characterized by bank defaults, plunging stock markets (triggering a withdrawal of funds, reflecting a loss in investor confidence) and beggar-thy-neighbour devaluations which harked back to the 1930s. Moreover, Japan too became mired in recession while the United States was facing a slowdown.

Against this backdrop, Europe's economic position looked relatively comfortable as it entered an upward phase of the economic cycle and domestic demand improved. It was not overdependent on any of the collapsed emerging markets. For instance, although the EU is Russia's major trading partner, exports to the former heart of the Soviet Union represent only a tiny fraction of its exports (3.2 per cent in 1997). Again the failure of EU exporters generally to penetrate Asian markets to any great extent left them relatively unexposed to the fallout. Furthermore, central Europe (the Czech Republic, Hungary and Poland), where western Europe placed its main trading hopes, was comparatively free of the corruption which had stifled Russia's emergence as a free market economy (Hawkins, 1988). Wolf (1998) considers that 'Europe has a golden opportunity to become the prime source of demand for the world economy.' Moreover, the new president of the ECB made a speech suggesting that the EMU project insulated Europe from the global turmoil, that the continent, which he characterized as 'an oasis of peace', had become a self-contained unit with minimum influence on the outside world ('We do what we can, but there is not much we can do') (Kaletsky, 1998). Conversely, the continent is bound to be affected by any general slowdown in global economic activity and faces the uncomfortable prospect of export dumping by countries desperate to offload goods. Moreover, its stock markets will reflect the uncertain position and the exposure of some western banks, particularly in Germany, to emerging markets is not helpful. Such an environment is far from ideal to launch EMU.

THE FUTURE OF EUROPE

The history of the European Union suggests that its well-laid plans can often be blown off course by unexpected events. The first oil shock postponed early moves towards monetary union, while the September 1992 ERM crisis again drove the process sideways for a time. As launch day neared, another global economic slowdown was taking hold. The immediate past has been framed by an optimistic scenario surrounding the single currency which may or may not be vindicated over time.

An optimistic assessment of the EU would posit 'ever closer' economic union, driven by the single market and EMU, bringing the full fruits of globalization. The SEM is the largest and most successful example of the elimination of trade barriers between national markets, inspiring imitators, notably NAFTA. In January and June 2002, euro notes and coins come into circulation following a preliminary three-year period starting on 1 January 1999 when parities are fixed irretrievably and a single monetary policy begins operating throughout the euro-zone. The conundrum of whether a single currency will seal the success of the single market or prove a spectacular and divisive failure was but one of the major question marks hanging over the continent's economic future as it faced the new millennium. The prospect of enlargement to the east promised, in political terms, to end the division of Europe enshrined at Yalta in 1945, but portended economic headaches, especially if the assimilation was not highly selective and extended over many years, even decades.

During the 'long boom', western Europe not only managed to achieve full employment, it was able additionally to employ millions of migrant workers. Over the period 1973–83, however, EC employment fell by 3 million, compared to the creation of 15 million jobs in the United States. In fact, from the mid-1970s to the late 1990s, the EU generated relatively little new employment, while the United States created 30 million jobs. A further worrying trend was the rising average duration of EC unemployment: six months, against one month across the Atlantic (Ball and Albert, 1983, 10). One key difference between the two continents is that, notwithstanding the single market, cultural impediments, such as language and nationality, remain in Europe. Americans losing their jobs in one state will generally pack their bags and move to another state where work can be found. In Europe this is more the exception than the rule. Against this, it should be said that the official statistics do not tell the full story. Across Europe, as elsewhere, the black economy has become much more significant, no more so than in Italy where a large number of 'unofficial' factories produce official goods. While the extent of official unemployment remains worrying, especially in an international context, the headline figures disguise the true state of affairs. This factor, together with more acceptable levels of welfare, also helps to explain why migratory workers are less a feature of the European economy than of the American one.

The early 1990s witnessed the lead-up to the much-vaunted single market, yet official unemployment continued stubbornly to rise, a feature absent from the EC's major competitors; at the end of 1993, the first year of the single market, the unemployment rates of the United States and Japan were 6 and 10 percentage points lower, respectively, than the EC average (McDonald and Deard, 1994, xxxiii). Moreover, the trenchant criticisms of the Ball and Albert report remain. Take venture capital markets: at the end of 1997, the US Nasdaq index of high-technology stocks listed 5500 companies, compared with only 385 for its three European equivalents (Easdaq, Euro-NM and AIM); Nasdaq's venture capital for 1997 was seven times greater than that for Europe; and Nasdaq companies were responsible for creating 16 per cent of all new jobs in the United States from 1990 to mid-1994, employing nine million people by 1997. The European Commission itself recognised that 'There remain a number of pernicious barriers – regulatory, economic, fiscal, cultural – that need to be addressed as a matter of urgency' if SMEs were to flourish (Champion, 1998, 7).

Resolving the growing unemployment problem is perhaps the biggest dilemma facing the EU as it enters the twenty-first century (see Mitchie and Smith, 1994). With unemployment on a rising trend since at least 1990, the European Commission (1993) published a White Paper on the problem. By 1998, 18 million were jobless. Moreover, in November–December 1997, the booming American economy created more jobs than Europe managed in 10 years. Gingrich (1998) considered the EU's structural unemployment problems 'staggering', adding that 'I am told that there is not the political will to solve them.' The French resorted to traditional-style solutions with a public sector job-creating programme and a plan to reduce the working week from 39 to 34 hours in January 1998. In truth, this proposed 'remedy' ignored the more fundamental problem of the rigidities in the labour market created by safeguards against dismissals.

While it is true that Europe has experienced problems unique to its experience which have helped push up unemployment levels (the fallout from German reunification and revolution in eastern Europe, the lead-up to EMU), some commentators also discern a more fundamental underlying reason – the constitution of the economic model. The Anglo-Saxon model, as practised by the United States and Britain, is predicated on a free enterprise economy, labour market flexibility, a relatively low tax regime and deregulation as the pillars of job creation. By contrast, the so-called Rhineland model, based on Germany but emulated elsewhere on the continent, has a number of characteristics which, its critics argue, create inertia. For instance, job protection is regarded as a management objective; the return on capital is not a top priority; large banks are the chief providers of capital rather than the stock exchange or venture capital; wages are much more uniform owing to the strength of trade unions; employment is heavily regulated; and there is universal backing for welfare provisions, which generate high spending on social security. The problem with such a view is that there is a middle way between the two models embraced by the intermediate economies, such as Denmark and Sweden. The Netherlands, for instance, in recent years has outperformed France and Germany. It has done so through embracing reforms within the 'Rhinelandish' model and yet still managed to sustain a reasonable level of welfare spending while generating new jobs (see van Zanden, 1997). That said, it is the performance of the continent's three leading economies (Germany, France and Italy) which will determine economic prosperity.

The need for 'social disarmament' across western Europe became a pressing one by the mid-1990s. Sir William Beveridge's idealistic vision that people would simply 'visit' safety nets, thereby ensuring the financial rectitude of the welfare state, failed to foresee what lay ahead: persistent unemployment, which especially afflicted the young and old (as employers became more discriminatory in a buyers' market), a breakdown of family values (as symbolized by the rise of one-parent families and the homeless), technologically-driven unemployment and the extension of welfare provisions to cover all manner of circumstances. On the continent, even more comprehensive welfare provision was the order of the day, not least in West Germany, where it was recognized that the lack of a social safety net had helped to propel Hitler into power amidst the mass unemployment and associated deprivations of the early 1930s. While social stability was engendered, it came with a price and the inevitable outcome (see Table 6.6) has been to place a heavy burden on public expenditure.

Pressure on governments to reform benefits and create a meaner, leaner welfare state arose from two principal directions. The first, all-embracing, pressure emanated from escalating welfare costs. These effectively represented a tax on jobs through often punitive non-wage costs. As Table 6.6 indicates, only Britain and the United States impose comparatively low burdens on employers, and the correlation between this and falling unemployment from the mid-1990s is clear. The UK's success also owed much to its opt-out from the Social Chapter, which helped to attract the biggest share of inward investment in the EU. The second source of pressure was the desire to comply with the budgetary requirements of the Maastricht provisions and subsequently to remain on an acceptably converging path within the euro-zone. There was increasing recognition, too, of the not-too-distant 'pension time bomb': a situation

Table 6.6 Labour costs and benefits (Deutschmark, per hour, 1996)

Country	Labour cost	Benefits	Benefits as % of labour cost
Italy	27.9	14.1	50.5
France	30.8	14.8	48.1
Germany	47.3	21.3	45.1
Netherlands	35.7	15.6	43.6
Spain	32.6	13.4	41.1
Japan	24.0	13.4	41.1
UK	22.7	6.5	28.6
USA	26.6	7.4	27.7

Source: Szamuely and Jamieson (1998, 59).

where, with the population living far longer, birth rates declining and unemployment rising, pensioners outnumbered those in work. In such a scenario, a government's tax take will be insufficient to fund state pensions and it will be forced to resort to borrowing on a grand scale, thereby pushing up interest rates.

Although it was not difficult to identify the sources of escalating welfare costs, in practice meaningful cuts were not easy to achieve. Welfare systems acquired the status of sacred cows, with vested interest groups anxious to defend the level and continued existence of their particular benefits. A growing element of fraud, by definition impossible to measure with any precision, provided a further headache for central governments. Even the British Conservatives' concerted attempt to 'roll back the state' and slash central spending over almost two decades was doomed to failure: by the end of the second Major government, its spending as a proportion of GDP was the same as when 'tax and spend' Labour left office in 1979. 'New Labour', which swept into office in May 1997, signalled that the time had come to act. When the Green Paper on welfare reform was published in March 1998, however, it marked a retreat from its slogan of 'thinking the unthinkable' and spoke lamely of a 10 to 20-year period being needed for transformation to occur. It was no wonder that the minister responsible resigned after his radical proposals were quashed on political grounds.

As Table 6.7 indicates, Britain's ratio of social security transfers to GDP in 1995 was 15.4 per cent against an average of 20.4 per cent for the EU 15. By 1997, France had a social security deficit of FF244 billion, while Germany's public pension problem loomed ominously in the near distance as it has a faster ageing population than Britain (Ball, 1998, 180). The same was true of Italy, whose population had the longest life expectancy in Europe, where, by 1997, pension costs were already consuming 15 per cent of GDP (Fletcher and Morgan, 1997, 10). The German social security system, where unemployment benefits averaged about 70 per cent of previous net earnings, was placing a huge burden on the state and taxpayers and stifled job creation. Mushrooming unemployment partly reflected the shedding of around two million jobs in manufacturing in the former East Germany, but the rising trend was also apparent in the more prosperous western part (Richards, 1998, 7). Only the Americans have truly 'grasped the nettle', reducing the maximum time on welfare benefits to five years (two years continuously) under the Clinton administration. But they have also seen their prison population rise to over 1.5 million and it is extremely unlikely that the Europeans will ever seek to introduce the American model.

Table 6.7 Public expenditure ratios in 1995

	PER	Consumption ratio	Social security transfers
USA	34.3	15.8	13.1
Japan	28.5	9.8	13.4
Germany	46.6	19.5	18.6
France	50.9	19.3	23.2
Italy	49.5	16.3	18.9
UK	42.3*	21.3	15.4*
Canada	45.8	19.6	14.7
Australia	35.5	17.3	11.4
Austria	48.8	20.2	22.0
Belgium	53.3	14.8	24.3
Denmark	59.7	25.5	21.5
Ireland	39.2*	14.7	14.6*
Netherlands	52.1	14.3	25.1
Spain	41.5	16.6	17.3
Sweden	64.0	25.8	23.4
Switzerland	36.7	15.0	17.6
EU (15)	49.2	18.7	20.4
OECD	38.9	15.9	15.7

Note: * 1994.

Source: OECD (1997).

The debate over the euro's prospects is reminiscent of George Bernard Shaw's famous quip that 'If you laid all the economists end to end, they still wouldn't reach a conclusion!' For every positive slant there is a negative counter and vice versa (see Rattner and Walter, 1998). The lessons of history are not encouraging for the long-term survival prospects of the single currency unless political union is brought about. The best historic examples of monetary unions are the Latin monetary union and the Scandinavian currency union which both lasted from the late nineteenth century to the First World War – though neither boasted as many members as EMU. The former was originally a bimetallic union, based on silver and, later, gold. It revolved around France and the inter-linked economies of Belgium, Italy and Switzerland. Formed in 1865, and joined three years later by Greece, it complemented German monetary union (1857–1918) and was committed to a balanced budget and fiscal rectitude. The Scandinavian currency union, conceived in 1873 by Denmark and Sweden, who were later joined by Norway, was a conspicuous success because of shared political and economic objectives. Neither union, however, was able to withstand the seismographic shock of global conflict, when the gold standard was suspended and currency volatility accompanied by roaring inflation swept in like a whirlwind (Lyons, 1998, iii). At the very least, it seems likely that increased fiscal harmonization will have to develop once the euro has become established, if only to augment the armoury of the ECB. There are echoes here of the inter-war period (see Chapter 4 of the present volume) when European economies struggled to rejoin the gold standard in the mistaken belief that a golden land of milk and honey lay beyond. On the other side, it might be argued that there are no pure historical precedents for a monetary experiment on the scale of EMU and it may well succeed against all the odds.

Continuing enlargement dictates that consensus, or more often compromise, will result from a community which is being transmuted from an exclusive club into a continent-wide organization. If all the eastern applicants are admitted, they will add 1.1 million square kilometres and a total population of 106 million, representing 29 per cent of the extended EU's population and 33 per cent of its area. The admonition that 'size isn't everything' was never more true. In 1997, the 10 supplicants combined managed a GDP of under 4 per cent of the current membership and were not expected to reach half their average GNP for 25 years. Worse still, two World Bank economists estimated that, even taking the best performing applicants, it would take the Czech Republic 15 years and Hungary 41 years to attain 75 per cent of the projected EU average GDP per head, while Poland would never do so (Szamuely and Jamieson, 1998, 19; Barbone and Zalduendo, 1998). This worst-case scenario is probably wide of the mark, but eastern Europe has always tended to 'play catch-up' with western Europe and is liable to remain at least one step behind notwithstanding its modernization programmes.

Eastern enlargement was implicitly on the agenda when the Soviet bloc regimes collapsed in 1989 and in politicostrategic terms it made sense to consolidate the ideological transformation from repressive police states and command economies to democracies and market economies. The protracted troubles in former Yugoslavia acted as a reminder of the dangers of conflict on Europe's periphery which, if not contained, threatened to light another conflagration in the Balkans. At the London conference on enlargement in March 1998, the British Premier, Tony Blair, argued that it was impossible for the EU to be a 'fortress of wealthy countries with the poor at its gate'. Yet, equally, there is the danger of the EU taking on too many new net recipient members. The enlargement process, creating what Santer has referred to as 'greater Europe', will extend the boundaries of Europe as far east as the borders of Ukraine, Belarus and Moldova, and as far south as Cyprus. Just as the Titanic's compartmentalized defences were overcome when sea water poured into too many sections, so the EU ship faces a potential capsize unless it is highly selective about the extra non-paying passengers allowed on board and also succeeds in the ambitious 'Agenda 2000' reforms. To avert such a disastrous scenario, the EU will need both to stagger the entry of new members and, sooner or later, to raise substantially the GDP ceiling on contributions to its increasingly strained budget. The disappointing economic performance of Greece, still the EU's poorest member, highlights the fallacy of the assumption that an enlarged Europe will instigate genuine transfers of wealth to the east.

As Szamuely and Jamieson (1998, 19–20, 41) suggest, once new eastern members become ensnared in EU rules and regulations, the bureaucracy could reinforce rather than release them from their backwardness by taking away their greatest asset – low-cost production. Indeed, the first-wave applicants received a foretaste of what was to come when they received the *acquis communautaire* containing around 90 000 pages of EU directives and legislation mainly related to social and employment regulations to which they must conform (Champion and King, 1998, 16–17). Vaclav Klaus, the former premier of the Czech Republic, informed the Davos World Economic Forum in 1997 that 'The key question is "how successful will be the dismantling of over-regulated and over-paternalistic welfare states in Western Europe?"' To burden the former communist states with the same faults will not help their international competitiveness. The sterile debate about whether the EU should be widened or deepened in fact misses the point that the two are interlinked; widening on a grand scale cannot succeed unless there is deepening, which means that more power must reside with Brussels if fundamental reforms are to succeed. Even so, the result is still likely to be a two-tier Europe comprising an inner core of richer members and an outer core, unsuited to EMU, chugging along in the slow lane.

The last quarter of the twentieth century found Europe grappling for ways to recreate the 'golden age'. In just five of 18 years (1980–97) did the EU manage to attain or exceed a growth rate of 3 per cent. Over the period, the United States beat the EU's average growth rate of 2.13 per cent by 15 per cent and Japan, despite struggling since 1992, by nearly 30 per cent (Szamuely and Jamieson, 1998, 45). Nor, unlike the United States, and Japan, has the EU come remotely close to replicating the full employment conditions of the 'long boom'. By the start of 1998, over 18 million (10.6 per cent of the workforce) were unemployed across the union, reflecting the failure to break the rising jobless trend dating from the early 1970s, in contrast to the United States, which managed to create 30 million new jobs (albeit many of them low paid), the best level achieved since 'the roaring twenties'. 'Agenda 2000's' strategy for growth, competitiveness and employment is but the latest manifestation of a misbegotten remedy for Europe's economic ills. As it faced the new millennium, the EU was struggling with an enormous formal agenda that incorporated enlargement, agricultural reform, employment programmes, institutional change and the introduction of a single currency. It was less a crossroads, more a maze which held out as many prospective dead-ends as potential solutions to a plethora of policy dilemmas facing decision makers. This was in stark contrast to Europe's position a century earlier when, with two of its economies in the world's top three performers, a rosy future seemed assured.

BIBLIOGRAPHY

Aldcroft, D.H.(1993), *The European Economy 1914–1990*, 3rd edn, London: Routledge.

Aldcroft, D.H. and S.Morewood (1995), *Economic Change in Eastern Europe since 1918*, Aldershot: Edward Elgar.

Ball, J. (1998), *The British Economy at the Crossroads*, London: Financial Times/Pitman.

Ball, R.J. and M. Albert (1983), *Towards European Economic Recovery in the 1980s*, Brussels: European Parliament.

Barbone, L. and J. Zalduendo (1998), *EU Accession of Central and Eastern Europe: Bridging the Income Gap*, Washington, DC: World Bank.

Barnes, I. (1996), *The European Union and World Trade*, Hull: Hidcote Press.

Barnett, V. (1998a), *Kondratieff and the Dynamics of Economic Development*, London: Macmillan.

Barnett, V. (1998b), 'Watch out dollar', *Financial Times*, 23 April.

Bergsten, F. (1997), 'The dollar and the euro', *Foreign Affairs*, 76.

Bideleux, R. and I. Jeffries (1998), *A History of Eastern Europe: Crisis and Change*, London: Routledge.

Bojnec, S. (1996), 'Integration of Central Europe in the Common Agricultural Policy of the European Union', *The World Economy*, 19.

Boltho, A. (ed.) (1982), *The European Economy: Growth & Crisis*, Oxford: Oxford University Press.

Cecchini, P. (1988), *The European Challenge: 1992 – the Benefits of a Single Market*, Aldershot: Wildwood House.

Champion, M. (1998), 'Capital heeds no barriers', *The European*, 6–12 April.

Champion, M. and E.Culp (1998), 'Welcome to euroland', *The European*, 30 March–5 April.

Champion, M. and T. King (1998), 'Long road ahead to the European Union for eastern supplicants', *The European*, 6–12 April.

Chote, R. (1998), 'Cliffhanging imprudence', *Financial Times*, 23 March.

Cook, G. (1998), *The Single European Currency*, Hull: Hidcote Press.

Corzine, R. (1998), 'Why OPEC blinked first', *Financial Times*, 2 April.

Crafts, N. and G.Tonioli (eds) (1996), *Economic Growth in Europe since 1945*, Cambridge: Cambridge University Press.

Delors Committee (1989), *Report on Economic and Monetary Union in the European Community*, Luxembourg: Office for Official Publications of the EC.

Done, K. (1996), 'Keen buyers for western products', *FT Exporter*, October.

Drewnowski, J. (1982), *Crisis in the East European Economy: The Spread of the Polish Disease*, London: Croom Helm.

Dyker, D. (ed.) (1992), *The European Economy*, London: Longman.

Eichengreen, B. (1997), *European Monetary Unification: Theory, Practice and Analysis*, Cambridge, MA and London: MIT Press.

Eichengreen, B. and C. Wyploz (1998), 'The Stability Pact: More than a minor nuisance?', *Economic Policy*, 26.

EP News (1998), 'UK Minister praises the single euromarket', March.

European Commission (1985), *Completing the Internal Market*, White Paper COM (85) 310 final, Brussels: European Commission.

European Commission (1993), *Growth, Competitiveness, Employment*, Brussels: European Commission.

European Commission (1995), *The European Union and World Trade*, Brussels: European Commission.

European Commission (1997), '*Agenda 2000*', Brussels: European Commission.

European Parliament (1984a), *Report on the Plan for European Economic Recovery Part A*, Brussels: European Parliament.

European Parliament (1984b), *Report on the Plan for European Economic Recovery Part B*, Brussels: European Parliament.

Fletcher, M. and O.Morgan (1997), 'Italy groans to get in shape for EMU', *Financial Mail on Sunday*, 25 January.

Frank, A.G. (1994), 'Soviet and East European "socialism": a review of the international political economy on what went wrong', *Review of International Political Economy*, 1.

Garton Ash, T. (1998), 'Chancellor Kohl trips up on his cardigan', *The Sunday Times*, 1 March.

Giersch, H. and O. Bertola (1990), 'Firing costs and labour demand – how bad is Eurosclerosis?', *Review of European Studies*, 57.

Giersch, H. and F. Wolter (1983), 'Towards an explanation of a productivity slowdown', *Economic Journal*, 95.

Gilbar, G. (1997), *The Middle East Oil Decade and Beyond*, London: Frank Cass.

Gingrich, N. (1998), 'EMU: putting the cart before the horse?', *The Week*, No.150, 25 April.

Graham, R. (1998), 'Bottom of the euro class', *Financial Times*, 23 March.

Grant, C. (1994), *Delors*, London: Nicholas Brealey.

Hawkins, P. (1988), 'Central Europe fends off dose of Russian flu', *The European*, 14–20 September.

Henley, J. (1998), 'Jobless pièce de résistance', *The Guardian*, 20 January.

Jacquemin, A. and L.R. Pench (eds) (1997), *Europe Competing in the Global Economy: Reports of the Competitiveness Advisory Group*, Cheltenham, UK and Lyme, US: Edward Elgar.

Jacquet, P. (1998), 'EMU: a worthwhile gamble', *International Affairs*, 74.

Jenkins, R. (1994), *A Life at the Centre*, London: Papermac.

Johnson, C. (1996), *In with the Euro, out with the Pound*, London: Penguin.

Jones, R. (1996), *The Politics and Economics of the European Union*, Cheltenham UK and Brookfield, US: Edward Elgar.

Kaletsky, A. (1998), 'Oasis or backwater?', *The Times*, 24 September.

Kuper, S. (1998), 'Euro likely to fluctuate', *Financial Times*, 23 March.

Lambert, R. (1998), 'Big partner takes care not to rock the boat', *Financial Times*, 5 January.

Lloyd-Jones, R. and M.J. Lewis (1998), *British Industrial Capitalism since the Industrial Revolution*, London: UCL Press.

Lyons, G. (1998), 'Survival depends on political union', *Financial Times*, 23 March, 'EMU' Survey.

Mahler, V.A. (1994), 'The Lomé Convention: assessing a north–south institutional relationship', *Review of International Political Economy*, 1.

McDonald, F. and S. Deard (eds) (1994), *European Economic Integration*, 2nd edn, London: Longman.

Meadows, D.H. *et al.* (1972), *The Limits of Growth: A Report from the Club of Rome's Project on the Predicament of Mankind*, New York: Universe Books.

Mills, J. (1998), *Europe's Economic Dilemma*, London: Macmillan.

Milner, M. (1994), 'Bloc bigger than NAFTA "from many points of view"', *The Guardian*, 1 January.

Mitchell, J. (1994), *An Oil Agenda for Europe*, London: RHA.

Mitchie, J. and J. G. Smith (eds) (1994), *Unemployment in Europe*, London: Academic Press.

Monti, M. (1996), *The Single Market and Tomorrow's Europe*, London: Kogan Page.

Munchau, W. (1997), 'Life will not be the same under EMU', *Financial Times*, 21 November.

Munchau, W. (1998a), 'Europe's big opportunity', *Financial Times*, 23 March, 'EMU' Survey.

Munchau, W. (1998b), 'Only politics can destroy EMU', *Financial Times*, 23 March.

Mundell,R.A.(1961), 'A theory of optimum currency areas', *American Economic Review*, 51.

Nagorski, A. and S. Thiel (1998), 'Building an engine run on euros', *Newsweek*, 4 May.

Norman, P.(1998), 'Waigel triumphs against the sceptics', *Financial Times*, 23 March.

Obstfeld, M. and G.Peri (1998), 'Asymmetric shocks: regional non-adjustment and fiscal policy', *Economic Policy*, 26.

Odell, P.R. (1986), *Oil and World Power*, 8th edn, London: Penguin.

OECD (1997), *OECD Historical Statistics 1960–95*, Paris: OECD.

Olson, M. (1982), *The Rise and Decline of Nations*, New Haven, CT: Yale University Press.

Olson, M. (1996), 'The varieties of Eurosclerosis: the rise and decline of nations since 1982', in N. Crafts and G. Toniolo (eds), *Economic Growth in Europe since 1945*, Cambridge: Cambridge University Press.

Owens, R. and M.Dynes (1990), *The Times Guide to 1992*, London: Times Books.

Portes, R. and H. Rey (1998), 'The emergence of the euro as an international currency', *Economic Policy*, 26.

Prodi, R. and A.Clo (1976), 'Europe', in R. Vernon (ed.), *The Oil Crisis*, New York: W.W. Norton.

Rattner, S.L. and N.Walter (1998), 'There are two sides to this coin', *Newsweek*, 4 May.

Richards, H. (1998), 'Why monetary union may derail Germany', *The Times Higher Educational Supplement*, 3 April.

Rostow, W.W. (1985), 'The world economy since 1945', *Economic History Review*, 33.

Shwadran, B. (1986), *Middle East Oil Crises since 1973*, Boulder: Westview Press.

Sirc, L. (1994), *Why Communist Economies Failed*, London: Centre for Research into Communist Economies.

Smith, A.H. (1983), *The Planned Economies of Eastern Europe*, London: Macmillan.

Smith, D. (1998a), 'EU promises to cut goods prices', *The Sunday Times*, 22 March.

Smith, D. (1998b), 'Free trade genie is out to stay', *The Sunday Times*, 27 September.

Sumner, M. (1992), 'European monetary integration', in D.Dyker (ed.), *The European Economy*, London: Longman.

Szamuely, H. and W. Jamieson (1998), *A 'Coming Home' or Poisoned Chalice?*, London: Centre for Research into Post-Communist Economies.

Temin, P. (1997), 'The Golden Age of European growth: a review essay, *European Review of Economic History*, 1.

The Economist (1998), 'Slicing the EUs shrinking cake', 21 March.

Van der Wee, H. (1991), *Prosperity and Upheaval in the World Economy 1945–1980*, London: Penguin.

Van Zanden, J.L. (1997), *The Economic History of the Netherlands 1914–1995*, London: Routledge.

Venn, F. (1986), *Oil Diplomacy in the Twentieth Century*, London: Macmillan.

Von Tunzlemann, N. (1992), 'The main trends of European economic history since the Second World War', in D.A. Dyker (ed.), *The European Economy*, London: Longman.

Welsh, M. (1998), 'Pointing the way: how the single market came about', in M.Fraser (ed.), *Britain in Europe*, London: Stratagems Publishing Limited.

Werner, P. (1970), 'The Werner Report', *Bulletin of the European Communities*, supplement II.

Whitney, C.R. (1998), 'Chirac exits Brussels with a victory, his reputation as a "bulldozer" intact', *International Herald Tribune*, 4 May.

Wolf, M. (1998), 'Averting the worst', *Financial Times*, 9 September.

Wood, A. (1994), *North–South Trade, Employment and Inequality: Changing Fortunes in a Skill-driven World*, Oxford: Clarendon Press.

Young, H. (1998), 'Europe is a dream, not a nightmare', *The Guardian*, 6 January.

Index